IMI AN
ROPOLIS.

The Spitel fielde.

The Spiral fielde.

V Geener winders B.

THE TOWRE

Winchester ho.

S. Mary evere

Sterles

Cum Privilegio.

quillam Rerumpub. pacem, & ad modestam ado
dam, instituta: plurimor, Regum, ac Principe
Magnæ Moscouiæ, nec non Flandriæ, ac Brabant
tutib. exornata fuit. Habet ea quatuor Empori
ciuitatum negotiatores resident, suosque mercatu
ni, domestica œconomia nitet, habens domum Gildebal

STUDIES IN HISTORICAL GEOGRAPHY

English Towns
1500–1700

STUDIES IN HISTORICAL GEOGRAPHY

Editors: Alan R H Baker and J B Harley

Also published in this series

Southern Africa
A J CHRISTOPHER

Finland
MICHAEL JONES

Rural Settlement in Britain
BRIAN K ROBERTS

Mirrors of the New World
J M POWELL

Climatic Change, Agriculture and Settlement
M L PARRY

STUDIES IN HISTORICAL GEOGRAPHY

English Towns
1500–1700

JOHN PATTEN

DAWSON · ARCHON BOOKS

First published in 1978

© John Patten 1978

Wm Dawson & Sons Ltd, Cannon House
Folkestone, Kent, England
Archon Books, The Shoe String Press, Inc
995 Sherman Avenue, Hamden, Connecticut 06514 USA

British Library Cataloguing in Publication Data

Patten, John
   English towns 1500–1700.—(Studies in historical geography).
   1. Cities and towns—England—History
   I. Title
   941'.00973'2   HT133   77-30665
ISBN 0-7129-0793-9

Archon ISBN 0 208 61721 6

Printed litho in Great Britain
by W & J Mackay Ltd, Chatham

For my father

Contents

Figures

Tables

Preface and Acknowledgements

This book represents original research on the urban structure of pre-industrial England, as exemplified by one of its regions. But it is also grounded in the work of many other scholars on the towns of the rest of the country during the sixteenth and seventeenth centuries. Its first aim is largely descriptive, to paint as clear an overall picture as is possible of the structure of English towns then; its second aim is to discuss their changing geography over two centuries as far as sources, and the work of others, will permit. Thus I am deeply indebted, in the construction of what is, in part, a synthetic work, to a great number of writers whose pages I have plundered; to those who generously allowed me to quote from and refer to their unpublished theses; as well as to those who have offered advice, criticism, and sometimes the fruits of their unpublished research. Individual acknowledgements of thanks are not possible here, but are self-evident in the notes to each chapter. One vital work does not, however, appear in them. This is Osbert Lancaster's *Draynflete Revealed* (London, 1949), a volume which I recommend to every student of towns, and which was recommended to me in my turn by my old friend Frank Emery, Fellow of St Peter's College, Oxford. Kept close at hand, it serves as an antidote to urban anecdote, and as a continuous reminder of the need to concentrate on broader issues than the curious and the local.

I am grateful to the editors of this series for the close attention that they gave during the preparation of the manuscript, which was most carefully typed by Mrs Ellen Collier with Mrs Cynthia Bunday. Miss Penny Timms drew the maps and figures, and the index was compiled by Mr Paul Coones of Christ Church, Oxford.

Louise Rowe read the whole book in draft, and contributed greatly to its style and content. Dr H. S. A. Fox provided many rare references. The writing of the book, which I was encouraged to undertake by Professor Clifford Smith, took place during leave allowed me by the University of Oxford and by Hertford College, in 1976–77. Hertford itself has provided a most congenial home, and a scholarly and invigorating atmosphere. I am particularly grateful to two of my colleagues in College. Firstly to Andrew Goudie, for all his encouragement during the preparation of this volume. Secondly to Professor Jean Gottmann. His kindness has known no limits and his massive and far-reaching contribution to urban studies has reached even that of the English pre-industrial town, as the pages of this book clearly demonstrate.

Lastly, I am deeply indebted to my father and my late mother who have given me continuous support. My father's all-seeing eyes on tours of towns, both at home and abroad, have added much to my appreciation of them, and this book is affectionately dedicated to him.

October 1977

John Patten
Hertford College,
Oxford

1

The English Pre-Industrial Town

The historical geography of English pre-industrial towns during the sixteenth and seventeenth centuries with which this book is concerned is only slowly being drawn. The forces which promoted change within towns and in their interrelationships, and the processes which initiated lasting growth in some and temporary or permanent decay and decline in others, are imperfectly understood. In some interpretations the pre-industrial town presents the very picture of stability; in others a story of quite remarkable growth; yet in others it represents no more than the first and uncertain stirrings of a later and more massive urban change that was to explode permanently onto the English landscape, and the Englishman's consciousness, from the late eighteenth century onwards.

Any attempt to discuss these forces on a national scale, or in a general way, is still largely a matter of manufacturing intellectual bricks without the benefit of abundant factual straw. Despite an increasing number of detailed studies of single towns, and a very much smaller number of studies of different aspects of several towns together (normally within a county setting, or in a regional context), remarkably little is known about their basic structures. Descriptions on any scale of the structure and nature of their populations, their occupations, and much else besides have tended to be limited in scope and partial in cover. This book examines these basic structural aspects from a national viewpoint; it does not set out to provide a national gazetteer of structural factors in all English towns, but rather a national description and discussion of them. The problems presented by the analysis of the huge surviving quantities of varied and often rather intractable sources – which is necessary for the discussion of even simple urban structures – prevent any basic

15

géographie historique totale of the English pre-industrial town from being undertaken at present. A regional study of all the towns of the populous and wealthy counties of Norfolk and Suffolk does however provide a particular worked example of contemporary urban structures, and offers a comparative framework for them nationally.

Nothing so hazardous as the construction of a national explanatory model is attempted, nor is one particularly desirable except in the most general terms for the urban geography of this period; example rather than theory is that which is both needed and offered here. The lack of overall national economic integration in pre-industrial England would make model-formulation possible only on a regional level, and even then differences between and also within regional systems have to be clearly recognized. The south-east provides an example of the often profound differences within regions: for there were few big towns in Sussex compared with those in Kent; Canterbury in the latter was twice as big as Chichester in the former. Yet, compared with East Anglia's urban system, even that of Kent appears underdeveloped: the great provincial capital of Norwich was more than twice the size of Canterbury.

Population, occupation and the relations between town and country are the focus for this study as a whole, and for the regional case study which exemplifies it. Within its span much is omitted on the administrative, political, cultural and social aspects of urban life, even when such studies might throw light on the bare bones of urban structure. Very little on the fascinating topic of urban topography and morphology is included, and only a little on the almost untilled field of the complex urban social geography of the day. Explicit spatial integration and consideration is delayed until the last chapter, and then is discussed in terms of one region rather than in the nation as a whole.

Three Themes

Although the focus of the book is structural and descriptive, some basic themes do run through it. The first amongst these is that *change,* not *growth,* was the diagnostic characteristic apparent within individual towns and within the growing urban system, a system which, albeit dominated by the continuous and growing economic primacy of London, altered relatively little and slowly in its main lineaments over these two hundred years. A second theme is that the towns of the day existed in a world that made them inherently frail, both demographically and economically. Fires, plagues, and the ravages of warfare both civil and foreign, all had significant and lasting effects on the towns that suffered them. The recovery from these disasters, always painful in the days before insurance, the welfare state and government emergency assistance, could sometimes be a lengthy business; nothing could really be further from our contemporary urban experience than this. Thirdly, the towns of the day were deeply penetrated by the countryside – the exact reverse of today's situation. Ploughland, meadow, orchards, farms and gardens marched boldly into the back streets of even the biggest towns, whose streets were often full of livestock and of people bringing foodstuffs from field to consumer. Furthermore, the rural-born served to replenish urban populations just as much as rural produce filled urban bellies. No growth in the size of towns was possible without these immigrants, because the extremely high urban mortality rates would otherwise have prevented any population replacement, apart from any actual population increase in towns. Town and country were indivisible; urban interests were so often also rural that any study of the urban system of pre-industrial England divorced from its rural context would be profoundly unreal. As individual towns, particularly the larger ones, led by London, became more sophisticated and diverse in the range of manufacturing and services they offered, some slow and progressive loosening of these rural ties began; but it was slight. For example, London was to continue to depend on rural immigrants for its growth until well past the divide of the eighteenth century.

Sources and Approaches

A comprehensive view of pre-industrial urban structures must depend on a variety of often indirect sources, manuscript and printed, primary and secondary. As always in historical geography, sources are a dominant consideration – though they must never be allowed to dominate the very nature of the study itself and the interpretation it offers. To take one example, that of urban populations in a pre-census age; consideration of the size of individual towns is bound to be greatly influenced by the survival of indirect sources for population size, sources which were taken at particular and often widely separated times. These might be the lay subsidies of 1524–25 or the hearth taxes taken in various years between 1662 and 1674; indeed, until far more work is done on the direct evidence of parish registers (themselves often patchy in survival), it will be hard to consider actual population dynamics and growth in detail and on any scale. Such considerations are not ignored in Chapter 3 which examines town populations, nor is the static nature of the best available sources allowed to dominate its shape; instead, all available sources, such as those on rural–urban migration, are used to build up an admittedly partial picture of a more dynamic sort. Suffice it to say here that whilst not every individual source, any more than every individual English town, is considered and used in this book, most major *classes* of source are. Sources are thus set in their correct perspective for the period, in a place in which they can be seen to allow, but emphatically not to dictate, conclusions; and in which understanding of the conclusions they do allow is tempered by an appreciation of the problems of their interpretation.

This study is certainly not breaking new ground for historians, who themselves rarely choose their source before deciding on their area of interest, unlike some practitioners of historical geography in its earlier, exploratory period. Rather, the historian's approach until very recently has been essentially to study individual towns, very often apparently regarded as self-contained urban islands within their walls. Usually it is only the larger, corporate towns that took records, and it is these that have thus been studied, often to the exclusion of the vast majority of smaller towns which did not take and leave many records. To take some notable examples, in order of publication, Hoskins's[1] and McCaffrey's[2] Exeter, Hill's Lincoln[3], Atkinson's Winchester[4], or Dyer's Worcester[5]; or equally, the unpublished studies of Norwich by Pound[6], Ashby-de-la-Zouch by Moxon[7] or Winchester by Rosen[8]. Many texts on the economic and social history of the day whether older,[9] or more recent in publication[10] rather neglect the pre-industrial town, and rarely accord it treatment in a separate chapter.

It is at the same time an undoubted fact that the sixteenth and seventeenth centuries were periods of extensive urbanization occurring side by side with urban stagnation in many regions of Europe.[11] England was one of the most advanced urbanizing countries of the day, comparing well with Holland, where agricultural specialization, labour mobility and rural industry all facilitated urban and seaborne expansion and were not simply responses to urban growth.[12] Both countries contrasted strongly in their turn with the still economically lagging France, dominated like some present-day developing country by its great primate capital city, Paris. The majority of French urban growth at this period involved the expansion of existing towns and cities. There were about a score of new towns built in France between 1500 and 1800. These were of three main sorts, new ports like Le Havre, fortress towns like Nancy and settlements close to royal residences like Versailles.

England contrasted more sharply still with neo-colonial Ireland where in Butlin's words:

> The towns . . . were few in number, for the wave of town development in the north had yet to come. The principal towns were the seaport towns . . . without exception, all the larger towns were sited in sheltered situations at the head of estuaries or bays which facilitated the vital external links with Britain and also with France and Spain. In a sense, the urban system of Ireland at this time formed part of an imperial system, based on England.[13]

Even nearer home, many of the towns grouped around castles in Wales were relics of earlier royal plantations,[14] having appeared on a Welsh landscape in which 'the Dark Ages saw virtually the obliteration of earlier town life'.[15] Indeed, our period was in Wales one of relative economic decay and continuing economic localization.[16] Here the market town system was only slowly emerging and creating a series of towns closely tied to their market areas. The great difference in urban experience between these last two countries (as well as Scotland) and England, provides the reason for concentration on England alone in this book, rather than on the British Isles as a whole.

The Need for Comparability

Few studies of English pre-industrial towns have examined them within a comparative framework, or, until recently, have even systematically related them to their hinterlands. There are many dangers in a comparative approach: if, for example, it is unnecessary or too rigid in construction, particularly if framed in model form. As Wheatley has written: 'There is no virtue in a unitary constructed type that conceals very real structural change through time'; he also observes: 'it may be remarked that it is the purpose of generalization about the past not to demonstrate that everything is regular and repetitive but to what extent it is so'.[17] On the English pre-industrial town there is virtually no published comparative study by a historical geographer. The first by a historian seems no earlier than Hoskins's brief but influential view of the occupational structures of a small number of provincial towns that was published in 1956.[18] No full-scale book cast in a comparative mould appeared until some fifteen years later, when Clark and Slack's admirable volume of essays, *Crisis and order*, was published.[19] The stimulating editorial introduction to this book suggests a comparative framework, and some of the essays included in it stray deliberately outside the bounds of single-town studies. For the eighteenth century, Chalklin has, in his turn, provided the first full-scale comparative study of one aspect of urban life, the building process.[20]

Despite these books, Phythian-Adams correctly observes that: 'Full length modern studies of English provincial cities in the sixteenth century are pitifully few . . . '[21] Elsewhere he has noted that:

> One of the most difficult problems facing pre-industrial urban historians is the problem of comparability between towns. Unlike the nineteenth century, when the censuses can provide an instructive framework of reference, in earlier periods the accident of local documentary survival is the critical factor . . . we may perhaps look forward hopefully to a time when medieval and pre-industrial towns are systematically contrasted on a uniform basis.[22]

Such ideas have taken root slowly, and are taking even longer to flower into systematic contrasts. Indeed, twenty years earlier than he wrote, Checkland was suggesting that more generalized thought about the growth of cities and the evolution of societies housed in them was desirable;[23] and at the same time in America, Lampard was urging study of 'the generalities of urbanization in a way which may help in organizing and evaluating diverse materials available in the history of particular cities'.[24]

We must not be over-critical of the apparent lack of comparative approach, despite the exhortations of Hoskins, Checkland and Lampard in the mid-1950s.[25] The difficulties of large-scale comparisons without empirical underpinning have been clearly demonstrated for the even more intractable medieval period by Russell, concentrating as he does on the identification of functional urban regions:[26] the nature of the survival, arrangement and storage of sources – and also the very scale of research – militated against it. Hobsbawm cogently summarized the problem thus: 'Urban history also possesses a certain technologically determined unity. The individual city is normally a geographically limited and coherent unit, often with its specific documentation and even more often of a size which lends itself to research on the Ph.D. scale.'[27]

Clark and Slack recognize the need for comparability: 'There are some analyses of trade structure, political organization and demographic change in individual towns; but with a handful of exceptions we lack both studies of the urban community in all its interrelated functions and surveys of towns in direct comparison with one another.' Their work offers one of the first comparative frameworks for the study of pre-industrial towns, a mixture of theory and empiricism, filling in the details of a scheme briefly suggested in an earlier review.[28] It is interesting to outline their ideas here,[29] not only because they are original, but also so that what follows after from an historical geographer's point-of-view can be set against them.

Any pre-industrial English town, Clark and Slack postulate, had one, if not all, of four particular characteristics, and these were: a specialist economic function; a peculiar concentration of population; a sophisticated political superstructure; and a community function and impact beyond the immediate limits of the individual town and its inhabitants. Three tiers of English town made up English urban society in the two centuries 1500–1700. A bottom level, exhibiting only two or three of these characteristics, and having strong rural overtones, was the commonest urban type, of which there were several hundred. Secondly, there was a middle tier, all incorporated, that possessed all the four characteristics, had more inhabitants at a greater density, and greater economic specialization and sophistication; there were perhaps a hundred or more of these towns. Thirdly, in the first division were seven or eight major cities, besides London, that had a dominant quasi-metropolitan role in their regions: such places as Bristol, Exeter, Hull, York, Norwich, and Newcastle. These had all four characteristics, were relatively immune from urban crises, and had a dominating influence on urban and rural society over an extensive surrounding region.

Before one proceeds any further with examination of the similarities and differences between English pre-industrial towns, it is vital to pause and ask the question 'What exactly *was* a town in pre-industrial England?'

What was a Town between 1500–1700?

Contemporary observers of the urban scene can be of some guidance in answering this question. Endless lists of 'towns' were published in the topographical guidebooks of the day, often plagiarized one from another. For example, John Adams in 1690 listed 779 places, excluding the cities of London and Westminster under the heading *An Alphabetical Table of all the Cities and Market Towns in England and Wales*. Yet a near-contemporary observed of Bath: 'Tis neither Town nor City yet goes by the name of both: five months in the year 'tis as populous as London, the other seven as desolate . . .'[30] In such lists, what the 'towns' might be was not commonly defined. Some rare attempts to do this were made. William Harrison, for example, used a strictly demographic approach: a 'market town' had, he felt, two thousand 'communicants', whilst a 'village' had but two or three hundred.[31] A more 'ecological' or 'sociological' approach was espoused by the west-country man, John Hooker, who described a town as a 'civitas' in which were 'a multitude of people assembled and collected to the end to continue and live together in a common society yielding dutiful obedience unto their superiors and love to another'.[32] Most foreign observers of the English scene took a city or town as being too self-evident to be worth definition; Botero described what to him was obviously in modern parlance a primate-city system: 'in England, London excepted, although the country do abound in plenty of all good things, yet there is not a city in it that deserves to be called great.'[33]

Indeed contemporaries, while acknowledging the capital's unique size and dominance, were certainly not convinced that London was a coherent whole. For during much of the sixteenth and seventeenth centuries the cities of London and Westminster were morphologically and functionally distinct, and no 'west end' then existed; Southwark flourished by itself over the river; and to John Styrpe the expanding built-up area to the east of the Tower of London was by itself 'a great town'.[34]

It is particularly interesting to reflect that whilst contemporaries were prepared to suggest definitions of towns by their size, or what we would call their urban consciousness as a community, or by their general appearance, they do not seem to rest any definition of urbanity on distinctive urban economies other than the possession of a market. This is due not only to the lack of any really specialized urban economies – there were then no 'coke towns' nor 'pottery towns' – but also to the very nature of most pre-industrial economic activity which transcended urban borders. Farmers and cordwainers raised their 'raw material' in surrounding fields, and rural outworkers kept the urban textile manufacturers of the day 'fed' both with spun yarn and woven cloth. The town of the day was noted more for its integrating economic role as a collecting and distributing centre than as the centre for any peculiarly urban economic activities.

There is nothing odd to the geographer in facing the problems of urban definition, and textbooks on urban geography are littered with attempts to nail down this elusive reality. Historians have found it equally tricky. There is Tate's oft-quoted aphorism: 'Tempers have been shortened, and arteries hardened, in the vain quest of a way of isolating those essential attributes of a town that all can recognize but none can define. . . .'[35]; one can also cite Thernstrom's observation that 'The boundaries of the modern metropolis are elusive', and Robson's contention that 'Ever since the town has been studied there has been agonized debate about its definition', and 'we are still faced with a dilemma in that, however the city is defined, all operational definitions still leave unanswered the conceptual problem that a city cannot be isolated as a functional operating unit in spatial terms'.[36] Often both historians and geographers fall back on dichotomous measurements of size as a framework; for example:

> Whatever its social meaning, there can be no doubt that the urbanity of a place is at least partially a function of its size. . . All that can be said is that the dichotomy is useful for some purposes, but, due to its deficiencies, not for all purposes. We commonly use dichotomous measurements and find them useful, even though reality presents us with a scale. A person 'has a fever' or he does not 'have a fever' . . . Life would be very difficult without such . . . devices, and so would the study of urbanization. In most cases there are additional indices and measurements if we need to go further in the matter.[37]

We need to examine some of these additional indices and measurements quite closely, for even size cannot provide us with a clear measure of urbanity at the bottom of the urban scale, at the points where town and country merged. Indeed, the functions of town and country merged all the way up the urban scale at least until London was reached. One such additional index might be legal or burghal status. But legal status does not necessarily confer urbanity on a place: for example the legal Borough of Dunwich was mostly under the sea by the seventeenth century, and Old Sarum in Wiltshire was sending members to the House of Commons when, for most of the time it was an uninhabited hill outside Salisbury. Similar examples could also be found abroad; on the U.S.A. Gottmann observed: 'Virginia remained throughout the eighteenth century a region with a scattered rural population, with small *boroughs* performing the indispensable functions of local marketing and administrative centers, *most of which could be described as villages by British visitors*'[38] [my italics]. On the other hand, even quite large and long established towns in England could flourish without incorporated legal status as a borough. Worcester, for example, was not incorporated until 1555 and did not become a mayorality with county status until 1621, despite being the county town of its shire and an important textile manufacturing and collecting centre.[39] Similarly, the county capital of West Suffolk, Bury St. Edmunds, once an ancient place of pilgrimmage, did not become incorporated until the beginning of the seventeenth century, despite being – besides an important marketing centre – a place of growing fashion and resort for the gentry who lived around it. Important changes in other parts of the urban system of England would be overlooked, too, if incorporation and legal status were to be our sole criteria for urban definition. By 1650, Manchester had a trade 'not inferior to many cities in the kingdom';[40] and Birmingham, equally a village in status, was in fact a booming manufacturing centre. Holt criticizes the standard *History of Birmingham*[41] for referring to it as a 'village' where 'one would not expect to find such a trade as a goldsmith'.[42] It is axiomatic that freedom from the often economically tiresome and restrictive practices of old established borough towns, with their sometimes inward-looking freemen and guilds, was a positive economic advantage for non-corporate towns at the time.

A second key indicator of urban status, also not without its drawbacks, is the possession of a market. In some cases this could be nothing more than the possession of the *right* to hold a market, which, if not exercised, is as poor an indicator of urbanity as were Old Sarum's corporate status and members of parliament. A live market was a different thing, but still not necessarily a clear indicator of urbanity. A market during the sixteenth and seventeenth centuries was an institution, and as such it was important for the status of any place and for the vitality of its economic life. The income from tolls and dues was of minor importance, although they gave some return for the outlay on the very simple market buildings, stalls, shambles (*ad hoc* and often lean-to shacks and sheds erected by market authorities in the market place, especially for butchers), and cleaning services, which the market authorities provided. Much more important were its resale and distributive functions, attracting buyers and sellers from the surrounding area, affecting the availability of commodities and goods, and acting as the vital focus for the trade of the town itself. A successful market acted as a social centre too, where the food and drink trades catered for those who came to market as much to gossip, see and be seen as to buy and sell. The market could have been as important a centre for the collection and dissemination of news as for foodstuffs, for here national and local news, technical news and that on the state of the market would be exchanged.

The mere presence of the institution itself, the right to hold a market, was no guarantee that all these benefits would accrue to a place and make it a town. Indeed, some places with markets were merely small villages, where once a week a few country folk would bring baskets of eggs, vegetables and capons for sale. For example in Suffolk, Blythburgh was described as having just 'some footsteps of a market', while in mid-sixteenth-century Sussex, the term market town was 'rather misleading since as will be seen many of the market centres, including some of the boroughs, were . . . little more than small villages.'[43] The market function is only one of the many economic functions of a town, and urbanity is best expressed through the town's total occupational and economic structure. A word of warning must be given here against the use of contemporary lists of 'market towns' as evidence of what people of the day thought were towns. These were almost invariably lists of places that had the institution of a market. The use of the word 'town' by contemporaries is often misleading. 'Town' for example appears in many Hearth Tax listings over those taxed in hamlets of three or four houses, sometimes as an abbreviation for 'township'. To take just one example, a protectionist diatribe of the 1630's questioned 'How many Townes there be in the champion parte and how many of them Markets?', and 'How many Ploughs in a little Towne, in a middling Towne and in great Towne?'[44] Every place seemed to be termed a 'town'; 'towne' by itself was used, it appears, both for a 'village' and for a market town, or at least a place where a market was held. It is wrong to start off from the supposition that in the sixteenth and seventeenth centuries in studying towns one is, *ipso facto*, studying market towns. Everitt maintains that there are very few adequate histories of the market towns of England, unless they have also been county towns (like Worcester and Lincoln), or have developed into industrial cities (like Leicester and Leeds), or into watering-places (like Cheltenham).[45] One would agree with this contention if the word 'market' were deleted, for it automatically imposes much on our outlook about towns of the day.

Most workers on medieval towns also tend to discount the 'market' or the 'borough' as an indicator of urban status. Palliser and Pinnock, in their study of the markets of Staffordshire, suggest that the chief economic function of these markets was as centres of distribution to the surrounding areas through shops, markets and fairs. In the larger centres, many people gained a living by working in shops and workshops, selling raw materials and foodstuffs, and in some cases processing them before sale. But the smaller market centres were not urbanized even in this sense; they were ordinary villages, earning a living mainly from agriculture and distinguished from neighbouring settlements only by the privilege of holding a weekly 'market'. Palliser and Pinnock conclude that 'the term "market town" as used here implies no more than a settlement with market rights, irrespective of whether it was large or small, or whether it enjoyed economic specialization or not'.[46] It would perhaps be better to try to drop the term 'market town' altogether from our vocabulary for medieval as much as pre-industrial England, in order to avoid inbuilt assumptions. Certainly the two most stimulating studies of the medieval English town to date, those by Hilton and by Bridbury, do not deal with the market alone. Hilton, in discussing little places like Cheltenham, Stratford-upon-Avon, Stow-on-the-Wold and Tamworth, wrote: 'The outstanding characteristics of these small towns . . . was that in spite of their size, they shared with much bigger towns and cities a sharp functional differentiation from the agricultural hinterland. Their inhabitants were overwhelmingly concerned with commerce and manufacture and the weekly market . . .'[47]

It would be wrong to elevate the market to any greater role than Hilton ascribes to it here, all the more so in the pre-industrial period when many smaller market centres failed altogether, and developing urbanization in the larger centres resulted in towns with many more functions than that of the hitherto all-dominating market function. It is their overall *centrality* that we need to penetrate. As Bridbury observed in his study of medieval towns in the fifteenth century:

> In the later middle ages, as at all times, towns were generally speaking no less productive than farms or workshops, though their products were more various and included the provision of services as well as the making of things. They were in no sense parasitic on the countryside – the self in-dulgence of an affluent society. Their main business was to release farmers from having to market their own produce and turn their own raw materials into finished goods. In doing this they in fact raised the quality of the goods and services available by making manufacturing and dis-tributing their full time concern. In short, towns were indispensable com-ponents of the economic system. No economy has ever advanced without them. *To study them is to study the entire system at a vital confluence of flows* . . . [my italics].[48]

To him a place became a town when more than a tiny minority of its inhabitants could earn a livelihood by devoting their working hours to manufacturing and service industries rather than farming.[49]

Medieval studies of English towns do not help much in the task of telling us exactly what a pre-industrial town was, although they do help to set the market institution and the market mechanism in their correct context. Cross-cultural analogies can be as unhelpful in urban definition. For example, in Russia during the sixteenth and seventeenth centuries the frontier may have been as powerful a force in shaping the town as it is held to have been on its nineteenth century North American counterpart.

> The Russian town of the seventeenth century was quite distinct from its Western counterpart. Having absolutely no form of real autonomy, Russian towns were mere points of administration for their surrounding territories, under the complete domination of the State. On the southern frontier, towns had important defensive functions, the inhabitants both of towns themselves, and of their surrounding districts holding their land (in small amounts) in return for military and ancillary services. . . . There were no sharp social differences in this respect between town and country, and the whole was tied into a single military-economic system.[50]

There is not much here to help us understand the English town of today. Cross-cultural and cross-temporal models of what was urban before the industrial revolution prove equally impractical. The greatest of these, Sjoberg's *Pre-Industrial city*[51] is an intellectual *tour de force*, but like many of its type its strength lies more in inspiring ideas and controversies than in providing instruction in particulars. Its drawbacks as a general source for, *inter alia*, urban definition have been succinctly discussed elsewhere. Sjoberg distinguished his universal pre-industrial 'city' from the rural community by its size, its density of population and buildings, by its heterogeneity, and by the presence of full-time specialists. McGee observed that medieval social theorists like Ibn Kaldun and Botero had stressed these differences between rural and urban society in no less definite a fashion.[52] Wheatley perhaps summed up the problem of definition most aptly when he wrote: 'Urbanism is the most protean of terms', and there 'is in fact no *a priori* reason to suppose that all the multifarious groupings of population both past and present that are and have been conventionally designated as "urban" should necessarily be subsumed within a single logically coherent field'.[53] We have to face at least the possibility that in pre-industrial England there may well have been regional variations in what constituted a town. This may well have been the case between faster developing, more populated and wealthier lowland England on the one hand, and less advanced upland England on the other. There certainly were differences between English towns and their Scots, Welsh and Irish equivalents.

We have, then, a clear problem of definition in a book on English pre-industrial towns; we have some cross-cultural and cross-temporal analogies; we have a number of definitions of what the pre-industrial English town might have been; we know what it was not, or rather that corporate status or market rights do not define it; and we have some suggestions of what a definitive framework for them might be. Most notable of these last is Clark and Slack's fourfold framework,[54] though there are, of course, others. For example, Burley suggested that 'the fundamental attributes of a town may be defined as: a place of more than average population density usually but not always expressed by an active corporate life, by an urban self-consciousness and by the existence of ruling elements.'[55] In his study of Essex, using the Hearth Taxes as an index of density and bearing these assumptions in mind, Burley isolated thirty-three 'places' as 'towns'; needless to say not all those places referred to as market towns in contemporary lists for Essex are to be found amongst his thirty-three towns. As Burley observes, a market centre in Essex had a very small core of permanent residents and need not have been different in density from its neighbouring hamlets, although swollen in size once or twice weekly by market visitors.[56] We must conclude that one is chasing an elusive goal in asking the essentialist question, 'what is a town?'; all that we can hope to do is to attempt the answer to the nominalist question 'what do we mean by the word town?'

Life in Pre-industrial Towns

In examining the English pre-industrial town, it is important to discuss their general appearance and the characteristics and tempo of life of their inhabitants. We must naturally turn first for illumination to those who could actually see what they and their inhabitants were like, to the recorded written observations of contemporaries.[57] Contemporary descriptions of medieval topography, including those of medieval towns are comparatively rare and of medieval urban life even rarer. Of pre-industrial towns they become much more common, under the liberating influence of the printing press and the proliferation of the book. This does not mean that the increasing

numbers of urban descriptions as the years of two centuries un-
folded necessarily always means an increase in our knowledge. As
Moir observes:

> John Leland had blazed the way and a large band of later Tudor
> topographical writers followed his lead. Perhaps the greatest of them was
> William Camden, though he can scarcely qualify as a tourist. For, setting
> out upon the herculean task of covering the entire country, including the
> outlying islands, from the Scillies to the Shetlands, he was forced to turn
> to a band of correspondents, for information about those parts which he
> could not visit himself . . . later authors were to go even further,
> depending not merely upon their friends for help but lifting accounts
> wholesale from earlier works, and compiling treatises which were little
> more than guidebooks listing noteworthy sites.

Nonetheless, the better writers can be a mine of information about
the general topography and appearance of the town, though
perhaps less so on their economy in general; detail of townsfolk's life
is usually merely anecdotal. In the case of urban topography it is
clear that 'Many of the more prosperous towns were paved by this
time [i.e. Tudor] and a few had even progressed towards some form
of elementary sanitation, though such developments were by no
means common.'[58]

Generally speaking, descriptions of urban economic activity
improved by the late seventeenth and early eighteenth centuries; for
example Fiennes and Defoe were acute observers of the activities of
the towns that they visited. On their arrival, the first thing that both
set out to discover was the particular staple commodity of the place.
So, we learn from their works that Leicester and Nottingham were
renowned for their stockings; Bedford famous for its hats and bone-
lace; silk-weaving was carried on at Canterbury; ribbon-making
and the tanning of leather at Coventry; and Newcastle had a great
reputation for its pottery. Within a comparatively small area of the
West Midlands, we get quite detailed economic information; we are
told that Birmingham specialized in guns, buttons and buckles,
Walsall in bits and bridles, Dudley in nails, and Wolverhampton in
locks.[59]

Earlier writers were, sadly, much less systematically informative,
only the very economically remarkable struck them as worth
recording from the scenes they observed. Camden, for example, saw
the rising manufacturing star of Birmingham, with its unusual concentration of metalworking as 'Brermicham, full of inhabitants and
resounding with hammers and anvils, for the most of them are

Smiths'.[60] Leland had picked out the same sort of thing earlier, in 1538, but whilst it was a fairly rare comment on urban manufacturing, it was not necessarily accurate. For,

> when John Leland visited Birmingham he observed that 'a large part of the town' was 'maintained by smiths'. The great number of their workshops beside the main road would certainly give him this impression. If he had made a more thorough investigation he would have found that tanneries and fulling-mills accounted for as much capital as the smiths, although most of them, standing by streams at a distance from the streets would not be seen by passing travellers.[61]

Of other equally interesting places such as Manchester, we are told little, merely that 'Manchester, on the south side of the Irwell River, standeth in Salfordshire, and is the fairest, best builded, quickest and most populous town of all Lancashire.'[62] But we are not told why it was [economically] 'quick', or to what its burgeoning population could be attributed. We have to wait for nearly two centuries for Fiennes to tell us of its large market place taking up two streets' length full of linen cloth and cotton tickings, then its main manufactures.[63]

The work of contemporaries is thus full of pitfalls. It often tended to laud the not very remarkable, for example Sir William Breretons described Newcastle-upon-Tyne in 1635 as 'beyond all compare the fairest and richest towne in England ... inferiour for wealth and building to noe cittie save London and Bristow,' whilst Munday compared tiny Penryn in Cornwall with Constantinople![64] Conversely other observers may pass over points of import to us, with the result that we come to doubt the value of the source for anything more than random and anecdotal economic information; William Smith for example dismissed Lavenham, with its once mighty broadcloth industry, with the words: 'Laneham standeth upon the head of the same river [as Hadleight], six myles northwest from Hadley'. Economic information, when given, is too often embedded in an anecdotal and confusing morass, Baskerville, for example, observing of Leicester in the 1670's that 'it is now an old stinking town; situated upon a dull river inhibited for the most part by tradesmen, viz. *worsted combers and clothiers*, for the streets being then a sweeping and cleaning against the judges coming in the next morning the stinking puddles of ... and water being then stirred, made me go spewing through all the streets as I went to see it.'[65] Yet he ignored Leicester's important leather trade in exactly the same way as Leland had overlooked Birmingham's a century and a half earlier. Economic and other information derived from Government papers and reports is often equally perfunctory. The late sixteenth-century port of Whitehaven, booming by the eighteenth-century, is described by Commissioners reporting on Cumbrian ports merely as having but one ship of nine tons,[66] and Lord Leicester writing to Walsingham of Southampton found that it was merely one of the 'decayed parts of the realm'. Very much more detail would be desirable from such sources, reasons for decay being as illuminating of the urban conditions of the day as reasons for growth.[67]

If we know something about the general appearance and topography of towns and about their economy and markets from contemporaries, they were very reticent about attitudes to urban life. A little can be learnt indirectly, from the actions of contemporaries; for example in the extension of the area where bills of mortality were taken in London. This spread from the tightly-packed area within the city walls in the sixteenth century to Westminster and outlying districts in the seventeenth century, demonstrating not merely a stronger administrative control but also a growing awareness by contemporaries of a 'functional greater London' that had long in fact been in existence.[68] Some direct evidence on attitudes can be found, for example one elderly inhabitant of later sixteenth-century Southampton observed disapprovingly of his fellow townsfolk ' . . . then downe with old houses, and new sett in their place: for the houses where the fathers dwelt could not content their children. Then must everie man of good calling be furnished with change of plate, with great store fyne lynnen, rich tapistre, and all other things which make showe of braverie'.[69] Urban life was the subject of at least one contemporary debate between the rural-dwelling Vincent, fond of field sports and fresh air, and his urban cousin Valentine. This was cast in the form of a recorded debate on the merits of urban life; this sort of 'dispute' was a very typical medium of the sixteenth century in particular, for example about whose country was nicest between the English and French or on the economy of the day as is found in the *Discorse*.[70] In this verbal battle, Valentine is very revealing of some contemporary attitudes:

> The manner of most Gentlemen and Noblemen also, is to house themselves . . . in the suburbs of the Cittie, because most commonly, the ayre there being somewhat at large, the place is healthy, and though the distaunce from the bodye of the Towne, the noyse not much . . . Also for commoditie we find many lodgings, both spacious are roomethy, with Gardaines and Orchardes very delectable . . . our water is excellente and much better than your have anye, our ground and fieldes most pleasaunte, our fier equall with yours. This much touching the site of our Towne dwellinge and the Elements.[71]

Vincent was won over, and on the last page he vows to give up his bucolic country ways and head for the city, just like so many other pre-industrial rural migrants.

For a greater appreciation of the nature as well as the quality of urban life we must turn to the less direct evidence offered by numerous documents and papers. Certainly life in the towns and cities of Tudor, Stuart and Restoration England was probably picturesque only at a distance. Nearer to hand, for the great majority of their inhabitants actually experiencing it, urban life was undoubtedly difficult and not very comfortable. Dickens has summed conditions up very lucidly. He wrote that it would be

> unwise to dwell too exclusively upon the picturesque aspects of life in the Tudor city. It was an age when moralists ceaselessly preached the virtues of industry and parsimony, when mastery in a craft remained difficult to attain, when the number of holidays diminished, when wages were not readily adjusted to the constant inflationary process. The journeyman worked in winter from down to sunset, in the summer from 5.00 a.m. to 7.00 p.m. or 8.00 p.m., with only two and a half hours for breakfast, dinner or drinking. And if official valuations of their goods bear any relation to realities, artisans and most tradesmen cannot have boasted more than a few poor sticks of furniture and very few of the domestic comforts taken for granted by all classes since Victorian times. For more than two centuries after the death of Elizabeth I, the men and women of York had to accept a constant cycle of epidemics, a short life span, much unassuaged pain and frequent bereavements. The harsh lot of the average townsman was far from originating with the rise of factories and industrial slums.[72]

Life in town houses was cramped, one or two rooms perhaps housing all the functions of family life cheek by jowl with domestic manufacturing. Fireplaces were rudimentary, windows small, through ventilation often lacking, running water largely non-existent and internal sanitary arrangements primitive in the extreme. Outside in the streets, which were often the ultimate destination of these primitive sanitary arrangements, mire, filth and butchers' offal mingled on unpaved and undrained surfaces rarely swept or attended to by the town scavenger whose work was often done even in London by the now nearly extinct Red Kite; pigs might be found roaming the streets in some towns until well into the seventeenth century. Towns were usually unlit and not very safe at night; certainly places where the chances of being jostled by an apprentice, or by a drover's cattle, of being drenched by the filth thrown up by the wheels of a coach or that thrown down from an upper window were quite high. The clean town was something to be remarked on.

Bristol seems far more salubrious than most of the towns of the realm. As William Smith could say in 1588, 'there is no dunghill in all the city' and Speed could point to its underground sewers removing 'all noysome filth and uncleaness'.[73] Nottingham, too, was noted for 'her Market Place . . . large, sweet and cleane'.[74]

The streets were the focus of life for the town-dweller. Through them vagrants and other unfortunates were whipped, and through them marched the guild and religious processions that bound the town's life, punctuated its year and gave it so much rhythm; the role of urban ceremonial, as Phythian-Adams has pointed out, was great.[75] The life of the town was periodic. It did not know exactly when the next plague, or pestilence, killing winter, or food shortage would come; but the town did know that such evils would come, for bitter experience had proved this to be the case. It did, however, know when the next procession, or the next mayor-making was to be. And it certainly knew about the market days, three or four a week in one or more market places in the bigger towns, and the fairs, three or four a year often lasting for several days in the larger centres. Early morning countryfolk with their foodstuffs and manufactured wares poured down the streets before dawn, and so too passed the richer grain factors, maltsters, wool broggers and clothiers. Stalls would often be set up in the streets, for much marketing could not be accommodated in the market-place alone. Out of market or fair time lesser towns would relapse into quietude. One contemporary visiting Winchester in 1623 on a day other than a market day described this cathedral and market city as:

> like a body without a soul; and I know not the reason of it, but for ought which I perceived there were almost as many parishes as people . . . but I am sure I walked from the one end of it to the other, and saw not thirty people of all sorts: so that I think if a man should go to Winchester for a goose, he might lose his labour, for a trader cannot live there.[76]

Yet a few years later a travelling lieutenant who arrived in the same city when the judges were there saw a completely different scene. Winchester was where he had 'as much adoe to obtayne a fayre Quarter, as I had in all my travell: for this old City was then crowding full'.[77] Yet he 'soone obtayn'd' a 'good inn' after his arrival at Portsmouth,[78] presumably on a quiet day.

Much of the economic life of the market and fair took place outside the formal market place.[79] This was usually conducted in the inns, as the daily life of many townsfolk was dominated by the local ale-house, where fire, company and news could be obtained;

Everitt says that 'the Elizabethan and Stuart inn has no exact counterpart in the modern world. It was the hotel, the bank, the warehouse, the exchange, the scrivener's office and the market place of many a private trader'.[80] The inn, whose role has been surveyed in depth by Chartres, played an extremely significant part not only in the towns in which it was predominantly to be found, but in the economy as a whole in a period of importance in England's steady development.[81] In particular in a predominantly illiterate age before the newspaper, the inn was a vital centre of information for the town. The higher up the urban ladder they were, the more literate, it seems, the townspeople became.[82] But even they had sometimes to rely on word of mouth for news on politics, prices and plagues, for broadsheets were often printed in London and tardily distributed, with the result that in-depth treatment of disasters were often not read until long after the event; an example was the *Lamentable News from the town of Darnton [i.e. Darlington] in the Bishopricke of Durham . . . where was burned 273 houses, uppon the 7 day of May . . . 1585 . . .*[83]

The social structure of the English pre-industrial town was very different from that of towns in modern England.[84] There was no equivalent to today's middle class, but generally a wide gap between a few very rich and comfortable and the great many poor and uncomfortable. Anything up to fifty per cent of the town's population might be poor in the terms of the day, existing at subsistence level or below. Table 1 illustrates the incidence of poverty in a variety of towns of different regions of the country at the end of the

Table 1: POVERTY IN ENGLISH TOWNS AT THE TAKING OF THE HEARTH TAXES, 1666–72

Those exempt from paying tax because of poverty

Bristol	20%	(PRO. E179/116/541)
York	16–20%	(PRO. E179/218/180)
Norwich	55%	(PRO. E179/254/701; E179/336)
Leciester	25%	(*VCH. Leices,* IV, 1958, p.156–9)
Rotherham	18%*	
Doncaster	19%*	
Richmond	27%*	
Bicester	30%*	

*Purdy, J. D. 'The Hearth Tax Returns for Yorkshire', Unpubl. M.Phil. thesis University of Leeds (1975), 360, 361, 334, 328.

seventeenth century. Certainly as much as a third of the population of some towns was too poor to take a very significant part in any economic acitivities. The aged, infirm, vagrant and work shy, who made a perilous living as sweepers or as pedlars of cheap drink, were susceptible to the frequent short-term fluctuations in the prosperity of the pre-industrial town.[85] Poverty, like filth, was everywhere to be seen on the streets, and existed next to the sometimes ostentatious life style of the top five per cent or so of older men, sherrifs and other leaders of the urban community who, as the merchants, clothiers or grocers of the day, might own some two-thirds of the property, and control much of the wealth, of the town. It was the poor who suffered most from the exigencies of poor supply, and from the cold. In the tiny town of Congleton, for example, 'It was . . . • the poorer craftsmen who were hardest hit by any dislocation of life and unemployment. For example, the "great snow" of 1614–15 caused great hardship'[86] Welfare was rudimentary and not particularly generous, reacting with 'outdoor relief' to only the most terrible situations, although a sometimes surprisingly humane system of 'indoor relief' (where the recipient was taken into an institution, e.g. an almshouse) on a longer-term basis was developing for the young, old and infirm; bones were set, haunches of veal provided weekly, and suits of clothing kitted out the young apprentice. On the other hand, fires and plagues – whose devastating effects are outlined later in Chapter 2 and 3 – struck at the poor and the rich with indiscriminate force: if a human life was frail, so was the town he or she inhabited.

The definition and distribution of different social and occupational groups within cities and towns is the constant preoccupation of both the modern urban geographer and the historical geographer. It is an easier problem for the former to tackle as he can observe the streets and interview the population for himself, but the historical geographer is hindered by the poverty of his sources. Whatever conclusions on the internal structure of pre-industrial towns may be reached, they are bound to be dominated by two overriding influences. The first is that the physical form of any pre-industrial town in England was very compact; and even in those larger places with some surburban growth outside the walls or outside the town liberties, houses pressed close to each other. The compactness of towns was in large due to the constraint of distance, for those who lived in pre-industrial towns walked almost everywhere, and journey-to-work patterns were likely to be very short. In many cases people lived where they worked at their craft or sold their goods from their houses, literally 'living over the shop'. The tiny towns that supplied the basic urban functions for the countryside of pre-industrial England, were very often a couple of streets crossing each other with fields running to the very backs of the houses that lined them, and it would have been possible to walk from end to end in a very few minutes. In the larger towns, even the great capital of London, the tyranny of distance produced a 'walking city'; Defoe and even Johnson could still comfortably walk across London in a day.

Within this compact area, without the liberating influence of, for example, the bicycle or organised intra-urban transport save for the very grand, townfolk were not entirely integrated. There is evidence that in many cases residential differentiation was vertical, not horizontal. The archetype of the ground floor shop with manufacturing sheds behind, the master and his family living above the shop on the first and second floor, with apprentices, journeymen and women 'servants' huddled in the attics and garrets, may not have been universal. But it was certainly common in many town centres.

'Horizontal' residential differentiation certainly existed too. As Ward succinctly observes:

> Residential differentiation is not, of course, unique to modern cities for from their beginnings urban settlements have displayed in varying degree some of the complexities of their social and economic organizations in the internal arrangements of the land uses . . . Within the most precocious of medieval European cities, traditional social patterns persisted alongside new institutions and it was not until the sixteenth or seventeenth centuries that rent yield rather than customary use or social obligation began to influence the assignment of urban land uses and encouraged the utilization of increasingly valuable central urban locations for more specialized commercial activities rather than for a mixture of residential and commercial uses.[87]

Sjoberg[88] clearly demonstrated that residential differentiation was closely linked to occupational differentiation in many cases, though his universal cross-cultural and cross-temporal models are open to many doubts, refinements and departures. Examples abound in English pre-industrial towns as much of occupational and residential heterogeneity as of homogeneity: to take just one such example, in Southwark, just over London Bridge from the City, a plan of a piece of civic property showed that in 1686 this block contained a tavern, and in addition a brazier, an upholsterer, a plumber, a sword cutler, a pewterer, a tinman and a boxmaker.[89] Wealth, occupation and residence were correlated.

Indeed, one of the most common preconceptions about pre-industrial towns is that the rich commonly lived in the commercial centre of them and that the poor lived on their edges, and although the distance separating the two was not very great there is much evidence to suggest that this sort of pattern *generally* obtained. In the Medway towns, the Hearth Tax assessments in the 1660s and 1670s showed that in Rochester the largest houses, and hence presumably the wealth of the town, were concentrated in a small area around the cathedral. Here was the commercial centre, along the High Street, and to the south the homes of such fashionable society as the town could boast. Elsewhere off the main street the average number of hearths per household dropped rapidly to the level of the surrounding rural area. Similarly in Gloucester the most valuable properties clustered to the west of the cross in the centre of the town, whilst other parts of the city near the northern and southern boundaries were squalid, crowded and poor.[90]

The reality of pre-industrial urban differentiation was much more complex than the foregoing general and preliminary discussion can indicate. Two major theoretical frameworks dominate this topic, Sjoberg's,[91] and Vance's.[92] The internal structure of Sjoberg's 'feudal' pre-industrial city was dominated by the marked social cleavage between a feudal elite and the 'rest'. Hence there was a rich central area, not only because it was an economic focus, but also where religious, ceremonial and political activities were concentrated and from where the power that they generated flowed. Outside this dominating core there was a steep downward gradient as status diminished outwards, the poor living beneath and beyond the walls. In Vance's view, by contrast, the social geography of the precapitalist city was dominated not by the exigences of 'feudal' life, but by the guild system. The guild was the pre-eminent spatial organizer within the city. Vance felt that 'to exist within a guild area was necessary for the proper practise of a trade and for the receipt of the social benificience of the organization . . . the place of residence and occupation, coextensive in handicraft technology, were located close to those of other members of the same guild . . . by occupational accident rather than by rent-paying ability'.[93] The result was occupational zoning and the mixing of social classes. We would not expect either of those models entirely to fit the English pre-industrial urban experience, an England whose urban social structure was certainly not dominated by a feudal patriciate in Sjoberg's sense, but in which, powerful though guild organization may have been, there was little evidence for guild-dominated spatial expression in the way which Vance postulated.

We would not expect it to be so, and geographers for far too long have depended on such archetpes with little empirical investigation. Until, that is, Langton's first excursion into the subject of residential patterns in pre-industrial cities.[94] He examined Dublin, Exeter and Newcastle at the time of the Hearth Taxes in the 1660s and 1670s. Numbers of hearths per house were used as a surrogate for wealth, and very similar patterns of wealth were discovered between the towns. Houses of various sizes were unevenly distributed, and quite marked peaks existed in each city. In all of these places, Langton says, peaks were located in proximity to the castle, either between it and the main place of worship or the guildhall. This location did not correspond to the main marketing and commercial centre, though this was not far away. The central market place was usually the dominant commercial focus only in the smaller towns, most of the larger towns having a number of markets for different specialist goods in different streets; markets and marketing were not market-place bound. Indeed, in Newcastle, the main market area was relatively low-ranking in terms of wealth.[95] Glass, using the evidence of the Tax on Birth, Deaths, Marriages, Bachelors, Spinsters etc., taken in 1695, comes to a similar conclusion for London (in which there were numerous markets), stating that the City was 'an area with a fairly distinctive pre-industrial topography. The proportions of upper status households were higher in the centre, and the lower status households showed the greatest relative frequency on the periphery.'[96] Langton concludes that Sjoberg's model of the pre-industrial city provided a much better approximation of patterns of wealth distribution which actually existed in four of the largest British cities in the late seventeenth century than that of Vance,[97] though there was, in Newcastle at least, the tendency for occupational subgroups to be concentrated and separated in the case of mercantile, service and manufacturing activity, and there was no clear clustering around a central business district. He states:

> Predictably, the social geography of Newcastle in the mid-seventeenth century was more complicated than any of the archetypes of Sjoberg or Vance. But it was not just more complicated: it was fundamentally different. Newcastle was not a feudal pre-industrial city, nor was it [in Vance's terms] a pre-capitalist or capitalist city. A merchant clique was pre-eminent in wealth and municipal power. Its social dominance was ex-pressed geographically in the existence of a mercantile quarter in that part of the city, where its economic purposes were best served and where the institutions through which it dominated the city were located. In addition, the city possessed other residentially patterned occupational

districts which were in some areas reinforced by 'class zoning', and in others countervailed by it. If the city [Newcastle] must be fitted into the schemes of Vance and Sjoberg, then it could be said to represent some hybrid . . .[98]

Many more such studies, which will produce different sorts of conclusions, will be needed before we can speak with certainty on the social geography of the pre-industrial English towns. Such studies will probably be restricted to London, the great provincial cities and seaports, and to county capitals and manufacturing centres which had distinctive social geographies, and what can be achieved by such studies will be limited severely by available data. The Hearth Taxes are a suitable source for the study of the internal social and economic structure of late seventeenth-century cities, but comparable sources for such structures are sadly lacking for the sixteenth and early seventeenth centuries. More detailed work on intractable sources such as rentals and borough court records presents the main opportunities for these years.[99] By contrast, the several hundred small urban centres would typically have had a very simple social geography to match their equally simple topography. In the smallest towns there was often merely a couple of streets, with perhaps in addition a market area – a space by the church or around a market cross – and informal market buildings, the whole being surrounded by fields that were both visible from their centre and the economic preoccupation of most of that place's townsfolk. The social geography would have been equally simple in a slightly larger town of a couple of thousand people A few more substantial houses at the centre perhaps, the owners of whom would have been equally as concerned with the management of the fields and even manors that they owned in the neighbouring country. Around these, along the few streets, the houses of the few local tradesmen – a tailor, a shoemaker and cordwainer, a weaver or two, a turner and one or two others – would be scattered, too few to be grouped significantly either by wealth or by occupation. The fact that many of the townsfolk in these small and medium-sized towns would have been very directly concerned in the surrounding land which they farmed daily, introduces a new dimension into the study of their social geography.

For most English pre-industrial towns, even the greatest, were much influenced by the country. This is the last general dimension of life in pre-industrial towns that must be considered. The short streets of the smaller towns in particular ran out into the surrounding countryside, and their inhabitants were often as much concerned with the prices of sheep and corn as with the simple craft and service occupations which supplied the immediate needs of the town and surrounding country. Better-off townsfolk were as likely to own rural land as urban lots.[100] Country rhythms often dictated urban rhythms. The whole economy even of larger towns would stop at harvest time; John Taylor, searching for a reason for the quiet of Winchester when he visited it, postulated: 'it may be they were all at harvest work', and at Birmingham nailmaking was such a seasonal activity that dealers spoke of difficulties in getting nails at harvest time when the nailers were busy with the crops. In March industrial work again stopped 'as it was ploughing time.[101] To try to understand towns divorced from their fields is to wrench the study of the urbanism of the day from its socio-cultural context. Laslett has indeed gone so far as to suggest that true rural/urban differences only existed between London and the rest of the country.[102]

Braudel recognised that 'The towns are so many electricity transformers. They increase tension, accelerate the rhythm of exchange and ceaselessly stir up men's lives'; he continued: 'There is no town, no townlet without its villages, its scrap of rural life attached'.[103] Everywhere one looks in Western Europe at the time the same picture obtains. Only a few suburbs spilled out into the country, whilst the green fingers of farmland penetrated into every town.

> Padua remained plunged in her rural pursuits, and Bayand and his companions in 1509 saw the city engaged upon agricultural tasks . . . 'every day much hay was harvested', relates the *Loyal Serviteur*, 'and in that quarter the loads were so great that they almost had to be forced through a gateway'. The same sight could be seen at Brescia . . . pigs were reared in large numbers inside the city walls. These scenes from agricultural life . . . show how open sixteenth century towns were, whatever the cost, to their surrounding countryside. How else could they have survived?[104]

The fact of this rural influence on urban life in pre-industrial England must be borne in mind as we examine their nature and historical geography. To utilize in this context the words of Carlo Cipolla writing about the classical world: 'The town was not an organism in itself but rather an organ within the broader context of an urban-rural continuum', is to sum up this relationship most succinctly for the majority of pre-industrial England other than London.[105]

2

Antecedents, Patterns and Forces for Change

The Pre-industrial 'Period'

This book is confined to an examination of English towns in the period between 1500 and 1700, denoted as 'pre-industrial' within this work. The choice of dates needs explanation for, like any dates encompassing a 'period', it must be recognized that they are imposed on the past, in the hope of reflecting both the actuality of the time and an author's preconceptions about it. The word 'period' is, like the word 'town', a nominalist rather than an essentialist ascription: thus, the 'pre-industrial period' as adopted here, is a slice through the urban historical geography of the day: it does not represent any completely coherent and self-contained reality. Many facets of the pre-industrial town between 1500 and 1700 owed much to their medieval antecedents, whilst others represented new developments which carried on into the eighteenth century and beyond. A crude ranking of towns during the medieval period, as seen in Table 2, shows that whatever else was happening to towns over these 350 years, they were undoubtedly changing their relative standing as measured by wealth. The sources used for this table – different sorts of taxation – were compiled on different bases for different ends, and are far from being properly comparable, so that some apparent changes in rank may be due to the nature of the sources. But, even taking this into account, the table clearly shows the rise to prominence of some towns and relative decline of others. Medieval conditions of wealth were not simply to be replicated amongst the towns of pre-industrial England, and sometimes underwent considerable alteration. It can be assumed that the same observations could be made about population, as urban size was

Table 2: THE RANKING OF 43 ENGLISH PROVINCIAL TOWNS (EXCLUDING LONDON AND ITS SUBURBS) IN 1334, 1524/5, AND THE 1660s–70s[1]

Town	1334	Rank 1524–25	1660s–70s
Bristol	1	2	3
York	2	11	2
Newcastle	3	*	4
Boston	4	22	7
Great Yarmouth	5	20	
Lincoln	6	15	
Norwich	7	1	1
Oxford	8	29	8+
Shrewsbury	9	26	12
Kings Lynn	10	8	18
Salisbury	11	4	13
Coventry	12	3	16
Ipswich	13	6	9
Hereford	14	19	
Canterbury	15	17	10
Gloucester	16	17	22
Winchester	17		
Southampton	18	27	
Beverley	19		
Cambridge	20	28	6+
Newbury	21	21	
Plymouth	22		
Newark	23		
Peterborough	24		21
Nottingham	25		24
Exeter	26	5	5
Bury	27	13	
Stamford	28	30	
Ely	29		
Luton	30		
Reading		9	
Colchester		10	14
Lavenham		12	11
Worcester		14	
Totnes		16	15
Hull		18	
Hadleigh		23	
St. Albans		24	
Leicester		25	17+
Chester			19
Portsmouth			20
Rochester			23
Dover			

[1] This table is based on assessments of relative wealth from the taxation of 1334, the lay subsidies of 1524–25, and the hearth taxes taken in the 1660s and 1670s.

* Not taxed that time, or not taxed previously.

\+ Excludes the colleges.

usually closely correlated with urban wealth. If wealth and population were changing it is certain that some other of the influences on, and characteristics of, the medieval town were to change in the pre-industrial period also, either in their balance, or into something entirely new.

What, then, did the pre-industrial town owe to its medieval forerunners? By attempting to answer this question we can hope to isolate what was new in pre-industrial urbanization. The basic urban framework was essentially medieval, resulting from the large number of towns instituted in that period. By comparison, few new towns were established on the English landscape in the two centuries following 1500, though some established ones changed in relative importance and some villages gained sufficient prominence to be classed as towns. The total share of the country's population living in medieval towns was small, but their influence was much greater than size alone would indicate. The author of the most recent book on the *English Medieval town*, C. Platt,[1] has pointed to their twin characteristics of small scale and rural nature: 'Medieval England was never intensively urbanized . . . Units of population which, for one reason or another, could be described as 'towns' were plentiful, but they were often very small . . . It was not just that the English town was small; frequently it also retained many rural characteristics that blurred its distinctions from the countryside'. Throughout the sixteenth and seventeenth centuries the total urban proportion of the country's population increased only slowly, whilst the effect of the countryside, diminishing in importance though it was on the larger towns, remained an important influence on lesser places. However the characteristic role the town played in medieval peasant society, so clearly summed up by Rodney Hilton,[2] may have changed considerably between 1500 and 1700, as the very nature of society itself changed away from a 'peasant' and neo-feudal economy. Their small size and the patent rurality of the smaller ones notwithstanding, medieval towns were a vital part of high medieval English society and economy, and according to A. R. Bridbury at least, played a marked role in maintaining the economy during the national slump of the fifteenth century.[3]

Alan Everitt has postulated three types of English towns in terms of their origins.[4] These were planted towns, founded *de novo* by royal grant or charter, like Stratford-upon-Avon; a more numerous group comprising hundreds of what are described as 'organic towns' or *vills* which dated from before the conquest and which from the eleventh century onward gained some sort of urban status, such as

Ashford in Kent or Lutterworth in Leicestershire;[5] and primary towns which, to use Everitt's words, 'probably antedated the Norman conquest in origin and are amongst the earliest of English towns to be established, apart from those of Roman foundation'. Such, for example, were Banbury and Charlbury in Oxfordshire, Melton Mowbray in Leicestershire, Oundle in Northamptonshire, and Maidstone, Charing, Wye and Milton Regis in Kent. These primary towns, Everitt suggested, weathered the economic storms of the fifteenth century better than many of the 'organic' towns, although he observed that 'Many of them, it is true, remained very small. In the mid-sixteenth century at least the thread of communal life in places like Charlbury, Charing and Wye was certainly exigious. Yet the fact remains that it did not die out completely, and even today such places are essentially little towns rather than large villages.' Indeed, there was a strong continuity between, for example, fourteenth- and sixteenth-century Banbury. In the fourteenth century, Banbury was already quite a large place by the standards of the day, with 325 names recorded on the Poll Tax list which must have represented a population of a thousand. The occupational information given in this list – though far from complete – demonstrates that the town was quite sophisticated, with 11 merchants, 6 dyers, 8 tailors, 11 tanners, 6 butchers, 6 victuallers, 3 smiths and 6 bakers, amongst others, whilst larger places such as York tended to be equally complex.[6] Several Oxfordshire boroughs, such as Burford, Chipping, and Henley, had merchant guilds, 'with all their implications for urban strength,' too.[7] In other parts of the country many medieval new towns became rapidly and notably wealthy; for instance, in 1296 the richest taxpayer in Newcastle-upon-Tyne paid as much tax as the king obtained from six ordinary villages west of the town, and in 1332 the two new towns of Stratford-upon-Avon and Henley-in-Arden in Warwickshire were worth as much to the exchequer in tax collected as the old county town of Warwick.[8] It can be seen that in dealing with the sixteenth- and seventeenth-century pre-industrial town we are not dealing with any notably new phenomenon, as Banbury and numerous other towns demonstrate.

Much of the regional differentiation of urban life had also been established in medieval times. The south and East Anglia had most of the main trading centres (though few on the south coast itself compared to the sixteenth and seventeenth centuries) and most of the big towns, in R. E. Glasscock's words:

... lay south of the Trent and the Severn. In the north, only Newcastle, York, Beverley, Nottingham, Hull and Scarborough were of comparable importance to the towns of the south and in the west and south-west only Bristol, Shrewsbury, Hereford, Gloucester, Exeter and Plymouth. Secondly, all the leading towns were ports or centres of cloth manufacture. Thirdly, there was the overwhelming predominace of London, a city of perhaps 50,000 people, which had more wealth than the three leading cities, Bristol, Newcastle and York combined.[9]

London's towering domination of the urban system of England, to become so marked and such a runaway feature of the urban scene in the sixteenth and seventeenth centuries, was already clear as early as the twelfth century. As R. A. Donkin observes: 'From 1183 comes the famous description of the city by William Fitz Stephen ... To the port of London "Merchants from every nation that is under heaven brought their trade in ships ..."',[10] and Sylvia Thrupp suggests that London was 'a metropolis, bearing far more resemblance to the great cities of northern continental Europe than to any other town'.[11] Equally, the questions that Veale asks of the fourteenth-century city are very much the same as we might pose for its sixteenth- or seventeenth-century successor:

Could London craftsmen satisfy the requirements of exacting customers drawn from the City's wealthy and sophisticated society? Or were the bulk of luxury goods acquired of foreign origin? ... What was the effect of the concentration of an increasing range of governmental activity in the capital and the size of its transient population? How important a contribution to London's economy was the need to supply the vast range of services required ...?[12]

Other urban characteristics showed similar continuity, the street pattern and even street names go back to Norman times.[13] This continuity has been observed in towns all over Western Europe; Hansen, in a study of two Danish market towns in the seventeenth and eighteenth centuries, observes that their social and economic segregation was influenced by ancient street and block patterns: 'First of all a kind of predetermination lies in the different size of the burghers' plot and with that the difference in accommodation in reference towns, and size of rooms, which again is pictured in the functional possibilities of the house. These were to a certain degree determined ages ago.'[14] H. S. A. Fox speaks of thirteenth-century English towns and the services they offered in terms almost exactly appropriate for many sixteenth-century towns:

They were the producers of simple manufactured goods for distribution to rural populations, consumers of agricultural surpluses, and with village market places functioned as centres between town and country ...

certain basic trades were to be found in rural settlements with no claim to urban status; bakers, carpenters, cobblers, smiths and brewers were contained among the populations of most villages. By contrast, the towns contained less common trades indicating that, for some of their needs, rural communities relied on town-made goods.[15]

A New Beginning in 1500?

The pre-industrial town was thus not a totally new organism when compared to its medieval forebears. Why, then, begin the study of pre-industrial towns at 1500, and why attempt to separate 'medieval' and 'pre-industrial' for the purposes of urban study? The answer can be found in two factors. Firstly, 'pre-industrial towns' represented the apogee of urban development before the great modernization of late eighteenth-century England began, and show may of the incipient trends of that modernization. The second and far more important reason is that the fifteenth century represented an undoubted nadir in the fortunes of the country and most of its towns, some of which were still in a state of decay by 1500, before population and economic growth began anew and with it urban growth and change. It is a year, chosen for its roundness, which thus represents symbolically the new beginning in English towns, influenced by medieval antecedents though they were, that would become notably more modern in the period to 1700 and beyond.

Decay and uncertainty are characteristic of English towns at the turn of the sixteenth century, although certain exceptions managed to thrive in the relatively poor economic context of the day, on wool, cloth or tin.[16] Laments and complaints of urban desolation were recurrent throughout the fifteenth century. In the 1460s, for example, a petition from the town of Yarmouth on the Norfolk coast to the Crown for financial assistance adduces 'The causes of thencrease and prosperite of the Towne of Great Yarmouth in dayes past and the causes of ruyn and decay nowe in these dayes'. Comparing its state with the mid-fourteenth century, the town's petition rehearses the fact that

> . . . where as is aforsaid were belonging to the said towne, 80 shippes with forcastelles there is nowe but oon and where there were thanne 140 small shippes nowe be but 24 fisshers and crayers [small trading vessels] . . . And where as the benefice was of the yearly value of 700 marc. is nowe of the value but of £50 . . . And where there died in oon yere [i.e. 1349–50] as is rehersed, 7,000 men there be not nowe in nombre in the said towne abiding 1,200 men and women . . .[17]

Apart from being a remarkably early contemporary population estimate of 1,200 men and women which, if reasonably accurate and counting adults only, must have represented well over 2,000 souls in all at Yarmouth at the time, this petition is a fine example, exaggerated for effect though it may have been, of countless other fifteenth-century petitions from towns in a similar plight.

The situation had not greatly improved by 1500. In many towns there was not only little 'industry', but much obvious dereliction in the way of empty and overgrown lots, half-rotten houses and poorly maintained streets. Acts of Parliament as well as town ordinances were resorted to in an attempt to improve matters. One such reads:

> Forasmuche as there have ben in tymes past divers and many beautiful Houses of Habitaecion within the walls and libertyes of the Cities Burroughes and Townes . . . and now are fallen downe decayed and at this day remaine unreedified and doo lye as desolate vacante grounds, many of them nygh adioyning to the high stretis replennyshed withe much unclennes and filthe with pittes, sellers and vaultis lying open and uncovered . . . and some houses be feeble and like to fall down dangerous to passe by, which decayes are to the great impoverishing and hinderance of the same boroughs and towns.[18]

Towns, large, medium and small all suffered. In Norwich, one of the great provincial capitals of England, there was much trouble caused by vacant ground: here, the Mayor and Corporation were reduced to ordering that land vacant for more than two years should be rebuilt, or at least stone-walled; if these conditions were not complied with the land would automatically revert to the corporation.[19] Equally, in the northern provincial capital of York a marked degree of desolation reigned, as authorities such as Sellers,[20] Bartlett,[21] Miller and Dickens,[22] and Palliser[23] have demonstrated. Decay was present as much in the manufactures as in the buildings. Its Mayor complained of ' . . . the lack of cloth making in the said city as was in old time accustomed which is now increased . . . in the town of Halifax, Leeds and Wakefield for that not only the commodity of the Water Milles is there nigh at hand but also the poor folk as spinners, carders and other necessary work folk . . . have kine, fire and other relief good and cheap which in this city very dear and wanting . . .'[24] Lesser towns had as much devastation of houses and trade, and sometimes were not to recover and blossom as did Norwich and, to a lesser extent, York. One such was the old clothing town of Lincoln from which, like Winchester and others, the medieval textile manufacture disappeared, never to return. In Lincoln the worried city fathers in 1515 ordered the constables of the different wards to stop people pulling down houses and other buildings;[25] but no such ordinance could halt the evident decay of a number of parish churches within its bounds.

At Southampton, as elsewhere, according to Ruddock, 'An outstanding feature of the economic changes of the sixteenth century was the rapid decay of some of the chief provincial towns ... Southampton was one of the principal seaports affected in this way, declining in less than a hundred years from one of the most important centres of the country's medieval trade to the status of a decayed port in Elizabethan England'.[26] Yet it was not only the disappearance of trade once brought by Italian carracks and galleys, but the increasing concentration of England's overseas trade in the hands of London capitalists that sapped Southampton's vitality. All the way down the urban hierarchy similar stories can be told. Leicester in 1509 was in a sad and derelict state,[27] as were many other county towns of the day, and tiny places like Grimsby told the same tale. Here, as in mighty York, according to Gillet:

> All the time the authorities were struggling against the appearance of waste plots and ruined houses in the town. The penalty of £10 could be inflicted on anyone who actually pulled down a house or building near the highway. It was more difficult to prevent decay from natural causes. Nevertheless all those who failed to repair their decayed 'pentices' [primitive shop fronts] in the market were threatened with a fine of five shillings.[28]

This problem of decay did not disappear magically after 1500, but lingered on in such small places as Grimsby, where in 1555 seven persons were given two years to rebuild on their waste plots,[29] and in larger ones like Norwich, where in 1545 weeds were said to be a problem near the market place.[30]

In 1500 neither the national economy nor national population were buoyant. Growth in the economy and in population began again after 1500, although rates of growth varied regionally, between town and country, and between town and town. As Petchey observes so succinctly for the tiny Essex port of Maldon, 'Decay and prosperity were, indeed, coexistent' in the sixteenth and seventeenth centuries.[31] What happened thereafter to English towns is unclear. That some changed is quite obvious, whether by flourishing or by declining though many more changed precious little, and merely survived through the next two centuries. Whatever did happen cannot be conveniently summed up solely by the word 'growth', with all its implications of dynamism, self-generation and self-perpetuation. Change was accompanied and influenced by the onset of uncertain but upward population advance from the 1510s and 1520s, which led to a rise of at least a quarter in total population before 1550; pre-1349 population levels were achieved again by the middle of the reign of Queen Elizabeth I, and were to double by the mid-seventeenth century. This movement in population was attended by a price inflation – at least partially influenced by population growth itself. Food prices, followed by those of manufactured goods of most kinds, rose sharply in the 1520s (parallel with the recovery in population growth) and more than doubled by mid-century, doubling again by 1600.[32] In the 1630s, even after the great foreign trade slump of the 1620s, prices still stood at well over five times their level in 1500. Towns, as centres of trade, as consumers and producers of manufactures, and as great lures to rural migrants, could not fail to change under the influence of these forces. London in the 1520s was perhaps the exception in that it was experiencing self-perpetuating, self-generating urban advance, for it possessed the scale to overcome troubles, ranging from plagues and fires to changes in trade and warfare. Only there were the conditions that allow us to use the word *growth* in a modern sense safely and surely.

But, there were signs of growth elsewhere. There was the growth of an urban *rentier* class,[33] a seemingly sure early swallow indicating coming urban modernity. There was the great rebuilding of many towns that began in the second and third quarters of the sixteenth century, a phenomenon in need of the same attention as has already been given to the great rebuilding of rural houses. This process was marked in places as widely separated and different as the port of Kings Lynn[34] or the cloth manufacturing and market centre of Worcester[35] Our view of what all this means, however, is open to a number of possible interpretations offered by recent authorities.

We have already noted that Petchey saw growth and decay existing next to each other.[36] Clark and Slack conclude, even more forcibly that ' . . . English urban society from 1500 to 1700 witnessed a major collison of continuity and change. Within the apparently ordered framework of pre-industrial society many communities underwent a severe reorientation, affecting all sectors of urban life';[37] but these authors stress at the same time threads of urban continuity expressed in factors like the small proportion of urbanization at both dates, the rural penetration of towns, the sameness of their topography, and the stability of the regional pattern with its southern and eastern concentration of towns.[38] Bridbury emphazises much more the continuity with medieval times: 'The towns were too small, both in the thirteenth and in the sixteenth century to have been able to relieve more than a tiny fraction of the desperate social and economic pressure that we can discern in the surviving records'.[39] Bridbury's view can be contrasted with that of Phythian-Adams, who argues, from a cultural and social point of view, that 'For urban communities in particular, the middle and later years of the sixteenth century represented a more abrupt break with the past than any period since the era of the Black Death or before the age of industrialization. Not only were specific customs and institutions brusquely changed or abolished, but a whole vigorous and variegated popular culture, the matrix of everyday life, was eroded and began to perish'.[40] Views on urban growth seem as numerous as the writers uttering them. Chartres, for example, considered the Tudor period as one which was '. . . to have been an awkward period of adjustment for English towns';[41] an opinion sharply contrasted with Dyer's more optimistic statement that in the history of towns in England the sixteenth century saw 'one of its most important and dynamic phases . . . for then began a process of growth which, despite changes in momentum, has never since been stopped'.[42] Arguments like these may be resolved according to each writer's definition of 'growth'. Alternatively, they may change as the spatial and temporal scales within which towns are examined change; Bridbury's view,[43] based on a survey of several centuries, is very different from the compressed and concentrated view of the urban facts of life arising out of Dyer's study of sixteenth-century Worcester.[44] Both historians' comments can be usefully contrasted with those of the historical geographer A. R. H. Baker. Looking at the period 1334–1524 overall, he concluded that

> the fortunes of English towns during this period were very varied and were characterised by great diversity, both in time and place. Even so, some general changes can be discerned, such as the relative decline and later recovery of many of the old coporate towns, the close association of the condition of towns with the state of trade, and the increasing economic upsurge of towns and of London in particular. A comparison of th subsidies of 1334 and 1524 shows that urban wealth constituted a far larger proportion of total lay wealth at the end of this period than at the beginning. The fortunes of individual towns differed but collectively they strengthened their grasp on the national economy.[45]

For a last example of the range of views, this time looking forward to the Industrial Revolution rather than backwards to medieval times, P. Burke has set the pre-industrial city in one more possible context, in an extract worth quoting at length. He writes that he does not wish

. . . to suggest that the Industrial Revolution made no impact at all on cities or that the early modern period was where the action really was (*sic*). I wish only to argue that the effects of industrialization are sometimes exaggerated or misinterpreted. They are misrepresented in at least three ways. (1) Differences in degree are often presented as differences in kind. Post-industrial cities may well have contained a higher proportion of long-distance immigrants or streets which were paved than earlier cities did, but they did not originate the immigration or paving. (2) Differences between large cities and small towns are sometimes confused with differences between pre-industrial cities and post-industrial ones. (3) Differences between rural society and urban society are sometimes confused with differences between pre-industrial cities and post-industrial ones.[46]

None of these eight varying opinions is mutually exclusive; to say that they are would be, to echo Burke, to see 'differences in kind rather than differences in degree'. Nonetheless, it is important to bear them in mind not only for the rest of this chapter (which considers the basic forces promoting and inhibiting movements in and between towns) but indeed for the rest of the book. This writer's own preferences are to look for and evaluate against each other, things which on the one hand promoted, and on the other hand inhibited, change, rather than imposing twentieth-century notions of urban growth on a period for which they may be singularly inappropriate. To take this view may be academically tame, but at least it avoids too many preconceptions about an urban scene, many major aspects of which have yet to be firmly established. Before these aspects are examined in their turn, it is vital to have some idea of the general pattern of English urbanization in 1500.

English Towns in 1500

In and around 1500, a relatively small proportion of England's population was urban. Indeed, the same observation could safely be made for the nation in 1700, though the proportions had changed, towns slowly gaining a greater share. It is very difficult to estimate the proportion of the nation's population that lived in towns at either date, since problems with urban definition mean that we are not even sure what a town was then. When a rule-of-thumb definition is adopted, as in the regional case study examined in Chapter 6, the problems of availability of information on both rural and putatively urban populations still make it difficult to be certain of this figure. On a national scale vast amounts of work remain to be done before estimates can be produced that are based on any firm empirical evidence.

It may be helpful to look at the 'towns' of the day as existing on two levels, one type being economically effective and the other not, rather like the dual economy of both present-day developing countries and perhaps also pre-industrial England itself. For it is certainly the case that in the pre-industrial world there was a very small proportion of people living in what we would instinctively recognise as towns, and indeed most lived in much smaller places. As Lampard has observed, 'Before the nineteenth century it is doubtful whether cities of, say, 5,000 and more inhabitants at any time accounted for more than 3 per cent of world population, or more than 15–20 per cent of population on a local or regional basis'.[47] In England there was nothing like such a high proportion as 15 per cent of the population in towns of over 5,000 even in populous and rich areas such as East Anglia or the south-west by 1700. Additionally, as has been argued above, we may need to differentiate carefully between the more and the less economically effective towns, in the same way as we recognise that there were more and less effective sectors of the economy. This last fact is clearly indicated by the huge poor section of urban society in particular which was a drain on, rather than a contribution to, national well-being – even if it may be inappropriate to label this actually as a 'dual economy' in the modern sense.

Though there were numerous towns there were clearly very few *large* towns in 1500. There was London, with its population of perhaps 50,000 in 1500, though this figure does not include the considerable suburban area outside the city and its liberties, as for example, already sprawled across the river at Southwark, and east of the Tower. There were the few great regional capitals, namely Bristol, Exeter, Newcastle-upon-Tyne, Norwich and York, which had populations then of not less than 5,000, but not more than 10,000. The location of these large towns is important. Firstly, they were on the coast or quite near the coast, and easily and quickly linked to the sea by good river connections. Secondly, and strikingly, they were unevenly distributed within England. Not only were but two of them north of the Bristol–Wash line, but there was none at all in the Midlands, the geographical heart of England, nor in the north-west. The size of England, with its small population of less than 2½ million in 1500, its slowly advancing and poorly integrated economy and its relatively undeveloped transport infrastructure, simply could not support and did not demand, very many big towns; only one political, economic and demographic capital like London was needed, or could be supported by a small island country. Nonetheless, even within the limited land area of England there were quite marked regional disparities in the provision of larger towns. These can be crudely summed up in the difference that existed between richer, more prosperous and populous, predominantly lowland, southern and eastern England, and northern and western upland England, which was more thinly populated and certainly much less prosperous.[48] The number and location of larger towns accurately reflects these basic patterns in the economic and population geography of the day.

Below the regional provincial capitals were a network of county towns, spread fairly evenly across the country, for most 'shires' naturally would have their 'shire towns'. They were unlikely to have reached a population of 5,000 in 1500. If they did, it was because of some manufacturing speciality that had led to a greater concentration of population than did the normal functions of shire towns – marketing, legal and social functions. Exceptions included Salisbury or Coventry, with their medieval cloth-manufacturing inheritance, even though this was a manufacture then in decline. Many other shire or county towns were not particularly buoyant, as we might anticipate, remembering the state of urban life at the turn of the sixteenth century. We have mentioned Leicester as a county town in a poor condition, and Stamford in Lincolnshire and Canterbury in Kent were almost equally badly-off. But for the average shire town, like Nottingham, capital of its county, or Bury St Edmunds, the 'capital' of west Suffolk, prosperity, while not over-abundant, was at least not tenuous. Historical and geographical advantages of location, and the benefits of scale, small though these may have been, prevented their decay and decline in size then or later. No shire town was to vanish from the urban map. They were the basic urban net of England, and differences in size between them were so small as to make unprofitable any attempt to differentiate between them. This is not to deny that there were other places in different counties or regions which were not of the same – or sometimes larger-size and economic importance as their historic county towns. In 1500, Southampton was probably of comparable size and importance to Winchester in the relatively poor and thinly-populated county of Hampshire, while in wealthy and populous East Anglia, Kings Lynn and Great Yarmouth were of the same order of size and importance as the county towns of Ipswich and Bury St Edmunds, although all four palled in comparison with the dominant provincial capital of Norwich. The importance of the sea for coastal and foreign trade, was marked in encouraging the locational advantages and prosperity of towns situated on the bank of the 'great river' that flowed around the coast of England, carrying with it much of the nation's trade. Once again, there were marked regional differences, north-western England in particular being poorly served by such ports.

London, the provincial regional capitals, county capitals and other towns of such standing (usually ports) made up the safe and well-founded urban superstructure of England in 1500. These were the socially and economically durable towns of the country; many of them did not flourish, but all of them were to exist and survive through the two centuries under review. Below this economically effective group of places was the other part of the dual urban system of pre-industrial England. Perhaps 500 places were in existence as towns in England in 1500. Some of these were prosperous centres with regular and well patronized markets and fairs, such as Tiverton in Devon, Preston in Lancashire, or Ludlow in Shropshire; some, rather different in character, had already growing manufactures, such as Birmingham in Warwickshire; others had established manufactures, such as Lavenham in Suffolk. Others again were still small places, but soon to become spa towns, or to serve the needs of war – as in the case of Portsmouth and Plymouth and the Medway towns with their shipbuilding. Such towns had, or were to have, a permanent economic and social rationale, though all were vulnerable to sudden changes of fortune, such as through a fire, or by alterations in trading patterns or fashion (as in the decline in demand for broadcloth made at Lavenham in Suffolk). The most sensitive to misfortune were the lesser 'towns' of a few hundred people, which were sometimes classed as boroughs, and which might have anything from a flourishing weekly market to a very rare one. This group was at the margins of urbanity, being at the very point where the rural dwellers (probably comprising at least ninety per cent of the country's population in 1500) came into contact with a 'town', or at least a place where services and trades not located in the village could be found. Some of these places simply lost their usefulness, and went into total decline over the two centuries; others managed to stagger on; yet more managed to flourish in their own terms at least. All had some claim to urbanity, though this was sometimes to be found in no more than the most tenuous of urban acitivities.

Despite the lack of evidence, an outline picture is undoubtedly there. It shows many towns, unevenly distributed across the English landscape, some of which by 1500 were economically effective and assured of a future, while others were much less fortunate. Having painted this urban canvas, we must now turn to the equally difficult task of evaluating the major forces that were to change towns of all sizes and types, both in themselves and in their regional and national relationships. These were the changes that were to bring about the English urban network of 1700, a description of which concludes this chapter.

Forces for Change

The major forces acting on pre-industrial English towns can be divided into those tending to promote change, and those tending to inhibit it. Many of these forces were external and acting upon towns; but others were internally generated by and from within the towns themselves. In looking at towns at any time in the past there seems to be an instinctive, if ill-founded, tendency to seek growth first and foremost. Any intrusion into the urban world of the past carries with it many dangers: Wheatley has correctly and colourfully observed: 'the irruption of a twentieth-century mind into the conceptual framework of the ancient world inevitably induces cultural refractions of such magnitude that the image of the quarry at best undergoes distortions, at worst is wholly lost from sight'.[49] In contemporary twentieth-century society we seem obsessed with the growth of our nation's economic performance. Success or failure of industries, public companies, and policies, is measured by the percentage growth achieved. But a glance at the sixteenth and seventeenth centuries shows that growth was not the dominant phenomenon in population, in agriculture or in industry. Indeed, writers of the time stressed, and often lauded, social and economic stability; and they observed economic change about them more than they did economic growth. I do not believe that statements like Millward's – 'The evolution of the medieval town into its Georgian successor represented changes as revolutionary as any imposed by the Victorian on the urban face of England'[50] – stand up to close scrutiny. In looking at forces for change, we must not be led too far astray by the examples of relative tearaway urban growth that did occur occasionally over these two hundred years in some spa-town, naval dockyard or manufacturing centre. We must instead firstly recognise those forces inhibiting change, such as the small scale of the country itself, its low population, and its weak economy and the effects of fires, plagues, wars, and of the weather. Secondly, we should distinguish those forces promoting change, for example, population growth, economic advances, new urban phenomena demanding new sorts of towns (often *de novo*, such as spas and dockyards), and the uniquely self-generating growth and influence of one huge primate city, London. Perhaps it is most sensible to begin our categorization of forces of change with a discussion of those that inhibited change, for it was these that were the rule, not the exception for most towns of the time.

Forces Inhibiting Change

Most recent books on the English economy of the period tend to stress the role of growth. This is a theme which runs through, for example, much of L. A. Clarkson's admirable survey, *The pre-industrial economy in England, 1500–1700* (1971). But, as Ramsey said of it in a review: 'The standpoint of the book is that of an economist of the 1970s rather than of men of the time, this being emphasized by the repeated comparisons between pre-industrial England and un-developed economies of the twentieth century. This is legitimate enough, but an over-riding concern for growth and productivity may tend to neglect the preoccupations and anxieties of contem-poraries'.[51] In addition, this can distort our view of the total English economy of the day so much that forces for growth, including those acting on towns, are allowed to dominate the picture. In looking at the economy of pre-industrial England we are examining the countryside, for it was here that most English people dwelled and earned their living, and the towns were deeply embedded in this countryside. It is difficult to be precise about the exact proportion of people that were employed in agriculture, as opposed to all other pre-industrial occupations, whether manufacture or commerce; indeed, the search for such estimates may be fruitless, for many people involved in agricultural pursuits also had other economic in-terests and vice versa. There was to an important degree a joint labour force for agriculture, manufacture and trade.

More people, as the onset of the economic advance of the later eighteenth century drew nearer, may have become occupied full time in non-agricultural activity, as more undoubtedly became urban-dwellers. Yet the indivisibility of town and country and the all-pervasive influence of the countryside remained, as did the rural interests of urban and country weavers, merchants, and scriveners.

Much of the reason for the slow change in towns is to be found in the slow pace of economic change in the countryside itself.

This situation was set within a national economy which, like its population, was growing erratically; an economy which some have termed 'stagnant'.[52] Such a society was undoubtedly characterized by a high incidence of poverty, a poverty which would have forced many country-dwellers into non-agricultural activity. Economic activity in pre-industrial England was labour-intensive, yet productivity was undoubtedly low. It was, with a few simple tools and inexpensive raw materials, not overly hard for most countrymen to engage in 'manufacturing' activity. This fact acts as a good indicator of the nature of low-level economic activity at the time. In the same way that the yearly tasks of farming were quickly learnt from an early age by those on the land, so most basic manufacturing techniques, such as spinning, the weaving of flax and wool, or working in wood and even leather, could be assimilated quite rapidly, and without much formal training. Yet it must be clearly recognized that the force behind the growth of non-agricultural activities inside the usually tiny towns of the day, as much as outside them in the countryside, was a simple one: it was frequently the imperative of survival, rather than the lure of true economic improvement, let alone any ever-rising expectations. Embedded in such an economy, English pre-industrial towns were unlikely to experience great growth unless other forces were to intervene. Any period which is best understood as a nationally unintegrated market economy, and one much hampered by poor productivity and unsophisticated and slowly developing economic institutions, is not likely to provide the best framework for urban growth. Few producers however were completely isolated from the market, which determined much of the pattern of economic activity. National government played almost no part in economic life beyond raising taxes and regulating private enterprise, possessing as it did neither the knowledge nor the bureaucratic means of organizing production and distribution, and was unlikely to promote urban growth, save in the case of dockyards and military establishments.

In the countryside, irregularity and a certain disregard for the demands of the clock, were the characteristics of the daily economic round. In agriculture, from which much of the supplies for urban manufactures as well as food for urban bellies came, the busiest time was between May and September. But in winter there was much enforced idleness because of the exigences of the cold and damp northern climate, a climate which was being affected during the sixteenth and seventeenth centuries by the work of a 'little ice age',[53] and which led to the terrible decades that ended both centuries. All economic activity was affected by this strong seasonality, not only in agriculture, but also in seafaring and fishing. Much of the carriage of vital raw materials and goods to towns, even inland ones, was by coastal traffic; but the weather forced boats plying on this trade to lay-up during the winter period. Mining, road making and repairing, shipbuilding and quarrying all suffered in the same way, as Holderness has pointed out.[54] Some of the national labour force spent some of its time in enforced idleness.

> Things [in town and country] could have been worse if many trades had not reached the peak of their annual production at times when agriculture was relatively slack. Brewing (following the annual harvest), milling, tanning, soap boiling, rope-making (especially active at night) and many trades which required the use of watermills were concentrated in the months from autumn to spring. Weaving, nail-making and other cottage crafts were less depedent upon the seasons, but tended to be suspended in high summer when the calls of the farm or of neighbouring farmers were pressing. Industrial entrepreneurs grew accustomed to the summer break in production, not least because many of them were also farmers who needed casual labour in the hay or the corn fields. Moreover, the prevalence of dual occupations in the countryside was sustained by the ease of transfer from one kind of employment to another. Even substantial capitalists saw little conflict of interest in their diverse commitments; thus a Wiltshire linen draper in the eighteenth century held up an order for his cloth because 'a plenty of apples now imploys many workmen making syder'. This ability to comprehend different kinds of employment in the course of the year did not solve the problem of underemployment as such in the pre-industrial economy.[55]

There was as much manufacture in the countryside as in the towns of pre-industrial England. There were to be advances in manufacturing technology in this period, but they were not dramatic, while the scale of production in all manufacturing activity remained small. Manufacturing was probably only slightly less craft-based in 1700 than it was in 1300. Many manufacturers were self-employed and essentially jobbing artisans, working on jobs as they were demanded by consumers. They owned little plant; had little working capital which they might invest, other than stock-in-hand; were often only able to expand seasonally in their production. Lampard has concluded: 'Indeed, there is little in their evidence before the sixteenth century A.D. to suggest, the growth of medieval capitalism notwithstanding, that many units were rational maximizing agencies in the strictly economic sense, or to indicate that locational decisions were precisely governed by an exact price calculus of costs and benefits'.[56]

Advances in the production of manufactured goods often tended to take hold in the countryside, to the manifest disadvantages of the towns. In the countryside wages might be lower, and the activity itself free of the restrictions that were such an irritant and sometimes such an inhibiting force on economic advance in towns. In textile manufacture, for example, Coleman points out: 'The ability of a rurally produced fabric to undercut a town-produced fabric of the same type – indeed, probably an imitation of it – is well documented by innumerable complaints, be they from sixteenth-century York or seventeenth-century Venice'.[57] If one of the factors inhibiting urban growth was the low productivity and low economic buoyancy of the countryside leading to relatively low demand for urban goods, services and facilities, another was undoubtedly competition from the countryside itself where manufacturing could often be as (if not more) conveniently located than in the towns.

Finally, in any discussion of the general characteristics of the English pre-industrial economy which might inhibit urban growth, the state of England's European and world trade must be noted. Foreign trade was most uncertain, not only in the sense of trade cycles with their troughs and peaks with which we are depressingly familiar today, but in the sudden, often permanent fractures in trade to which urban manufacturers and merchants had to adjust. Changes in the sixteenth century falling into this category were, for example, a number of crises in the North Sea trading areas, and later the dramatic alterations in English relations with the Antwerp market.[58] The first half of the seventeenth century saw, in Supple's words, a 'chronic depression [which] engulfed the English economy for more than a quarter of a century . . . all the evidence supports the view that the fluctuations of the time did reflect a real and prolonged crisis arising from a radical adjustment of English foreign trade'. Supple further observes of the conditions obtaining during this same slump: 'At first sight the organization of England's economy might not seem to bear out the conclusion that there could be an intimate relationship between events overseas and prosperity at home. The nation was both small and poor. [Here was] an economic balance which could be alarmingly susceptible to commercial disturbance.'[59] The effects on towns and their inhabitants were alarming. The Essex clothing towns, for instance, felt repercussions from the effect which the Thirty Years War (1618–48) had on Baltic and European cloth markets. In Pilgrim's words, 'Under such conditions regular exports must have been impossible, hence the violent fluctuations from year to year. Years must have occurred in which the clothiers would sell no cloth; those with sufficient wealth probably retired from business, and their employees found themselves idle'.[60] A picture emerges, therefore, of England as small in area and population and with an economy unlikely to encourage urban growth.

The low level of the economy was not the only factor which inhibited or retarded urban growth of those generally rather small towns which did exist, however. As we have already noted only towns the size of London and the provincial capitals were able to resist the effects of natural disasters which occurred with monotonous regularity throughout the two centuries, and which could affect towns in two entirely different ways. Firstly, they could, by their regular occurrence, simply slow down and disrupt any advances a town might otherwise be making. Continuous loss of population, for example, by a series of plagues, could have a very debilitating effect upon urban vitality. Secondly, some of these forces could have such a catastrophic effect and do so much damage to a town's human or physical fabric that fortunes were grieviously affected; in such circumstances any potential growth could be set back for several decades.

The major inhibiting forces to be considered are fires, plagues, the weather, natural catastrophes and physical changes (such as silting) and warfare. In no way can the relations between these events and urban change be regarded as systematic, for they were truly fortuitous in their occurrence if devastating in their effect; but the very fact of their habitual appearance makes them very much part of the urban context, even if they cannot be analysed in a systematic way. Such disrupting forces were simply part of the everyday life of pre-industrial towns and were so common as to be expected and accepted philosophically.

The most sudden and most alarming event in the life of any pre-industrial town was undoubtedly a major fire. One writer has held that in the eighteenth century, to 'a certain extent fires replaced the plagues as the chief physical hazards to be faced by urban communities',[61] and for a town like little Beccles in Suffolk which experienced as many as four great fires in the sixteenth and seventeenth centuries, this may well have been true; as the age of plague drew to an end after the 1660s this can be seen to be the case. (See Tables 3 & 4.) It is easy to find the reason for the frequency of damaging fires in pre-industrial towns. They were compact places, the majority of the houses being linked on their frontages or through the mess of backyards and back buildings. There was little formal

Table 3: NOTABLE URBAN FIRES, 1500–1700

Chester, 1564[1]	
Blandford, 1579[2]	
Darlington, 1585[3]	'273 houses burnt'
Wolverhampton, 1590[4]	'A five day fire, little left untouched'
Tiverton, 1598,[5]	
Bury St Edmunds, 1608[6]	'The town devastated'
Tiverton, 1612[7]	
Dorchester, 1613[8]	'£200,000 damage'
Banbury, 1628[9]	'A third of the town destroyed'
Bere Regis, 1635[10]	
Marlborough, 1653[11]	'224 houses destroyed'
Southwold, 1659[12]	
London, 1666	'The Great Fire'
Honiton, 1672[13]	
Wallingford, 1675[14]	
Northampton, 1675[15]	'The town devastated'
Blandford, 1677[16]	
Bungay, 1688[17]	'£30,000 damage, only one street untouched'
Warwick, 1694[18]	'£110,000 damage'

1 Morris, R. H. *Chester in the Plantagenet and Tudor Reigns* (Chester, 1893).
2 Weinstock, M. B. 'Blandford in Elizabethan and Stuart times', *Notes and Queries for Somerset and Dorset,* **XXX** (1975) 119.
3 'Lamentable news from the town of Darnton' (London, 1585).
4 'Fires and pre-industrial towns', *The Local Historian,* 10 (1973) 395.
5 Hoskins, W. J. *Industry, trade and people in Exeter, 1688–1800* (1935) 13.
6 Patten, J. H. C. 'The Urban structure of East Anglia during the sixteenth and seventeenth centuries', Unpubl. Ph.D. thesis, Cambridge University (1972).
7 Hoskins, *Exeter.*
8 Porter, 'Fires and pre-industrial towns', 396.
9 Crossley, A. *A History of the County of Oxford, V.C.H.* X (1972), 7–8.
10 Meekings, C. A. F. *Dorset Hearth Tax 1662–1664* (Dorchester 1951), xxxi;
Jones, E. L., 'The reduction of fire damage in Southern England, 1650–1850', *Post Medieval Archaeology,* 2 (1968), 141.
12 Porter, 'Fires and pre-industrial towns', 396.
13 *Ibid.* 395.
14 *Ibid.* 396.
15 'A true and faithful relation of the late dreadful fire at Northampton (1675)'.
16 Porter, 'Fires and pre-industrial towns', 395.
17 *Ibid.* 396.
18 *Ibid.* 396.

terracing, but much overcrowding, with the overhanging eaves of houses in some streets almost touching those opposite as can still be seen in the picturesque street known as 'The Shambles' in York. Flames leapt easily from one to the other. Very many houses outside the slate-producing areas were still thatched in a period when tile-making and tile laying was developing but slowly. Chimney construction was often rudimentary, the linings of some chimneys being

Table 4: NOTABLE URBAN 'PLAGUES', 1500–1700

Worcester[1] 1558, 1593–4, 1603, 1609, 1618, 1637, 1644–5
Leciester[2] 1564, 1579, 1583, 1593, 1604, 1606–7, 1610–11, 1625–6, 1636, and 1638–9
York[3] 1604
Loughborough[4] 1610
Dudley, Worc.[5] 1617
Birmingham[6] 1626
Salisbury[7] 1627
High Wycombe[8] 1631
Newcastle[9] 1636
Stafford[10] 1640
Banbury[11] 1643
Stockton-on-Tees[12] 1643, 1648
Chester[13] 1647
Southwark[14] 1663
Birmingham[15] 1665
Derby[16] 1665
Colchester[17] 1665
Winchester[18] 1665
Norwich[19] 1665

1 Dyer, A. D. *The City of Worcester in the Sixteenth Century* (Leicester, 1973), 45; Johnson, J. A. 'Developments in Worcester and Worcestershire 1563–1851', *Trans. Worc. Arch. Soc.,* 3rd Series 5. (1976), 54–5
2 Kerridge, E. W. J. 'Social and economic history, 1509–1660', *V.C.H. Leicester,* IV (1958), 76–109, and Wilshere, J. E. O. 'Plague in Leicester, 1558–1665', *Transcriptions Leicester Historical Society,* XLIV (1968–9), 47
3 Everitt, A. *Perspectives in English Urban History* (London, 1973) 54
4 Griffin, N. 'Epidemics in Loughborough, 1539–1640', *Trans. Leicester Archaeological and Historical Society,* XLIII (1967–8), 30
5 Roper, J. S. *Dudley, the seventeenth century town* (Dudley Public Library Transcripts, 5, 1965)
6 Gill, C. *History of Birmingham,* I (1952), 48
7 Clark, P. and Slack, P. A. (eds.) *Crisis and order in English towns, 1500–1700* (1972), 172
8 Ashford, L. J. *The History of the Borough of High Wycombe* (1960)
9 Clark and Slack, *op. cit.* 7–8
10 Adey, K. R. 'Seventeenth century Stafford: A country town in decline', *Midland History,* II (1974)
11 Crossley, A. *V.C.H. A history of the County of Oxford,* X (1972)
12 Sowler, T. *A history of the Town and Borough of Stockton-on-Tees* (Teesside, 1972), 78–79
13 Armour, C. 'The trade of Chester . . .', Unpubl. Ph.D. thesis, Oxford University (1956)
14 Johnson, D. J. *Southwark and the city,* (1969)
15 Hutton, W. L. *The History of Birmingham* (Birmingham, 6th edn. 1835), 51
16 Hutton, W. *The history of Derby* (1891), 233
17 Cal. Treasury Books, ii (1688) 296
18 *Ibid.*
19 Hudson, W. H. and Tingay, J. C. (eds.), *The Records of the City of Norwich,* II (1910), CXXVII–CXXVII

a mixture of dung and mud applied to a timber framing. Not only did the frailty of roofs and chimneys aid the starting, spreading and stoking-up of fires, but the very construction of houses and the materials in their walls and floors were equally likely to promote fire damage. Most walling materials used outside the stone-producing districts were very readily combustible, especially in dry periods: timber framing filled with lath and plaster and timber floors and staircases presented an ideal environment for the rapid spread of fire from house to house. And the rapidity with which fires sometimes spread through whole towns is almost as remarkable a feature as their undoubted frequency.

One of the most famous seventeenth-century fires, in Northampton, can serve as a convenient example. When fire struck that town in 1675, buring over 500 houses in a few hours, a townsman about two miles away from the town on a hilltop saw 'The Fire at one End of the town then newly begun, and that before he could get to the Town it was burning at the remotest end, opposite to that where he first saw it.'[62] Huge losses could be incurred because of such fires, and houses needed to be rebuilt although often radical rebuilding did not take place thereafter. Very often houses were run-up in the same materials and were as tightly packed on old building lines as they were before the fire which destroyed them. The loss to life, terrible though it sometimes was, is unlikely to have equalled that caused by plagues. But the loss to, and disruption of, trade could be enormous; cloth manufacture in Tiverton, for example, suffered terrible dislocation because of the fires of 1598 and 1612, as much from the loss of houses and stock as from the loss of looms, which were a relatively small part of any weaver's capital equipment.[63]

In pre-industrial England, the potent force for physical and economic change presented by fires was a threat everywhere and it is difficult to pick out any clear regional pattern of the incidence of urban fires. The steep reduction in the number of fires in the late seventeenth and throughout the eighteenth centuries can be more easily explained, however, It was not due entirely to improvements in fire-fighting techniques, although towns did attempt to improve their fire-prevention systems. Dorchester bought 'a brazen Engine or spout to quench fire' in 1649, and the corporation of Reading followed suit in 1665.[64] Most towns by the seventeenth century had some sort of arrangement by which buckets were stationed in a central position, and ladders and poles with hooks on the end for removing burning thatch from roofs were provided and maintained.

Such efforts at reducing the effects of fires may well have been more important symbolically than practically, and about as much use as the one or two 'suits of towne armour' generally kept for civil defence in time of war. As Jones observes, 'changes in the organization and technology of fire-fighting thus seem neither abrupt nor powerful enough to account for so remarkable a decline in the number of fires. The decisive shift is more likely to be found in rebuilding in less combustible materials.'[65] The corporation of Norwich was busy legislating about the materials to be used in new buildings early in the sixteenth century; at the little Berkshire Thames-side town of Abingdon in 1661 the council adopted a policy of replacing wood and wattle chimneys by stonework in its leasehold property, and by 1697 they were ordering that a clause be inserted in the leases of corporation properties to bring about a change from thatched to slated or tiled roofs.[66] In the tiny port of Grimsby in the sixteenth century, because of the risk of fire, no one was permitted to have a tenant living in a shop without proper provision of chimneys; and it was made unlawful to carry live embers from one house to another in a pot lacking a proper cover. The little port town also did everything that it could to encourage building in brick to prevent fire hazard, and when James Byrkes, a bricklayer, was admitted as a burgess in 1515 he paid part of his entry fine by working 'at tiler craft'.[67]

Nevertheless, such attempts by towns at ameliorating the effects of fire were not very effective during the pre-industrial period. Evidence of the sorts of fires and of the damage that they did can be seen on Table 3, a far from complete, but not totally unrepresentative selection of such events. A very popular subject for pamphlet literature was the after-effects of such fires. Peoples' imaginations were titillated by such tracts as that describing the then little town of Darlington in Yorkshire.[68] Fires such as that at Northampton (see Table 3) almost a hundred years later excited much attention, as the pamphlet 'A True and Faithful Relation of the late Dreadful Fire at Northampton', demonstrates.[69] Relief-funds were raised after such disasters in the great parish churches of London and in counties all over England, to help the stricken places. Preachers were able to draw from the pulpit interesting parallels between the visitation of such fires and biblical events, whilst appealing for funds. In the case of Northampton, where fire spread so readily, the conflagration began in the stock of merchants returning heavily laden from Stourbridge fair outside Cambridge.[70] The results were devastating in loss of houses, stock and life, but a county town such as Northampton could quite quickly reassert its dominance in local trading. Thomas Baskerville, writing a few years later, thought very little of its neighbouring shire town of Leicester, but rather more of Northampton which had, in his opinion, 'Phoenix-like, risen out of her ashes'.[71] The larger the town, clearly the more buoyant it was, and the more able to recover quickly from this sort of depredation; London after the last great fire of 1666 provides the best example, with its rapid rebuilding on old street lines, typical of most post-fire urban reconstructions; but Southwark across the river, which escaped the Great Fire of 1666, suffered terribly as late as 1776.[72]

The further down the urban hierarchy, the more lasting the effect of fire was likely to be. In 1628, about a third of the town of Banbury was consumed by flames in a massive fire, which probably started in a malt house; over a hundred dwellings were lost, and in 1644 another fire dispatched yet another hundred houses.[73] The contemporary observer John Sprigge, writing three years after this latter fire, said of Banbury that there was 'scarce one half standing to gaze on the ruins of the other'.[74] When such disasters occurred markets had to be held elsewhere. A place the size of Northampton, or the smaller Banbury could stand the physical and economic strain, but for even smaller places it was much more difficult. Blandford in Dorset was hit hard by fire in 1579, the old guildhall destroyed and marketing severely disturbed, affecting its relative standing compared to that of Dorchester and nearby places of like size. It is not surprising that the town account book notes: 'this day ordered by the amount of the whole town that whatsoever he be which in this town after this present day that have any chimney in his house to be afire that he shall loose to the maintenance of the town 11/s 111/d to be levied by distress by the bailiffs . . .'[75] This was apparently to no avail, for in 1732 the town was again devastated by fire, being subsequently rebuilt in the charming Georgian brick still so evident today. The little town of Bere Regis, not far from Blandford, had only a hundred taxpayers or so by the 1660s and 1670s Hearth Taxes, representing a population of perhaps 500. It has been described as 'a rather declining market town which had suffered a severe fire in August 1635'[76] Here again, fire had struck at its fortunes in a way that would be entirely unfamiliar to us today; perhaps the contemporary equivalent would be the effect still visible ten or twenty years after earthquakes had struck towns in Turkey, Yugoslavia and Italy during the twentieth century.

The effects of epidemic and endemic disease could be as wide-ranging (see Table 4). 'Plague' and diseases of various other kinds were virtually endemic in pre-industrial England, and their continuing depredations were often taken for granted by contemporaries. Major epidemics, however, did strike with terrible ferocity, carrying off large numbers of townsfolk of all ages, rich and poor alike. The conditions under which epidemic disease and 'plague' in all its manifestations thrived were remarkably similar to those which encouraged fire in towns. Houses cheek by jowl, built of organic materials in which rats could flourish were almost copybook environments for disease. Added to this was a lack of through ventilation in many of them, and appalling sanitary arrangements – a bucket emptied now and then into a midden in the back yard a few feet away from living space – 'plague' could not fail to flourish, whether or not it was carried by the constantly present rats. As was the case with fires, plagues were likely to have a more long-lasting and devastating effect on the smaller places. Table 4 shows some of the most noteworthy urban plague and disease catastrophes in pre-industrial England. London of course suffered from bubonic plague in 1666, when between 70,000 and 100,000 people perished. But its sheer scale and dominating position meant that it recoverd quickly and suffered less disruption than most places. Moreover London, whose growth was only made possible by massive immigration throughout these two centuries, continued to rapidly replace those lost by such demographic disasters.

Provincial capitals tended to suffer rather more dislocation, even if it was not permanent. The results of the same 1666 plague which had hit London so hard, seemed to dislocate Norwich's trade quite severely. A government agent reported of the city on 11 July 1666 that 'The city looks sadly; most of the chief shopkeepers in the market are gone and the shops shut up;' he thought that in ten days a quarter of the city's population would have left in the face of the plague, and that this might cause trouble, with the poor (a large proportion of Norwich's population) trying to take over empty houses. Another report said that many of the aldermen had left on 11 July, and that thousands of people would be out of work at Norwich and in need of 'collection'.[77] 'Plague' was largely confined to urban areas, whereas virus diseases affected both town and country. The typical pattern when plague hit towns was that the more fortunate (usually members of town government, merchants, manufacturers and leaders of the commercial community) left for the country; for the plague whilst being no respecter of riches, was usually confined to urban areas. Many of the wealthier of the urban community maintained rural property to which they could retreat; certain Oxford colleges had agreeable country homes to which, in the seventeenth century, the Fellows and their servants could repair from such pressing danger. But for the poorer elements of the town, however much they wished to escape the urgent and deadly risk of infection, the countryside did not always present much of an alternative. There was little shelter to be had, and in a vagrant-fearing age people who had tramped from known plague centres across the countryside were not welcome visitors to other towns and villages. Generally speaking, it was the more economically active who were able to leave, so the disruption of trade, and particularly weekly marketing, would have been all the more marked.

This general situation was clearly the case with the plague which hit York in 1604. It has been estimated that a severe outbreak carried off almost a third of the city's population, and the city's markets were closed down completely. The rich merchants left with understandable alacrity for nearby market towns like Tadcaster and Selby. There they set up shop as best they could and traded in those markets, staying on with commendable prudence after the first and, as it turned out, premature reports of the abatement of danger in York. This was obviously damaging to York's trade, and caused much alarm in a city which by then did not have many important local manufactures on which it could rely for prosperity. The corporation threatened its mercantile deserters with heavy fines unless they returned immediately; for the tradesmen who were left behind in York were in danger of becoming impoverished, and it was maintained that their departed colleagues were drawing gentry and other customers away from the city.[78] It is apparent from the examples of Norwich and York, just how rapidly, even late into the seventeenth century, the economy of big provincial cities would be disturbed. It is also a reflection of how mobile trade, as well as manufacture, could be in the sixteenth and seventeenth centuries compared with out twentieth-century experience.

The longer-term effects of plague in holding back urban change are harder to assess, but they must have been evenly felt throughout the country; a town might be lucky enough to be missed in a 'plague year', but statistically it was unlikely to escape a visitation during the next outbreak. In the major coastal city of Newcastle, for one example, Howell suggests that 'The devastation worked by the plague probably accounts for the fact that the population of Newcastle-upon-Tyne was not much greater in the mid-seventeenth century than it had been in 1547'.[79] Similar effects, although not always so serious, must have resulted from the regular outbreaks of plagues that occurred in other large towns whose general development would have been similarly inhibited, and whose population was dependent on continuous immigration for further growth.

As in the case of fires, the smaller the town, the worse the impact of plague. We noted the effects of fire on the Midland county town of Northampton; the effects of plague on the neighbouring county town of Leicester were equally deleterious. In 1610–11, for example, a serious epidemic hit this market town, with its cloth and leather industries. Some 700 deaths occurred out of a population of perhaps 3,500, some 20 per cent of the total, and this was only one of many such occurrences.[80] The resulting situation in Leicester is most clearly summed up by Kerridge:

> While the secular trend in Leicester economy in this period may be described as the simultaneous growth both of industrial capital and the control of commercial capital over small masters, the course of develop-ment was not smooth, but was distorted by short-term movements and in particular by harvest crises. Such crises occurred, for example, in 1558, 1587, 1595, 1608, 1622, and 1629–31. Deaths were often accompanied or followed by pestilence, of which there were outbreaks in 1564, 1579, 1583, 1593, 1604, 1606–7, 1610–11, 1625–6, 1636, and 1638–9. These plagues are indicative of famine, near-famine, and post-famine conditions and constituted the main impediment to population increase in early seventeenth century Leicester. The periodic harvest crises and pestilences merged in the general crisis between 1625 and 1640, with plague in 1625–6, dearth from 1629 to 1631 and plague again in 1636 and 1638–9.[81]

The demographically inhibiting and economically retarding effects of regular plagues on provincial towns like Leicester must have been enormous, hard though they are to quantify. The sum total of the effects of the continuous lesser plagues probably far outweighed the effects of the few really devastating ones in dictating the long-run fortunes of medium-sized towns. Conditions in Derby after the severe plague of 1666 were certainly as bad as those in the larger town of Norwich in the same year. In Derby, 'The town was for-saken; the farmers declined the Market-place; and grass grew upon that spot which had furnished the supports of life', lamented one Victorian writer. In Birmingham in 1665, recently troubled by the Civil War action which had burnt down eighty houses in 1643, in-fection was said to have arrived in a box of clothes taken by a carrier to the inn where he lodged. So overpowering was the ensuing effect that the churchyard was not big enough to take the victims. Their bodies were carried a mile or more to Ladywood to be buried on waste land which was to be called 'the pest ground'.[82] The effect of that year's great plague was widespread all over English towns; two years later the Farmers of the Hearth Tax, getting less than they thought because of many empty houses on which they could not levy tax, complained of houses 'continuing void . . . as in Colchester, Winchester, etc.'[83] Undoubtedly the less well-recorded after-effects of earlier, sixteenth-century plagues must have been as bad. The losses in Norwich caused by the mid-sixteenth century crises were economically most enervating, and population growth in this city in the sixteenth century became consequent on Flemish immigration (the English population of the city in 1610 was little more than 12,000 – its approximate total size in 1524).[84]

As far down the urban hierarchy as we look, the same depressing tale is to be seen. The troubles of the two already declining ports of Southampton and Chester were enhanced by plague. Heavy losses of population occurred at Southampton in 1583 and 1604, and as Merson records, 'the number of burials recorded in the French church register alone rose from an annual average of five, to seventy-one and over 150 respectively. In 1596 the population was recorded as 4,200, including 397 aliens; during 1665, when the town was again swept by plague, it was reported to have lost 1,700 of its inhabitants'. Groombridge notes that Chester too suffered terribly in 1603–04.[85] In Stockton-on-Tees, the little town was devastated in 1643 and 1648.[86] In Loughborough, in 1610 the whole town moved out of the plague-riddled buildings and death-filled air: they '. . . removed themselves and their belongings to the Great Meadow, a stretch of common land just outside the town, and built a temporary shanty town on a patch of land that afterwards was known as Cabin Lees . . .'[87] As a last example, in tiny High Wycombe the population, hard hit by disease in 1631, was struck a double blow by plague in 1665 and 1666, and the trade of this market town took a long time to recover.[88]

One of the greatest forces inhibiting urban change in the sixteenth and seventeenth centuries was the slow and uncertain rate of urban population growth. Plague and other demographic disasters are undoubtedly to blame. Like fires, they could induce terrible short-term disruptions of urban marketing, manufacturing and life in general. Whole populations could be impoverished, at least temporarily, and many orphaned children thrown on the charity of the town and county for relief. Little towns could not undertake this sort of basic social service provision on their own resources. Hence the cry for help from the then small town of Dudley after the plague of 1616–17. A petition for aid was presented to Worcestershire Quarter Sessions on behalf of 'the poore distressed town of

Duddeley' in April 1617 on the grounds that the plague had left many people destitute, and 150 children orphaned.[89] Larger towns, like Lincoln in the plague decades of the 1580s and 1590s, were forced to introduce schemes for such relief on their own resources.[90] Unlike fires, the almost constant attendance on the town scene of plagues and diseases had a continuously draining effect upon urban demographic, and therefore economic, vitality; no sooner was one plague over and consigned to memory, than the next was either upon a town, or causing concern by raging nearby. This stop-go cycle greatly upset economic continuity, and was therefore a great inhibitor of urban 'growth' in the modern sense. Even the constant influx of immigrants was not enough to fully and immediately set right the imbalances so induced, although without these factors it is unlikely that even the most plague-free and fortunate could have replaced themselves.

Warfare (see Table 5) could also be an inhibitor of urban change. The English mainland was free of warfare throughout the sixteenth century, although very occasionally coastal ports suffered raids. During the eventeenth century, however, the effects of the Civil War must not be underestimated. The workings of the Civil War on the population, economy and standing of the towns it touched have scarcely been properly and systematically examined. These effects must have varied regionally. Many Midland towns suffered whilst most of their East Anglian counterparts were completely untouched. A few towns suffered badly, such as Colchester after its lengthy siege; more had relatively slight damage or disruption of trade. Yet all escaped the ravages towns on the continent had regularly felt, the experience of many of the Palatinate towns during the Thirty Years War, providing an obvious example.

London was fairly free of Civil War damage and disruption. Of the provincial cities, Norwich and York were equally undisturbed, but Bristol and Newcastle-upon-Tyne suffered quite badly from both the direct and indirect effects of the war. In Bristol, the Civil War and its aftermath notably disrupted the city's trade. It had to withstand two sieges; and it was much affected by the interruption to commerce and manufacture in the areas from which it obtained its agricultural goods and raw materials and to which it sent imported goods and Bristol manufactures in return. Much of Bristol's economy depended on its ships, whether involved in the continental, Irish or south- and west-coast English trade. These were liable to be siezed by one side or the other, for their cargoes or for their use in

Table 5: OTHER URBAN CATASTROPHES, 1500–1700

Civil War damage in the 1640s
Bristol[1]
Newcastle-upon-Tyne and Gateshead[2]
Chester[3]
Leicester[4]
Birmingham[5]
Lancaster[6]
Stafford[7]
Banbury[8]
Wallingford[9]
Faringdon[10]
Dudley[11]
Woburn[12]
Bridgenorth[13]

Silting
The port of Chester[14]

Washing away of Quays and Houses
Brighton[15]

---

1 McGrath, P. 'Merchants and merchandise in seventeenth-century Bristol', *Bristol Record Society,* **XIX** (1955) XIX–XX
2 Howell, R. *Newcastle-upon-Tyne and the puritan revolution* (Oxford, 1967), 274, and Manders, F. W. D. *A history of Gateshead* (1973), 16–17
3 Armour, C. 'The trade of Chester . . .' Unpubl. Ph.D. thesis, Oxford University (1956)
4 Clark, P. and Slack, P. A. (eds.) *Crisis and order in English towns, 1500–1700* (1972), 26; and Simmons, J., *Leicester past and present* (1974)
5 Gill, C. *History of Birmingham, I* (1952), 52–54; and Hutton, W. *The history of Birmingham* (Birmingham, 6th ed. 1835), 50
6 Clark and Slack, *Crisis and order,* 26
7 Adey, K. R. 'Seventeenth-century Stafford: A country town in decline', *Midland History,* **II** (1974)
8 Crossley, A. *V.C.H. A history of the County of Oxford,* **X** (1972)
9 Porter, S. 'Fires and pre-industrial towns', *The Local Historian,* 10 (1973), 395
10 Moir, E. A. L. *The discovery of Britain: the English tourists 1540–1840* (1964), 26–27
11 Roper, J. S. *Dudley, the seventeenth-century town* (Dudley Public Library Transcripts, 5, 1965), 396
12 Porter, 'Fires and pre-industrial towns', 396
13 *Ibid.,* 396
14 Stephens, W. B. 'The overseas trade of Chester in the early seventeenth century', *Transactions of the Historical Society of Lancashire and Cheshire,* **CXX** (1968), 23–34
15 East Sussex Record Office, Qo/EW 7p/100 and *V.C.H. Sussex,* VII, 245

the war.[91] Bristol's north-eastern coastal counterpart, and
counterweight in the coastal trade of the 'great river around
England', Newcastle-upon-Tyne, suffered more directly from the
fighting itself. Much fighting went on on the edges of the city;
Gateshead's economy in particular was hit hard and its coal trade
severely disrupted.[92] Newcastle itself had been compared on the eve
of the war, in 1635, by an enthusiastic local, Sir William Brereton,
with the greatest provincial towns in the kingdom. He was flushed
with patriotic pride for his home town, ranking it with Bristol and
asking 'whether it may nott deserve to be accounted as wealthy as
Bristow I make some doubt'.[93] The trade and economy of Newcastle
were shattered by fighting around the town, and the weeks of
conflict in the Durham and Northumberland coal-field saw the
destruction or damage of a great number of mines and workings.
Large parts of the town itself had been destroyed, and the Tyne was
blocked for a while by sunken ships. As a result, trade picked up
only slowly between 1645 and 1652.[94] It is very difficult even in the
case of a well-documented example such as Newcastle to fully assess
the capital loss, or the length of the recovery period. The effects
must not be underestimated, but neither should they be
overestimated; the laments of contemporaries on Newcastle and
elsewhere – 'there being in view nothing but many hundreds of
almost naked people, wanting all things but misery'[95] – must be
taken with a pinch of salt.

A number of county towns and ports also suffered Civil War
damage. Particularly vulnerable were those suburban areas which
were fast becoming not only notable morphological features of
English towns, but also important areas for manufacturing. At
Chester[96] the siege by parliamentary forces took such a heavy toll of
these buildings that a French tourist commented: 'under the usur-
pation of Cromwell the town was almost utterly ruined after having
sustained a long siege'.[97] At Worcester the Civil War and its two
sieges caused considerable physical damage, like Chester mainly in
the suburbs. The town was held by the King until 1646, and it is inconceivable that it did not feel the effects of this long period of
occupation;[98] both sides, apparently, indulged in extensive demoli-
tion. Trade as in Bristol, Newcastle and Chester, was distorted and
heavy fines were imposed on Worcester by the republican government which took its toll on prosperity.[99] Civil War fighting raged
primarily in suburban areas of the burgeoning metal-manufacturing
town of Birmingham, which had already suffered from a bad plague
in 1626, when fairs were stopped and restrictions imposed on

wayfarers to prevent the spread of disease. In 1643 there was considerable disruption following a Royalist attack, though law and
order were quite quickly restored. But immediate prosperity did not
automatically follow. The years of civil crisis were not happy ones
for trade in Birmingham. Contracts for weapons and munitions kept
some tradespeople employed while the war lasted,but when these
contracts ended there was probably a severe slump in local
manufacture. As was the case with the little town of Dudley after
plague in 1617, so in 1650 an applicant for relief after civil disruption, at the Warwickshire Quarter Sessions spoke of the 'deadness of
trading' in Birmingham.[100] At nearby Stafford, which was far from
thriving economically during the whole two centuries, and constantly suffered from the competition of Lichfield, there is evidence of
quite large-scale depopulation of the town during the Civil War.
The parliamentary committee ordered many people to leave
Stafford. Others must have left of their own volition since the town
was virtually under martial law. Catastrophic mortality was
induced by plague and infection there in the 1640s, some of which
must have been due to the effects of war, a mobile population, and a
transient soldiery, and made worse by inefficient food supplies. The
effects of heavy net out-migration plus heavy mortality due to plague
and other infection seriously depleted Stafford's population. Adey
has estimated that it was not to reach its immediate pre-war 1640
size again until the 1680s.[101] It took this town, therefore, some thirty
or forty years to regain its earlier equilibrium. For a last example of
the effects on a county town, armed conflict took its toll on Leicester
in 1645, and many houses were pulled down when its defences were
strengthened, causing considerable capital losses.[102]

Further down the urban scale, the effects of the Civil War sieges
could still be felt. Banbury was severely damaged, and the interruptions to the town's life were disastrous. As in Stafford, a number of
its inhabitants probably left very early in the war, and epidemics
flourished, some of which must have been connected with, or exacerbated by, the war, and there was a series of plagues between 1643
and 1645. Between March and November 1644, for example, at least
161 plague victims (specified as such in the Banbury's registers)
were buried.[103] Few people in the middle years of the seventeenth
century could fail to take notice of the effects of the Civil War and
the scars it had left on some parts of the country. In John Taylor's
Wanderings to see the Wonders of West, published in London in 1649,
the effects of civil war are constantly noted. At Faringdon, a small
but not locally unimportant Berkshire market town, he graphically

reports the situation. Here the Royalists had burnt one part of the largely timber-built little town, and the Parliamentary forces had fired part of the rest. Ashes and rubble were still evident, although by 1649, it was being rebuilt again,[104] as was its trade. Ending discussion of these examples, as in the case of plagues, with tiny High Wycombe in Buckinghamshire, the effects of civil war were marked, though not too disturbing. A Royalist raid did some damage; the town was later to become the head-quarters of a parliamentary army, which must have been a mixed blessing to local trade.[105] Disruptions due to the conflict were slight, and this in fact must have been the experience of many similar towns of mid seventeenth-century England; far more escaped Civil War damage than avoided plague and fire.

Fire, plague, and civil war, were thus the great triad of extraneous disasters which could inhibit or disrupt change in all pre-industrial towns. There were also other events which could not have made urban life easy (see Table 5). We have already noted the effect of a bad winter on one tiny town, Congleton, in the 'great snow' of 1614–15[106] The effects of wet autumns on harvests, and thus on food supplies for towns, must have been very deleterious for town populations. Hoskins has given us a good survey of the harvest fluctuations which occurred between 1480 and 1619.[107] He observes, for example, that 'The disastrous harvest of 1551, following as it did upon two other bad harvests, was of infinitely greater moment for the mass of English people than the commercial crisis of 1551–2, on which so much has been written'.[108] Towns had to take action to try and ameliorate the effects of such famines. Large towns with strong local governments did this quite effectively and with relative ease; by 1556, having learnt the lessons provided by the famines of the earlier part of the decade, both Norwich and Great Yarmouth in Norfolk established permanent town stocks of grain, in place of the *ad hoc* action during previous years of hunger.[109] For smaller places with fewer resources, the suffering and disruption was less easy to mitigate, particularly for the poor who were likely to suffer as much as their country brethren in the surrounding villages.

Whilst the weather may have only been a minor irritant for many towns, simply a part of the rhythm of life that was exacerbated by famine years, for coastal towns the action of the sea in an age before sea-defence could sometimes be a great threat. Waves could have a damaging effect, washing away not only harbours and piers, the basis for the often-precarious trading prosperity of little ports and creeks, but sometimes actually eating up houses. In some cases a town could be permanently ruined as in the well-documented case of Dunwich on the Suffolk coast. In Sussex at the fishing port of Brighton, the lower part of the town often suffered badly; in 1676 for example, it was stated that 'the towne of Brighthelmstone in the County of Sussex is a Maritime Towne and that by the rageing and swelling of the sea the same hath lately suffered great losse and damage and is impoverished';[110] there are similar reports for the north Norfolk coastal port of Cromer. Such little places, with their poor or non-existent natural harbours – often tiny vessels were simply drawn up on the beach behind the protection of a frail artificial spit placed between it and the prevailing winds – were unlikely to grow to any importance.

On other stretches of coast, the effects of the sea could be quite the reverse, and yet be as dramatic in the result of their actions as at Dunwich; the retreat of the sea and silting could be as disastrous as erosion. A number of Cinque Ports of the Kent and Sussex coast, like Winchelsea, were suffering from sea-retreat by medieval times, and it led to their total decline. Perhaps the best-documented case of silting is Chester, where fortunes in the Irish and coasting trade had been linked to relative ease of navigation up and down the river Dee. By the sixteenth century silting and braiding on this river, which contemporary technology was quite unable to deal with, was a major problem and one of the reasons for the relative decline of Chester itself. It is too well-known a story to describe in detail here,[111] suffice it to say that the rise of a port like Liverpool[112] became inevitable in order to take over Chester's Irish and coastal trading functions. Other ports were to suffer from the unstable demands of foreign warfare and political exigency; Portsmouth and Gosport, for example, declined as towns after their abandonment as naval bases for nearly a century after 1540.[113]

Chester can indeed provide us with a fitting conclusion to this brief account of the role of 'natural' forces in inhibiting urban change. In addition to its other problems Chester also suffered badly from fires, perhaps not on the scale of that which devastated Northampton in the 1670s, but it was certainly damaged by lesser ones, as in 1564.[114] It was racked by civil war siege with consequent physical destruction and disturbance to trade. It was hit hard by devastating plagues, which temporarily reduced its total population and provided incessant interruptions to any smooth upward progression in its numbers, while its declining economic stature did not provide any encouragement to potential immigrants from North

Wales, Cheshire and Lancashire who might collectively have boosted its size. The silting of the Dee provided a final strangulating blow to its fortunes by trade. Chester thus presents us with a useful compound picture of just how forces such as fire, disease, warfare and the rest, could inhibit the fortunes of the pre-industrial town; it is a point that will be hard ever to quantify, but which must be constantly borne in mind.

Forces Promoting Change

In some cases, the very things which have been hitherto adduced as factors inhibiting change could equally be represented as factors promoting it. This was obviously not the case with such phenomena as fires and plagues; but population, for instance, could prove as potent a force for urban change as it had been an inhibitor elsewhere. The major factors to consider are: population and the economy (both previously looked at for their inhibiting role); the nature of towns themselves; new forces, stimulating such growth and change in certain towns as to make them appear like 'new' towns; and last but not least, the role of London in the urban and general economic life of the country in which it was the primary city. The effects of all these forces could vary between towns of different sorts and sizes at different times, and between regions.

It is quite clear that the English population grew between 1500 and 1700. Fertility, mortality, age of marriage, in- and out-migration and all other demographic forces (which are discussed in Chapter 3) must be examined to explain how and why population did advance. Consideration must also be given to a variety of extraneous forces such as plagues and famines, inadequate and intermittent food supplies, low levels of nutrition, poor public sanitation and water supply, low standards of personal hygiene, overcrowding and poor ventilation, and so on. Statistics can tell us the general order of the growth. In 1500 the population of England stood at 2·25 millions, little more than it had been on the eve of the great demographic disasters of the mid-thirteenth century. This figure was to double between the early sixteenth and the early eighteenth centuries – when it reached about 5·5 millions – much of the increase taking place before 1650, followed by a period of relative population stability. This bald statement tends to give the impression of a steady upward progression over two hundred years, but scholarship during the post-war period has revealed a number of demographic fits and starts, with periods of quite rapid growth followed by some very dramatic falls. A graph purporting to represent this picture would not be a gently upward-sloping line, but rather an erratically fluctuating one.

Such a graph would represent a substantial increase of population in the first half of the sixteenth century, by something like three-quarters of a million, the first sustained increase since the later thirteenth century. From the 1550s population pressure was marked, and food production was not keeping pace. There was considerable inflation, with food prices rocketing to levels which threatened the less well-off urban dweller with no land of his own. Undernutrition, if not actual famine, affected many people, and when combined with the influenza epidemics of the second half of the 1550s, produced an actual fall in population of perhaps 10 or 20 per cent. Urban mortality was endemically high for towns of all sizes; towns might only replace themselves and recover from demographic setbacks by constant immigration.

The setback of the 1550s was followed by renewed general growth, but population took time to re-establish itself and was probably not back at its 1540 level until 1570. From 1570 until the 1600s there was rapid population increase, during which time perhaps a million people were added to England's population. This growth was despite a check to population during the 1580s and 1590s. These were decades of bad weather, with up to seven consecutive lean and hungry years; food supply was short from the still slowly advancing agricultural sector, prices were high, and there were outbreaks of influenza, 'pox' and 'plague'. But population nevertheless managed to grow, and by the mid-seventeenth century it must have been approaching about 5·0 million for the country as a whole. To have produced this figure, rates of growth similar to those occurring during England's rapid late eighteenth- and early nineteenth-century industrialization must have obtained. This growth was, however, accompanied by falling real incomes for many people, and the increase in national demand was largely for fundamental foodstuffs like bread and beer. After about 1650, for a variety of reason still not wholly understood, sluggish growth replaced the earlier spurt, although with considerable regional variation. The village of Colyton in Devon described by Wrigley[115] had a small surplus of burials for the rest of the century; but Wigston Magna in Leicestershire, as studied by Hoskins,[116] showed considerable new growth after the 1660s. This diversity may merely reflect the differences inherent in their location: the one relatively isolated Devon parish, the other a big village not far from the centre of the important county town and leather-manufacturing centre, Leicester. Considerable growth took place in towns such as Birmingham and others like it nearby in the West Midlands, and also to the east, in Nottingham,[117] while growth was certainly very marked in London and the Home Counties. Migration must have played a major role in fostering such growth, much of the migration coming from north-western England, where, unlike during the first half of the century, there was a marked tendency for parish registers to record an excess of deaths over births.[118] The period of slow and uncertain growth after 1650 was accompanied *not* by falling real incomes and rising demand for basic foodstuffs, but by rising real incomes amongst the wage-earners, together with a demand for dairy and meat products as well as for manufactured items from the towns and the countryside. Much of the economic change of the sixteenth and seventeenth centuries can be seen as closely interrelated with, if not an actual response to, changes in the rate of population growth. In addition, the doubling of population over the period added greatly to the capital stock of the nation and certainly to that of the towns – many of which had not extended their areas much, and were bulging at the seams, with houses being divided again and again into tenements and single-roomed lots.

By the end of the seventeenth century the slow overall growth of population had important implications for future economic growth in England, particularly in its larger towns; these, as will be seen in Chapter 3, were often rapidly increasing in population whilst the average picture for the countryside remained one of but sluggish advance. If a population is growing slowly, the bulk of savings which it generates can be devoted to increasing the capital per head. This in turn eases the pressure of population on the land in a primarily agricultural society by facilitating the growth of non-agricultural enterprises, such as manufacturing in the countryside, and with it the general enterprise of towns. In England in 1700, the annual rate of saving was probably between 3 and 5 per cent of the nation's income.[119] This is a low saving rate, yet there were undoubtedly important additions to per capita savings. With such a low saving rate, capital per head could increase significantly only if the rate of population growth was negligible. A population growth rate of even as little as 1 per cent per annum would absorb virtually all potential savings; in England in the later seventeenth century, it was much less than this. Savings that this low population growth rate allowed were very important for towns in a society which was notably 'modernizing'[120] *without* industrializing in an 'industrial revolution' sense; population growth had been sufficiently small as not to hinder the development of institutions, like banking, which were most important for towns.

North and Thomas have proposed a model within which to study such institutional change.[121] They suggest that the stimulus behind institutional change is population growth, a growth that changes the relative cost of land and labour, and which also encourages more efficient economic organizations. The sixteenth century, it is argued, was the critical period in this process of population growth and institutional change in the western world, for in England it was a time of considerable population growth. North and Thomas recognize that such a process would bring about diminishing returns in agriculture and a drop in real wages, as indeed it did in much of England, but that it would also create a greatly expanded market for manufacturers and merchants alike. The result would be that profits derived from production for this expanded market would bring about institutional improvements that further hastened and expanded the rate of economic advance. Enclosures, and a well-defined system of property rights in country and town were two such changes; the growth of urban freeholding and the development of urban *rentier* classes would have important implications for the organization and development of towns. Three other institutional changes are suggested by North and Thomas: the growth of joint-stock companies; the development of well-integrated banking and credit systems; and growing control of the quality of goods. All these certainly took place in England. The inception of such institutional change, linked to a period of low population growth, allowing capital accumulation, was vital for urban change. Their model of the effects of population growth seems to fit the English pre-industrial experience, although clearly the impetus behind institutional change was not population alone.

Movements in population played a dynamic as well as an inhibiting role on urban change. The economy of the day has already been adduced as a reason for the slow rate of urban change, but it can also be looked to for important evidence of forces which promoted change. We must look to the market and market mechanisms for the first of these economic forces promoting change. In Chapter 1 it was argued that 'no town doth a market make', at least not automatically; but certainly all large and successful towns had important formal institutionalised markets and fairs, as well as performing more general marketing functions. It was the market, not the state, which helped to determine the rate of economic change. Central and local governments did intervene in trade, it is true, central government encouraging or barring certain imports, local government hedging the marketplace around with regulations against 'forstalling', 'regrating' and other anti-social marketing habits, as well as trying to ensure certain minimum standards, such as the weight of loaves or the freshness of meat. But the market was essentially free. Towns were the major market-places, both in a formal and informal sense, for pre-industrial England. As such they would lead and reflect any economic change in the country as a whole. But whilst the market was an engine of growth, it was one of small capacity, limited by considerable institutional difficulties. Guild and trading monopolies had a limiting effect, but as these became weaker (to some extent as a function of the increased size of towns, for the larger and more transient the population, the more difficult such monopolies were to enforce) other marketing institutions such as joint-stock companies and the growth of early banking (as merchants or goldsmiths began to discount bills of credit) appeared to encourage urban change. Equally, slow and irregular communications, much dependent on the vagaries of the weather, confined the trading areas of all but London and the largest of the other cities, and small trading areas meant a small total market. Yet, as population grew and transport improved, marketing improved also; the benefits were to be largely reaped in the eighteenth century, but the very growth of the larger towns, particularly London, had a stimulating effect upon marketing in the seventeenth century.

Technical changes also had some, though slight, effect on urban change. Organic raw materials and animate power were nearly as important in the urban economies of 1700 as they had been two centuries earlier, though the replacement of wood by coal – 'sea-cole' from the Newcastle-upon-Tyne region in particular – as a domestic fuel was a noted trend in towns, but one which brought with it rather more pollution than economic activity. Both invention and innovation in manufacturing were limited. In the seventeenth-century cloth industry for example, clothiers sought to devise new types of cloth by changing the weave or colour, rather than seeking to develop new techniques to cheapen the cloth which they were already making, a situation which is not surprising at a time when labour was cheap and capital relatively scarce.[122] New techniques often caught hold faster in the countryside than in the towns. The most important development in towns may well have been that of mass reading and writing, which speeded up the flow of information about the market, new products, and much else. The important evolution of banking and trading techniques has already been mentioned, but these techniques spread very slowly down the urban . hierarchy from London in the seventeenth century. Their economic effects in inducing 'change' in towns may well have been as important as the changes in the techniques of manufacture, in an age when the levels of skill of the labour force *en masse* were not high. As Clarkson concludes

> . . . as long as markets remained static and the growth of demand was limited by small populations, low incomes and poor transport, there was little incentive to change methods of production. It is no accident that the most important technical advances in pre-industrial England occurred in agriculture, since it was this sector of the economy that felt the pressures of increasing demand from the growing population [including urban population] most strongly.[123]

Certainly the general trend was towards increasingly commercialized production and increasing regional specialization for a domestic market influenced by urban demand, and dominated by the redistributive role of urban markets; the first hints of clear and lasting division between retail and urban functions can be seen. Thompson observes that, 'The structure built by merchants and putters-out in the seventeenth century gradually evolved into the kind of market organisation necessary for a commercially centred and specialized economy'.[124]

Urban change consequent on economic change occurred but it was uncertain and generalized in effect over most towns. There were however, some centres in which real economic growth of a nineteenth-century sort can, with hindsight, be seen. Liverpool's phenomenal growth as a port and a refining centre is a case in point, and the growth of Birmingham as a manufacturing centre is another,[125] worth describing in more detail here. Its medieval growth had been slow, but by the end of the sixteenth century as elsewhere in England, population was accelerating. Already Birmingham's proximity to iron and coalfields had led to iron-working emerging as a most important manufacture by 1500, although tanning was also still significant.[126] As the sixteenth century developed, Birmingham was selling its metal goods to an increasingly wide market, an expansion in production which was achieved by the spread of the industry into surrounding rural areas. Some of this growth was due to iron manufacturing moving from older centres in the ironfield, such as Wednesbury, towards Birmingham in a search for water power and charcoal. Here was clear economic growth, with important results for the growth of the town. By the mid-seventeenth century, there were about fifteen main streets, like Digbeth, Corn-market, Bull Street and High Street, with some 900 houses and 5,000 people. Between 1650 and 1700 a quite amazing rate of growth took place; the number of streets nearly doubled, there were at least 2,500 houses, and population grew (largely due to immigration) to well above 10,000. Cases of urban growth that we would recognize as such today were therefore not absent from the pre-industrial urban scene; but they were not frequent or widespread, and were mainly restricted to the seventeenth century, with the exception of London. The changing economy must have influenced men's attitudes to the towns and cities. The continuous growth of London in particular reflected a new attitude towards town life by more and more people.[127] Towns were slowly becoming potent force for change in themselves.

Before 1700 there was no true urban (or rural) industrialization in England; there were urban neo-industrial communities, it is true, such as Birmingham, Leeds, Manchester and others. Yet they did not at that stage outpace the general rate of change of old-established traditional centres. All the cities at the head of the pre-industrial urban hierachy like Bristol or Exeter (with the probable exception only of York) advanced at a pace similar to the newer, neo-industrial communities right up to the turn of the eighteenth century. These traditional cities had benefits of long-establishment, location, and scale which, when viewed strictly within the confines of the period, allowed them to maintain their position; even if when standing back from the period and viewing it in a longer-run context it is apparent that their position was steadily worsening *vis-à-vis* many newer centres.

For it is clear that it was mainly the 'open' towns which were to expand most quickly in the seventeenth and eighteenth centuries. Such places as sixteenth- and seventeenth-century Birmingham and Manchester were essentially post-medieval towns in their nature, with little if any of the urban traditions and institutions of medieval times. Even when such burgeoning villages achieved corporate status and developed corporate institutions in the sixteenth or seventeenth centuries, they remained persistently open and comparatively free economic communities. Looking at one regional example, the towns of eastern Yorkshire provide a good case study. The great provincial city of York, ecclessiastical and legal capital of the north, represented a typical corporate medieval foundation whose scale had allowed it to pass relatively unscathed through the economic and demographic degradations of the late fourteenth and fifteenth centuries, but whose institutions and manufacturing traditions (and some locational disadvantages) had constrained its rate of pre-industrial change. By the end of the pre-industrial period it was quite 'closed', and not very successful. A contemporary aptly observed of York's slow economic self-strangulation:

> Our magistrates have been too tenacious of their privileges, and have for many years past . . . as it were locked themselves up from the world, and wholly prevented any foreigner from settling any manufacture amongst them. The paying of a large sum of money for their freedoms, with the troublesome and chargeable offices they must often undertake, would deter any person of an enterprising genius in regard of manufacture, from coming to reside at York.[128]

The port of Hull, not far to the east, and the clothing centre of Leeds to the west, were by comparison more open and more successful places. They emerged, through the sixteenth and seventeenth centuries, as the textile manufacturing, collecting and marketing as well as commercial, centres for one of England's most vibrant new manufacturing and exporting areas. It would be too easy to use such phrases as 'freedom from the stranglehold of the guilds' in an explanation of why all this happened, as the picture was far more complicated than that, even though it is noticeable that in traditional centres which did thrive in the seventeenth century, guild regulations on manufacture and on certain aspects of trade had been relaxed. Such was certainly the case in Exeter, and moving with the economic times by becoming more open was as much the hallmark of the more successful traditional centres as it was of increasingly buoyant new centres, such as the port of Liverpool on the opposite coast from Hull, facing the new colonial markets as well as the old one presented by the Irish.

If the scale and locational advantage of some towns, and the openness and free institutions of others, were likely to promote change, there was another characteristic of urbanity then which was also likely to promote urban change. That was the attraction of the pre-industrial town of any size or prosperity for the dwellers in a countryside which was becoming increasingly crowded, and in which incomes and savings were likely to fall, especially during the sixteenth and earlier seventeenth centuries. The medieval German aphorism, 'stadtluft macht frei', sums up part of the lure represented by towns for countless thousands of rural–urban migrants at that time. It is not, however, entirely applicable to pre-industrial England, for people moving from village to town were not fleeing the oppression of medieval serfdom and feudal regulation. Rather, they were usually impelled by a combination of the lure of hoped-for economic and social advantage and the compulsion provided by the knowledge of the limitations of opportunities at home. Sometimes urban immigrants were attracted to the towns from a safe and secure country life and prosperity, as in the case of the younger sons of yeomen and gentry; but more often it was not so much the lure of the town as the hopelessness of life in the country in poverty, exacerbated by bad weather, famine and plague, which almost literally *drove* poor rural folk to the towns. For them, coming perhaps from some overcrowded open village, where land was short and manufacture failing, the attraction of the town and its supposed opportunities was no less of an illusion than that presented by towns in the less-developed countries today.

Migration to towns as a demographic phenomenon is considered in the next chapter, and as a spatial phenomenon in Chapter 5. As urban death rates far exceeded urban birth rates for most pre-industrial English towns, the maintenance of urban life was dependent on massive and consistent rural–urban migration. Thus urban change and most of the growth in the population of sixteenth- and seventeenth-century English towns was dependent on and promoted by migration to them. We must recall that these were fragile towns, with hesitantly developing economies consequent on the slow contemporary rates of invention and innovation, with sometimes restrictive economic institutions (whether guild restriction or primative credit facilities), and with ever-present disease. That they changed at all must have been due in no small part to the effects of migration, through both the sheer numbers involved and the skills and entrepreneurial spirit that the newcomers brought.

Other forces existed to promote change in certain types of towns, sometimes inducing remarkable growth rates. There were few absolutely new towns as such in the sixteenth and seventeenth centuries. Towns such as Birmingham, Manchester and Liverpool proceeded by slow accretions to their pre-existent, even if poorly developed, manufacturing or port-trading bases. The activities in them were not new, but rather tended to increase in scale. Certain other towns changed because of the injection of new urban phenomena into their physical and economic landscapes, although their numbers and importance should not be overrated. For example there was the spreading fashion of taking the waters which led to the growth in popularity of some spas and wells. A number of these places developed into towns that were to reach their acme in the elegance of Georgian Bath or the Victorian solidity of Harrogate. Dr McIntyre observes of this urban change: 'By the opening of the seventeenth century, the search for mineral springs was well under way, and many resorts could trace their first discovery to these years . . . old towns expanded and new ones appeared'.[129] At Bath, the new fashion revived the economic life of the little town whose Roman antecedents as a spa town had been almost forgotten. At Tunbridge Wells and Epsom, tiny places, hardly accounted as towns despite their little markets, considerable growth was engendered around their spas, population shot up, and with it houses and accommodation for the increasingly social activity that surrounded the taking of the waters.

The other increasingly important enterprise promoting rapid urban change was the building, provisioning and repairing of ships for the Royal Navy, whose activities, because of foreign warfare and in the colonial spheres, grew in the seventeenth century. Plymouth had experienced a considerable growth in the sixteenth century, and Portsmouth and Gosport, having gone into a decline from 1540,[130] experienced an enormous boom in marine activities, with resulting growth in population, from the time of the Cromwellian wars onwards[131]. Other dockyards, such as the Medway towns, experienced similar increases. Such dockyard towns may well have represented 'the most spectacular cases of urban expansion',[132] but their overall effect on the urban system of the day was very limited, and to devote too much attention to them is to fall into the trap of looking with eager and instinctively twentieth-century eyes for 'growth'.

Last, and by no means least, of all the forces tending to promote change in pre-industrial towns was the influence of London; it was truly a 'great capital' in Vaughan Cornish's terms. The Scandinavian scholar Ekwall stressed the greatly diversified nature of the capital during the twelfth and thirteenth centuries,[133] a city which he suggests was some 40,000 in size by the beginning of the fourteenth century; already it was one in which occupational diversification was made apparent by residential diversification, with different city wards having their own highly localized activities and personalities: Queenhithe Ward for fishmongers, Castle Baynard Ward for 'the poor', and Cheap Ward for merchants.[134] In pre-industrial times London shared the advantages of scale, or traditional and well-established economic interests, and of location, also enjoyed by the great provincial cities like Bristol; but it had much more beside. Its scale was overwhelming, its control of the nation's trade dominant, it had the monarch, the court, the inns of court, the two houses of Parliament, the law courts; and it had glamour and fashion. Only one such city could have existed in pre-industrial England, and that was London. It was not, however, a major manufacturing centre for the rest of the country. Its parish registers show that many of its inhabitants were merchants and in finance; or wholesale traders, such as mercers, haberdashers and grocers. There certainly were manufacturing areas on the eastern and north-eastern suburbs, and in the urban areas south of the river at Southwark; brass was founded and copper smelted down river. But most in the manufacturing trades were engaged in satisfying the needs of the hundreds of thousands of London inhabitants, or in the refining of imported goods for re-distribution. It was essentially a trading, rather than a manufacturing city in the national context, increasing its share of national trade through most of the two centuries, and probably handling at least two-thirds of that trade by the end of the period.

Its stupendous scale left a deep mark on contemporary observers, as Stow's Survey shows.[135] Many royal proclamations, such as one put out in 1522 by Henry VIII, tried to regulate its progress and expansion – in this case by attempting to stop brickmaking within one mile of the city.[136] To a foreigner's eyes London was a great marvel. The Duke of Würtenberg's secretary, on a visit to London, conveys a vivid impression of its crowded bustle – 'It is a very populous city, so that one can scarcely pass along its streets, on account of the throng'.[137] Its suburban spread was equally noticed in an age when many European cities were packed within their walls – even though the walls were continuously being extended in an ever-widening circle to accommodate growing population, as was the case in Vienna and other capitals. Busino, during his travels in 1617-19, wrote: 'Around the liberties of London there is such a patchwork of suburbs that they look like so many monsters who have been converted after being tamed by the Goddess Circe, the greater part being inhabited by an inept population of the lowest description'.[138] Later Mission de Valbourg described the London suburb of Islington as a 'spaw village' to which fashionable and criminal alike resorted during the seventeenth century, for pleasure or (illicit) profit. It was to him a 'large village, half a league from London, where you drink waters that do you neither good nor harm, provided you don't take too much of them. There is gaming, walk-ing, dancing; and man may spend an hour there agreeably enough.'[139] All the attributes of a great European, indeed world, capital were to be found in London by the turn of the seventeenth century; centrality, many people, much suburban sprawl, sophistication and fashion.

In the sixteenth century, Braudel tells us that demographic growth favoured all towns in Europe indiscriminantly whatever their size.[140] His proposition does not hold good for England's great capital, for the immigration engendered by its great centrality favoured its position markedly over all other English towns. He does go on to state that 'In the seventeenth century political success was concentrated on a few towns to the exclusion of others. Despite the depressing economic situation they grew increasingly, and con-tinuously attracted people and privileges. London and Paris led the most.'[141]

By the seventeenth century London was certainly in the lead over all European capitals, and was one of the biggest and economically most effective. It sprawled down the lower Thames as the city and Westminster joined up, and 'Southwark-over-the-river' developed fast; its suburbs were a vital component of its change: 'Just as a strong tree is never without shoots at its foot, so towns are never without suburbs. . . . Suburbs were made up of the poor, the craftsmen, the watermen, the noisy malodorous industries, cheap inns, posting houses, stables for post horses, porters' lodgings'.[142] The outward spread of London's immediate influence was most marked in the counties of Kent, Surrey, Middlesex and Essex; of the effects of the capital on Essex Burley observes: '. . . it is difficult to overstress the influence London had on the local economy. It is clear also that most of the development traced in this branch of the economy [i.e. especially the agricultural] owed their opinions to the influence of London, either directly or indirectly.'[143] Gottmann's wonderful elucidation of the dynamics of large cities sums it up well;[144] cities like London, then as now, 'continued to direct, finance and manage manufacturing production, controlling the marketing of the goods produced from the offices of the central places. The cities may also have kept an incubator function for the new in-dustrial technology created by the Renaissance'[145] London certainly had this vital and dynamic 'incubator' effect on changes that subse-quently spread through the rest of the nation's economy and society.

Lampard has suggested that 'The presence of an overly-large city in a pre-industrial society may act as a curb rather than a stimulus to wider economic growth. Its growth and maintenance have been somewhat parasitical in the sense that the profits of trade, capital accumulated in agricultural and other primary pursuits have been dissipated in grandiose urban contruction, servicing and consuming'.[146] London was no such curb and was not a conspicuous, enervating consumer of a small nation's resources. It was exactly the opposite; its continuous growth must have moulded a new attitude towards urban life by more and more people: in Thompson's words, 'The growth of London in the seventeenth century must have meant that more and more of the lower classes were thrown into the commercial world'.[147] It stimulated and drove, rather than inhibited change. Its role usually increased in advance of the nation's own economic advance. It became a European city; Voltaire sang his first praises of the concept of the city not to Paris, but to London. London was the Athens of modern Europe:

> Rival of Athens, London Blest indeed,
> That with they tyrants had the wit to change
> The prejudices civil factions breed.
> Men speak their thoughts and in its pease
> In London, who has talent, he is great.[148]

The detail of the make-up of the city, how it worked, exactly how it grew, its precise influence on the rest of the towns and the rest of the economy, remains to be filled in. The overall picture has been clearly drawn in model form by Wrigley in an influential article.[149] Before the plagues of the mid-sixteenth century, the population of the whole London area may have been approaching 100,000. This would make London more than three-quarters of the size of Antwerp, which was then the trading and financial centre of Europe, half that of Venice yet double the size of some important German cities such as Frankfurt (am Main). London was not yet in the same class as the European giants with several hundred thousand population, such as Naples or Paris. Indeed, the plagues of the 1560s may have claimed up to quarter of the capital's population.[150] Yet it managed to re-establish its population in a matter of another few years, to reach 250,000 by 1600, when it was well on the way to the runaway rates of growth which took it to 575,000 by 1700. Immigration was the mechanism for this growth. London as an area of surplus mortality acted as a safety-valve against potential over-population in other parts of the country which might have surplus fertility. It doubled its population during the seventeenth century while other European capitals, which had been its leaders in the mid-sixteenth century, virtually stood still. Wrigley points out how

London fostered agricultural advances, broke down regional barriers, integrated local economies, and stimulated the growth of a truly national economy.[151] It seems to me that rather than change and innovation cascading down the urban hierachy, much of it was 'sucked in' from town and country alike by the capital. In this way modernization was very different in pre-industrial from industrializing society.

This growth could not have failed to have had a tremendous effect on the emergence of new forces in the economy, and on the towns of the day. London by 1700 contained at least ten per cent of England's population, compared to the perhaps two or three per cent of France's population dwelling in Paris. Wrigley has suggested that from such an advance traditional custom-based patterns of behaviour broke down and new patterns – including those of consumption – arose. He tells us that the ever-developing and expanding London market was a forcing ground elsewhere in the country for change in marketing, manufacturing and agriculture, as well as leading to slow change in the transport systems of the nation. The domination of the country was complete by the time of Defoe's writings. If the story of Defoe's towns have one single theme, it is London's unique place in England's economic geography, and especially the wide extent of its trade connection.[152] Innovations from London then diffused through the economy, passing down the urban hierarchy to the provincial capitals and to smaller towns. If it was one of the inherent functions of large urban centres to act as the focus for such innovations, then the processes of change themselves became dependent on the continuous change of such centres. This must have been London's effect on English pre-industrial provincial towns. Provincial towns attempted increasingly to copy the capital's style, but they were never able to compete with it. London was the self-generating metropolitan nucleus of a country that was in many ways being increasingly bound to it.[153] Out of London flowed not only judges on assize, and re-exported and refined exotic goods, but fashion, ideas, innovations and demand, all of which increasingly helped to change English towns economically and socially, and advance the slow but sure process of their modernization.

All these factors promoting change had had their differing effects; as also did those inhibiting it. Many of the changes going on inside individual towns and within the English urban system can be seen, with benefit of the hindsight available to us, to be factors paving the way to later genuine and self-sustaining urban growth. Much else that went on, as will be illustrated in the next four chapters, introduced a measure of gentle re-structuring and change inside individual towns and within the English urban system. It would have been difficult for the most prescient of observers alive in 1700, even with the object lesson of runaway growth presented by London, to have predicted the gathering and quickening pace of general urban growth in the eighteenth century. The intention of this book is to examine the urban geography of the two centuries in their own terms as much as possible, rather than to support any particular theory of urban growth or change, or to pad out the theoretical bones of some structural model. But a survey must be made of the state of towns in 1700, the date marking the end of the examination. This chapter began by examining the medieval forerunners of the pre-industrial town, discussed the reasons for picking on 1500 as a year marking the beginning of the period, and posed the question of whether or not there was a new beginning in 1500. Therefore we must ask whether the year ending the period marked a new beginning also.

A New Beginning in 1700?

It was quite easy to advance the logic for 1500 as a year (symbolically) opening the 'pre-industrial' period for English towns. It marked the end of a century of decline and stagnation, which had produced physical and economic decay in the towns; it was a year which, viewed in retrospect, showed the first signs of revitalization in towns, and of population growth and economic change on a national scale. Even if many towns displayed medieval topography and institutions, these were soon to be altered, and the continuity represented by such survivals from the past was far outweighed by the breaks with the past that were hardened by the economic and demographic stagnation of the fifteenth century. On the other hand it is less clear why 1700, rather than, for example, 1675, 1725, or 1750 is suitable as the date ending the period. For there was nothing like the fifteenth-century standstill which helped to demarcate medieval from pre-industrial towns. The year 1700 does not represent a new beginning in the way that 1500 did. Indeed it was a year which, if a long-term view of urban historical geography is taken, is located fairly early on in the genesis of eighteenth- and nineteenth-century growth. Many of the things that were to happen later were undoubtedly dependent on the foundations laid for them during the sixteenth and seventeenth centuries. Yet urban change had not, with the exception of London and a few incipient manufacturing, dockyard and spa towns, produced much obvious self-generating urban growth up to 1700. In as much as 1700 did represent a new beginning, it was the time when processes of 'change' increasingly altered in character to become processes of 'growth'. The uncertain foundations laid over the two centuries after the medieval slump became not only able to bear the strain but positively to encourage urban growth throughout the urban system in a form which we would clearly recognize today.

The period from 1500 to 1700 can therefore be viewed in two ways. It can be thought of as a coherent urban period in its own right, and it can be thought of as two hundred years which were the preparatory part of a longer process of urban growth which found its roots in these two centuries of uncertain but vital urban change. But as Lampard observes, we must not restrict our examination of urban change to towns alone during this period, for if we look 'only for conspicuous changes in rates and levels of urbanization before 1700 [we] will overlook important structural movements in society that were scarcely reflected in the city'.[154] To divorce town and country completely is to open the way to serious misunderstanding of the urbanism of the day. To do this and thus miss the early growth of regional and national marketing orientation to London, or the emergence of early forms of enterprise in and around open towns would be to miss an important engine of urban change and, as Otsuka observes, to miss a pre-condition of 'industrial revolution'.[155]

Up to 1700, change hardly seems to have touched many towns, however. In-depth scholarly examinations of individual pre-industrial towns show remarkably little change. Rosen's study of one from 1520, finds that 'An examination of Winchester in the late seventeenth century reveals much that had scarcely altered',[156] A hundred miles further north, in the busy manufacturing county of Staffordshire, its own county town of Stafford was barely increasing in population.[157] An Exeter mercer of Henry VIII's time would have little trouble in finding his way around that west-country metropolis in the time of William and Mary. Monastic houses might have vanished, there would have been some new building and the suburbs would have extended, but the scene, the scale, the sort of activity carried on would have been familiar to him in a place which had maintained and enhanced its position in the national urban hierarchy since Henrician times. Yet whilst the basic urban pattern of counties like Sussex (see Figure 1) changed very little over two

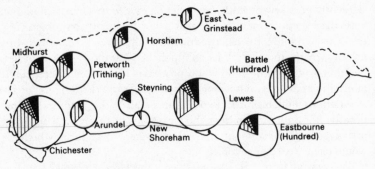

1a Wealth and taxpayers in Sussex towns, 1524-25

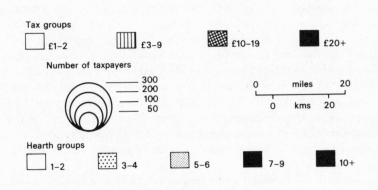

Tax groups

☐ £1–2 |||| £3–9   ▦ £10–19   ■ £20+

Number of taxpayers

300
200
100
50

0   miles   20

0   kms   20

Hearth groups

☐ 1–2   ▦ 3–4   ▦ 5–6   ■ 7–9   ■ 10+

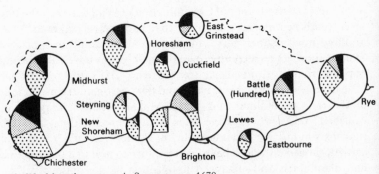

1b Wealth and taxpayers in Sussex towns, 1670s
(Based on G. O. Cowley, 'Sussex Market Towns, 1550-1750', Unpubl. M.A. thesis, Univ. of London, 1965).

hundred years, the urban map of England *had* changed. Little places like Bury in Lancashire which had been described by Leland as 'Byri . . . 4 or V miles from Manchester, but a poore market' were growing by 1700.[158] Urban life too had changed, had become more modern within the town walls and in town suburbs. Newspapers, for example, existed in London by 1700; as disseminators of information and advertisers of new, sophisticated goods, they are key indicators of increasing urban refinement. There were *The Athenian Mercury*, *The True Protestant Mercury*, *The True News* and others. Their pages offered the services of those ready to fit artificial eyes and teeth, and told readers where to get parakeets and Virginian mocking birds, where to buy fishing rods, and where to obtain quotes for fire insurance and inspect machines that turned saltwater fresh. A measure of this change can be found in the language of the advertising copywriting of the day, perhaps more familiar to those alive in the reign of the second rather than the first Elizabeth; copywriters trumpeted the virtues of, for example, beehives that 'profit threefold more than in the usual method!' Oil burning street lamps began to appear, too, in the 1680s and 1690s.[159] Towns were recognizably more modern, if not recognizably more industrial.

Yet, 'In spite of changes during the seventeenth century there were not many more large towns in 1700 than in 1500'.[160] By the 1720s Birmingham, for example, had grown to near 15,000[161] so the picture of stability obtained from looking at the towns at the top of the hierarchy is to a degree illusory. Nevertheless, most of the big towns in 1700, as in 1500, were still in the south and east of the country. Chalklin feels that by 1700 still only about 22 or 23 per cent of the population of England and Wales were town dwellers, between a third and a half of these living in the capital.[162] Similar proportions obtained in the individual regions in 1700, although in well-developed East Anglia the proportion was higher, while in the north-west it was probably lower. Chalklin feels that the rate of urban growth in 1700 was higher than that in 1500, and getting much faster after 1700; at this date there were six or seven towns only outside London with a population of much more than 10,000, but by 1750 there were at least fourteen or fifteen.[163] The country was well endowed with towns by 1700, but most were still tiny; Liverpool may have grown by nearly five times between the 1670s and 1700, from 1,500 to 5,000, but it was one of the urban exceptions, not the urban rule of the last quarter of the seventeenth century, which was a stable period for the majority of towns. The urban map of the day, though we can see the germ of later developments

spawning forth on it, is set in proper context by what was to come
after. Chalklin again sums it up:

> In 1820 between three-fifths and two-thirds of the population were still
> country-dwellers. Many market towns had grown no faster than the total
> population of their districts over the previous 120 years. On the other
> hand industrial changes, and to a lesser extent the growth of trade and
> rising popularity of resorts and the needs of naval warfare, brought into
> prominence fourteen or fifteen centres which have dominated the urban
> map of England ever since. These were the ports of Liverpool, Bristol,
> Hull, Newcastle, and Sunderland; the manufacturing centres of
> Manchester, Birmingham, Leeds, Sheffield, Nottingham and Leicester;
> the dockyard towns of Portsmouth and Plymouth. In 1700 there was only
> one provincial town (Norwich) with more than 25,000; by 1820 there
> were fifteen.[164]

The urban map of 1700 bore much more resemblance to that of two
hundred years before than to what was to come within the next
hundred years. It shows the apogee of the pre-industrial town,
whose characteristics of population, economy and relationships with
their surrounding countryside will now be explored.

3

Town Populations

Town populations, their numbers, the forces changing them, and
their role are central to any consideration of pre-industrial urban
geography. It has already been demonstrated that the level of population change, and its generally erratic course, could be both inhibiting and innovatory forces in urban life. Sometimes towns grew
faster than the countryside, sometimes they grew more slowly,
sometimes urban populations grew at a faster rate than overall
national population; sometimes it was the larger towns, and
sometimes the smaller that experienced faster growth rates; there
was considerable regional difference too. With the exception only of
London, the course of the population history and geography of all
English towns was uncertain and hesitant. Unfortunately, we still
know only very little about the actual numbers that were living in
any one town at any one date, and even less about the working and
interrelationships of the processes of birth, death and migration
which determined those numbers; of the forces working on these
processes, ranging from levels of hygiene and nutrition to social
customs, famine and epidemic disease we know even less.

In the sixteenth and seventeenth centuries we do know that
Europe's population grew by only one quarter of one per cent per
annum, and that English population growth was probably faster
than this, achieving an overall rate of about one third of one per cent
per annum between the beginning and end of these centuries, and
reaching one half of one per cent by the second part of the
eighteenth century. It was not until the mid-eighteenth century that
the impact of the demographically dominating force of mortality
was lessened, and towns became able to reproduce themselves; it
was then that the impact of modernization of agrarian systems and
production, and of the marketing and distribution of foodstuffs

began to lessen the affects of famine and malnutrition on population. It is clear that the sixteenth century saw a rise in most European urban populations; in the Mediterranean, for example, 'All categories of towns shared in this increase, from the very small and modest communities to important towns and great cities, whether characterized by industrial or artisan production, by bureaucracy or commerce . . . everywhere in the sixteenth century man was on the increase'.[1] Braudel observes that numbers are not the only consideration in a study of a town, and that the town only exists as a town 'in relation to a form of life lower than its own'; but numbers do help to determine the character of the town, for before 1500, 90% to 95% of towns known in the west had fewer than 2000 inhabitants,[2] and the character of European town changed as its size changed.[3] In England it is reasonably clear that there were considerable and quite systematic variations in rates of growth between towns of different sizes; demographic growth did not favour all towns indiscriminately, whatever their size. Generally the larger the town the greater and more certain the rate of growth was for them, however small it may seem compared to eighteenth and nineteenth century experience. What is quite clear in England is that London's population forged ahead, that of a few other favoured centres steadily increased in size, and most English towns experienced at least some stirring in their population. As far away as the Balkans the same situation can be observed.[4]

Population is quite rightly accorded a central role in the study of English towns in sixteenth and seventeenth centuries. Population change probably played the dominant role, too, in determining secular changes in the real wage of the population, both urban and rural, in urban and rural rents, and in the terms of trade between manufacturing and agriculture, and hence in the terms of trade between country and town.[5] This is why town populations must be examined before occupations, marketing and other economic facts of urban life are considered. In this examination, one thing remains central: that for most of the two centuries a sort of homeostatic regulator, the force of which was determined by an exogenously varying mortality, dominated population change in town and country, with the exception of London. The word 'change' is used advisedly for, whilst we are left with the impression of great variation in population of pre-industrial England generally and in its towns, however hard one looks at both there is no radical structural alteration to be seen during these two centuries.

Sources

Such an examination must in the first place be descriptive of the
sizes and characteristics of English urban populations, for we can
hardly begin to argue about what caused them to change in their
size and characteristics until we have firmly ascertained these basic
facts. Even this is an impossible task to expect *ever* to complete with
accuracy. Sources which will enable us to estimate town populations
with any certainty at any particular date are few and far between;
indeed we are tied for basic estimates to a few sources, cross-
sectional in their nature, taken at widely spaced dates (*viz.* the
1520s, 1560s, 1600s, 1660s and 1670s), and indirect in the information that they offer. We can find only tax lists, episcopal enquiries as
to the number of families in a parish, or records of the number of
hearths or of communicants in any place, rural or urban. Direct
counts of people are extremely rare, and the discovery of one such
rightly excites great attention. Whilst there were no censuses until
1801 in England, there was meant to be continuous registration for
all places, ostensibly from 1537.

Thomas Cromwell's edict laying down that parish clergy should
maintain registers of the births, deaths and marriages occurring in
their parishes, reinforced by penalties for non-observance that were
strengthened from time to time, did not produce the demographic
goldmine of information we might expect. There were three main
reasons for this: the mendacity and low educational standards of at
least some of the clergy and their servants, who were charged with
administering these registers; the exigencies of storage over many
centuries; and population numbers themselves. First of all, the
clergy in the sixteenth and seventeenth centuries were mostly in
towns outside the cathedral and old monastic centres, likely to be of
a relatively low educational standard, like the hedge priests, their
country brethren; and the turmoil of reformation did not ease these
problems in the first half of the sixteenth century. As literacy and
numeracy increased amongst the clergy in the later sixteenth and
seventeenth centuries, so there is considerable evidence that the
attention to duty of some incumbents, including those of urban
parishes, decreased. Low-paid curates and clerks were given the
charge of both the cure of souls and the keeping of records; registers
were sometimes entered up long after the event, and population
totals, causes of death, places of origin were haphazardly set down.
Secondly, whilst there may have been greater pressures to maintain
registers in larger towns, there is no evidence to suggest that they

were any better stored in the parish chests of urban churches. The continuous process of the amalgamation of inner city parishes led to the loss and dispersal of some records; damp, rats, careless clerks unaware of their value, fire and other accidents led to the destruction of many others. Therefore large gaps often appear in those series that do survive for urban parishes.

Finally population growth itself in towns, or rather its peculiar nature, militated against accurate registration. The rate of natural increase of most urban populations was determined by the rate of immigration, for there was probably not a town in England that consistently replaced itself by indigenous births for any length of time during these two centuries. Immigrants poured into towns, and in the larger of these it was difficult for the clergy – with very few effective sanctions against non-registration – to ensure that the demographic events were always carefully recorded, or indeed recorded at all. Many migrants achieved permanent residence and thus permanent record of the bare details of their life; many more, journeymen, pregnant girls fleeing parental wrath, vagrants seeking shelter and relief, were the transients of the day, unsung, unloved and often unrecorded. Occasionally in parish registers we catch a glimpse of their existence, as a 'poore childe' or an 'old and impoverished woman' are laid to rest; but often such folk escaped even the little bit of immortality afforded by a parish register entry.

The framework of ecclesiastical administration in the larger towns served only to exacerbate the three types of registration problem. For whilst the smallest market town might have but one parish covering all its area and people, a large city such as Bristol or York had a good number of them. The level of recording in some was much higher than in others and the survival rate of the three different registers of births, deaths and marriages could vary greatly, not only within the records of individual parishes, but between the parishes that went to make up any larger town. It is a relatively rare event to find all the vital birth and death registers for all the parishes of any large town surviving for the number of years that would make it possible for techniques of aggregative analysis to produce reasonable population totals from them. While parish register material can begin to tell us, after much labour, something of the dynamics of population change, and of the periodicity and rate of population advance, they are still a fairly intractable source for totals of population at any one time.

Rough estimates on size can be gained from indirect sources and these can be valuable even though widely separated in time. These

sources can be conveniently itemised thus: in 1524–25 the lay subsidies were levied which were taxations on lay wealth; in 1563 a
survey of the number of households and/or parishioners in different
parishes survive for some of the bishoprics in which it was made; in
1603 a 'census' of communicants, recusants and non-conformists
was made in most of England, to help inform the new King, James I,
of the religious state of his new kingdom; between 1662 and 1674
were levied hearth taxes in a number of years, the records of which
give details of those paying the taxes, and those exempt from it; in
1676 the so-called 'Compton' census endeavoured to obtain the
same sort of information as was sought in the 1603 communicant
returns; and lastly there was in 1695 a tax on Births, Deaths,
Marriages, Spinsters, Bachelors, etc. which should have provided us
with a great demographic domesday for the late seventeenth century, but in fact the records have been lost for much of the country.
To get near approximations of population from these sources it is
necessary for some sort of multiplier to be applied to represent the
section of the population not counted in the records. For example,
family size in the 1520s may be held to have been 4·5 persons per
family, and every taxpayer to be the head of a family; ignoring for
the present the problem of the number of those exempt from the tax
and hence missing from the records, the number of taxpayers in any
town multiplied by 4·5, supposing our assumptions about average
family size are valid, should give a total estimated population size. It
can immediately be seen both from the pitfalls mentioned and those
not dismissed here, that figures derived by such calculations are of
the most approximate kind, and that the calculations themselves
belong to the realm of political arithmetic with which the late-
seventeenth century demographer and political scientist, Gregory
King would be immediately familiar, rather than the world of
sophisticated techniques of modern historical demography. Figures
derived in this way are mere indicators of the relative order of size of
towns, rather than exact totals. Any figure for any large town which
is not rounded to the nearest thousand, or for a tiny one, that is not
rounded to the nearest 250, is held to be immediately suspect. It is
impossible from such sources and by such methods to be any more
accurate than this.

It is probably true to say that not even every source for the population of every English town has yet been properly listed, let alone
transcribed, tabulated and subjected to analysis to achieve population estimates. We are not yet in a position to offer a gazetteer of
town populations based on the sources just discussed, though such

has been possible on a regional scale for East Anglia – as illustrated in Table 12 in Chapter 6; for the rest, Tables 6, 7, 8 and 9 show a heterogenous collection of population estimates for many of the towns mentioned by name in the pages of this book, together with the sources from which they have been drawn. They should not be taken as anything more than approximations to reality, but each set of sources, and the population estimates that they allow us to derive, are worth examining here to show the sorts of problems encountered in compiling them.

Sources 1500–49

The major sources for the population of towns in the first half of the sixteenth century are the lay subsidies, taxes levied on personal wealth in 1524 and 1525. It is generally thought, though by no means universally accepted, that taxpayers recorded represented all adult males over 16 years of age; they might be thought to represent a family, the average size of which in a century which was not noted for extended household units, might range between 4 and 5 persons.

Table 6: ESTIMATES FOR URBAN POPULATIONS 1500–49

Town	Year	Estimate
Leicester	1509	3,000[1]
Oxford	1520s	5,000[2]
Birmingham	1520s	1,000[3]
Stratford-upon-Avon	1520s	600-700[4]
Maldon, Essex	1520s	1,000[5]
Oakham, Rutland	1520s	600
Uppingham, Rutland	1520s	300[6]
Rye, Sussex	1520s	2,000
Eastbourne, Sussex	1520s	400
Chichester, Sussex	1520s	2,000
Lewes, Sussex	1520s	1,500
Arundel Sussex	1520s	400
Petworth, Sussex	1520s	600–700
Midhurst, Sussex	1520s	500–600
Horsham, Sussex	1520s	600
Battle, Sussex	1520s	400[7]
Birmingham	1535	1,200[8]
Richmond, Yorks.	1547	1,200[9]
York	1548	8,000[10]
Guildford	1520s–1530s	2,000[11]

1 *V. C. H. Leicester,* 76
2 C. I. Hammer, 'The mobility of skilled labour in Late Medieval England: Some Oxford evidence' *Vierteljahrschrift für sozial und Wirtschaftsgeshicte* 63 Band, Heft 2 (1976)

3 R. A. Holt, 'The economic development of Birmingham before 1553', Unpubl.
   M.A. thesis, Birmingham University (1975), 108
4 *Ibid.* 109
5 W. J. Petchey, 'The Borough of Maldon, Essex 1500–1688', Unpubl. Ph.D. thesis,
   Leicester University (1972), 40
6 Both Rutland references from J. Cornwall 'The people of Rutland in 1522', *Trans.
   Leicester Hist. and Arch. Soc.,* 37 (1961–2), 22
7 All Sussex references from G. O. Cowley 'Sussex Market Towns 1550–1750',
   Unpubl. M.A. thesis, London University (1965), 60–76
8 Holt 'The economic development of Birmingham', 108
9 R. Fieldhouse 'Social structure from Tudor lay subsidies and probate inventories', *Local Population Studies,* 12 (1974), 12–13
10 D. M. Palliser 'Epidemics in Tudor York', *Northern History* VIII (1973), 46
11 E. M. Dance 'Guildford Borough Records, 1514–1520', *Surrey Record Society,*
   XXIV (1958), xiv

The level of exemptions from the tax on grounds of poverty, age and inability to pay, is not known, although there is evidence in some parts of the country from the earlier Muster of Harness taken in 1522, that these reached at least 10 per cent.[6] Thus, the number of taxpayers, plus a notional 10 per cent for exemptions, multiplied by 4·5 (representing supposed family size) can produce an approximation of the population of most towns for which the records survive (see Table 6). The whole subject of the lay subsidies has been exhaustively studied by Dr Sheail[7] and the information provided by the gazetteer to his important doctoral dissertation can be the basis of estimates for the sizes of many towns in an England with a population of some two and a half millions. The information given about the level of taxes can also tell us about the relative riches of different towns; these figures in turn closely correlate with population numbers; the City of London, being the wealthiest town, yielded £8,262. 10s. 1d. in 1524.[8] Such information is printed in the record series for many English counties, such as Dorset[9] and can tell us much of the relative standing of towns by wealth and thus by implication give information about their population. We can see from these subsidies that Buckinghamshire and Rutland[10] were fairly poor and little urbanized; Sussex was relatively rich,[11] with some towns; and Suffolk[12] was very rich with a number of important towns by the standards of the day. In Buckinghamshire 8,000 persons paid £1,084, in Sussex 12,000 persons paid £2,237[13] and in Suffolk 17,000 paid £3,520.

In Buckinghamshire, Aylesbury, a town important within the county, had only 199 taxpayers in a population of between 700 and 900 people and was certainly not a very well-off place. Those surveying the Aylesbury inhabitants' wealth in order to assess them for tax liability, were unusually detailed in their observations; we are told of John Bray, 'decayd by evyll dettes and corn' and the merchant William Bassett, 'decayd by evyll servants in loss of wares'. In tiny, almost totally rural Rutland, England's smallest county, the two most important towns Oakham and Uppingham had populations of only 600 and 300 each; Uppingham with its market was described by the early tourist and topographer Leland as having 'one meane streete, and . . . a very meane churche' – it certainly had no more people than nearby villages like Langham and Lyddington. The wealthier county of Sussex had its tiny towns too, like Petworth with only 165 taxpayers, and its poor and empty areas like the Sussex portion of the Weald (see Fig. 1). It also had its share of disasters, affecting population and thus ability to pay; the inhabitants of Westbourne were exempt because of recent fire damage, and those of Brighton were exempted presumably in consideration of being burnt by French raiders in 1514[14]. In Suffolk, one of the richest and most populous English counties, there were two substantial and wealthy towns, Ipswich and Bury St Edmunds, with populations of several thousands each, far larger than any town in Buckingham, Rutland or Sussex, as well as a number of places of over a thousand in size in the broadcloth producing areas such as Sudbury. It is quite possible from these subsidies to get good enough population estimates for most English towns to serve as a baseline for their study in the 1520s; the date itself is fortuitously chosen, for population growth was just reviving in the 1510s and 1520s; but the subsidy was not levied in the Duchy of Lancaster or the Palatinate of Durham, so north-western and north-eastern English urban populations must be estimated from other, less accurate sources. Subsidies were taken for much of the rest of the sixteenth century, but covered an increasingly narrow band of taxable people according to increasingly outdated taxation formulae as the years passed, making such records useless as approximate measures of population or even accurate measures of wealth. The Chantry certificates of 1547 are the only comparable source to the lay subsidies for the first half of the sixteenth century. These can give approximate totals of population for some towns, recording for instance 1,200 'houseling people' at Richmond in Yorkshire,[15] but are not sufficiently systematic to allow us to place much reliance on their use.

Sources 1550–99

As was the case during the first half of the sixteenth century, there is only one major cross-section source for population in its second half, the 1563 episcopal survey. The lay subsidies continued to be taken, but an inspection of those for Surrey (where only 18 paid in Epsom and 75 in Reigate for instance)[16] Worcester[17] or Derbyshire[18] in the 1590s shows them to be useless for population purposes. Taxes had been collected for the past three hundred years[19] leaving records of use to historical geographers, but it was only after the Reformation that religious enquiries leaving comparable documentary evidence began to appear. The Chantry certificates of the late 1540s enquired about numbers of parishioners incidentally to their main purpose of surveying Chantries and their associated endowed wealth. In 1563, however, the first of the three great sixteenth- and seventeenth-century religious surveys was begun, with Bishops enquiring as to the numbers of families and parishioners in their diocese. Not all of these surveys survive and, as with the 1524–25 lay subsidies, not every part of the country can be covered; for example the returns for Norwich are no longer in existence.

In counties that are covered, such as Hertfordshire[20] valuable information can be derived from these returns, generally in terms of numbers of families; this is a more direct form of information by comparison with the lay subsidies of 1524–25, where taxpayers can only be assumed to be the head of families or households. In Buckinghamshire[21] the survey asked, *inter alia,* for the number of households in each parish or chapelry; there were 351 in

Table 7: ESTIMATES FOR URBAN POPULATIONS, 1550–99

Town	Year	Estimate
Leeds (whole parish)	1550s	3,000[1]
Gloucester	1563	4,068–4,250[2]
Worcester	1563	4,250[3]
Stockton	1563	1,000[4]
Blandford, Dorset	1564	500–700[5]
London	1560s	90,000[6]
Liverpool	1565	700[7]
Leicester	1560s to 1570s	3,000 to 4,750[8]
Northampton	1570	3,500[9]
Gateshead	1576	3,000[10]
Southampton	1596	4,200[11]
Leicester	1599	3,500[12]
Bristol	1599–1600	12,000[13]
Birmingham	1599–1600	1,700[14]
Newcastle-under-Lyme	1599–1660	660[15]

1 G. C. F. Forster 'From the foundation of the borough to the eve of the industrial revolution', being pp. 131–45 in *Leeds and its region*, (1967), 136

2 P. Ripley 'The parish register evidence for the population of Gloucester, 1562–1641', *Trans. Bristol and Gloucester Arch. Soc.*, XCI (1972), 199–206

3 A. D. Dyer 'The city of Worcester in the sixteenth century' (Leicester 1973), 26

4 T. Sowler *A history of the Town and Borough of Stockton-on-Tees* (1972), 50

5 M. M. B. Weinstock 'Blandford in Elizabethan and Stuart Times', *Notes and Queries for Somerset and Dorset*, XXX (1975), 119

6 G. D. Ramsey *The City of London in international politics at the accession of Elizabeth Tudor* (1975), 33

7 F. Walker 'The historical geography of south-west Lancashire', *Chetham Society*, CIII (1939), 45

8 J. E. O. Wilshere 'Plague in Leicester, 1558–1665', *Trans. Leicester Arch. and Hist. Soc.*, XLIV (1968–69), 47

9 A. Everitt 'Urban growth, 1570–1770', *Local Historian* 8 (1968–69), 118

10 F. W. D. Manders *A history of Gateshead* (1973), 11

11 A. T. Patterson 'A history of Southampton 1700–1914', *Southampton Record Series*, 11 (1966), 6

12 Wilshere 'Plague in Leicester'; see also *V. C. H. Leicester*, IV, 76

13 P. McGrath 'Merchants and merchandise in seventeenth century Bristol', *Bristol Record Society*, XIX (1955), ix

14 R. A. Holt 'The economic development of Birmingham before 1553', Unpubl. M.A. thesis, Birmingham University (1975), 108

15 K. R. Adey 'Seventeenth-century Stafford: A country town in decline', *Midland History*, 11 (1974), 166–67

Buckingham proper, 145 in High Wycombe, 139 in Amersham and 123 in Newport Pagnell; the application of a multiplier of 4·5 giving population totals of about 1,575, 650, 625, and 550 respectively. Yet the survey was far from a census, and the question about number of households probably seemed rather incidental to the pressing religious questions which were central to the enumerator's enquiries; in most cases it seems the returns are clearly estimates, often in suspiciously 'round' totals, and we can only treat figures of 3,000 for Leicester, or 4,250 for Worcester, shown on Table 7, with caution. 1563 is quite a good base line for studies using parish register material where this is available, as in Exeter,[22] or at Gloucester, where Ripley says that the town had a population of between 4,068 and 4,520 in 1563.[23] Certainly parish registers bring out the secular trends of the advance of population in towns like Gloucester, which was to reach nearly 5,500 in 1671–2, despite major set-backs during the 1590s and 1630s, years of heavy mortality induced by near-famine conditions and epidemic disease. There is no doubt that where evidence is available from parish registers surviving for a whole town and is carefully analysed (as in Gloucester or Worcester) the results are far more impressive than those derived from any similar surviving survey.

Sources 1600–49

For the first half of the new century there is again only one major cross-sectional source for population estimates, the 'communicant census' of 1603. This was a survey asking direct questions about numbers of communicants taking the sacrament on Easter Sunday and about those that were absent from church that day because they were recusants, or dissenters. Many of these are published in different county record series;[24] but many others are not and remain surprisingly little used. They have all the intrinsic defects which we might expect, having examined the 1563 Religious Survey, particularly in that incumbents charged with making returns often treated the question as requiring only an estimate. In one Suffolk archdeaconry,[25] for example, 53 per cent of answers were given in round figures, and indeed some of them were quite clearly estimates, given in terms of 'about 600', etc. The numbers of recusants and dissenters recorded are often suspiciously small, leading one to suspect that parish clergy were over-anxious to give a good impression of the state of the established church in their parishes. Using the figures that are available showing numbers of communicants, different assumptions have to be made and different multipliers used, to achieve population totals comparable with the lay subsidies. For in this source we are dealing not with entries that represent male heads of households, but entries which represent those over the age of taking Holy Communion; in other words, adults of both sexes. In order to achieve total population estimates, we need to know the usual age of first communion, and what proportion of the total population we might expect to find under that age. The age of first communion by the beginning of the seventeenth century seems to have reached about sixteen, and the proportion of the total population under that age seems to have been about 40 per cent from both contemporary evidence and model life tables;[26] thus if the total number of communicants, recusants and dissenters are assumed to be adult males and females over sixteen, the addition of 40 per cent gives a total population estimate.

Figures of town sizes in Table 8 gathered from this sort of source, tell us of the relative sizes of Grimsby, a struggling port of about 1,000 people; Hastings, another port of some 1,400 people; and Birmingham, which with its population of between 2,000 and 3,000 was just beginning to grow rapidly. A number of other sources for the first half of the seventeenth century may be of some use; in 1642 for example the Protestation returns were made. These were lists of those people subscribing their name or mark to a document giving support to the King, and population figures for Liverpool based on these returns have been suggested by Stewart-Brown,[27] but here the

Table 8: ESTIMATES FOR URBAN POPULATIONS 1600–49

Town	Year	Estimate
Birmingham	1603	2–3,000[1]
Grimsby	1603	1,000[2]
Winchester	1603	3,000[3]
Nottingham	1600s	3,540[4]
Stafford	1622	1,550[5]
Salisbury	1630s	6,800[6]
York	1630	12,000[7]
London	1633	34,000[8]
Leeds	1626	5–6,000[9]
Liverpool	1642	2–2,500[10]
Worcester	1646	8,300[11]
Hull	1649–50	6,000[12]
York	1649–50	12,000[13]
Canterbury	1649–50	6,000
Rochester	1649–50	3,000
Maidstone	1649–50	3,000
Dover	1649–50	3,000
Ashford	1649–50	1,000–2,500
Sevenoaks	1649–50	1,000–2,500
Faversham	1649–50	1,000–2,500
Deptford	1649–50	1,000–2,500[14]

1 C. Gill *History of Birmingham* (1952), 49
2 E. Gillet *A History of Grimsby* (1970), 67
3 A. B. Rosen 'Economic and social aspects of the history of Winchester, 1520–1670', unpubl. Ph.D. thesis, Oxford University (1975)
4 A. C. Wood 'A note on the population of Nottingham in the seventeenth century', *Trans. Thoroton Society,* 40 (1937), 111
5 K. R. Adey 'Seventeenth-century Stafford: A County town in decline', *Midland History,* 11 (1974), 154
6 P. Slack 'Poverty and politics in Salisbury, 1597–1666', being pp. 164–203 in P. Clark and P. Slack *Crisis and order in English towns 1500–1700* (1972), 176
7 D. M. Palliser 'Epidemics in Tudor York', *Northern History,* VIII (1973), 46
8 I. Sutherland 'When was the Great Plague? Mortality in London, 1563–1665', being pp. 287–320 in D. V. Glass and R. Nevelle, *Population and social change* (1972), 307–8
9 W. G. Rimmer 'The evolution of Leeds to 1700', *The Thoresby Miscellany,* 14 (1967), 118
10 R. Stewart-Brown *The inhabitants of Liverpool from the fourteenth to the eighteenth century* (1930), 10
11 A. D. Dyer *The city of Worcester in the sixteenth century* (1973), 26
12 *V.C.H. Yorkshire, East Riding,* 157
13 D. M. Palliser 'The trade guilds of Tudor York', being pp. 86–116 of Clark and Slack (eds.) *Crisis and order,* 87
14 C. W. Chalklin 'A seventeenth century market town; Tonbridge', *Archaeologia Cantiana,* 76 (1961), 152

list contained the names of only 371 people when there were, as we know from other evidence, some 450 freemen working in the town and a total population of at least 2,000; thus the Protestation returns can be seen to be of limited use as a basis for population estimates. A variety of other sources peculiar to certain towns also begin to appear; increasing town government and increasing literacy lead to increasing urban record-taking, as town governments were faced with the problems consequent on urban growth, like famine relief or vagrancy. There was a special survey made in Stafford in 1622 for example, listing 385 households, a population of approximately 1,550.[28] Subsidies continued to be levied, but on fewer and fewer people; only 24 burgesses out of a population of over•1,500 were taxed in Stafford a few years later in 1640,[29] and very few in Macclesfield,[30] so they are by now useless for population estimates. No other sources survive that allow rapid calculation of size for a number of towns in a regional or national context. Close examination of parish registers for individual towns where they survive, will undoubtedly prove the most reliable way of achieving estimates in the future. In Salisbury, for example, Slack is able to use the baptism registers for three parishes, together with the numbers of residents in almshouses, to get a population estimate of some 6,850 for that cathedral city in the 1630s.[31] However, parish registration often failed during the period of civil war and parliamentary government from the 1640s and there are alarming gaps for many towns in different parts of the country.

Sources, 1650–99

After a period of civil turmoil and some upset in record-taking, the restoration of the monarchy brought about a return of clear episcopal authority, with restored parish registration everywhere. There was also increasing activity by the monarchy in raising taxes, with far greater levels of accuracy in administration and record-taking. In particular, the great series of Hearth Taxes levied on the number of chimneys and hearths any householder had, taken between 1662 and 1674,[32] gives a mine of information; if the records are missing for one year in any town, they tend to be present for another. It is unfortunate that the same cannot be said for the Tax on Births, Deaths, Marriages, etc. of 1695, sadly missing for most towns, though available for some like Bristol.[33] There is thus a plethora of cross-sectional information to be had, reinforced by the last of the great pre-industrial religious surveys, the so-called

'Compton Census' of 1676. The latter asked exactly the same questions about numbers of communicants, recusants and dissenters as
had been posed some seventy-five years earlier in 1603. It can be
treated in exactly the same way in order to achieve total population
figures, and provides valuable substantiating evidence for population size to that given by the Hearth Taxes. In Norfolk and Suffolk,
for example, the two sources used together give closely correlated estimates for most towns. The Hearth Taxes are analagous to lay subsidies in that the taxpayers recorded can be taken to represent the
heads of households, and a multiplier of 4·5 or 4·75 can be used to
obtain population estimates. However, the numbers of those exempt
from payment because of poverty must be taken into account.
Sometimes they are enrolled on the returns, but on many occasions
they are not; in larger towns, the poor sector of society could be as
much as 30 or 40 per cent of the whole. Great care must be taken in
their use, though often the actual certificates of exemption accorded
to individuals can be found in local or national record offices.

In a modernizing country, as England was fast becoming during
the second half of the seventeenth century, records such as these
began to excite the attention of contemporaries such as Graunt,
Petty, and above all Gregory King.[34] King used such figures to
produce national population estimates, and treated them in many
ways as though they were virtually census information, which they
clearly were not. The problems of estimating population figures for
that period from such sources are as severe in England as they are in
North America at the time.[35] A number of guides to their use are in
existence,[36] their relative profusion, and the interest shown by those
studying the eighteenth century in the base-line provided by
seventeenth century records has ensured that a great number of estimates have been based on them; these are shown in Table 6. The
volume of printed hearth tax material is considerable, more than for
any other comparable source. Use of hearth taxes can proceed with
some degree of certainty, for contemporaries like Gregory King and
others treat them as usable sources for the study of 'political
arithmetic'. Wherever one looks in the country they can be found: in
Suffolk,[37] for the town of Chester with a population of about 8,000,[38]
in Oxfordshire,[39] and for the town of Newcastle-upon-Tyne.[40] For
the latter the tax roll of 1665 gives a total of 2,510 names, 1,472
liable to pay the tax and the very high number of 1,038 exempt from
it; a multiplier of 5·0 suggested for this expanding coal-exporting
and manufacturing town, gives a population of some 12,500. Similar
sorts of information can be obtained for the towns of Somerset,[41]

Staffordshire,[42] Surrey,[43] and Warwickshire, where little market towns like Kineton were smaller than many of the more populous villages.[44]

It is quite clear from a survey of sources that as time and national population advanced, so the information available to us on the sizes of English towns becomes more profuse, whilst parish records become more accurate, and survive in greater numbers. The information on births and deaths which they give, is vital to any understanding of the dynamics concerning population growth and change. We should not feel inhibited from the use of these registers by their drawbacks, for exact numbers escaped even contemporaries; as Gregory King said in the 1680s: 'What ye true Number of ye people of England may be, is not only uncertain but very difficult to compute, by reason of the great neglect and ommissions in all the Publick Registers and Assessments.'[45] But such records are our only real source of information on population dynamics.

Table 9: ESTIMATES FOR URBAN POPULATIONS 1650–99

Town	Year	Estimate
Birmingham	1650	5,472[1]
Exeter	1660s	9,400[2]
Newcastle-upon-Tyne	1660s	12,550[3]
Stafford	1660s	1,300[4]
Birmingham	1660s	6,000[5]
Bury, Lancs	1660s	1,000[6]
Leicester	1660s	5,000[7]
Liverpool	1660s	2,000[8]
Macclesfield	1660s	2,875
Stockport	1660s	1,480
Chester	1660s	7,600[9]
Congleton	1660s	1,830
Congleton	1660s & 1670s	1,200[10]
Colchester	1662	10,305
Colchester	1666	4,114[11]
Cambridge	1670s	9,000[12]
Bury St Edmunds	1670s	5,000[13]
Gloucester	1670s	5,397[14]
Brighton	1670s	2–2,500
Arundel	1670s	8–9,000
Petworth	1670s	1,500
Midhurst	1670s	900–1,000[15]
Maldon (Essex)	1670s	1,069[16]
Sheffield	1670s	1,900–2,500
Rotherham	1670s	1,200–1,500
Doncaster	1670s	2,000
Richmond, Yorks	1670s	1,500–1,800

Town	Year	Estimate
Beverley, Yorks.	1670s	2,500–3,100[17]
Dudley, Worc.	1670s	2,250[18]
Winchester	1670s	3,100[19]
Stockton-on-Tees	1670s	2,000[20]
Lichfield	1670s	2,500[21]
Northampton	1676	4,500[22]
Lincoln	1676	4,100[23]
Warwick	1676	3,300[24]
Chichester	1676	2,500[25]
Faversham	1676	2,000[26]
Guildford	1676	1,750[27]
Hertford	1676	1,670[28]
Lewes, Sussex	1676	2,500[29]
Nottingham	1676	3,328
Mansfield	1676	1,390
Newark	1676	1,247[30]
Birmingham	1700	10,000[31]
Liverpool	1708	7,000[32]
Kendal	1695	2,195[33]
Penrith	1688	1,000
Workington	1688	945[34]
Chichester	1700	2,500–3,000[35]
Lichfield	1700	3,300[36]
Hull	1700	7,500[37]
Exeter	1688	13,000[38]
Southampton	1697	3,000[39]

1 H. Hamilton *The English Brass and Copper Industries* (1926), 125
2 W. G. Hoskins 'The population of Exeter', *Devonshire Notes and Queries,* XX (1938–39), 242
3 R. Welford 'Newcastle householders in 1665'. *Arch. Aeliana,* VII (1911) 55–56
4 K. R. Adey 'Seventeenth century Stafford: A county town in decline', *Midland History,* 11 (1974), 152–67
5 C. Gill *History of Birmingham,* 1 (1951), 49
6 M. Gray 'The History of Bury, Lancashire from 1660 to 1877'. Unpubl. B.Litt. thesis, Oxford University (1963), 9
7 *V. C. H. Leicester* 76
8 D. J. Pope 'Shipping and trade in the Port of Liverpool', Unpubl. Ph.D. thesis, Liverpool University (1970), 8
9 S. I. Mitchell 'Urban markets and retail distribution 1730–1815, with particular reference to Macclesfield, Stockport and Chester', Unpubl. D.Phil., Oxford University (1974)
10 W. B. Stephens *History of Congleton,* (1970), 48–49
11 I. G. Doolittle 'The effects of the plague on a provincial town in the sixteenth and seventeenth centuries', *Medical History,* 19 (1975), 333–41
12 *V. C. H. Cambs.* III, 501–4
13 *Suffolk Green Books,* 13 (1905), XIX
14 P. Ripley 'The Parish register evidence for the population of Gloucester, 1562–1641', *Trans. Bristol Gloucester Arch. Soc.,* XCI (1972), 199–206
15 G. O. Cowley 'Sussex market towns, 1500–1750', Unpubl. London M.A. thesis (1965) 65, 70, 73, 74

16 W. J. Petchey 'The Borough of Malden, Essex, 1500–1688', Unpubl. Ph.D. thesis. Leicester University (1972)

17 J. D. Purdy 'The Hearth Tax Returns for Yorkshire', Unpubl. M.Phil. thesis (1975) 328, 334, 360–61

18 J. S. Roper *Dudley, seventeenth-century town* (1965) (1974) 11

19 A. B. Rosen 'Economic and social aspects of the history of Winchester, 1520–1670', Unpubl. D.Phil. thesis, Oxford University (1975)

20 T. Sowler *A history of the Town and Borough of Stockton-on-Tees* (1972), 99

21 H. Thorpe 'Lichfield: A study of its growth and function'. *Coll. History Staffordshire,* (1950–51), 183

22 Compton Census, Ms. William Salt Library, Stafford, fo. 329

23 J. W. F. Hill *Tudor and Stuart Lincoln* (1956), 210

24 *V. C. H. Warwickshire,* VIII, 418

25 Compton Census, Ms. William Salt Library, Stafford, fo. 329

26 C. W. Chalklin *The provincial towns of Georgian England* (1974), 18

27 E. R. Chamberlain *Guildford* (1970), 9

28 L. Munby *Hertfordshire, population statistics, 1563–1801* (1904), 34

29 Cowley 'Sussex market towns', 69

30 E. L. Guildford 'Nottinghamshire in 1676', *Trans. Thoroton Society,* 28 (1924), 107–9

31 Gill *Birmingham,* 49

32 Pope 'Port of Liverpool', 8

33 J. D. Marshall 'Kendal in the late seventeenth and eighteenth centuries' *Trans. Cumb. and Westmorland Antiquarian Society,* LXXXV (1976), 188

34 R. Millward 'The Cumbrian town between 1600 and 1800', being pp. 202–28 of C. W. Chalklin and M. A. Havinden (eds.), *Rural change and urban growth 1500–1800* (1974), 209

35 Cowley 'Sussex market towns', 66–67

36 Adey 'Stafford', 167

37 *V. C. H. Yorkshire, E. Riding,* 158

38 Hoskins 'Population of Exeter', 242

39 A. T. Patterson *A history of Southampton 1700–1914* (1966), 6

Basic Patterns in the 1520s, 1600s and 1670s

The population of England was somewhere between 2 and 2·5 million in the 1520s, had reached about 3·5 million by 1600, and was fast approaching 5 million by the 1670s. The urban proportion of these totals is still not completely known, and indeed depends on the definition of a town adopted. The evidence from one region, East Anglia, which is discussed in Chapter 6, suggests that urban population rose from at least 20 per cent of the region's population in 1524 to 25 per cent in 1603, and to 30 per cent by 1670. These figures are dependent on a detailed definition of 'urban', and also on the fact that these counties were amongst the most densely populated and wealthy in the whole country; they were counties where one would expect to find larger than average towns. Over the whole of the country it is likely that the proportion of town-dwellers rose from about 10–12 per cent of the whole population in the 1520s, to between 20 and 25 per cent of the whole population by the 1670s.

In the 1520s London's population was probably about 50,000, excluding suburbs over the river like Southwark and the area further down the river beyond the Tower. It stood in a clearly primary position in relation to the towns of the rest of the kingdom, as it had from the years before the Conquest. It was five or six times larger than its nearest rivals in size, the provincial centres of Bristol, York and Norwich, with their populations of under 10,000. The rest of the country's towns were much smaller; important ports like Newcastle, Chester and Southampton were a few thousand in size, as were some traditional manufacturing centres like Coventry or Salisbury. Below these were many county towns like Leicester or Northampton, with populations of 2,000 or 3,000 at most, and a great network of towns of much smaller size, down to a few hundred people, differentiated only from villages by a few small marketing and manufacturing functions.

To take one county as an example, in Sussex in the 1520s there were only three towns with a population of over 1,000; these were Chichester, Lewes, and Rye.[46] The next biggest, Brighton and Hastings, were not far behind, but still had not recorded 1,000 inhabitants. Chichester was the biggest of the towns, with over 2,000 in 1524–25, an important corn-marketing and coasting centre, with Lewes the biggest of the downland towns – not far behind in size with some 1,600 people. One third of its population dwelt in the large suburb of Southover, and writers from Camden's time onwards were impressed by the borough's populous nature, singling out the suburbs of Southover and Cliffe for special mention. Other downland towns were tiny: Arundel by the early sixteenth century contained little more than 400, and Steyning little more than 600 people. In the Weald, average town size was even smaller. Midhurst had a population of only 500 or 600, as did Horsham, and lesser places like Hailsham or Storrington, accounted as towns by contemporaries contained only 300 people. Like most other English counties, Sussex had its decayed and decaying market towns, notably Ditchling which contained little more than 150 people in the 1520s.

The number of tax-payers living in the major Sussex towns is shown on Fig. 1; the table has limitations as a population indicator as it does not include those exempt from the tax, but it serves as a good indication of the relative sizes of the towns. On a national scale, a similarly indirect measure is given by Fig. 2, which shows taxation levied, excluding London; the dominance of Norwich,

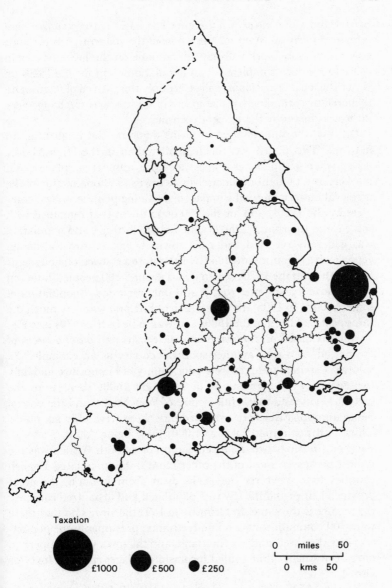

Taxation

£1000   £500   £250

| 0 | miles | 50 |
| 0 | kms | 50 |

2 Taxation in English towns, 1524-25
(Based on Sheail, 'The regional distribution of wealth in England as indicated in
the 1524-5 lay subsidy returns', Unpubl. Ph.D. thesis, Univ. of London, 1968)

Bristol and like centres is apparent. The basic pattern shown here remained fairly constant for the whole of the sixteenth century; but very much more work will have to be done on the lay subsidies in order to produce complete urban population maps for the 1520s on either the local or national scale. Certainly the pattern of towns, and their relative standing by size in broad outline was to change very little over the rest of the sixteenth century.

By 1600 the same 800 or so towns made up the English urban network. This figure was much smaller than in the High Middle Ages, when as many as three times the number of places held markets and thought of themselves as towns. Rationalization of the medieval pattern under the impact of declining population was complete by the 1520s, and for the 800 or so towns that remained with some claim to urbanity, the decline in both fortunes and population was generally reversed and most towns began to grow, although very slowly. A county town like Northampton showed obvious signs of growth from the 1570s (when it had about 3,500 people), but even two hundred years after that it still only recorded a population of some 7,000.[47] In 1600, the urban map of England was very much the same as it had been in the 1520s and was to be in the 1670s (see Fig. 3 which is based on the communicant census and other sources of the period). To take another southern county as an example, the thinly populated and relatively poor county of Hampshire had only two places with populations of 3,000 by 1600; these were the cathedral city and marketing centre of Winchester, and the port of Southampton. Elsewhere in the county there were only six places which had populations of over 1,000; these being Alton, Andover, Fareham, Basingstoke, Petersfield and Portsmouth.[48] Such was the typical picture in most of the other more thinly populated English counties too. Wherever one looks away from London, the great provincial cities and the few well populated and urbanized counties, the picture is the same. In Grimsby in 1603 the vicar said that there were 500 communicants and no recusants; presumably the population was then well under a thousand, and the town would appear to have been smaller than some Lincolnshire villages such as Hoxey or Crowle.[49]

By the 1670s, 150 years of growth had still failed to distort the urban pattern present in the 1520s. Only two or three provincial cities like Bristol and Norwich had even reached a population of more than 20,000 people. No more than a dozen or so had populations of 7,000–12,000: such were Canterbury, Coventry, Exeter, Ipswich, Kings Lynn, Salisbury, Yarmouth and York. Thirty or

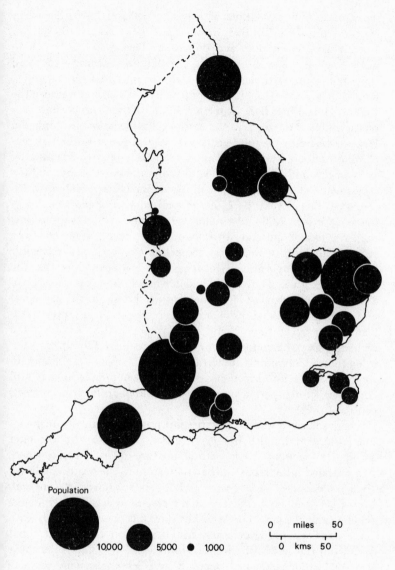

Population

10,000   5,000   • 1,000

0   miles   50

0   kms   50

3   Estimated population of English towns, *c* 1600

more places had populations of between 3,000 and 7,000, the hearth
taxes reveal: towns like Bury St Edmunds, Leicester, Northampton,
Nottingham, Shrewsbury and Worcester. The seven hundred or so
other English towns did not have populations reaching even three
thousand people, although by this stage the minimum size of a town
tended to be nearer 1,000 than under 500 as had been the case in the
1520s. Thus little had happened both in the pattern and size
relationships of the basic urban network. Fig. 4 shows the number of
Hearths taxed in the top twenty-five English towns of the day, excluding London, and gives a measure of their relative standing by
both wealth and population. Fig. 5 shows the yield of the land tax
assessments of 1692 from English towns, including London, which
reinforces this picture. By 1700 the total number of people living in
towns with over 2,000 inhabitants outside the capital was still less
than the total population of London.[50] In the last quarter of the
seventeenth century we have some actual examinations of English
towns by contemporaries. Gregory King's enquiries show that the
little market town of Sevenoaks had 206 houses in it, a population of
891 people at a density of 4·3 persons per house; in the cathedral
city of Lichfield some 655 houses gave shelter to just over 3,000
people, at an average of 4·7 persons per house; while in the
cathedral city and county capital of Gloucester, 1,126 houses were
in existence, containing an average of 4·22 people, a population of
some 4,750 in all. Most evidence for town populations is still
derivative for the period up to the first, although far from perfect,
census of 1801.[51]

Three southern English counties illustrate the relatively unchang-
ing pattern of English provincial urban populations in the later
seventeenth century. Kent, with its mixture of weald and lowland,
had changed little in basic urban pattern since the beginning of the
sixteenth century.[52] There were perhaps sixteen towns in Kent with
over 1,000 people in them, but the largest was still only in the
middle rank of English towns of the day; this was Canterbury with
some 6,000 people. Rochester, Maidstone and Dover had about
3,000, but the rest of the Kentish towns were no larger than those
like Ashford, Faversham, Deptford and Sevenoaks with between
1,000 and 2,500 people. There were still many small towns of only
500–800 inhabitants, like West Malling or Tenterden, but there
were the stirrings of quite rapid growth from a relatively low starting
point in the Medway towns, whose population was being boosted by
shipbuilding.

The story in Sussex, a county whose urban pattern in 1524 we

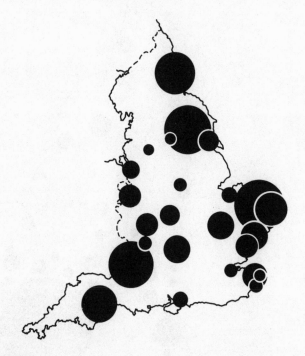

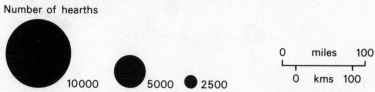

4 Number of hearths in English towns, 1670s
(Based on C. A. F. Meekings, 'Dorset Hearth Tax, 1662–64', Dorchester, 1951)

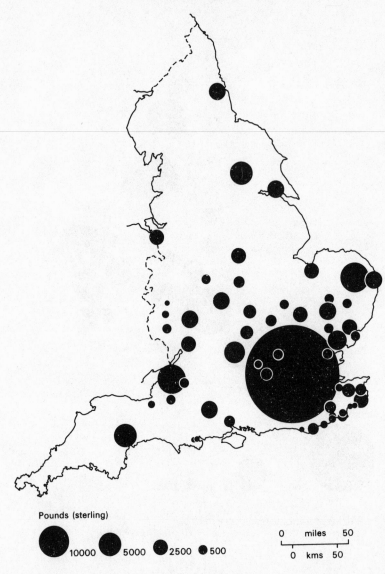

Pounds (sterling)

10000   5000   2500   500

0   miles   50

0   kms   50

5   Land tax assessments in English towns, 1692
    (Based on J. H. Andrews, 'Some statistical maps of Defoe's England',
    Geographical Studies, 3, 1956)

have already noted, is rather similar at this date (see Fig. 1). This wealden and coastal neighbour of Kent had only one town of 3,000 people, Chichester,[53] a place which had grown by about 1,000 since the 1520s and was as a result only half the size of Canterbury. Sussex contained some examples of towns which had once been quite important within their county, but which had declined; Rye being a case in point. In the early sixteenth century this cinque port had a population of approximately 2,000 people, but by the time of the taking of the Hearth Taxes it had fallen to only about 1,500, a decline undoubtedly due to its total failure as a port, consequent on the silting of its harbour facilities. The story of the smaller cinque ports was very similar, with the total decline of Seaford and Pevensey having set in by the 1670s. The third town which had dominated the urban pattern of Sussex in 1524 (see Fig. 1), Lewes, had proceeded to grow at the same sort of pace as Chichester had up to the 1670s, increasing its size from some 1,500 to about 2,500 people. Other small towns like Arundel, little more than 400 in the 1520s had advanced proportionately, to about 800 or 900, and Midhurst likewise from 500 or 600 to not more than a thousand.

Further west, Dorset was another English county which could claim none of the first or even second rank of English towns within its borders.[54] Dorchester was its largest town, but it still had a population of only about 1,500–2,000. Meekings observes that of all the Dorset towns, it was the only one to be compared with such towns in the west as Bath, Cirencester, Marlborough, Newbury, Taunton and Wells[55] at the time of the taking of the Hearth Tax. An extensive quotation from Meekings about this county's towns brings home the low level of urban life away from the provincial capitals and the few counties with above average urban populations, such as Devon, Essex, Norfolk or Suffolk. About Dorset at the time of the taking of the Hearth Taxes he writes:

> Of the towns with between seventy-five and a hundred taxpayers (a population of 500–750), some of which had markets and all of which were centres of a little district, we may note the following: Broad Windsor, in the west, Puddletown, the largest place in the Puddle Valley and athwart the Dorchester-Salisbury road, Sturminster Newton in Blackmoor Vale, Sturminster Marshall in the lower Stour Valley, Cerne Abbas, the only place of any size in the northern hills, and, probably, Cranborne, the only place of any importance in the wooded and heathy north-west. Beaminster, for all that it was once a sessions town, and Corfe Castle, the smallest corporate and parliamentary borough in the county, had barely seventy taxpayers. The other little market towns, Evershot, Frampton, Milton Abbas and Stalbridge, have fewer taxpayers than many of the

populous villages of the Stour Valley, such as Okeford Fitzpaine, Shapwick, Marmhull and the five towns.

It is clear that too much must not be made of the few obvious tales of growth – except of course, that of London's, which is difficult to overstate – and that much more should be made of stability in any discussion of basic patterns of urban population in the sixteenth and seventeenth centuries. Darby writes:

> In spite of changes during the seventeenth century, the five largest towns (London apart) in the early years of the eighteenth century were still the same as in 1600 – Norwich, York, Bristol, Newcastle and Exeter; each seems to have had between ten and twenty thousand inhabitants. Daniel Defoe in the 1720s, however, could speak of some towns 'lately encreas'd in trade and navigation, wealth and people, while their neighbours decay' . . . he had much to say about the rise or decline of individual towns.[56]

Whilst Darby certainly underestimates the size of the larger towns, for by the earlier eighteenth century Bristol and Norwich had populations of nearer 30,000, with Newcastle-upon-Tyne not far behind, he equally certainly encapsulates the position; and when Defoe speaks of those towns 'lately encreas'd' he was using the term advisedly for the rate of growth of the majority of the bigger towns was faster after 1670. This was not a purely English phenomenon. It was true of Dublin, with a population of 60,000 in 1680 making it three times the size of the next biggest Irish town, Cork, for example. In Dublin there was noted suburban growth towards the end of the century.[57]

Urban Growth

'Urban growth' in the sense that we would use it today is thus clearly a phenomenon of no earlier than the eighteenth century. Yet, there was obvious relative growth and change of urban populations in the sixteenth and seventeenth centuries within the context of the geography of the time. The actual rate of growth of the national population was not great, as previously noted in Chapter 2, the rate being probably highest in the middle and later sixteenth century, while in the seventeenth it became more erratic and uncertain and may well have been levelling off entirely towards the end of that century. A population growth curve for the whole two centuries would probably approximate to a straight line (sloping upwards), thus implying a decreasing rate of growth, as Eversley has pointed out.[58] Changes in population densities and distributions were limited both in their scale and in a regional sense, such changes being most marked in some midland and north-western counties, and they were nothing to compare with the rates of change that occurred in these areas in the eighteenth century.

Indeed, change over the whole of a country experiencing broadly stable population distribution and limited population increase, may have been most marked in towns, fed as they were by streams of immigrants. Certainly in East Anglia (see Chapter 6) it was the increase of urban population which was most marked. Here, whilst population grew overall by some 50 per cent between the 1520s and 1670s, the share of the population which was urban grew from less than a quarter to nearly a third. Most significantly, towns increased in size by nearly 50 per cent between 1603 and 1670, while the countryside at large grew by only 11 per cent; it was the larger towns, too, which saw most of the growth, the top twenty in size increasing by 55 per cent between 1603 and the 1670s, the twenty smaller growing by only 20 per cent.[59] The picture for other regions is not yet clear, but is unlikely to have been radically different. This must be set against what we know of English pre-industrial population trends overall,[60] and our knowledge of the relative standing of rural and urban populations. As Deane and Cole observe: '. . . between 70 and 80 per cent of the occupied population was primarily engaged in agriculture, though of course many of them must have pursued secondary occupations in industry and trade. The strictly rural population (the inhabitants of the villages and hamlets) accounted for about three-quarters of the total, and London with its spreading suburbs outside the walls for about 10 per cent.'[61] In discussing urban populations outside the almost separate phenomena of London, we must be quite clear that we are discussing a fairly narrow band of the total population of the nation, between 15 and 30 per cent of the whole at any time, however much these figures may vary regionally; and the population living in the larger towns where most of the growth took place was perhaps only 10 per cent or so of the whole – certainly not more than 15 per cent of the country's population was resident in towns over 5,000 by 1700.[62] Thus the section of population under discussion is small, however important that section may have been because of location in a number of densely packed marketing, manufacturing and communications centres that made up pre-industrial towns. It must also be remembered that such urban growth was almost certainly outpacing the long-term rate of growth of *per capita* production between 1500 and 1750, being only 0·2 per cent per annum[63] compared with urban population growth of 0·3 per cent per annum.

Marked growth in urban population, outside London and the established provincial centres, probably took place in those areas where *per capita* production growth was also fastest, outstripping average national population growth in pace by the end of the seventeenth century. Such places as Halifax, Leeds, Liverpool, Sheffield, Sunderland and Wakefield began to feel the impact of the processes that were to cause rapid growth of both population and production in the eighteenth century. By the first half of the eighteenth century the fastest-growing towns were Liverpool, the centre for the West Indies trade, and Birmingham, the centre for the metal industries; Birmingham probably increased four and a half times between 1675 and 1760.[64] This process was clearly under way by 1650; from a population of about 1,000 in the 1520s[65] Birmingham grew to between 2,000 and 3,000 in 1603,[66] to 5,000[67] in 1650 and to 15,000 by 1700,[68] though this last figure may be somewhat optimistic. But old established towns also grew more rapidly than the population as a whole,[69] not only in East Anglia but all over the country. Between the mid-sixteenth and mid-seventeenth centuries several towns to the west of the country, like Exeter, Plymouth, Tiverton and Worcester, doubled in size: Exeter's population grew from 9,400 in 1662 to 10,650 in 1672, and 13,000 in 1688, for instance.[70] In the Midlands, the traditional county town and marketing centre of Nottingham, whose fine buildings and clear wide streets had so pleased Celia Fiennes when she visited it towards the end of the seventeenth century, doubled in size between 1660 and 1790. In Worcester the increase in the city's population was rapid enough to make visual impact. Early in the seventeenth century the council discussed the need for more burial ground, because 'the multitude of people do daily increase'.[71] Leeds, too, whose whole parish area had contained 3,000 people at most in the mid-sixteenth century, began a process of growth that led to the doubling of its population in the next two generations; and though, as Forster observes, this was 'a rate of increase which was probably not maintained in the early seventeenth century', as in much of the rest of the country it laid the foundations for later growth.[72] Towns such as this became fuller, with more hands to man the looms, but also with more mouths to feed; 'It is observed by clothiers and others, who employ great numbers of poor people, that when corn is extremely plentiful, that the labour of the poor is proportionately dear, and scarce to be had at all (so licentious are they who labour only to eat, or rather to drink),' disapprovingly noted Sir William Petty.[73]

Smaller towns in the West Midlands were stirring too. Frost has shown that Walsall, with a population of only about 800 in the 1520s, had reached between 1,300 and 1,400 in 1563, nearly 3,000 by the time of the taking of the first hearth taxes in the early 1660s, and some 3,200 when the Compton census was taken in 1676; Wolverhampton in the same region doubled in size between the 1520s and the 1660s, from about 750 to over 1,500,[74] and Dudley in Worcestershire shot up from a few hundred to about 2,500 in the 1660s.

For the best example of urban growth we must turn to the capital itself, whose overall population advance, so brilliantly plotted and evaluated by Wrigley,[75] had led it to increase from around 50,000 people in 1500 to over half a million two hundred years later. London stands alone as the one clear case of urban growth, in the twentieth century sense, taking place in England. Exponential self-generating growth is what London experienced in pre-industrial times, an experience alien to the rest of the country's towns; if London must dominate our consideration of the English pre-industrial urban system, it must not blind us to what was going on elsewhere.

It is just as instructive and illustrative to look at parts of London – its suburbs for example – as to consider its mass as a whole. The burgeoning suburbs to the east of the Tower provide a good case study which focuses attention away from basic patterns and figures of town populations to the processes that brought urban growth about, both in London and elsewhere. The parish of Stepney provides an example of such development. At the beginning of the seventeenth century this parish was already very large, with between 12,000 and 13,000 people living in it. It extended from Whitechapel in the west, to the river Lea to the east; it was bounded by Hackney in the north and by the Thames to the south. In 1600 the parish consisted of numerous hamlets. Inland there were Bethnal Green, Bow and Mile End, Spitalfields adjoined Whitechapel and Shoreditch; whilst Blackwall, Limehouse, Poplar, Ratcliff, Shadwell and Wapping lay along the bank of the Thames – these were the most populous parts of the parish. A close examination of the parish registers over the five year period 1606–10 by the Population Study Group of the East London History Group,[76] shows a great excess of burials over births; there were 2,620 burials compared with 1,752 baptisms, clearly indicating a natural decrease of population. This excess of burials over baptisms is quite apparent even when the deaths caused by plague outbreaks in 1608, 1609 and

1610 are discounted. Some 2,078 people, who died from causes other than plague according to the evidence of the registers, were buried between 1606 and 1610, compared with the 1,752 who were baptized. Yet Stepney's population not only maintained itself, it increased; this increase continued over the rest of the century, despite a constant net natural decrease consequent on an ever present excess of burials over baptisms.

The cause of population growth exemplified by Stepney, but probably to be found in almost every English town up to 1700, was immigration; they could not replace themselves otherwise. Such immigration brought with it huge problems for London and elsewhere. It put a strain on accommodation and on employment; the large numbers of vagrants and poor brought with them increasing demands for indoor and outdoor relief. It has been suggested that Spitalfields in Stepney parish for example, might already in the first decade of the seventeenth century, have been assuming its now traditional role as the last refuge of the miscreant.[77] Control of the poor was becoming a severe problem everywhere by the 1550s, especially in London, and crime as a major social phenomenon was marked in London in the seventeenth century, an increase being noted particularly from the 1660s, at exactly the same period when there was much legislative activity against overcrowding.[78] As London became larger and more modern, with huge development in commercial activity after the mid-seventeenth century, resulting in more shops, more goods on display, and more wealth, so crime rates soared, a phenomenon in which immigrants played a major dynamic role. From this example, we are forced to recognize the dynamic role of immigration above all else in the demography, the society, the economy and most other features of the pre-industrial town. Immigration provided the numbers of people that increased urban populations; but it provided much more in terms of social and economic vitality. We must now turn our attention to the processes that promoted and inhibited population growth and change in towns: births, deaths, and above all immigration.

Processes of Urban Population Change

A traditional approach to the processes determining the rate and nature of urban population change in modern England would probably commence with an examination of whether or not towns were experiencing natural increase or natural decrease, consequent on levels of birth rates and death rates, and the interplay of fertility and mortality. Migration, as a demographic, social and economic force, would nowadays generally be accorded a residual place, to be discussed after the explanation afforded by study of birth and death rates. In pre-industrial towns of any size in England, and probably in much of Western Europe, this approach has to be reversed. Occasionally in towns, or some parishes in them, baptisms may have exceeded burials for certain years. The consistent picture was, however, that burials exceeded baptisms in every English town in the pre-industrial period. A few places by 1700 may have been able to reproduce themselves, but for most this was not the case; they were experiencing natural decrease. Yet, as we have seen, they grew, London enormously, some others quite quickly, and migration is clearly the key to an explanation of their growth.

Migration

Growth can be almost wholly attributed to net gains of population by towns from immigration, most of it from within England, although there are a few cases, mainly in East- and South-coast towns like Kings Lynn, Norwich, Colchester, some of the Kentish towns, and Southampton, where substantial numbers of foreign immigrants (usually religious refugees from the Low Countries, or France) took up residence, swelling town populations. Even these places, however, continued to depend for most of their population growth on constant increments of English born and bred immigrants coming from near and far, from countryside and other towns alike. Emigration undoubtedly occurred, from towns to other towns; to the countryside by those who had made a success of life and bought country estates, or those escaping the control of the city fathers on the practice of their occupations; or indeed to the colonies of the new world. Yet it was minuscule both in importance and in numbers compared to the effect and size of immigration to towns. Within towns, studies of replacement rates using registers of births and deaths have been made, as we have seen in the case of Stepney; these are extremely difficult to calculate, but we are slowly getting a clearer picture of urban fertility and mortality rates in at least quasi-quantitative terms.

Actual rates of immigration into cities are extremely difficult to calculate; because of the nature of the evidence, we are unlikely ever to be able to produce estimates of any accuracy, and must always argue by implication and inference from imperfect figures. Yet no other inference can be drawn from our knowledge of the predominant natural decrease of pre-industrial towns, sometimes alarmingly rapid after plague years, than that immigration provided the dynamic for growth in numbers. Their economic and social well-being was equally dependent on continuous influxes of labour to fill urban manufacturing, trading and service occupations. 'Migration', as Morrill observes 'is of fundamental importance to the development of the human landscape';[79] it was vital to the development of the urban landscape throughout the pre-industrial period. This was the period of which Chambers wrote that 'Towns had been proverbially the graveyard of successive generations of migrants, consumers of, rather than contributors to, the new growth that constantly flowed in from the surrounding country; but . . . from about 1750 this trend was checked and before the end of the century was put into reverse. The urban population, for the first time in its history, was on the point of recruiting itself by a normal annual increment from its own natural increase.'[80] The urban landscape before 1750 was astonishingly mobile, and astonishingly varied. A large amount of immigration may have been casual and transient. The substantial and ever-changing vagrant population of England, moving back and forth across the country like so much detritus on a beach – perhaps on the unfounded rumours of work to be had at harvest, or of generous poor relief, but most likely performing rather aimless day-to-day movements – must have made towns their target on many occasions. This is a process which we are only dimly able to perceive, assisted by such few studies as do exist.[81] Much of the immigration for which we do have evidence is of those people clearly seeking betterment, however illusory the opportunities might have turned out to be in practice.

Indeed, 'The movement from country to town . . . is motivated by the possibility, held out by the town, of considerable or even dazzling advancement; an opportunity held out to all, though in fact it is only a few of those who move who will achieve it. The call of Bow Bells to Dick Whittington – "Lord Mayor of London"! In their sound we have a symbol of the enchantment'.[82] The words of Sir John Hicks aptly sum up the lure of town and city for all men and women at all times. The present day shanty towns marring the edges of São Paulo or Brazilia bear witness to just that same force which impelled the growth of London and other English pre-industrial towns.

Sources for Rural–Urban Migration Data

The types of sources concerning migration that may be used have been examined in some depth.[83] They can be briefly listed here as: records of the enrollment of those entering into the freedom of towns, and thus gaining the right to trade and manufacture, as well as of those entering into apprenticeship agreements to learn the trade practised by some freeman; parish registers, which sometimes give place of origin of those marrying in a town, though rarely of those dying in it; poor law removal orders and settlement papers, which usually record the place of origin of the vagrant and transient sections of pre-industrial society; court records, particularly the deposition books of civil and ecclesiastical courts which often give potted biographies of witnesses appearing within them, including details of where they had lived and changes of residence; and occasional nominal listings which give the same sort of information on migration and movement, though these are very rare. All of these records tell us about sectors of pre-industrial society that are highly selective by age, ambition, occupation and standing. Even if records like these are all present for a town in any one year, they are only going to tell us about a part of the total immigrant population. It is very rare to get the chance to do even this, and there is as yet no study which uses all possible sources to try to calculate immigration rates for any town; if such figures did exist, they would not be likely to be as good as for example, what we know from parish registers about fertility and mortality. Even if such parish register data are only to be had for one or two of the several parishes in a town, they can indicate general trends of natural decrease or increase, where the information exists for the whole town[84] it can reveal a good deal about rates of population change and thus indirectly about immigration rates. That portion of growth which cannot be explained by the trend of births and deaths as shown in parish registers is the portion which must be explained by immigration.

The level of explanation possible will depend on the particular characteristics of available sources of immigration. *Freemen's rolls* record the names of people who have been given the freedom of the town, their occupation, and quite often their birthplace. If this information is not given, it is a possible indication that the man being made free was born in that town. These people were the reasonably successful ones – for quite substantial entry fees had to be paid – members of the urban community, usually of mature years; they were the economically dynamic additions to a town. But the

granting of freedom should not necessarily be equated with the date
of arrival in a town, for the bestowing of freedom generally
represented at least one stage away from initial immigration to the
town, and usually occurred after some period of domicile and training, unless it was purchased by a 'foreigner' directly on entry. Unfortunately for the historical geographer, information about where a
locally trained apprentice and journeyman originally came from,
many years before his eventual enrolment as a freeman, may not
have seemed very important to the recording clerk of the company
or city corporation.

Apprentice indentures, which contain the indentures of young
labourers going in to training in trades and crafts, are of a similar
character to freemen's records, and are in many ways complemen-
tary to them. They are, perhaps, better immigration records than
freemen admissions; for they do represent first employment, and
usually first entry into a town. Such records are much more likely to
give place of origin, and thus indicate if the apprentice was an
immigrant. Apprenticeship records do share the drawbacks of
freemen enrolments in only including entrants (usually male) to
relatively prosperous occupations – those which towns thought it
important to control might thereby be thought of as being relatively
prosperous. Not only are apprentice records usually sex selective,
and in a way income selective, they are also age selective; most
apprentices were aged between 15 and 20 when they were enrolled.
Therefore they need to be carefully evaluated, as they only represent
the entry into towns of a young, mobile, ambitious and
predominantly male sector of society. On the other hand, it may be
that the relatively young would represent quite a reasonable sample
of the total migratory population which, because of short life expectancy, had such a large proportion of its members between 14 and
25 years old; these are the years for which the probability of migration is highest under normal conditions. Freemen and apprentice
registers are not a bad surrogate for general patterns of immigration
of one stratum of society, the more economically effective part of it,
but give only a very partial picture of the numbers involved. They
only exist for certain towns, the corporate places which kept such
records, and although many of the non-corporate towns for which
they are absent were rather small, this category did include such important places as Leeds and Manchester which began to grow fast
by the later seventeenth century.

Parish Marriage Registers are another source which may give the
place of origin of those being married, and thus some possible

indication of the volume of immigration; in contrast to freemen and apprentice registers they are not restricted to the corporate and generally larger towns. Yet it is dangerous to assume permanent residence from such evidence. People marrying in urban parishes might have been only temporary residents, or those returning home simply for the marriage ceremony. Like apprentice records, marriage registers are most likely to represent the younger section of the population, but drawn possibly from a wider social spectrum. As Peel concludes, 'The place of residence data are not . . . definite proof of local origin or subsequent settlement'.[85] All in all, marriage registers are likely to give us only the most general indication of the volume of immigration.

A further important source for information on rural–urban immigration may be found in the *settlement papers and removal orders* which recorded the control of vagrants and transients. These records derive from parish administration, like marriage registers, and only appear in number after an act of 1662. This act had set out to ensure, *inter alia*, that an influx of poorer people should not become a charge on the receiving parish, by making the sending parish responsible for them, unless a permanent settlement was granted. These records have both advantages and drawbacks for the study of pre-industrial migration in comparison to the sources already discussed. A major drawback is that they exist only from the mid-seventeenth century, while a major advantage is that they include people of all ages. They also record the lower strata of society, missed in many records; yet these were not the out-and-out poor, for settlement papers were issued to all those in residential property worth less than £10 per annum. Certainly there is no guarantee that all those who should have obtained a settlement paper did in fact do so, for there would have been numerous opportunities for evasion, particularly in larger towns. These settlement papers often increase in number after the amendments made in 1697 to the earlier, more restrictive act of 1662. There were also earlier records of vagrants taken by individual towns. Yet vast numbers of the vagrant folk, who swelled the numbers of the town, must have gone unrecorded. In Salisbury, for example, the survival of registers of vagrants' passports, and in Colchester a list of all vagrants punished amongst strangers expelled, and in Norwich the Minutes of the Court of Mayoralty recording the punishment of expelled vagrants, enabled Slack to examine vagrancy as a phenomenon in early mid-seventeenth century England. But, as he observes:

The limitations inherent in the records are, however, evident. The amount of information they provide is uneven, only names and places of origin being regularly recorded . . . it is never clear how far variations in the numbers of vagabonds punished from year to year reflect changing levels of enforcement or a change in the actual volume of vagrancy. Certainly those apprehended were only the tip of the iceberg and *can tell us little about the quantitative as distinct from qualitative features of the vagrant phenomena* [author's italics].[86]

Vagrancy, and indeed poverty, became an increasing problem towards the middle and end of the sixteenth century, as national population grew and often outstripped both production and increases in income. The poor became a major sector, and a major problem in large towns and amongst them immigrant vagrants were in their turn a notable sector, in Norwich in 1570 at least half the city's poor were not local born.[87]

It is the migratory history of those at the upper end of the social scale which was recorded in the *deposition books* of civil and ecclesiastical courts.[88] The detailed biographies of witnesses before different civil and religious courts that record such information may reveal the sometimes quite numerous changes of residence made during an individual's lifetime. Work on the depositions was pioneered by Cornwall,[89] and taken up in detail by Clark;[90] it has revealed the great mobility of all sorts of people in pre-industrial England. In using these records, it is important to realize that the type of migrant and type of information about him or her can vary with the level of court whose records are consulted: in the case of the ecclesiastical courts, for example, there were the prerogative courts of the two archbishops, the consistory courts of the various bishops, and the multitude of arch-deaconry courts, usually two or more for each county. There is a discernible bias as to the people recorded in these different levels of courts, depending on their wealth and on where they lived. When depositions were taken from countrymen, they seem often to have been the older and more respectable members of the community; in towns this is not always the case. Despite this apparent bias, given a big enough sample, much could be learnt of the demographic and economic role of migration in urban populations by comparing the proportions of deponents recorded who had never moved from the towns, with the proportion and origins of those that were migrants. Yet such comparison will be able to tell us very little, because of the unsystematic and biased nature of the sources concerning the actual volumes of immigrants. In addition, ecclesiastical deposition books decline in coverage during and after the Civil War, with the temporary abeyance, and subsequent steady diminution of the Church's administrative control.[91] Other ecclesiastical records such as *wills*, occasionally yield information on the deceased's origins, as do various civic records noting everything from fines to the costs of entertainments.

It is clear that even if all of these sources survived in any number for any decade in any town, the information that they could offer would give a far from complete count of all the immigrants arriving. If the decade in question were one for which reasonable population estimates are available, such as the 1660s or 1670s, so much the better, for then some idea of the ratio of recorded immigrants to estimated total population could be suggested. This picture would be strengthened if all the birth and death registers for all the parishes in the town were available in well preserved and accurate form, for then mortality and fertility rates could be calculated, and with these the rates of annual and decadal natural change. If, as is likely, there was natural decrease combined with a clear population growth as revealed by both parish registers and indirect sources, then the annual or decadal shortfall consequent on high mortality – which would have to have been made up by net immigration – could be suggested. This apparent total could then be related to what *was* known about volume of immigration for the sources discussed. Unfortunately there is to date no study of this kind that examines all available sources in this exhaustive way for even one English town, to give us a case study of exactly how and in what numbers immigration made up the shortfall of population and promoted growth. Yet there is plenty of evidence that immigration did take place in almost every English town in every year during the pre-industrial period. We still have alarmingly little quantitative evidence on the most dynamic force behind urban population growth.

Processes of Replacement and Growth by Migration

Replacement by immigration happened, on occasion, with apparently astonishing rapidity. To take the case of a plague-stricken city, it is clear that very large numbers of people, sometimes a quarter, or even virtually half of the total population could be killed. Yet after the considerable setback that this represented, population often seemed able to recover itself and even began to grow again after a hiatus of only a few years. Both the pace of recovery from such economically and socially debilitating mortality, and the pace of growth during periods of normal mortality suggest very high rates of migration.

In Colchester, for example,[92] it is quite clear that whilst epidemics of plague might have provoked flight from centres of infection, they equally drew in an influx of strangers, some vagrant, to fill empty houses when the crisis was over,[93] and to restore the seemingly shattered population. Colchester had many setbacks because of plague visitations, in common with most English towns, as discussed in Chapter 2. The town suffered attacks of plague and epidemic diseases in 1579, 1586, 1597, 1603, 1626, 1631, 1644 and, like London and many other provincial capitals and county capitals, during the last terrible plague visitation of 1665–66.[94] In the last plague it is estimated by Doolittle that between 4,500 and 5,000 people died in Colchester; perhaps half of the town's population was destroyed in these two years. He further estimates that Colchester's population fell from 10,305 in 1662 to 4,114 in 1666. Yet after only five years it had climbed again with astonishing rapidity to 9,526, levelling out to reach nearly 10,000 by 1675. It is striking how quickly the town recovered its original numbers, even if the estimate based on the 1662 Hearth Tax returns may be over-generous. At the same time, 'as a concomitant of this demographic recovery'[95] the town showed a considerable economic resilience in the face of the havoc wreaked by the plague.

It is possible that quite a substantial amount of the recovery in Colchester was due to internally generated growth in numbers. Parish register evidence (unfortunately rather deficient) suggests that the number of burials in the years immediately after the outbreak of disease in 1665–66 fell to their previous yearly average, if not below it. Baptisms recovered rapidly, regaining their earlier numbers within two years of the epidemic. Better evidence exists in the registers of Colchester after the earlier plague outbreak of 1626; one parish in the town showed twice the average number of marriages in the years following it. This sort of post-plague spurt in marriages and consequent numbers of baptisms is a phenomena noted all over pre-industrial England, both in town and countryside, as for example in Staffordshire.[96] Severe epidemics were often followed by an upsurge in baptisms and marriages. Such an upsurge could not have accounted for the rapid rebuilding of Colchester's population, however; by the seventeenth century even in plague-free years baptisms in Colchester rarely kept pace with burials. Colchester's recovery must have been partly due to immigration, the inference from the evidence being clear. Just as the bulk of parish register material is deficient, preventing the calculation of the exact size of internally generated replacement, so lack of many of even the imperfect sources for immigration commonly available for English pre-industrial towns equally prevents measurement of the annual rates of immigration that must have played the major role in the rapid re-establishment of Colchester's population.

The most dramatic role that immigrants played was thus to restore the population of plague-stricken towns up to 1666; but both before and after that watershed in the history of epidemic disease in England, their most constant role was to counteract urban natural decrease and promote urban population growth. The most important single population movement in pre-industrial England was the tremendous flow of people into London, the power-house of the process of modernization. This allowed and promoted the city's great rate of growth compared with other English towns or European capitals. Perhaps upwards of one million people came to London between 1550–1750, and newcomers were arriving in late seventeenth-century London at the rate of 8,000 or 10,000 a year. At certain times, half of the natural increase of provincial England was probably absorbed by London. It is almost certain that the greater part of this mass movement was made up of young people; indeed Wrigley has estimated an average age on arrival of about twenty.[97] The high mortality rates of a number of London parishes have been examined, and the Hollingsworths suggest a great excess of burials over baptisms combined with a growth rate of at least 1·5 per cent per annum.[98]

Rolls recording the admissions to apprenticeship and freedom of various city companies illustrate the very small numbers of London-born who were enrolled. Of the 3,780 boys entering the small Stationers' Company as apprentices between 1562 and 1640, only 678 (18 per cent) were actually recorded as born in the city,[99] and of the 1590 admissions to the Freedom of the City by apprenticeship in 1690, only 317 (20 per cent) were London-born.[100] Immigrants were at least as important in the suburbs of the city.[101] The excess of deaths over births in some of the crowded eastern parishes beyond the Tower of London, ranged between 15 per cent and a staggering 130 per cent.[102] In a detailed analysis, Power has examined these fast-growing suburbs, and has suggested that decades like the 1580s, 1600s, 1620s and 1680s stand out as periods of especially marked immigration. In these decades the annual number of immigrants reached over 4·0 per cent of the total population each year. Even these bare figures may do much to conceal the nature of the actual movement taking place, and its astonishing vitality, for as Glass observes of London 'figures of net migration may easily hide much larger numbers of inward and outward migration.'[103]

Many of the migrants were apprentices, or if not formally apprenticed, were likely to be young. There are many printed lists of apprenticeship returns,[104] and their social and geographical origins have been given considerable attention.[105] Their impact on London society is of great importance to social historians of towns in this period; as Smith says: 'Belonging to a recognized economic order, possessing their own literature and their own heroes, seeking some set of ideals, sought after by reforming politicians and preachers, the apprentices developed a set of values for the subculture, values which were not accepted by all apprentices, but which did help to define apprenticeship in the minds of many'.[106] For the historical geographer concerned with urban population growth their impact is important in terms of fertility and population growth. Young people, marrying quite young, not only boosted actual population, but also population potential. Data for London in 1695, partial though they are, give a generally similar picture to that given by data for the 1851 census, namely a large proportion of single males and females. This would be expected with a relatively high age at first marriage – as was the case in England and Wales in 1851 – and particularly in the largest urban centre with substantial employment opportunities for young, unmarried men and women and, in 1695, with a heavy emphasis upon apprenticeship opportunities for young men.[107] The latent affects of migration on fertility were as great as they were on every aspect of London's society and economy. Glass concludes: 'No less important is the fact that the London apprenticeship system brought together young men from all over the country to the largest urban centre in Western Europe and certainly one of the major intellectual centres of the period'.[108]

In much smaller towns like Worcester, which doubled in size between 1540 and 1640, as did Shrewsbury, it was of constant importance. Some towns seemed more able than others to generate their own growth by substantial natural increase from time to time, and there were considerable differences between towns in this respect, although no clear picture of marked regional differences is apparent. In Worcester, for example, Dyer has plotted the factor of natural increase, showing sometimes quite marked excesses of christenings over burials for considerable periods, interspersed though these were by bouts of crisis mortality. He estimates that natural increase accounted for over half the population rise from

4,000 to 8,000 between 1540 and 1640, immigration supplying the rest; the reasons for natural increase changed in emphasis during the period, high fertility in the sixteenth century – present since its first decade – being replaced during the last quarter of that century by a lower rate of mortality.[109] It must be realized, however, that a substantial amount of the christenings recorded could be directly attributed to immigration; many new-born were the children of recently arrived or recently married immigrants. The proportion of native born apprentices was often just as low in provincial capitals as it was in the national capital. In Bristol of the 1,432 apprentices recorded as entering that important port between 1532 and 1542 only 404 (some 28 per cent) were apparently Bristol born.[110] In Nottingham, migration was responsible for much of the city's growth in the late seventeenth century, and for more than 90 per cent of the population increase in the first forty years of the eighteenth century.[111]

Urban Mortality

Against migration as a dynamic force on urban population must be balanced the factor of mortality. A good deal has already been said in the two introductory chapters to this study, on the role of mortality in towns by inhibiting growth, particularly in the 'plague' years. A rough picture has been painted of urban conditions under which high mortality – whether due to disease or poor quality and standard of life – could flourish in overcrowded houses with little ventilation, sanitation or fresh water; such living standards by no means necessarily improved as time passed, sometimes the contrary. The implications of high death rates have also been an obvious concomitant to discussion of the vital role of immigration. Mortality operated as a factor in the towns in two ways: firstly in terms of a generally high death rate which inhibited growth; and secondly, in those areas where population did achieve growth, the threat remained of an abnormal and debilitating death rate due to plague or epidemic. As Flinn observes: 'The outstanding feature of mortality behaviour in western Europe in all centuries before the twentieth has been a great instability. From the highly unstable mortality of, say, the seventeeth century, to the remarkable steadiness of the late twentieth century is a long and uneven process of the damping down of fluctuations'.[112]

Wherever one looks in the parish registers of English pre-industrial towns, high levels of mortality in non-plague years and very high levels in plague years are apparent. In York, for example, whose population increased from 10,000 in 1600 to 12,000 by 1630 and not much more by the end of the century, Forster argues, 'The registers show such a marked preponderance of burials over baptisms that it seems likely that only substantial immigration could have caused even this modest increase in population'.[113] Sometimes urban mortality would be highest amongst children, and sometimes amongst adults, whilst life expectancy also varied between men and women. There was considerable variation in these factors over the two centuries and in different towns: between Worcester and York, for example. Certainly the expectancy of life in modern England (approximately seventy years or so both for men and women) looks very impressive compared to those of the day, which ranged between thirty-two and forty-two years. Wrigley suggests that in the period 1538 to 1624 adult death rates conformed to an expectation of life of forty years, and that between 1625 and 1699 they give an expectation of thirty-two years; there was thus a substantially lower expectation of life in the second half of the seventeenth century than in Tudor England.[114] Palliser's important study of mortality in Tudor York shows the conditions in which ordinary and plague mortalities could all flourish:

> Warm weather activated disease in a dirty city, where many house-flies would be present to carry microbial diseases, as well as rat fleas to carry plague. Street cleaning was erratic, and what there was was often performed by scavenging pigs. The streets became repositories for butcher's offal and the contents of chamber pots. Amid this squalor the corporation valiantly battled for better standards of public hygiene, well aware of the connection between dirt, warm weather and disease ... In the city centre, health hazards were accentuated by population density and tightly-packed housing ... A net population increase of forty-five per cent was apparently squeezed into the existing stock of accommodation, probably a major cause of the terrible epidemic of 1604.[115]

In the consideration of the periodic bouts of very high urban mortality a clear distinction should be drawn between epidemics which coincided with harvest failure, and outbreaks of bubonic and related plagues, and other epidemic diseases,[116] though this is very difficult to do. It is also difficult to speak with any certainty of 'plague years' applicable to all the towns in the country at any one time: indeed it is not always possible to clearly identify the actual nature of the disease causing high mortality in any town at any one time. Sometimes it is clear from records that a disease responsible for high mortality was influenza, or the plague; on other occasions it is simply put down to 'the fever' or 'the sweat'. Whilst it is possible to find evidence of epidemic disease of some sort in London during

almost every year of the pre-industrial period, epidemic years in
other towns varied. For example, Reading was badly hit in 1543–44,
Bristol in 1544–45, York in 1550–52 (coinciding with some other
English towns), but Norwich was the only English town struck in
the early 1580s,[117] as well as between 1589 and 1592. Yet Norwich's
northern counterpart, York, was almost free of plague between 1552
and 1603. There may also have been differences in the effects of
plague between towns because of their size, as well as their location
and the chance quality of plague outbreaks. One view is that 'It was
in the largest towns that epidemics had their most dramatic effects.
Partly this was a function of size itself: the absolute number of
casualties was greater than in smaller communities. Partly it was
because of other social problems, in particular the growing number
of poor requiring food and employment, were becoming more
serious in urban society in this period.'[118] This was certainly true of
England's largest provincial city in the later sixteenth century,
Norwich, but not of every large city; as has been mentioned above,
York was remarkably free at the same period. Why this should be so
is difficult even to speculate upon; preventative regulations may
have been better in York. Much must have depended on patterns of
disease diffusion, and on disease pathology itself with its seemingly
spontaneous outbreaks.

The plague also had dramatic effects on much smaller urban
communities. In Loughborough, for example, a serious epidemic
raged between 1609 and 1611; not only was mortality extremely
high and the little market centre put into quarantine by surrounding towns and villages, but in 1610 the townspeople
actually removed themselves and their belongings out of the town
itself to a stretch of common.[119] In nearby Leicester the plague also
raged in 1610–1611, with the markets closed and preventative conditions imposed; mortality was at least three times the average over
this two-year period. The 700 people that died in the two years
represented about twenty per cent of Leicester's estimated population of 3,500, most of the 700 being clearly 'plague' rather than 'normal' deaths.[120] There was no effective medical treatment for any of
the plagues and epidemics that raged. Isolation was the only possible palliative, isolation both for individuals who had a recognized
contageous disease in their household, and of towns themselves.
This sort of isolation was practised by towns attempting to stop
plague coming in; not only in large towns like York, but in small
ones like Faversham, where in 1630 three wardens were appointed
to examine all comers and keep out those who came from places

affected by the plague.[121] Similar measures were taken at Winchester[122] and Stafford, where anyone suspected of carrying the plague seems to have been quickly driven from the town.[123]

We know little about the types and courses of disease that induce crisis mortality; of the causes of the high levels of 'ordinary' mortality we know even less. Many parish registers and the early bills of mortality will pick out plague or like diseases as something worth recording from time to time. The death by starvation of some old person, or by malnutrition of some young vagrant child, may also be described in a marginal note, as may the death of a suicide. However, on the few occasions when cause of death is mentioned, it is in, to us, mysterious prose; 'died of a bloody flux' or of 'a great sickness' or 'ill-humours' or 'the sweat' or the like.[124] The conditions obtaining in pre-industrial towns, such as overcrowding or malnutrition, created ideal conditions for diseases like typhus to persist endemically, or influenza[125] to flourish epidemically. Starvation as a cause of death seems to have been present especially in some economically lagging rural areas, and amongst the poor and vagrant sectors of society in particular.[126] It is likely that townspeople, with their greater average purchasing power, more centralized marketing and occasional corporation stores, may have been more able to resist real starvation, though not avoid malnutrition; and as the years passed, national and regional communication and distribution networks improved greatly. Lack of food would have affected the poorest members of society most by direct suffering and even death, or because undernourishment made them more prone to disease.

The predominant view that food shortage and disease went hand in hand during both the inception and diffusion of an epidemic, may not, however, have applied to London. London might have been a special case in this, as it was in so many other ways in the geography of pre-industrial England.[127] It has been argued that an infectious disease of sufficient power to produce a mortality crisis may have had its own dynamic. Indeed, it appears in most areas that whilst sometimes epidemics slowed down or halted population growth in periods of low food prices, yet quite marked population growth could occur even when food was relatively short, if plague was absent. It has been found in London that there was little correlation between high bread prices and plague epidemics; in most, though not all, plague years, bread prices were average or even below average; equally years of food shortage when bread was available but at a price – and the urban poor had no alternative sources of supply or types of food to turn to – there were not necessarily epidemics, even though epidemic diseases were endemic in London at the time. Nutritional factors, in London, do not appear to have been important determining factors in inducing endemic disease to become epidemic. Appleby[128] has even cast doubt on the role conventionally ascribed to overcrowding in encouraging high mortality; he felt that as London grew, mortality from epidemic disease should have increased disproportionately, because the chances of exposure were greater; but the reverse seemed to happen, with the plague vanishing and typhus declining in importance. As Chambers wrote in his seminal work: 'we are now brought face to face with the irrevocable fact which historians have been loath to recognize, the fact of the autonomous death-rate, the death-rate which could override countervailing influences such as low prices, an abundance of free land, a shortage of labour, advising real wages'.[129] The autonomous nature and seemingly random timing and location of crisis mortality make it extremely difficult to adduce causes for it. In the case of 'ordinary' urban mortality – which was usually high – it is even more difficult to allocate cause, and doubt has been cast on the actual efficacy of long-accepted environmental influences, although they must have been important.[130]

Urban Fertility

In looking for factors which promoted or inhibited increase in town sizes, to search for those affecting population growth above all else may be as infelicitous as it is to look persistently for growth in economic terms. Population growth as such may be much less important in the context of the period, but we cannot ignore urban fertility itself. For it may be a mistake in the case of any town to hold that the only two important demographic variables were immigration and mortality (especially crisis mortality), even though they were certainly the most dramatic demographic dynamics. Urban fertility provided the solid basis for some measure of advance, though rural fertility, in its turn feeding the process of rural-urban migration, was an equally important factor; that is, however, outside the scope of this book.

We have seen, in the case of Worcester, that some towns apparently experienced quite consistent natural increases over long periods as evinced by parish registers. Worcester may well have been atypical of other medium-sized and probably all larger towns, although it is likely to have been more typical of smaller places. Natural increase was certainly never the case in London, but seems to have been fairly typical of the developing manufacturing centres of the seventeenth century. These 'open towns' free of corporate control and restriction, with their obvious economic opportunities, must have been as attractive to potential settlers as were the crowded 'open villages' of rural society, free of manorial control. Birmingham represents a classic case of this, with its population rising from some 2,000 or 3,000 in 1603 to about 6,000 in 1660, and at least 10,000 in 1700. Immigration was a very important factor in this, but it should be noted that excess of births, though slight at the turn of the sixteenth century, grew rapidly during the late seventeenth century.[131] Leeds, too, prospered demographically in the same way, particularly after 1580, when the amount of recorded baptisms doubled, so that by the time of its incorporation in 1626 the town had a population of between 5,000 and 6,000.[132] It may be that size itself was an influence on marriage and fertility, as much as environment and economic opportunity. Many more studies will have to be made of places like Worcester, Birmingham and York before we know whether the generalizations made about the predominant natural decrease in pre-industrial English towns are applicable only to the larger of them. Comparatively little work has been done on urban as opposed to rural nuptuals and fertility, though baptism series from registers have been plotted in print for a good number of towns.[133]

Pre-industrial nuptuality, and as a consequence, fertility, was probably as much determined by social institutions and habits as by conscious calculations of economic advantage.[134] Most of that which we know in detail about nuptuality and fertility is drawn from rural examples, like the classic study of Colyton by Wrigley.[135] Certainly the results of these studies suggest that in pre-industrial English society there was a very flexible response to economic and social conditions, with important implications for the general course of social and economic change in the country. Much less is known about the social and economic responses and behaviour of townsfolk in places of any size, and their effects on and interrelationships with demographic change. The semi-control conditions of demographic inspection which family reconstitution allows is largely denied us in most urban parishes because of the large turnover of population consequent on migration; Chambers is certain however, that fertility patterns differed between manufacturing and agricultural populations.[136] Despite advances in the study of fertility, it is true that we still know almost nothing about the growth of some sections of the indigenous population.[137]

Population Patterns within Towns

Lastly, it is important to consider the internal demographic geography of pre-industrial towns. A few facts about differences in mortality, household size and susceptibility to plague are known about some towns, but it is difficult to pronounce on their social geography with certainty, as already noted in Chapter 1, though there are one or two exceptions such as Gloucester and Newcastle-upon-Tyne.[138] Much more is known about the later seventeenth century than earlier years in this respect, largely because of the existence of one particular source, the Hearth Taxes of 1662–74. These tell not only the number of Hearth Tax payers, and of those exempt from paying it on many occasions, but of the numbers of 'hearths' or fire-places in each taxpayer's house. From such evidence it is both possible and permissible to infer something about the size of the house of each taxpayer, and by implication, something of his prosperity, family and household size. With the help of parish register evidence it is possible to do much to reconstruct the population geography of many pre-industrial towns and fill-in the framework offered by the Hearth Taxes. Such an opportunity does not exist for earlier years, though much can be done by painstaking study of late medieval urban rentals, as Langton has shown in Gloucester.[139] It is quite clear that family size varied between different socio-economic groups. An Elizabethan survey of about 450 poor families in Norwich shows that the average number of children per family was a figure between two and three, rather on the modern English pattern. Well-to-do citizens of Norwich and of Exeter, however, had on average between four and five children respectively. Differential infant mortality must have played its part in accounting for this discrepancy, as did the fact that poorer people could not expect to live as long and thus have as many children, as their better-off counterparts. With the poor sections of urban society sometimes constituting fifty or sixty per cent of the total populations, and the very well off representing probably less than five per cent in many cases, this differential must have been marked; it had considerable spatial as well as social and economic expression.[140] A census of the poor in late Elizabethan Ipswich shows this very clearly.[141] Some parts of towns were undoubtedly more overcrowded, and contained poorer and often smaller families than others; it is usual to discuss these within the parish framework of any town, the parish being the most convenient and indeed the only valid division of the often muddled urban topography.

In London, the old urban core of the city displayed marked socio-economic differences between its parishes in medieval times; differences which persisted and developed into the pre-industrial period, when a considerable phase of suburban expansion began. This was most marked in the eastern parishes in the sixteenth century, though during the later seventeenth century the movement to the west was beginning in earnest, particularly along the banks of the Thames. There was a spectacular increase in the population of East London in the seventeenth century, where the suburban parishes grew from a population of about 20,000 in 1600 to nearer 100,000 by 1700.[142] There was a general fall-off in the density of building away from the crowded eastern suburban parishes like St Katherines and Whitechapel (which had been built up in the sixteenth century) with a resultant general decrease in population density, although it remained high by the crowded and busy riverside. There is as yet relatively little known of the population geography of London and its suburbs in the sixteenth century, though more is known about the end of the seventeenth century. It is quite clear that plague mortality was most severe in the plague years of 1563, 1578 and 1593 inside the city proper, whilst plagues after 1603 like those of 1609, 1625, 1636 and 1665–66 struck hardest in the suburbs, particularly the 1665 outbreak.[143] It is probable that the population of the medieval core of London, overcrowded and prosperous, began to decline from the mid-seventeenth century:

> London was an area with a fairly distinctive pre-industrial ecology. The proportions of upper-status households was higher in the centre, and the lower status households showed the greatest relative frequency on the periphery and in many of the parishes without the walls. There was a huge range of wealth apparent, from just under five per cent of the population being liable to surtax in the 1695 tax, in the poorest parishes of the north-west and south-west edges of the city, like St Mary Staining and St Andrew by the Wardrobe, to nearly forty per cent in prosperous St Matthew, Friday Street, one of the central parishes; another, St Mary Le Bow had thirty-five per cent of its population liable to surtax and an average of two servants and four apprentices per home.[144]

Figure 6 shows this pattern for the late seventeenth century based on the 1695 Tax for Births, Deaths and Marriages, etc. There were three areas of substantial and prosperous population, one being the five contiguous parishes of Allhallows, St John the Evangelist, St Martin's, St Mary le Bow and St Matthew, Friday Street; there were also two other secondary areas of high prosperity, separated by a band of parishes of lower status. Parishes outside the wall on the

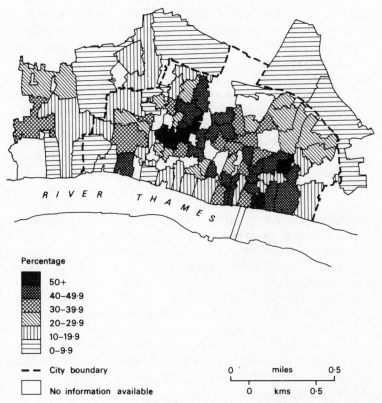

Percentage

■	50+
▨	40–49·9
▧	30–39·9
▨	20–29·9
▥	10–19·9
▤	0–9·9

-- -- City boundary

☐ No information available

0   miles   0·5

0   kms   0·5

6   Numbers of substantial households in London parishes in the later seventeenth
century
(Based on D. V. Glass, 'Notes on the demography of London at the end of the
seventeenth century', in D. V. Glass and R. Nevelle, *Population and Social Change*,
1972)

other hand tended to have most houses and least substance, a
gradient untypical in the modern city.[145] The poorer people moving
out tended to go to the manufacturing, refining and shipbuilding
parishes downstream from the Tower; whilst the wealthier went
west to escape what Sir William Petty called the 'stink' of the
town.[146] Growing urban congestion drove many of the wealthier
citizens to seek more salubrious places of residence in Westminster,
Covent Garden, and Bloomsbury, as well as the outer and still rural
reaches of Islington and Stepney.[147]

The same sort of overcrowding and social differentiation was
evident in the provincial cities and county capitals of pre-industrial
England; parishes that were poor or rich, crowded or capacious,

parishes with below or above average family size, greater or lesser susceptibility to plague and other epidemics, all can be differentiated. In Tudor York, for example, five out of every six people lived within the walls, between 10,000 and 12,000 crammed into just 260 acres, not all of which was available for building.[148] At the time of the taking of the Hearth taxes in the following century, the population and social geography of York can be clearly seen in outline. There was a compact group of eight parishes in the centre of York and on the west bank of the Ouse, where most of the substantial citizens lived in houses with an average of 3·2 hearths per home. At the other extreme were another eight parishes around the rim of the city with houses of less than 2·5 hearths on average, and up to fifty per cent of their total population exempted from paying any tax at all. Between the two extremes were thirteen 'middling' parishes containing forty-nine per cent of the households of the 'middling sort' of shopkeeper and craftsman.[149] Ralph and Williams demonstrate a very similar pattern in Bristol at the end of the seventeenth century, when open spaces within the city had almost disappeared.[150] The same sort of picture was apparent in Exeter. There were seven parishes with an average of four to five hearths, forming 'a compact nucleus in the heart of the city'.[151] Average size was 2·6 hearths per house, some forty per cent of the population being exempt on grounds of poverty; the five poorest of the city's thirteen parishes lay against or outside of the medieval walls, with up to fifty-five per cent of their inhabitants exempt by poverty from taxation.

In Exeter and in many other cities, differential mortality patterns can be seen; the plague struck hardest in the suburbs, as it did in London after 1603. The plagues of 1570, 1590 and 1625 in Exeter moved slowly across the whole town, but struck different sections with differing severity. On each occasion it was worst in the poor areas, plague burials often being twice the level in the poorer parishes like Holy Trinity or St David's than they were in central, richer ones like St Petrock or St Martin. The situation was almost identical in Bristol, where in some of the poorer parishes, like St John, plague burials reached about three times the recorded annual average.[152] This heavy incidence of epidemic disease amongst the poor, who already had a lower expectation of life, higher infant mortality and smaller family size than richer townsfolk and were usually grouped in peripheral parishes, may be one of the most conspicuous aspects of the demographic and social geography of medium and larger pre-industrial towns. As Slack observes of the towns whose epidemic history he has studied:

The increasingly marked incidence of plague in the poorest quarters of towns after 1560 might equally be explained by a change in their social geography. The subsidy returns for each town show that there were extremes of wealth and poverty in different areas in 1524–25, as there were at the end of the period. But the contrasts may have increased as these towns became important social centres for the gentry in the counties around them. By the 1630s the central parishes may indeed have become rather more exclusive than they were in the 1570s, and the suburbs, with their growing population, poorer.[153]

There was a great concentration of the poor in the suburbs of all fair-sized English towns, as great outside the walls of Leicester[154] with its strongly and typically differentiated social geography, as outside Canterbury,[155] where there was apparently the greatest concentration of squatters and misery, with a high incidence of crime and lower than average household size. The socio-economic polarization of wealthy and poor areas that was so typical of every pre-industrial town implied a demographic polarization of the most marked kind, with wide differences of household size, of mortality, of life expectancy, and possibly of nuptiality, fertility and peri-natal and infant mortality. Quite high levels of poverty were to be found in much smaller towns, too; whether in the Medway towns like Rochester and Chatham in the late seventeenth century, or Richmond in the north riding of Yorkshire in the earlier sixteenth century,[156] whether in Rotherham, Doncaster and Beverley or Lichfield at the time of the Hearth Taxes[157] or little Suffolk weaving towns at the Musters of Harness of 1522.[158] The general picture we have is bound to be altered as our knowledge of this period grows, as Langton has demonstrated for the socio-economic geography of Newcastle in the 1670s.[159] The very smallest places, tiny market towns with a population of several hundred or a thousand, had considerable extremes of wealth and poverty too, but had less clearly marked internal population patterns, having only one or two streets. These places with their simple topography made up the majority of English towns, though paradoxically we know least about their populations.

4

Town Occupations and Town Economies

We have seen that English towns generally became more populous during the sixteenth and seventeenth centuries. At the same time they became more modern and sophisticated. It would be surprising if these changes had not been accompanied by parallel changes in urban economies and occupations, and by changes in the inter-relationships between towns of different sorts and sizes. It is to questions of the urban economic geography of the day that discussion now turns.

Differences between the economies and relative importance of towns of different types and sizes were readily apparent. Writers of the day endlessly remarked upon the 'quickness of markets' or 'the slowness of trade', the fact that a town 'standeth most by draping' or that 'this place depends much on smiths'. Simple ideas of the ranking of towns familiar to geographers of the twentieth century were present in the mind of topographers of the seventeenth century. Peter Heylyn, for example, in his *Cosmographie*, published in the later seventeenth century, spoke of the different ranks of cities; to him Bristol was 'third in rank of the cities of England', Norwich the fourth city of the first rank, Oxford the first city of the second rank, and so on.[1] Defoe, writing nearly a century later, had a very clear idea of how urban economies might develop.[2] He postulated a model in which fifty farmers, having each been granted 200 acres of farm land rent-free on the condition that every one bought £200 worth of stock with him in order to help create a new town, were also given land and gardens rent-free if they promised to build houses there. The subsequent growth of the economy, Defoe suggested, might take place along the following lines: a butcher would arrive to serve

146

the needs of the newly settled farmers, erecting a shed until he could build a house and a shop; and since one butcher could not possibly cope with the demands of fifty farmers, certain farmers would be dependent on the nearest town until more butchers saw the opportunity afforded by the settlement, and moved in to join the first one. These would soon be followed by a baker who would set up an oven, while work would rapidly be provided for a variety of other basic trades: a smith or a farrier, two wheelwrights, an ironmonger, one or two shoemakers, a turner, an earthenware seller, a glover, a ropemaker and three or four barbers to service the farming and domestic needs of the community. Master carpenters would be needed to build houses, as would sawyers and bricklayers. Assuming that the town was on a post road, Defoe then posited the arrival of a victualler to set up an ale-house, soon to be followed by others. The next people to arrive, drawn by the obvious prospects of trade, would be shopkeepers such as grocers, chandlers, apothecaries, mercers, haberdashers and drapers. At this point the now-flourishing town would probably acquire a market and some fairs as well, also attracting specialist craftsmen like pewterers, coopers, brewers, and attorneys and surgeons.

Defoe was writing as the pre-industrial period drew to an end, and as the first stirrings of industrialization were becoming apparent. Yet, interestingly enough, in the construction of his general model of urban genesis and growth, he did not suggest mining or manufacturing activity as the nucleus around which a new town would spring up. If he had been writing in the 1820s rather than the 1720s he undoubtedly would have suggested a salt works or glass factory or iron manufactory as the nucleus for urban growth. As late as 1728, when England was still a rural society, with over two-thirds of its inhabitants living in the country and engaged in rural occupations, his model town sprang from that countryside. In his model, the town did not become a noted industrial centre and find its economic rationale in an industrial speciality. Instead it was to grow into a general service and 'shopping' centre of considerable occupational complexity, containing high-level legal and medical professional services. Any 'manufacturing' activity would be a later addition to this basic urban economy. Defoe's overwhelming interest in trade and commerce must be remembered, for this would have biased the construction of his model;[3] yet his neglect of agriculture, also evident from his writings, did not prevent him from clearly perceiving agriculture and the needs of the countryside as the apparent basis of urban growth.

There were in the sixteenth or seventeenth century no equivalents of the nineteenth-century one-industry towns; at the most there were only a very few specialized manufacturing towns slowly emerging by the latter part of the seventeenth century. Most pre-industrial towns were 'generalized central places' in that they were deeply embedded in the countryside, London obviously excepted. That is not to deny that certain towns had marked economic specialities generating urban growth and prosperity; but these specialities were as likely to be in the highly organized marketing of rural produce such as horses, cattle or corn as in manufacturing goods. Norwich had its textile speciality, as did Worcester, but it would be as wrong to call either place a 'textile town' as it would to call even later seventeenth-century Birmingham an 'iron town' – for that burgeoning Midlands centre was then still a very important leather manufactory.[4]

Hoskins thus seems to have misjudged the urban economies of the day when he writes of Elizabethan Leicester: 'there was a community of some three thousand people, the largest and wealthiest town between the Trent and the Thames, *which had no obvious means of livelihood*' [my italics]. Hoskins continues: 'The special interest to the economic and social historian is indeed that it had no industry worth speaking of'. Far from having 'no obvious means of livelihood' at the time, Leicester had an urban economic superstructure as typical of Stuart and Restoration towns as it was of Elizabethan towns.[5] The activities of building, brewing, provisioning, tailoring, weaving and the like in pre-industrial Leicester supported the basic economy of every pre-industrial town. Specialities in the manufactures of the day – usually textiles, iron and leather goods – when located in towns were invariable additions rather than the basis of their economies. They may have engendered prosperity and population growth, but were just as likely to attract the poor and the vagrant. It is clearly important to look at pre-industrial urban economies in their own terms rather than in ours.

Town economies and the nature and sorts of occupations that people followed in them did not remain static during the two centuries. They were subject to cyclical movements in the economy, various secular economic trends, and inflationary pressures from time to time. The most specialized towns dependent on foreign trade usually suffered most from economic depression, such as those of the 1550s and 1620s, and benefited most from the relatively stable prices obtaining from the 1660s. The role of towns, especially that of London and the larger centres, became more and more important in the economic geography of the day. Towns by 1700 had a greater share of national population than they enjoyed in 1500, and thus were bound, by this fact alone, to play a progressively greater role in integrating the nation.

Yet we know very little of the output of urban economies and of the value of production of urban goods, save in special cases of tightly controlled manufactures like textiles which left records. Of production per man or per unit we know next to nothing, and of the actual values of goods produced even less. Something of the value of raw materials or stock in trade is revealed in the probate inventories of (generally better-off) townsfolk. We can tell very little of turnover or levels of activity, although contemporary accounts give qualitative impressions. The national and regional location of manufacturing activities and of their locations within towns, is becoming clearer but there were of course no government statistics of industrial location as there are today. It is necessary to depend to a considerable degree on secondary evidence for town economies, presented by sources which give occupational information, and thus infer from the statistics of occupational structures of towns something about the changes in urban economies.[6]

Certain trends are quite clear from even these skeletal statistics. First, there was a slow increase in the numbers and types of occupations in most towns of any size over the pre-industrial period. Occupations became progressively more specialized and more sophisticated, often with more people being engaged in the different crafts. In York, for example, by 1700 there were a number of new crafts and an increased membership of others. This growth reflected a rising standard of comfort for some, and even luxury for a fortunate few. By 1700 there were to be found bookbinders, booksellers and stationers, soapboilers, tobacco-pipe makers, clock and cabinet makers, dancing masters and musicians.[7] There was a clear change in the status of some crafts, too; to become a surgeon was to join an occupation of much greater social standing and occupational sophistication in 1700 than in 1500, while on the other hand to become a grocer was to join an occupation of, if not lesser standing, at least lesser rarity value.

The second major trend was for higher-level occupations to filter down from the larger into the smaller centres over the period. By 1700 most smaller towns and indeed some larger villages had a far greater and relatively more sophisticated array of occupations,[8] a process which is illustrated in this chapter. Trades and crafts even as specialized as clockmakers and apothecaries were to be found in some of them, as were a proliferation of shops. The intermingled functions of fabricating, wholesaling and retailing goods were becoming progressively, if slowly, more organized, specialized and differentiated, itself a mark of increasing economic specialization. The trend was quite clear to writers of the day. The anonymous author of one tract on trade inveigled against it thus: 'For now in every country village, where is . . . not above ten houses, there is a shopkeeper, and one that never served any apprentice to any shopkeeping trade whatsoever'.[9]

These changes were, naturally enough, reflected in the economies of towns and their interrelationships. Most larger towns tended to forge ahead, as they had in the case of population growth, relatively faster than smaller towns. The smaller towns also experienced in general a relative increase in their economic sophistication, although many failed as urban centres between 1500 and 1700, owing to competition from larger towns nearby, which benefited from increasing economies of scale and improving transport. There was also genuine economic specialization in some towns. A few of them were becoming the specialized, one-manufacture 'coke towns' of the age; certain places were not only noted for but dependent on and totally dominated by activities such as the colonial trade, ship-building, the manufacture of iron goods, or mining. Yet in 1700 the trends that can be perceived in this direction are still insignificant compared to the dominant general and unspecialized economic role of most centres.

Occupational Sources and their Interpretation

Any approach to the internal workings and external economic relations of pre-industrial towns must recognize the part played by the individual. By and large, surviving economic sources tell what individuals did, rather than giving aggregate figures of production or output of large concerns. This evidence accurately reflects the economic realities of the day, for it was the individual, not the firm or the factory, who played the central role in the economy. If the individual was a great clothier at the centre of a putting-out system, then it was he rather than a works or plant, which was the economic focus; the individual was at the root of the urban geography of the time to a much greater extent than now.

Quite a range of sources survive for occupations. Actual direct counts such as those carried out by the censuses after 1801, are

absent, and, therefore, all sources that do survive are essentially indirect in their nature. Any study which hopes comprehensively to
examine a town's occupational structure must use all available
sources; and even these would give a far from complete picture of
urban occupations.

The problem is not simply the defects of the sources themselves
and the chance of their survival. The difficulty lies in the fact that
the occupations of a considerable proportion of the population of
any town were unlikely to be recorded at all, particularly with
reference to the poor, who might number forty per cent or more of
the whole population. Occasionally, surveys of the poor undertaken
by town governments do give a fleeting glimpse of what they did,
and thus of their role in the urban economy.[10] Yet the life-styles of
the urban destitute are still one of the great unknowns of the society
of pre-industrial England. The poor interrelated economically with
the more gainfully employed work-force from time to time as
fetchers and carriers, occasional labourers, sweepers and buriers.
On the other hand, they also represented a great drain on resources,
and constituted another economic and social world.[11] Their largely
unrecorded but numerically substantial presence must constantly
be borne in mind while the economic activity of those we do actually
know about from extant records is discussed.

Available sources of information are of two main sorts.[12] Firstly,
there are those records which were likely to include occupational information, since their essential purpose was as a record of the
control and regulation of what people did. This category mainly
consists of records of admission to town freedom[13] (i.e. the right to
trade and/or manufacture freely within a town); of enrolment into
apprenticeship[14]; and various lists of households, of those in particular sorts of trades, of aliens or 'foreign' workers (i.e. those not
made free) and sometimes of the poor, that might be taken from
time to time for particular purposes.[15] But an actual occupation,
even in the case of admissions to the freedom or apprenticeship, was
not always written down, the name and terms of entry being all that
might be included. Such sources as these generally recorded only a
proportion of the economically active population of a town. Many of
those gainfully employed – and who did not fall into the poorer
classes – were those who did not take up their freedom or necessarily served an apprenticeship, but simply worked for a master as a
journeyman or workman. These people were rarely subject to
control and record in the way that freemen and apprentices were.

These sources are, nonetheless, more direct than the second main category which might give occupational information in passing, or record details from which a man's trade might be inferred. In this case, control of what people did or control of the town economy was in no way part of their purpose. The main examples of this source are wills and probate inventories,[16] recorded in one or other of the ecclesiastical courts which administered them; either that of the two Archbishops, the Bishops or the Archdeacons; in addition, parish registers may record occupational data.[17] There are other un-systematically surviving indirect sources such as those derived from central government administration, especially notable amongst the latter being military muster lists[18] and taxation lists.[19]

The survival of records is clearly linked to the nature and size of different towns. Most towns with any corporate life kept records of the former type; in addition there is a good chance that those in the second category are likely to survive. But most English towns were not corporate, and therefore did not keep records to any extent. Many towns, including most of the smaller ones about which we know so little, either did not keep records, or did so sporadically. Thus, for them, the main occupational sources must remain those of the second category. Generally speaking, the larger and better governed the town, the wider will be the range of occupational sources and the greater the detailed information on the economic activities of individuals. Much depends on the intrinsic accuracy of the sources and upon their interpretation.

The problems of inaccurate, incomplete, partial or poorly surviv-ing sources are compounded by the occupational designations used in the records themselves. We cannot know for example if a 'tailor' recorded as being given the freedom of some town was in fact a sub-stantial merchant tailor with countrywide and even international business interests or a poorer man making a scant living repairing and mending. It was not only the scale of operation which seems so often confused, but also its nature. For instance, a grocer might have been selling over the counter, or importing and redistributing, or indeed making, refining and selling goods. Even if the recorded evidence seems at first sight to be precise and unambiguous, other sources can reveal that other activities were in fact undertaken by the same man. In sixteenth-century Great Yarmouth there was one person, ostensibly a barber who also mended fishing nets. Another barber in the same same town taught braiding and reading to local children; Paul Riseburgh was paid five shillings by the Yarmouth Corporation for every child he could teach to braid, and ten shillings for those that could 'read well in the bible'.[20] We also know about a man called John Batholomew who lived there and was recorded as a 'merchant'. Yet this seemingly sure evidence is shaken by other details given in an indenture of 1582 which enrolled an apprentice coming from the village of South Elmham 'as a *turner* and to John Batholomews *other trades, misteries and occupations*'. The activities of those called merchants such as 'Great' Tooley of Ipswich, could be surprisingly diverse,[21] as could those in other occupations.[22] Furthermore, individual craft guilds representing apparently separate activities can be found to include people doing entirely different things from those which their names suggest. The mercers in late sixteenth-century Coventry were deeply invloved in a 'who does and sells what' dispute with the cardmakers' guild – but these so-called cardmakers were by 1579 actually ironmongers![23]

The guilds that men entered did not always indicate their real business activity. In Leicester, Richard Barnes, vintner, bought and sold wool as well as wine, and Richard Swan, who belonged to the fishmonger's occupation, was a grazier and part-time gaoler. John Launder, who was recorded as a pewterer, had most of his capital invested in a malting business. Many tailors in Leicester got part of their income from investment in dairies, pigs, brewing and spinning. Others were practising ready-to-wear tailoring, and were not popular with the guild. In the early seventeenth century the tailors complained of one Shilcock 'not being content with the trade wherein he was brought up . . . nowe byes great quantities of cloth of furrien clothiers, makes them up into garments and sells and exports them ready to sale to the great impoverishinge of the drapers, mercers, taylers and other tradesmen'. The constantly fluctuating guild and craft structure of Leicester[24] presents problems of occupational information similar to Coventry's. In the 1620s the mercers' guild there swallowed up the previously separate linen drapers and the grocers, so that a comparison of the number of 'mercers' recorded in the freemen's rolls of Leicester before and after that time is invalidated by the change in their membership.

Of the occupations which by their nature embraced both making and selling, that of 'cordwainer' can serve as an example of the problems of interpretation. Etymologically speaking, a cordwainer was one who worked in Cordovan leather or in Spanish leather in general; and the term was used in the upper end of the trade for shoes in particular. In big cities, and especially London, the distinction in this sense between 'cordwainers' and other 'shoemakers' survived well into the seventeenth century. In many other smaller places, however, the name 'cordwainer' was never more than an interchangeable alternative for shoemaker and/or general leather-worker, making clothing or fastenings; it was a slightly euphemistic term, too, rather like denoting a butcher as a 'meat purveyor'. In Tewkesbury the cordwainers' guild was the one for all shoemakers trading on their own account; the other leather-workers' guild there, in existence by 1579, was for glovers, point-makers and pouch-makers.[25]

There could be equal confusion in the case of pure crafts, where no selling was involved, as with carpenters, for example. As Goodman writes: 'Judging from their tools there were, then as now, carpenters and carpenters. Some of them appear to have been "hedge carpenters"... but there were also a number of men working on the elaborate half-timbered houses of the wealthier merchants and similar high-class woodwork'. As with carpenters, so also with turners: 'One Bristol turner John Banghe, is down in 1604 as a turner and pumpmaker. In the Mayor's Audit for 1617 John Berrow, who took six apprentices between 1593 and 1623 as a turner, was paid: "... in full payment of his work for bringing of water to the New Fissle Shambles." '[26]

As far as the nascent professions and services in the towns are concerned, the apothecaries can be used to illustrate the linkages which commonly occurred between professional and service activities on one hand and trading and craft activities on the other. In the City of London apothecaries were not separated from the Grocers Company until 1617. The Grocers Company had itself developed from the Spicers and Pepperers. Many grocers sold 'physic goods' and mercers in country towns sometimes had a variety of very simple medical preparations in their stock,[27] on the use of which they must have given advice from time to time. Apothecaries' activities could be carried on conveniently amidst the dry goods being imported and sold ('merchant' activities) after being made up ('craft' activities) by grocers. Thus a good deal of medical activity may be entirely lost from sight, disguised under the bland title of 'grocer' or 'mercer'. It is equally difficult to determine how much barbering and how much surgical activity a so-called 'barber-surgeon' indulged in. For a final example, we can see how, by the seventeenth century, the 'scrivener' had developed into something far more sophisticated than his largely clerical sixteenth-century forebears. Coleman observed that in London, 'In addition to exercising their purely clerical art, they frequently acted as legal and financial intermediaries'. They drew up bonds and arranged mortgages, and acted roles as diverse as those of estate agents and accountants.[28] The rich complexity and diversity of pre-industrial urban life is concealed more than revealed by a term like 'scrivener'.

The observations of contemporaries seldom help to resolve these questions. The *Discourse of the Commonweal of this Realm of England,* an early sixteenth-century tract,[29] is an important source of contemporary perceptions on the relative importance of different occupations in town and country. One of the participants in a debate about the economic health of the country printed in the *Discourse* was the 'Doctor', who suggested that there were 'three sorts of Misteries'; 'some that bring money out of the country, some others spending again in the country and a third sort that bring treasure into the country'. In the first category were mercers, grocers and haberdashers who sold imported goods bought with exported English treasure; these received but scant approbation from someone living in a mercantilist age. In the second category were shoemakers, tailors, carpenters, butchers and others in similar trades who earned and spent their living within the country; these were thought necessary and acceptable. But it was those in the third category, for example clothiers, cappers and worsted makers, who were valued most and cherished by the Doctor, because they brought foreign treasure into the country from their exports abroad. His opinions, and those of others like him, illuminate the economic thought of the day but they do not help us to understand, for example, the differences between manufacturing and services; nor do they help us to see whether there were genuine differences between wholesaling and manufacturing activities – both of which are vital questions. We must avoid looking at the economic activities of pre-industrial townsfolk with twentieth-century preconceptions about 'industry', of 'wholesale', or of 'retail'. We must certainly not think in terms of distinctively 'urban' and 'rural' occupations, for, all the evidence given in inventories and other sources warns us the contrary. Many country-dwelling husbandmen or yeomen might have been part-time craftsmen or carriers. On the other hand, not only might some of their 'urban' counterparts labour in the fields at harvest time, but they might indeed have direct rural interests in lands, crops and beasts. Detailed study of those business papers that do survive for the sixteenth and seventeenth century is vital if we are to understand more about how people engaged in different occupations actually worked, to compare with our knowledge of farming at the time[30] or shopkeeping in the later eighteenth century.[31]

Economic Control, Direction and Restriction in Towns

Mirroring the limited information available about the economic role and occupations of that major section of urban society, the poor, as well as of journeymen and other unenrolled workers, is our ignorance of the activities in certain parts of most medium and larger towns, especially their suburbs. It is clear that a great deal of manufacturing and trading was carried on by those living outside town walls, and, therefore, outside town control and the regulation of standards of manufacture and trading. Most corporations tried hard to limit and direct the economic activity in their towns, perhaps by controlling the number of apprentices and journeymen any master could have at any time, by laying down and enforcing standards of manufacture (for example the width of cloths produced or the process by which leather was tanned) or by regulating the numbers of 'foreigners' who could trade in the town. Much of the impetus behind such control was obviously fear of competition, particularly from cheaper rural competitors. It was also undoubtedly due to perceptions about the nature of the English economy and the opportunity afforded by towns for those who ran town corporations. Very often, it seems that the national and local economy was regarded as a cake of fixed size, which had to be apportioned fairly. For much of the pre-industrial period urban economic philosophy, in so far as it existed, seemed more concerned with husbanding and sharing a range of economic possibilities that were perceived as finite than extending them. Such attitudes began to be modified in the seventeenth century, particularly in and close to the capital, and with such modification came a breakdown of tight urban economic control. Such control was already becoming difficult because of a population growth in larger towns making it as hard for corporations to oversee economic activities as it was for parish authorities to supervise and record the occurrences of births, deaths and marriages.

Town corporations tried to extend their control into and over the suburbs, in order to prevent unfair competition, superintend the poor, and garner local revenues and dues. Suburban dwellers, if not controlled by the town, were not recorded by them either, so much less is known about their activities than of townsfolks'. Suburbs spilled out beyond the town walls of Canterbury, for instance, and became a haven for the work-shy, the vagrant and the lawless.[32] The suburbs beyond the City of London were a persistent source of irritation to the corporation, and they made constant – and eventually successful – attempts to take areas like Southwark under their wing.[33] Complaints about surburban competition were continuous, and in Leicester suburban dwellers were characterized as '. . . like drone bees to the hyve, paying neither scot nor lot, lye lurking in the suburbs and other secret places, in and about this town, and robbe your suppliants of the work.'[34] The picture of urban activity available from surviving urban records, already limited because of the omission of the poor, is thus even more restricted because the records often did not cover the suburbs, which were vitally important – however much resented – component parts of the urban economy.

Within towns themselves control over economic activity can be conveniently separated into the control of what people did and how they did it, via craft and trading guilds enrolling members and often supervising the quality of what they made, on the one hand, and the control of the sale of goods in town markets and fairs on the other. The efforts of craft and trades guilds and corporations to limit economic activity sometimes had deleterious effects, for undue restriction on activity allowed the more entrepreneurial corporate towns, non-corporate 'open' towns and rural areas to take the economic advantage in costs and output. It may be naïve to ascribe all the decline from medieval greatness in cloth production experienced by Lincoln or Beverley to inward-looking and restrictive town governments, but they certainly played their part. There was an attempt to control the multifarious activities of craftsmen who had been given the freedom of the town and who thus were free to trade, as well as stopping those not made free from setting-up shop. As Unwin observes, a craftsman might be: a workman using his hands; a foreman, superintending the labour of his journeymen and apprentices; an employer, undertaking responsibilities of production and supplying capital for materials, food and wages (plant costs then, unlike now, being usually very low); a merchant in respect of the raw materials and final product of his trade (for there were not always those who would be recognized as wholesalers to undertake these tasks); and a shopkeeper.[35] It can be seen from this list, that even if the freeman class as enrolled and recorded by guilds represents a limited proportion of all those gainfully employed in towns, at the same time each individual so recorded equally represents someone who was at the focus of different parts of the urban economy. Thus bare occupational statistics of freemen are a good descriptive surrogate for total economic activity, when related to town size; in addition they represent the most systematic and comprehensive view of any town's economy at any time in the pre-industrial period that is available to us, even if it is a structural and undynamic view.

The study of guilds and their role in towns has a long history. All the evidence points to the fact that their power decreased over the sixteenth and seventeenth centuries, until by 1700 it has been suggested that only about a quarter of English towns had organized guilds.[36] Guilds of course were not primarily creatures of central but of local government; when borough interests could no longer be best conserved by craft companies, their death-knell was rung[37] and most records of the enrolment to freedom in different crafts over the whole medieval and pre-industrial period show this process at work, with a decline in the importance of guilds slowly setting in.[38] The changing guild structure of any town is extremely complex, for individual guilds were often at odds with one another over their trading rights,[39] and involved in endless amalgamations and take-overs.

York provides an example of one great English provincial city whose guild structure is known in some detail.[40] In medieval times, it had a very high rate of admissions to the freedom, and seemingly strong guild and corporate control. But, as Dobson observes:

> entry to the urban franchise was rarely compulsory for every male craftsman of a medieval English borough . . . the options available to particular city authorities remained bewilderingly open: many large English towns, notably Bristol, clearly accepted into their franchise only a minority of those economically qualified and personally prepared to set up as retailers . . . the neighbouring Kent towns of Romney and Canterbury were capable of manipulating the level of entry fine to quite different intents: whereas the freemen of Romney formed a large and broadly based social group, the Canterbury authorities preferred to envisage the presence in their city of a large class of non-freemen retailers subject to separate fine . . . No doubt the freemen admission rate in medieval York was so much higher than elsewhere just because enfranchisement remained in the great majority of cases a condition, although not of course a guarantee, of employment in most of the city crafts. It cannot . . . be sufficiently stressed that the size of the freemen class in any town was directly related to the rigour with which its city authorities enforced that condition. The fact that York admitted an average of more than eighty freemen a year in the fifteenth century – as compared to less than forty at Norwich and less than twenty at Colchester, Exeter, Kings Lynn, Leicester, Northampton and Hull – does not necessarily mean that it was either the most populous or the most prosperous city in the kingdom.[41]

York was certainly not the most restrictive as regards admissions, but it had problems with suburban competition, and 'foreign' penetration of its markets. By the sixteenth and seventeenth centuries, Palliser suggests, 'the volume of trade was increasing, many towns were specializing in particular products and selling them over wide areas, and the craft guilds of the corporate towns are often seen as anachronisms which were in decline in the prospering towns, and which dragged down those towns unwise enough to leave the system intact',[42] though Palliser goes on to say that '. . . there is no evidence that the York guild system changed greatly in the Tudor period, nor is it easy to argue that the retention of the medieval system proved an economic liability'.[43] There were some fifty-one guilds in York at the outset of the Tudor period, a number to be joined by the hat-makers' in 1494, the minstrels' in 1561, free labourers' in 1578, cobblers' by 1582, embroiderers' by 1590 and brewers' in 1600; a list of crafts drawn up in 1579, not all of them formally constituted as guilds, numbered sixty-four in all. Of this list the merchants' and tailors' guilds were larger than any of the purely handicraft ones, and both the numbers and the prosperity of the weavers declined in the face of 'the bleak wind of West Riding competition'.[44] By 1700 in York, as elsewhere, the guild's powers were waning, and restrictive corporate control was declining in importance as a locational factor.

The role of town governments was not altogether restrictive, however. They were sometimes active encouraging new manufac-tures in the town, though often this was when trading conditions were poor, or the poor themselves were becoming a problem. In Grimsby, for example, in a depressed condition economically throughout the sixteenth and seventeenth centuries, attempts were made to establish a woollen manufacture in the later seventeenth century. A maker of rugs and coverlets was lured from beyond the other end of the Lincolnshire diocese in Oxfordshire to teach the trade, the immigrant weaver being given accommodation rent-free.[45] In other towns spinning-sheds were set up to keep the poor at work, and in some ports sugar-baking refineries were funded by cor-porations. But generally the economic role of town corporations in the sale of goods was restrictive; this was the case even in small towns like Grimsby. Here the borough strictly regulated certain aspects of the economy: an ale-wife was bound to sell to anyone if she had four gallons in store, tanners were not to buy the skins of dogs or sheep after Mayday, and so on.[46] Such regulations abounded in every borough town in pre-industrial England, sometimes to the good of the consumer, sometimes to the benefit of town trade, but often hindering expansion.

Such regulations became increasingly difficult to enforce as towns became bigger and more economically diverse while bureaucracy remained small. Nowhere is the decline of guild control on manufacture, and corporate control on trading more evident than London, a decline which marks both the onset of more modern economic conditions and London's role as the leading city of the age. The system gradually broke down during the seventeenth century, despite many attempts by the corporation of London to legislate in order to prohibit the presence of those not free who had not served apprenticeship, while trying to bring suburban workmen into guilds.[47] As Jones observes:

> From at least the beginning of the seventeenth century, government by guild and municipality was ceasing increasingly to reflect the economic vitality of the metropolis as a whole. The growth of the suburbs, and the rise of unfree trading and manufacturing within them, diminished the value of both apprenticeship and freedom: more and more of the trade and industry which were nominally the citizens' exclusive right under successive great charters of London were being intercepted by the activity of the unfree trading and manufacturing in the suburbs. . . . Where typically the historian of the medieval merchant class would focus on question of guild monopoly, guild exclusiveness, and municipal control, a historian of the London mercantile community of the later seventeenth century must be concerned with the new world of stocks and shares, and with the increasingly large indirect intervention of the government in the workings of the economy which determined in as yet unspecified ways, the distribution of prosperity and depression within that country.[48]

Guilds and corporate control were an increasing anachronism.[49] In discussing corporations and guilds, however, we are not discussing administrative history, but phenomena with real economic implications, sometimes positive, sometimes negative.

Occupation and Economy

It is evident that we know a good deal about some aspects of urban occupations and economies, but little about others. We do know something about the general occupational structures of towns, whether specialized or not; the important growth of professions and services within the town; the development of shops and shopping; and a good deal on London itself which has to be treated in this context as a unique urban entity. On the other hand we know next to nothing about what the poor sector of urban society did, not enough about the part that rural activities played in urban economies of various kinds; little about individual economic behaviour; and even less about the internal economic geography of towns than we know about their internal social and demographic geography.

The small unit of production, operating in one fixed location, was the rule in pre-industrial towns. That is not to deny that there were in pre-industrial England units of production that were large and interdependent, although usually dispersed from any one location. The domestic putting-out system was the best example of this form of production: the often substantial numbers of people who were engaged in the component parts of a typical manufacture like the production of cloth – spinners, corders, combers, weavers, shearers, hat-pressers and the like – usually laboured as individuals in the home perhaps with the help of wife and children. They were not at any stage gathered together in a large unit. Indeed it would be wrong even to regard them conceptually as a functioning whole, as a spatially dispersed unit. They were not all members of the same unit for the same length of time. They could be engaged, whether consecutively of concurrently, in working for more than one putting-out master; equally they could be thrown out of work by a master the moment trading conditions changed, and in addition there was no or only little concept of continuity of production. Work was bargained for by the piece, it is true, but not within the context of piece-work on a continuous production line, typical of so many nineteenth- or early twentieth-century factories. Much domestic out-working was carried on in rural areas, particularly in textile manufactures, and not all of it was for urban masters. Throughout, capital was invested first in the stock in hand, on labour second, with investment in plant coming a poor third.

Even a large and well integrated domestic putting-out system centred on the individual, not on the factory or firm. There was little continuity of operation between generations, and no joint stock or public companies to ensure the continuity which exists in many industrial concerns today. Being the head of a great urban business almost invariably meant urban office-holding too. Yet, as in Winchester, 'Office-holding dynasties did not generally last for more than two generations, though there were exceptions, and trading dynasties too were rare. One reason for this was the high rate of failure of a family's male line, for about a third of all office holders (and other classes) died without surviving sons'[50]; the same was true apparently of York. When a man died his business, based on his own individual qualities, often died with him. Secondly, though we recognize the role of the individual, as much in the putting-out as the handicraft systems, we must not forget that there were some large units of centralized production in pre-industrial England, the iron or coal mine, the blast-furnace and the flour or

paper mill being the best examples. These tended not to be located
in towns in most cases, though many boiling processes such as of
dyeing, soap- or sugar-making could be urban, as could shipbuilding. Even in these units of production the capital invested and
labour force employed would generally have been relatively small,
and production irregular, dependent as it was on fluctuations of
wind, water and warfare as well as on demand.

Labour remained the most important factor in urban production
and thus in the urban economy. The products of masters, craftsmen
and artisan-retailers remained the largest single source of urban-
manufactured output throughout the pre-industrial town. Far-
reaching technical change revolutionizing manufacture was rare.
Advances in manufacture proceeded rather by the refinement of
processes, sometimes simply by slightly altering the appearance of a
product – such as a cloth – and changing its name. Increases in the
volume of production to meet increased demand at home or opportunities abroad were generally made by increasing the numbers of
people working on the product involved. Motive power in almost all
urban industries remained human, just as raw materials remained
largely organic, up to 1700. The rate of change in manufactures
between 1500 and 1700 was slight compared with what was to occur
later. The same manufacture might be located as easily in the
countryside as the town, and it is not possible to conclusively
differentiate between rural and urban manufactures, or even styles
of manufacture and organization of production. An urban clothier
might work in much the same was as his rural counterpart, as the
locational forces for any one manufacture were not necessarily
peculiar to town or country. In the seventeenth century there were
booming cloth manufactures not only in towns like Colchester,
Exeter, Norwich or Worcester, but also in the country areas of the
West Riding of Yorkshire, even though the latter relied first on
London and later on Leeds or Halifax for the marketing of their
cloth. The example of cloth is an apt one, for in 1700, just as in 1500,
the making of woollen textiles was still the country's biggest
manufacturing industry in town and country; and it still accounted
for over two-thirds by value of England's exports of home produced
goods.[51] However, the production of cloth was not the only
manufacturing function of towns. The peculiarity of manufacturing
activities in urban economies was not that towns contained
manufactures that were peculiarly urban; the reverse was in fact
true. Rather, the distinctively urban quality was solely in the concentration and array of manufactures and handicrafts located

together within the town boundaries. Add to this the varieties and numbers of professions and services which towns increasingly provided, the growing specialization in incipient wholesale activities in and outside of the formal market, the burgeoning retail activities through the innovation of the shop, and the nature of an urban economy is better described and understood as a whole than by exemplifying any particular urban manufacturing specialization. Concentration rather than specialization of activity was the touchstone of the town economy, in a way that is not wholly the case today.

Urban handicrafts constituted the core of economic life in towns,[52] and the largest source of manufactured production. We cannot now, and may never be able, to measure their output, for statistics of home-produced and home-consumed manufactures were rarely kept. If we cannot measure their output we can at least, as is exemplified in Chapter 6, plot their presence or absence in towns of different sizes and sorts via available occupational statistics, and consider the different activities and isolate those towns which deviated from the norm of generalized activities represented by the typical array of pre-industrial urban occupations. Such deviation might occur because a town developed a particular specialization, and grew faster than the rest. A model of the urban economy of the day must be as generalized as any model that tries to comprehend urban divisions of labour, for the masters and the men often worked side by side, with the merchant involved in some manufacturing, with the manufacturer participating in the selling process, and with the poor and semi-employed being a very apparent sector of the urban economy.

To look at the pre-industrial town is thus to look at an unspecialized economy; it is also difficult to analyse because of the deficiencies of the available sources for occupations, and the problems in their interpretation already referred to. As occupational specialization was not marked, and terms of occupational designation were confusing and interchangeable, any classification of the work force involves a considerable simplification of the actual situation, and possibly a misleading one. Clarkson was constrained to write: 'It might be concluded that because of the conceptual problems involved, as well as any difficulties arising from the quality of the evidence relating to the occupational distribution in pre-industrial England, statistics should be eschewed altogether'.[53] Nonetheless, he was able to produce a table which gives details of the occupational structures of over twenty rural and urban places in

England, derived from parish registers, freeman's rolls, muster rolls, probate inventories, wills and a taxation list.[54] It is clear from this evidence that half a dozen groups of crafts and manufactures – textiles, clothing, leather and metal working, building, and the processing and distribution of food and drink – dominated the urban workforce. Even where there were notable specialities, such as Worcester with its cloth, Newcastle with its coaling and the Medway towns with their shipbuilding, these occupations were present throughout the urban landscape. Every occupational study since that of the Tawneys[55] has illustrated this fundamental diversity; very few, if any, manufactures fell within the sole purview of any town, any more than any particular manufacture was likely to be found only in the town itself. Pewter might be expected to have been a specialist occupation, for example, but instead 'it was made for every conceivable domestic purpose ... the manufacture of pewter was widespread'.[56] To attempt to build a model of the economy of the pre-industrial town using occupations as a surrogate may be a rather difficult and deluding exercise because of the problems of sources, and the fact that they record far from all the occupations of all the people; it may be rather self-defeating too, because of the very generality of most urban economies. Over twenty years ago, Hoskins suggested that the clothing trades (between 14 and 15%), the food and drink trades (15–21%) and the building trades (4–7½%) together constituted some 35–40% of the working population of the average English provincial town; even in a specialized (though by then declining) weaving town like Coventry in the early sixteenth century those involved in these trades constituted over a third of the whole.[57] We may expect that the textile, leather and metal trades – which were just as 'basic' to the typically unspecialized and localized urban economies of the day as clothing, food and drink, and building occupations – made up at least another third. It may not be only simple but also accurate to accept this picture as fairly representative of all provincial towns of any size. The remaining 20–30% of occupations were likely to be generalized and varied too, and comprehended service activities, growing professions and the rest. This third of the workforce that was residual from the basic economic superstructure is also the area of the urban economy in which we may look for activities which made a pre-industrial town specialized – shipbuilding, for example. Yet any noticeable specializations were as likely to spring from a particular concentration on one of the activities that was typical of every pre-industrial town, as was the case with most noted 'cloth towns'. The basic economic structure was unlikely to vary much between towns, or at different times from 1500 to 1700, although genuine specialization was an increasing feature of some later seventeenth-century towns.

There are other ways of looking at occupational structures than by classifications based on product or raw material. An alternative approach is to focus on type of work.[58] Most work in the pre-industrial town was, in ascending order of numbers involved, first in the professions and services; second in merchant and trading activities; and with most people in 'artisan-retailing'. Then there were the poor. In any town outside the capital those involved in the professions and services, albeit a growing sector of employment between 1500 and 1700, were a tiny proportion of the whole workforce. Those in merchant and trading activities were also a small part of the whole, though they were economically very important because of the focus of trade they provided and the amount of economic activity they generated. The main part of the workforce numerically was undoubtedly in the 'artisan-retailing' sector. Artisan-retailing is an inappropriate term because of our imperfect perception of what occupational terms meant. Most people who sold also made – a tailor or a shoemaker for example, while many people who made also sold – for a weaver might sell some of his cloth direct to the consumer, at the same time as working for some larger putting-out master. This was not always the case, but it is dangerous to assume the existence of a permanent proletariat of full-time artisans who, in the style of an assembly-line worker today, never met and dealt with the consumer. We are not in a position to tell what proportions of people were involved in making and selling, as opposed to involvement in only one of these functions; the same person may have done both at different times in his working career, or indeed during the course of the same year because of the fragmentary and fluctuating nature of any urban worker's employment. Of the poor it is safe to assume thay made up at least a third of the population of most towns of any size, though not necessarily of its workforce.

The Generalized Urban Economy

In dealing with the non-specialized urban economy we are dealing with the majority of English pre-industrial towns. The characteristics of such urban economies have been outlined: certain sorts of

activities comprised perhaps two-thirds of any town's economy, the
majority of the workforce being 'artisan-retailers', with a substantial
poor sector also present. This is a picture demanding such a
generalized model as to hardly merit the term. Larger towns, not
surprisingly, had a greater variety of occupations than small ones;
they tended to have the professional, service and trading activities
which were not present in lesser places. Such activities developed
in style, complexity and number over the period 1500 to 1700
and tended to filter down into lesser places. Any large city such
as York or Bristol had at least a hundred different sorts of occupations in 1500, and at least 200 (including new, high-level activities) by 1700. How much of this increase was simply due to
different names being used for the same trade and how much
represented genuine divisions and growing sophistication of labour
is difficult to tell. Smaller places advanced proportionately to their
size, though there may have been an actual decline in the
occupational complexity of tiny places. The towns of East Anglia,
which will be examined in a regional context in Chapter 6, afford a
very good example of a range of places from the biggest provincial
city in England to tiny declining towns. The picture afforded is one
which provides a good framework for the rest of the country, a
regional model of broad applicability.

There were no very strong regional differences. It is true to
say that the towns of thinly populated, not very prosperous regions
in parts of the north and the west of England lagged in their
economic advance, although the largest places in them, such as
Chester or Newcastle-upon-Tyne, could be as occupationally advanced as southern and eastern cities.

Winchester, for example, which retained cloth manufacturing
throughout the sixteenth and seventeenth centuries, was not particularly economically or demographically buoyant, but had a
cathedral and an important school, was a market and assize town
and a social centre for the gentry of the surrounding countryside.
But Hampshire was a thinly populated and not very fashionable
county; by the eighteenth century 'Hampshire' was a generic term
of abuse in London for the worst and most boring of simple provincial society. It would not seem to be a very promising place to look
for growing urban economic diversity, perhaps, but even here there
was to be a noted growth in numbers of different occupations.
Between 1500 and 1549 there were sixty-five recorded; between
1550 and 1599 there were eighty-seven, including for the first time a
goldsmith and a stationer; between 1600 and 1649 about a hundred,

newly including a gunsmith and a tobacconist. This number held steady until the end of the century, though the trend of increasing sophistication continued, with booksellers, watchmakers and pipemakers appearing for the first time.[59] By comparison, in the Northern cathedral and market city of Ripon there were book-binders and goldsmiths by the 1550s, as well as merchants, drapers, tanners, butchers and pewterers; in the Midland cathedral city of Lichfield there were between fifty and sixty occupations in the early seventeenth century, ranging from apothecaries and attorneys to schoolmasters and stationers.[60] Towns of this size all over England, with or without cathedrals, were equally well served with general basic trades: Leicester, for example, in the words of Jenkin and Smith, 'emerges clearly as a town with no predominant industry or trade. It was economically a mixed community with a wide variety of trades, producing consumer goods and it was still a market town with a strong rural character'.[61] In the same way, the important livestock marketing centre of Banbury was held in 1600 to have as its most distinctive products 'cheese, cakes and ale'; otherwise its most numerous trades, not surprisingly in cattle-country, were those concerned with refining and making-up leather, especially shoemaking.[62]

The lower down the urban hierarchy, the greater the number of towns are present, but the less we know of them compared to provincial cities and medium-sized towns. As Moxon correctly observes in his splendid detailed study of one little place, Ashby-de-la-Zouch in Leicestershire, growing slowly between 1500 and 1700 from a population of 1,000 to that of 2,000:

> Although historians have realized the social and economic importance of small market towns, little attempt has been made to analyse the life of such towns in detail. In the seventeenth century the small market towns were probably far more important to the majority of the population than were the larger towns; local markets were presumably visited every week, whereas the larger towns were probably visited by men from beyond the immediate neighbourhood on only rare occasions. Yet social and economic historians have concentrated almost entirely upon villages and larger towns . . . It is not possible to know until further research has been done upon this type of town, whether or not Ashby was representative of all small market towns.[63]

It is probably true to say that by the seventeenth century, just as the tiniest towns were often going into decline, medium-sized places like Ashby – and there were hundreds of them in pre-industrial England – were experiencing something of a golden age. The smallest places of a few hundred people could only offer limited marketing facilities, and a range of occupations that was little different from that to be found in larger villages.[64] They suffered more than they gained from the economic effects of a slowly improving transport system which made it easier, and more worthwhile, for people to travel to larger places like Ashby which offered better marketing facilities and a greater range of occupations (and therefore goods and services offered) by the seventeenth century; such places prospered as they built up an economy more sophisticated than anything their lesser cousins could offer. By the mid-seventeenth century Congleton in Cheshire, noted for making 'great store of leather gloves, purses and points',[65] had its plasterers, innkeepers, mercers engaged in general trades, ironmongers, barbers and glaziers;[66] at the same time Gateshead had its apothecaries, grocers, pipe-makers, glaziers, 'distillers of all sorts of strong waters and other liquors',[67] though it was noted, too, for textiles and stocking-knitting. As a last example, High Wycombe by the later seventeenth century had a typical array of shoemakers, glovers, tailors, bakers, butchers, carpenters, coopers, fishmongers, grocers, ironmongers, tanners and wheel-wrights to be found in the average medium-sized town. There were surgeons, musicians and even a dancing-master,[68] and lace-making was its speciality.

A massive table of the occupational structures of towns like these, composed according to some classification scheme or another could be drawn up, though the national picture has not yet been systematically covered and sampled. It would however serve the purpose of showing only how generalized most towns were. Most would have their little specialities – Banbury and Congleton in tanning and gloving, Gateshead in stocking-knitting, High Wycombe in lace-making, and hundreds more like them. Deviations from the economic norm were small and simple in most cases, reflecting a low level of occupational sophistication consequent often on some particular produce of the surrounding countryside.

Any English county can be used to show how generalized its urban economies were, and how unspecialized. At the lowest level in the early sixteenth century was a tiny county like Rutland,[69] the economy of which was wholly agrarian. What was said about Rutland could apply to much of the rest of England too: 'What trade and industry there was existed solely to serve the farming population, and indeed nearly all the artisans and tradesmen were part-time farmers'.[70] There were only two little market towns, Oakham and Uppingham, and most of their inhabitants were still at least part-time farmers. The only features that made them different from other places in the county were their markets and the larger proportion of men engaged in trades; nearly a quarter of the men of Oakham plied one, but far more of its people worked on the land. In Oakham, in the 1520s, besides farmers of various kinds there were 2 barbers, 3 butchers, 1 grocer, 1 miller, 1 weaver, 1 fuller, 2 shearers, 2 dyers, 1 tailor, 1 draper, 1 mercer, 1 tanner, 2 glovers, 3 shoemakers, 1 joiner, 1 turner, 2 smiths, 3 pewterers, 1 furbisher; 1 chapman, 2 barbers and a minstrel. Uppingham had a few higher-level trades in addition, like a waxchandler and a haberdasher. This simple manufacturing, selling and service economy was typical of most towns in 1500; by 1700, perhaps at the height of the era of the medium-sized town, such places may have had a few more occupations of a sophisticated sort – an apothecary or a bookseller – but the basic structure of their economy as seen through occupational structures was the same.

Whole areas of England had few specialized towns of any sort, no large ones of any kind, and only the most generalized urban economies. One such area whose population was examined in the previous chapter, was the south-east, including counties like Sussex. In this region, cloth-making was still quite a marked urban activity in the sixteenth, though declining in the seventeenth century. In Hampshire it was quite important at Alton, Alresford, Andover, Basingstoke, Fordingbridge, Petersfield, Romsey, Southampton and Winchester, while in Surrey it survived into the seventeenth century in Godalming. By contrast in Kent, Canterbury, Cranbrook and Maidstone were all noted as cloth-finishing centres into the later seventeenth century. There were some other urban specialities such as brewing in Basingstoke, or paper-making at Canterbury and Maidstone. Much more typical was the economy of towns like East Grinstead, Battle or Tonbridge most of whose trades fell into the basic groups of food (in which the butchers were dominant), building (carpenters and joiners dominant), and clothing (tailors and shoemakers dominant). Generally speaking, manufacture on any scale was completely lacking in Sussex towns, with the sole exception of Chichester. This had specialized concerns in corn-marketing, malting, flour-milling and paper-making. The production of needles had been important on a domestic system in Chichester but it never recovered from the destruction of St. Pancras Parish by fire in 1643. Local trade was the most important part of any town's economy in Sussex. Even Chichester, despite its specialization, had a basic structure little different from that of

Table 10: SUSSEX TOWN TRADES 1680–1730

Trades	Chichester No.	%	Lewes No.	%	Horsham No.	%	Midhurst No.	%	Arundel No.	%	Battle No.	%
	*		*									
1 Rural	230	21.3	88	20.8	59	22.4	50	24.4	35	19.8	76	51.6
2 Victualling	222	20.5	85	20.1	50	19.0	33	16.1	44	24.8	17	11.4
3 Clothing/Textile	193	17.8	75	17.7	51	19.3	43	21.0	13	7.3	17	11.4
4 Building	148	13.7	31	7.3	35	13.3	30	14.6	28	15.8	10	6.7
5 Distribution	76	7.0	41	9.7	17	6.4	9	4.4	12	6.8	5	3.4
6 Service	70	6.5	27	6.4	9	3.4	8	3.9	17	9.6	11	7.4
7 Leather	43	4.0	36	8.5	22	8.3	20	9.8	7	4.0	5	3.4
8 Marine	17	1.5	3	0.2	—	—	—	—	7	4.0	—	—
9 Miscellaneous	83	7.7	37	9.3	21	7.9	12	5.8	14	7.9	7	4.7
TOTAL	1,082	100	423	100	214	100	205	100	177	100	148	100

*Suburbs are included.

Lewes or other inland market centres.[71] (See also Table 10). This picture is clearly shown in Figure 7. By the end of the seventeenth century higher-level occupations had appeared in most Sussex towns; between 1680 and 1780 for instance surgeons were working in Arundel, Battle, Chichester, East Grinstead, Hailsham, Horsham, Lewes, Midhurst and Rye; Chichester between these dates had at least six surgeons and twelve apothecaries. Most towns had a tallow chandler, and tobacconists were widespread by the end of the seventeenth century; such occupations were basic to town economies, but stationers, booksellers and bookbinders were restricted to the two biggest Sussex towns, Chichester and Lewes, and to Midhurst. Most of them had at least one representative of the metal trades such as an ironmonger or brazier, but gunsmiths were to be found only in Chichester, Lewes, Arundel, Horsham and Rye, whilst gold and silversmiths are recorded only for Chichester and Lewes.[72] Apart from tiny and declining places like Hailsham, most Sussex towns had basic marketing facilities, while one or two larger ones had some specialities not available in the majority. There was thus a very simple urban hierarchy. There were firstly the county capitals of East and West Sussex, Lewes and Chichester; secondly there was the great mass of middling-sized towns like Horsham and Midhurst, enjoying fair prosperity, and a number of tiny and declining places. Petworth was typical of the majority of the towns, in the second level of the hierarchy.[73] Here in the seventeenth century there were some forty or fifty different trades, crafts and professions;[74] together they helped serve the administrative,

Towns															
ast astead %	Petworth No.	%	Cuckfield No.	%	Steyning No.	%	Brighton No.	%	Hastings No.	%	Rye No.	%	New Shoreham No.	%
44·5	28	22·5	55	52·9	16	19·7	14	8·5	12	7·8	22	14·5	16	17·0
12·3	22	17·6	9	8·7	15	18·4	21	12·7	22	14·5	27	17·8	6	6·4
16·4	23	18·4	13	12·5	12	14·8	22	13·3	8	5·1	9	5·9	4	4·3
11·5	23	18·4	12	11·5	8	9·8	11	6·7	13	8·5	7	4·6	12	12·8
6·9	6	4·8	7	6·7	7	8·6	4	2·4	4	2·6	9	5·9	1	1·1
3·8	7	5·6	2	1·9	5	6·2	2	1·2	6	3·9	13	8·6	1	1·1
3·1	7	5·6	2	1·9	11	13·6	3	1·8	1	0·7	8	5·3	—	—
—	—	—	—	—	—	—	86	52·2	83	54·3	45	29·6	52	55·2
1·5	9	7·1	4	3·9	7	8·9	2	1·2	4	2·6	12	7·8	2	2·1
100	125	100	104	100	81	100	165	100	153	100	152	100	94	100

marketing and trading needs of perhaps a sixth of west Sussex, with
Petworth drawing its custom from a radius – on the evidence of inventories – of at least six miles.[75] In Petworth, those engaged in
merchant activities (mercers, grocers, etc.) and food and raw
material processing (millers, butchers and tanners etc.) accounted
for less than a third of those in the different occupations but owned
at least two-thirds of the wealth. Thus Petworth was a typical, non-
specializing town. Chichester was the only specialized large town in
the whole county, and there was – despite the presence of an albeit
declining Wealden iron and armaments manufacture – no town very
dependent on one particular occupation other than the ports. In the
sixteenth century Hastings, Winchelsea and Rye formed the
country's main shipbuilding centres, but with the decline of the
Cinque ports the emphasis shifted to Shoreham in the seventeenth
century.[76] The economies of Hastings and Brighton were also
focused on the sea, but on fishing rather than shipbuilding.[77] Over
half the heads of households in mid-sixteenth century Rye and
Hastings were fishermen, while in 1580 it was noted that the
Brighton fishery employed 80 fishing boats, 400 'able mariners' and
10,000 nets. The comparative galaxy of occupations to be found
during the early seventeenth century in Lewes, with its goldsmith,
wiredrawer, gunsmith, bellows maker, locksmith and watchmaker
was not to be found in the three fishing towns.[78] Seaports, shipbuilding, trading and fishing produced in Sussex, as elsewhere in
pre-industrial England, some of the relatively few examples of
specialized towns dependent on single activities.

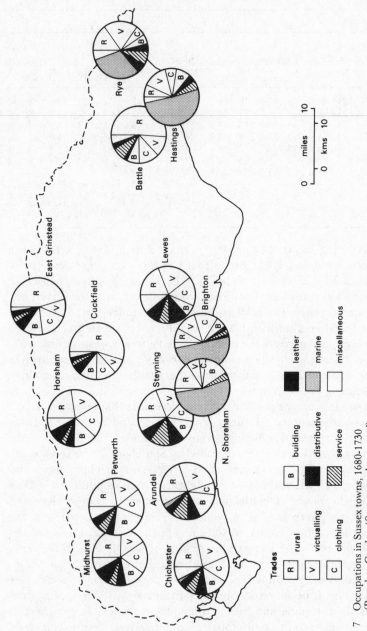

7 Occupations in Sussex towns, 1680-1730
(Based on Cowley, 'Sussex market towns')

Trades

R rural
V victualling
C clothing
B building

■ leather
▨ marine
□ miscellaneous

■ distributive
▨ service

Rye
Hastings
Battle
East Grinstead
Cuckfield
Lewes
Brighton
Horsham
Steyning
N. Shoreham
Petworth
Arundel
Midhurst
Chichester

0   10 miles
0 10 kms

The Specialized Urban Economies

Notably specialized economies were the exception rather than the rule amongst pre-industrial towns; they were not even the most noticeable urban feature, for it was economic unity, not economic diversity, which characterised towns. There were few equivalents to the 'coke towns', and very few new towns, whose growth we might safely ascribe to some special purpose or activity. Even in the latter decades of the seventeenth century, when growth in certain manufactures was under way, little if any of it was accommodated in new urban centres. Chalklin observes of one major English region: 'despite its expansion of agricultural output and the flourishing growth of its textile industries, no new town is known to have emerged in East Anglia'.[79] Towards the end of the seventeenth century the picture was much the same for other areas, though there were exceptions such as the growth of the port of Whitehaven on the Cumbrian coast for coaling, and of Wednesbury in the Black Country which combined coal and iron-ore making with nail-making.[80] But beyond that, it is clear that any new towns which did emerge were not the result of manufacturing activity.

What specialized towns there were generally included ship-building and fishing to create a number of specialized port towns, though far from every port on the English coast was the creation of a single economic activity. Coal and iron-mining led to no specialized industrial towns on the nineteenth-century model, though contributing much to the prosperity of coal-exporting ports like Newcastle-on-Tyne and Whitehaven. The manufacture of iron and other metal goods had long been the speciality of certain medieval towns, notably Sheffield, but it increasingly dominated the economies of a few towns by the later seventeenth century, especially Birmingham. The production of textiles generated noted economic activity in some towns, but it is probably true that while there were many places in which it played a vital role, such as Colchester, Norwich, Halifax or Leeds, and some where it dominated the manufactures of a town for a while, such as Worcester, there were no textile towns in the sense of the emerging Lancashire mill towns of the late eighteenth century. A few places relying for their growth and status entirely on resort activities, notably some spa towns, did emerge, but their efflorescence was not to occur until the eighteenth century. The growth of towns as county social centres, with a mini-season of balls and assize aping London, was again an emerging feature of the seventeenth century. While there were few resort towns, there were parts of some towns, especially London's suburbs, which depended on pleasure-seeking. These broad categories represent the markedly specialized towns, dependent especially on one activity; that is not to say that many places did not have economic specialities, though these were not to dominate the urban economy to the same extent.

Shipbuilding, ship-provisioning and fishing, for example, were highly specialized activities that dominated some ports. It is clear that ports were concerned with trade in the same way that inland towns would be, much of it based on internally manufactured goods which happened to be carried by one medium of transport – the boat – rather than another. The role of international trade on any scale was restricted to relatively few ports. Both internal and international trading functions of ports are discussed in the next chapter which focuses on the marketing role of towns and their relations with non-urban areas, but a glance at any pre-industrial port shows that its generalized urban activities within its own hinterland were often as important a feature of its economy as overseas trade might be. Southampton is a good illustration. It had been a great medieval outport for London in the Italian trade, but suffered markedly during the sixteenth century from changes in the patterns of international trading which increasingly, in south-eastern England, focused on London.[81] It remained an important port for trade with France, the Channel Islands and the coast of England. Merson's observations sum up the situation not only for Southampton but for most other English ports which neither had a speciality in shipbuilding and naval supplies, nor in international trade, re-export and refining. Examples of those that did included London, Newcastle, Hull, Bristol and Chester throughout the pre-industrial period, joined later in the seventeenth century by new ports like Liverpool involved in the growing colonial trade. Merson writes of Southampton that:

> The distribution of occupations in the town appears, from a study of the register of admissions to the freedom between 1614 and 1700, to have been much what one could expect to find in any market town of the period, except for the prominence of wine coopers . . . the distribution of trades did not change markedly, except for the appearance in the later seventeenth century of some new occupations, such as tobacco seller, tobacco-pipe maker, a 'confekt maker', (i.e. sweetmeat maker) and a 'perruque maker'.[82]

There was indeed nothing much to mark out Southampton from other English towns of its size, save for the numerous recorded wine coopers, who were engaged on containers for the French and Spanish wine trades. Like so many ports and ordinary provincial towns, it had a meagre specialized manufacturing base, though there was an influx of Huguenots who came after 1685 bringing some silk manufacture with them, and also a certain amount of paper making – largely outside the actual town itself.[83]

Shipbuilding was one coastal activity which did totally dominate the economy of some towns, and was stimulated by the needs of warfare and trade in the seventeenth century. The existence of shipyards in the early sixteenth century did not however imply continuous employment of men, the investment of capital, and the setting-up of ancillary trades, with their implications for urban economy and status. In the early sixteenth century there was indeed no large and permanent supply of skilled shipbuilding labour in any district. Rather, it was scattered over a multitude of small private yards especially on the south, east and west coasts. Much of the building of a 1,000-ton giant of the day like the *Henry Grace à Dieu* between 1512 and 1514 at Woolwich was through impressed labour, shipwrights being brought from as far as Cornwall and Yorkshire.[84] Shipbuilding was usually very scattered, tiny yards with a carpenter or two turning out vessels of a few tons, located in every little haven, which would also probably have its landing place and *ad hoc* coastal trade made up of small parcels of goods. Geographically speaking, the building of ships of any size was restricted to southern and eastern England, and within that area, to a few specific locations.

For most of the sixteenth century the main ship-construction areas were the Thames estuary and some of the East Anglian ports. Throughout the seventeenth century, however, East Anglian ship production at ports like Woodbridge and Ipswich suffered with competition from Dutch-built vessels,[85] as well as from the unwelcome attentions of Dutch and French privateers in times of conflict; from increasing competition from the north-east coast beyond Hull, in places like Whitby, and from increasing specialization in shipbuilding in the Thames estuary and north Kent coast. By the end of the seventeenth century Kent had four great dockyards, at Chatham, Deptford, Woolwich and Sheerness;[86] in Chatham alone the workforce in the dockyards grew from 40 in 1600 to 800 by the 1660s. The great expansion of the Navy under William III and the war of the Spanish Succession led to the remarkable growth of Plymouth and Portsmouth, and a substantial settlement arose in the late seventeenth century at Deal on the east Kent coast because of the importance of the Downs as a naval station.[87] These centralized shipbuilding undertakings were clearly not on a large scale even in the late seventeenth century except in places like Portsmouth which by 1700 was employing well over a thousand men in its naval dockyards. In the rest of the country's ports, shipbuilding played an important role, but generally not as dominating a position as in these highly specialized cases. In Chester, for example, it was significant in its urban functions although it was of less importance than the leather trades in the overall pattern of that city's manufactures; Celia Fiennes saw 'ships of 200 tons burden being built at Chester'.[88]

The picture presented in the Medway towns is entirely different, for here by the end of the seventeenth century the stranger could hardly tell where Rochester ended and Chatham began; the Navy and dockyards were vital, at least a quarter of the inventories surviving for Chatham after the 1680s being in these trades.[89] Apart from the dockyards there was no large-scale manufacture in the two towns, although there was a variety of craftsmen supplying local needs. Some textiles were made, and there was all the normal panoply of tanners, brickmakers, and food and drink trades. Dulley notes that: 'The other traders were primarily, if not entirely, retailers, meeting the day-to-day needs of the townsfolk and the country about within a radius of ten miles or so.'[90] Dulley goes on to make an interesting comparison with Petworth.[91] Over a comparable period much the same trades are represented at Petworth, but the average wealth is higher and the vast bulk of the trade was in durable goods, especially clothing, not in foodstuffs:

> butchers are quite numerous but there are no grocers and only one tallow-chandler. The clothing trades were much less specialized than in Rochester and Chatham, where retailers often dealt mainly in hats or lace or ready-made clothes, for the last of which there seems to have been no demand at Petworth. The most of the trade in Petworth would appear to have been a market-day one, with the inhabitants of a largely self-sufficient rural area. In the Medway towns on the other hand the shopkeepers for the most part were selling the day-to-day necessities to their fellow-townsmen.[92]

Just like shipbuilding, fishing was omnipresent in coastal towns. Fishing alone, however, does not seem to have generated urban growth in towns of any size. Great Yarmouth, the fishing port famous for its herring fairs when boats from all over north-western Europe stood off its haven, was equally as important as an outport for Norwich. In little places like Rye, Hastings and Brighton, however, fishing totally dominated the economy. In Hastings, of a total number of 280 heads of households, 239 were directly connected with the sea; 16 of them were called 'mariners', and 146 'fishermen'. Even in a place like Brighton with no proper harbour, a flourishing little fishing trade was built up, with over half of those gainfully employed being concerned directly with seafaring and fishing. Alternative employment could be as prevalent in seafaring as in agricultural communities, sailing and fishing and shipbuilding being very seasonal activities. Stocking-knitting in the close season was one typical by-employment of fishing communities;[93] indeed wherever a town is to be found, textiles are to be found too.

In the age of homespun cloth, the production of textiles was a common urban and rural activity. In certain towns it was a marked speciality; in a few it dominated the economy for a period. Manchester in the early sixteenth century was clearly seen by contemporaries as a 'textile town'. The preamble to one Henrician act, for example, referred to the 'Towne of Manchestre is and hath of long tyme ben a town well inhabited . . . an the Inhabitants of the same towne well sett a worke in making of clothes, as well of lynnen as of woollen;'[94] much of the flax and linen came from Ireland. Whole regions were becoming noted for, but not yet dominated by cloth production. Walker notes that 'As early as 1540 Middleton, Bury, Bolton and Manchester had all become quite important centres of the woollen industry, and by 1566 a start had been made in producing fustians and other types of mixed wool and linen cloths in the [then tiny] towns of Rochdale, Bolton, Bury, Leigh and Manchester'.[95] Growing regional specialization was accompanied by growing urban specialization.

In the West Riding of Yorkshire much of the growth of textiles production in the seventeenth century was in rural areas, with small independent masters and the domestic putting-out system.[96] Earlier, in the fourteenth and fifteenth centuries, manufacture was located only within towns such as Leeds, Wakefield and Halifax. In the pre-industrial period these remained seats of manufacture, but were as important as cloth markets. In the whole Halifax parish area – which was very large – 'most of the inhabitants were engaged in one way or another in the cloth industry'.[97] Indeed, by 1660–85, Halifax parish itself had come to accommodate over a quarter of those people who left 'textile wills' in the whole of Yorkshire. Within the town itself, rather than its extensive parish, the proportion of those describing themselves in their wills as clothiers, woollen manufacturers, and by other similar textile designations, had risen to over a third.[98] Halifax never assumed the first position in the West Riding, however. In the sixteenth century this place was held by

Wakefield, undoubtedly the centre for the clothing district when Leland travelled through the valleys in the 1530s.[99] By the seventeenth century it has been overtaken by Leeds, which, with its local industry already well established in the sixteenth century,[100] expanded rapidly in the early seventeenth. In the Hearth Tax returns Leeds had three times as many houses as Wakefield, and Wakefield ranked as the second largest town of the district, although it was not much larger than Halifax at the western end of the Calder Valley.[101] Leeds played an important dual role in the West Riding textile industry, which reinforced both its local dominance and its specialization. As well as manufacturing, it was very important for the finishing of cloth made locally; textiles from the south and west of Leeds were sent to the town for dressing, shearing (cropping) and dyeing. In addition, it became the centre for marketing, with increasingly wealthy local merchants, and the Brigg Market so graphically described by Defoe and other travellers was one of the commercial wonders of the age. Regional specialization in one manufacture had led to increasingly 'one-manufacture' towns in the West Riding and the north-west by the end of the seventeenth century, though this was little compared to the scale and concentration that was to come in the eighteenth and nineteenth centuries.

Elsewhere in England it is hard to find many other such 'textile towns'. Pound does not feel that this is the correct designation for Norwich, despite its important worsted manufacture. Not only was it also noted for hats, it also had far more important and varied functions as a provincial capital.[102] Worcester was another town which specialized in textiles. Dyer felt that 'The majority of Worcester's citizens were concerned in the production of goods, but only the cloth trades could really be called industrial, for only there were the producing and retailing elements separated', and further that Worcester's economy 'rested on the basis of the production of broadcloth of quantity and quality. Half of her citizens were engaged in the industry which was a source of great wealth to a few and of a moderately high standard of living to many. It did not show any well-developed form of the domestic system, but rested on the voluntary co-operation of a large number of independent artisans'.[103] Agriculture played a lesser part in Worcester than in many other towns of its size. If places with noted textile specialities like the north-western and West Riding towns were slowly developing into genuinely specialized towns, others began to show similar signs by the end of the seventeenth century, sure signs of the onset of modernization and industrialization. This trend can be seen from just one example of many. In Leicester the production of hand-knitted stockings was a well-established and highly organized manufacture by the mid-seventeenth century. Hosiery was being made on frames there by the 1670s, with the first mention of a 'hosier' in 1677; between then and 1700, seventeen different men and one woman were described as hosiers in the freemen registers;[104] yet by the 1740s, forty of the workforce were in the textile and particularly the knitting trades, and Leicester could be described as a 'hosiers town'.[105]

As in the case of textiles, there were some specialized metal-working towns in pre-industrial England, but only a few were very specialized by 1700; the picture is rather of the gathering pace of specialization that was to lead to true 'one-industry' towns only later. The pace of change and specialization in mining and metal manufacture was slow. In coal mining in the Midlands, for example (largely taking place away from towns), progress in the area between Coventry and Nuneaton, according to White, was 'painful-ly slow and fundamentally different from that of later times. Available evidence suggests very strongly that those developments which had taken place by 1703 sufficed for the rest of that period. It seems doubtful, therefore, whether the seventeenth century con-tained any significant precursive growth for subsequent years'.[106]

If there were no 'mining towns', Birmingham presents a case of an early specialized metal-working town. Leland visited it in 1538 and observed that 'a large part of the town' was maintained by smiths, and in the 1580s William Smith described it as a town where a 'great store of knyves'[107] were made – although both may have been struck by the unusual to an exaggerated degree. Yet there were still throughout the sixteenth century, at least, many inhabitants of Birmingham, such as Ralph A'Lees or John Elliot, who had marked farming interests.[108] Woollen manufacture also held its own within the town for most of the sixteenth century, and the leather trades were very active; in the reign of James I the old Folk House was turned into an inspection and stamping hall for leather and leather goods.[109] Gradually, however, as the seventeenth century advanced, the Birmingham metal-worker and ironmonger rose to dominate the town. The ironmonger in particular was of vital importance. He acted as a middleman, getting the bar iron from the forge and passing it on to the smith, and perhaps also marketing the final product. The ironmonger bore a close functional resemblance to the clothier, who played an equally important role in the cloth industry at the same period.[110]

Similar trends may be observed in the mostly unincorporated Midland towns in the sixteenth century; at Dudley, for instance, agriculture and cloth-working activities were progressively overtaken by nailmaking during the seventeenth century, a typical Black Country development.[111] Bromsgrove, West Bromwich, Wolverhampton and Handsworth experienced similar growth, founded on specialization. Even in the sixteenth century, parish registers show a high proportion of metal-workers.[112] A Fellow of Hertford College, Oxford, the distinguished topographer and scientist, Robert Plot, wrote of this area that 'the greatest excellency of the locksmith's profession was in the making of locks for doors, wherein the artisans of Wolverhampton are to be preferred above all others'.[113] Walsall too was known for its lorrimers rather than its blacksmiths, and there was a great concentration of the making of bits, spurs, saddlery and buckles. Yet, according to Rowlands:

> the metal workers still lived in basically rural societies. The towns of Walsall, Dudley, Bromsgrove, Stourbridge and Wolverhampton were taking on the aspect of industrial towns with small houses and workshops beginning to compete for space, but the overwhelming majority of the ironworkers lived in close relationship with agriculture, both in their own daily lives, and in terms of the economic balance of their communities . . . Nail-making was a seasonal occupation. Dealers spoke of difficulties in getting nails at harvest time, when the nailers were busy with the crops. . . . In March, industrial work again stopped as it was ploughing time.[114]

Due weight must be given to the importance of specialities in these and similar metal-working and textile urban economies, but it would be wrong to view them too much in twentieth-century or even in nineteenth-century terms as one-industry towns; these interpretations would deny the small scale, the seasonality and irregularity, and the low levels of capital investment and concentration which applied in urban manufacture in the pre-industrial period.

Except in a few cases like those of specialized shipbuilding, fishing, textile and metal-working economies it is therefore probably better to think of 'town specialities' rather than 'specialized towns' up to 1700. There are a few other exceptions, as in the case of spa towns; by 1700 Bath was already dependent on the visitors who came for health or pleasure. Buxton's development, though slight, had been stimulated by the sixth Earl of Shrewsbury who built the 'New Hall' to accommodate visitors in 1568, and there were 'galleries' there for visitors to walk in by 1572. Not too much should be made of the effects of such early developments or urban growth, and at Harrogate for example, where there was no inn until 1687, the site was described as a 'rude and barren moor'. Publicity for the new fashions, however, became quite prolific in the seventeenth century – notable examples were Deane's *Spadacrene Anglica* (1626) or Stanhope's *Cures without Care* (1632) – and the habit took hold, with many implications for urban growth.[115]

The fashionable visitors eventually brought prosperity to drapers, milliners and jewellers, and attracted tradesmen from outside. Bath was certainly not a flourishing community earlier in the seventeenth century; the abbey on which it depended had disappeared and woollen manufacture was in steady decline. The Mayor had complained to the government in 1622 that 'we are a verie little poore Citie, our Clothmen much decayed, and many of their workmen amongst us rehoused by the Citie'.[116] Yet by 1700 Bath had its gravel walks, bowling greens, tennis courts, and coffee houses, all based on the growing fashion of taking the waters. In the 1670s it was described as having 'Noble Buildings of Reception, that they appear . . . rather pretty palaces than common lodgings'.[117] A very short time after the laments of the 1620s, genuine specialized growth had transformed Bath and in fifty years turned it into the place Celia Fiennies described: 'the town and all its accommodation is adapted to the bathing and drinking of the waters, and to nothing else.'[118] Even more notable was the growth, from much humbler beginnings, of Tunbridge Wells; there the thermal springs had been noted from the 1600s, but there were only a few public rooms and booths of tradesmen in existence in the 1670s. In the 1680s, however, permanent settlements began to spring up, and the rapid growth typical of many an eighteenth-century spa town began.[119] Fiennies found that facilities were 'commodious' and that the shops were full 'of all sorts of toys, silver, and china'. These two were the only noted spa towns beginning their growth in the seventeenth century; Scarborough and Weymouth were still, in 1700, concerned with the sea and seafaring.

Rather like the spa towns, the university towns' future was closely tied to one institution, in this case the colleges; in the 1520s for example about a fifth of the taxable population of Oxford served the university directly,[120] and many more served it indirectly as bakers, butchers and vintners; then as now, wine merchants and tailors found a good living from the university. By the time of the taxing of Hearths in the 1660s, over 2,000 of Oxford's estimated 9,000 inhabitants were members of the University, their dependants or servants.[121] Cambridge was very similar. Elsewhere in England, however, we find that there were town specialities rather than specialized towns. In Macclesfield in Cheshire, for example, the button industry, which had originated in the late sixteenth century, was the staple trade of the town by 1700, and the town's main claim to fame in England.[122] But it would be ludicrous to call Macclesfield a 'button town', just as it would be to call Newcastle-under-Lyme a pottery town in the seventeenth century, even though it was already set on that course. By the second half of the seventeenth century Newcastle had developed its own specialized clayworks, especially for clay pipes which, though they added much to the total economy of the town, apparently did not contribute materially to the expansion of the pottery trade elsewhere in the north Staffordshire area, despite the corporation's activities in setting up corporate brick and tileworks in 1709.[123]

London

Discussion of the non-specialized and specialized pre-industrial town cannot ignore the unique status of London. London was at once the most generalized and the most specialized of all pre-industrial English cities. Its economy, like its society, was in a class by itself, and had been so since early medieval times. In fourteenth-century London, for example, there were over 180 different trades named in the records, and there was already acute specialization and division of labour. There was, for instance, in fourteenth-century London, one Robert Leg, practising as an *ageletmakere;* technically, he was concerned only with the making of metal tags to go on the end of laces, as on the end of the modern shoelace.[124] Some of the units of production organized on a household basis – master, journeymen, apprentices and servants – were quite large, although the biggest single recorded unit yet discovered, that of a pewterer, was still only eighteen people.[125]

In the pre-industrial period London increased its already established importance, tightening its grip on the economic as well as the political mechanism of a country that was increasingly bound to it by communications, by demand,[126] and by the fact that in the late seventeenth century nearly one Englishman in ten was a Londoner, and many more had received their training there. Yet despite a considerable amount of published work,[127] brilliantly codified into theoretical terms by Wrigley,[128] a full-scale socio-economic history of London during the early modern period is lacking. Of the Henrican period Stone observes that 'we know almost nothing about the occupational structure of London, or indeed of the distribution of wealth within it. No records survive as to give us anything like an overall picture: possibly the complexity of the urban economy in London and its large suburb of Southwark defeated all administrative efforts'.[129] At least twenty times larger than the next biggest English town by the end of the seventeenth century, it was clearly the country's primary city.[130] The English urban hierarchy was dominated by this primary-city relationship, one that existed within a very small total population and a small island land area.

The sixteenth and seventeenth century was the period in which London permanently consolidated its position in the country, so that not even the growth experienced by the great centres of the industrial revolution like Birmingham or Manchester could ever come near it. It was also during the period that London rose from being merely the most important town in England to becoming one of the great European cities, on a par with Paris or Naples. Ramsay, in a recently published book, rightly observes that, 'London in mid-sixteenth century was a lively trading city, much frequented by strangers. It was easily the largest urban unit in the British Isles while by European standards not outstanding in size; a position which dramatically changed by 150 years later.' Ramsay goes on, however, to illustrate a still widely held and fundamental misconception about the nature of the forces causing pre-industrial urban growth, whether in London or elsewhere in the urban hierarchy:

> the growth of Tudor London, exuberant as it was in some respects, rested on a *curiously narrow* base [my italics]. No doubt in part the city developed because it was the capital of the country, close by the administrative centre of government. Just outside the municipal walls the law courts were maintained, lawyers were trained and parliaments met. This helps to explain why inns and taverns were plentiful. *But London was not yet any great extent a seat for industry* [my italics]. . . London owed its economic ebullience and its aldermen their wealth to virtually one thing only – the English woollen cloth trade.[131]

This quotation illustrates the economic historian's predeliction for concentrating on those few aspects of economic activity that left quasi-statistical records, in this case of the sale and export of cloth. Ramsay's summary of the causes – or lack of them – of London's growth illustrates the misconception that any urban growth should be caused by one special industry, and that it is curious if one is not immediately apparent. London's success as the dominant centre by 1500, and its tearaway growth in the two centuries thereafter should rather be seen in the context of national population growth and economic advance which was both focused on and focused by the capital.

London's pre-eminence was due not so much to any natural advantages as a source of labour, or capital, or industrial specialization as to the fact that it was such a large consuming centre, of men and food, of political power and social influence and economic expertise. It enjoyed locational advantages, it is true, but its major advantage in 1500 was that it was there, and was, as it always had been, England's largest city. No other town in England enjoyed such marketing facilities. As the capital it had the Court, Parliament, the law courts, and, increasingly, fashionable society. Its manufactures were in existence as much to serve its own population as to make, refine and finish indigenous or imported materials. London undoubtedly fed on itself, as much as it fed on the country; it reached the point of build-up to a 'critical urban mass' during the sixteenth and seventeenth century which gave it its own economic velocity thereafter. We have the theoretical framework in which to ask the questions, but of the actual mechanisms of growth we know next to nothing; of what people actually did in the city itself we know certainly no more than for many a provincial town; and even less of what they did in the burgeoning suburbs which contained so much economic growth. The records of the city companies can give us details of the occupations of those made free and apprenticed; but an enormous amount of work must still be done to consolidate this information to produce breakdowns of occupational structures such as those already available for provincial cities like Southampton, Leicester or Norwich.

We do know something of the manufacturing geography of the capital, which must be looked at within the context of the great suburban growth out from the crowded core. Surburban growth was primarily eastwards, within which area much of London's growing and diversifying manufacturing and finishing activities were increasingly to be fostered. Besides its role as the major English textile marketing centre, textile manufacturing was also very important inside London as it was in many other provincial cities. Inside the city it was carried on in wards like Bassithaw, Cripplegate Within, and Vintry, and in the peripheral northern and north-western parishes. Silk-weaving, dominated by aliens in the city, was largely concentrated in Bishopsgate, but also in Spitalfields, and beyond; dyeing, requiring plentiful supplies of water, was close to the Thames at Queenhithe and other city wards, but spread down-

stream. Tailors were found all over London, and it has been estimated that they constituted as much as a fifth of the manufacturing
population;[132] they were very numerous in the suburban areas,
too. Metalworking was important in the city, especially goldsmiths and silversmiths, and cutlers dominated the trade of
southern England. Stow considered that 'at this day the best and
finest knives in the Worlde, are made in London',[133] but he railed
against Saint Paul's for being 'defaced by means of licences granted
to cutlers, Budget makers and others, first to build low sheddes, but
now high Houses, which doe hide that beautiful side of the Church'.
Outside the city proper, brass and copper-refining industries went
on downstream, while armaments were made around the Tower;
Busino speaks of this area as a suburb of gunsmiths.[134] There was
much tanning, both north and south of the river, with the great
leather market at Leadenhall, and gloving concentrated at
Smithfield. Breweries lined the river, and also dominated northern
and north-eastern suburbs, St Giles, Cripplegate and Southwark.
Shipbuilding and provisioning spilled downstream, as did various
noxious trades like soap and alum-boiling. As the seventeenth
century advanced new manufactures were set up like sugar-
refining, and the making of enamel, alum and gunpowder, almost
all of which were suburban. Nothing illustrates the difference
between modern industrial conditions and those of the seventeenth
century so much as the very small extent to which London's
manufactures were dependent on the export trade, or even on trade
with other parts of the country. Vital trading centre though London
was, only a very small fraction of the goods carried by the great
merchant companies with headquarters in London was of London's
production. Cloth was rather brought in from all parts of the
country to Blackwell Hall, leather to Leadenhall Market, lead sent
by sea via Hull from Derbyshire.

In the luxury trades, however, the capital did play a vital role in
the production of expensive light-industrial goods, such industries
as the making of silver and gold wire for cloth, for example, had
numerous spinning sheds in St Giles and Cripplegate.[135] London
was important for its essential marketing facilities, its refining and
entrepôt role, and specialized luxury manufactures that were unique
to it, but also for the growth of a new mode of trade occupation, the
shop and shopkeeper, and for the growth of a new strata of activity,
the services and professions.

The increasingly specialized retail shop, slowly disentangling
itself from craft and manufacturing activities, was a creation of

sixteenth-century London. From there it was to spread to the rest of
the country. There had been places that were earlier called shops,[136]
letting down boards and awnings from house fronts on which goods
were displayed, as well as being the 'workshops' from which the
term 'shop' is undoubtedly a contraction. In most sixteenth-century
provincial towns such places operated as retail outlets, mostly on
market day; for the rest of the time they were concerned with
making and fabricating in the back regions. This was how most the
'shoppys' of some English towns in the 1520s functioned: by the
turn of the sixteenth century in London there were, however, 'in
divers particular shopps in Cheapside, and other places', highly
specialized retail silk shops, for example.[137] Whilst there are some
studies of shopping[138] that deal with this period in brief, there is
nothing to compare with Alexander's authoritative *Retailing in
England during the Industrial Revolution*.[139] It is almost certain that the
origins of shop retailing must be pushed further back, particularly in
the case of London, than Alexander or Scola have allowed. Studies
by Willan of these involved in what might be considered retailing
and wholesaling activities in the sixteenth century demonstrate
these earlier origins, and the spread of the shop throughout one of
England's most economically advanced regions, East Anglia, was a
marked feature of the geography of the period.[140] In London the
shop was developing as a distinct entity, at least for luxury goods, by
the mid-sixteenth century. Shops existed alongside the trading
undertaken in permanent covered markets, street markets, fairs, and
from barrows and hawking, and were concerned with everything
from large-scale wholesaling to the selling of seasonal fruits and
vegetables like Kentish peas and pippins, in tiny lots to the small
consumer. Detailed work on shopping as an occupation in early
modern London is necessary to plot this advance. It is probably
still true that we know more about provincial shopping, whether
in Stuart Wiltshire,[141] Oxfordshire,[142] late seventeenth-century
Hereford[143] or eighteenth-century Kirkby Stephen[144] than we do of
pre-industrial London shopping. The diffusion of retailing as an
occupation from London was as rapid as that of fashions in dress
and conversation. By the early seventeenth century there were glass-
fronted shops replacing the wooden pentices (hinged shop-fronts on
which goods were offered for sale) previously lowered from house
fronts in central Ipswich: and by the end of that century at least one
contemporary observer remarked on the rich shops there.[145] Shops
were becoming concentrated in richer, central parishes near
markets.

London saw an equally early development of services and professions.[146] It had no university, it is true, but with Parliament and the courts as well as much church administration, it was naturally the centre of the legal professions and those connected to them. The Inns of Court acted as a finishing – as well as legal – school for young gentlemen from all over the country. There were rapid developments in the numbers, importance and division of the legal and medical professions in particular. Lowly creatures like the scrivener of the sixteenth century, writing wills and letters in a pre-literate age, sometimes developed into far more specialized professionals in the next hundred years. In the seventeenth century, in addition to exercising their purely clerical art, scriveners frequently acted as legal and financial intermediaries; they drew up bonds and mortages, and combined some of the roles of solicitors, clerks, accountants and estate agents. Merchants began to specialize in banking and broking at the same time. Further divisions took place in the medical professions, with surgeons and physicians becoming more numerous and somewhat more capable than the earlier barber-surgeons and bone-setters. Apothecaries, breaking away from close trade alliances with such activities as the grocers, became more specialized. This specialization spread, by example if not by direct diffusion, into provincial towns.[147] London was clearly the breeding-ground for the entirely new professions and services that appeared for the first time in sixteenth- and seventeenth-century England.

If London was important for innovation in pre-industrial occupations, it was equally important in fostering the large-scale growth of a new urban form with important economic implications, the suburb. Of course, medieval towns had had their suburbs. Leland's tour is full of observations on suburbs, such as the two outside Northampton to the south and west; so usual was it for towns to have them by the 1530s that he picks out Hull as being odd for having none. Such suburbs as these had been important manufacturing areas, being away from guild and corporation control. It was not the presence of the London suburb that was a new phenomenon, rather the scale and rapidity of its development. Suburban development had taken place in two distinct directions from the City. On the one hand, there was a slow westward development of residential suburbs especially around Covent Garden; but this was primarily an eighteenth-century movement. The other direction of expansion was eastward, down river from the Tower, a development of the late sixteenth and the seventeenth century, primarily for manufacturing, ship-building and refining. Suburban growth on this scale was entirely new: other towns had their suburbs, but they very often had open spaces within their walls too, which London certainly did not. By the middle of the seventeenth century London's manufacturing activity was increasingly to be found outside rather than inside its core, for the first time in the history of any English town. Suburban population grew enormously, as newcomers from all over England streamed into the area.

What were the reasons for this predominantly eastern development of the London suburbs? Firstly and most importantly, there was the proximity of a widening river Thames with as yet unbuilt-up banks which encouraged shipbuilding, repairing and provisioning. Secondly, there was the need to supply the people of London with necessities, and hence a rapid growth of food trades, brewing, tanning, soapmaking, starchmaking and sugar refining. Much of the material for supplying the construction industry came from here, too: there was brick- and tile-making, lime-burning and glassmaking. Thirdly, there was a concentration of textile-making, much of it by refugees from abroad who could be more easily and cheaply housed than in either the overcrowded city or the increasingly fashionable west.[148] Detailed occupational breakdowns of such parishes as Stepney, whose riverside was already quite crowded by the early seventeenth century, show the diversity of occupations already established there. It was quite as marked in its diversity as any provincial town or port; indeed the suburban population of London east of the Tower alone was larger than most English provincial cities by the end of the seventeenth century.[149]

London was the only town in pre-industrial England with suburban growth on this scale. The phenomenon was not restricted to the contiguous built-up area, for, uniquely amongst English towns, there was across the river for a long time an administratively separate but functionally intertwined town, Southwark. This was much more than a suburb *super flumen*. Here in Southwark was a considerable clothing and leather industry, and a great variety of other general trades and crafts. For most of their customers, the traders and craf smen of Southwark looked to the city. This was especially true of the victualling trades. The large numbers engaged as butchers, bakers and brewers, and in some cases the very scale of their activities, indicated that they were supplying an area greater than the borough. The city constantly, and eventually successfully, fought to get control of this place;[150] just as it struggled to impose its will on some of the peripheral northern parishes. Its position amongst the towns of England, therefore, was not merely as one of them writ large; it was instead entirely different. There seemed between 1500 and 1700 no foreseeable limit to its economy or its size, unlike even the most important provincial cities, like Bristol or Norwich. These had grown by no more than three, or at the most four, times between 1500 and 1700, when they had populations no bigger than 30,000. London had grown by eleven or twelve times over the same two centuries, from 50,000 to nearly 600,000. London could feed on itself, on the (albeit slowly) growing economy and population of the country, and on burgeoning overseas trade. Provincial capitals seemed by contrast limited, not stimulated, by the marketing, manufacturing, administrative and social roles they played within their regions and in relation to the capital. The 'excess' economic and demographic energies of the region were both siphoned off to, and increasingly during the sixteenth and seventeenth centuries directed by, London and *not* their regional centres. It is arguable that London was not to achieve ever again the order of overweaning dominance it had over other English towns between 1500 and 1700; if this was the period which saw them increasingly trying to ape the capital's style, it was also the period when it became lastingly clear that there would only be one primate city in England.

Unknown Aspects of the Urban Economy

There are at least five aspects of the economy of pre-industrial towns about which very little is known, compared with, for example, occupational structures or marketing. These can be summarized as: figures of urban output, whether by volume or value; the exact size, role and economic implications of the numerous poverty-stricken sections of society; the direct role of agricultural activity by town-dwellers; individuals and their economic behaviour; and the typical internal economic geography of a pre-industrial town.

Of urban output next to nothing is known in detail, except for the few exported manufactures which were regulated and recorded, like cloth. We sometimes know about their relative standing by virtue of the taxation that was levied on them,[151] but of their output and production we know very little. The proportion of the most economically effective sector in corporate towns is recorded fairly precisely; for instance about a thousand of Exeter's population of

11,000 in the mid-1670s were freemen, and the annual average proportion of merchants was about nineteen per cent of the yearly figure for all freemen. The merchant company comprised quite a large part of the economically and socially privileged section of the citizens.[152] Yet what they bought and sold, what they produced, is hardly known; generally only indirect evidence of this may be obtained from an individual's inventory records of his work. In Norwich by the later seventeenth century there was a growing concentration of weaving processes within the actual city,[153] rather than as before in the countryside around; what this meant in quantitative terms to urban cloth output and value can be surmised only from the qualitative evidence of contemporaries as to widths, lengths and numbers of cloths produced.

It is occasionally possible to measure the size of the – by modern standards enormous – poor sector[154] of a pre-industrial town's population; but what they contributed to the economy on the one hand, and what sort of drain on the urban economy they represented on the other is very hard to ascertain. The hardest thing of all is to define what 'poor' meant at that time. Rather than being the 'not very well off' and 'not as well off as we would like them to be', of our modern welfare society, they were clearly actually poverty-stricken; they often lacked even basic shelter, clothing, food and employment in anything like adequate supply. The most reliable indicators of the actual size of the poor sector are contained in the few tax returns which record those exempt from taxation: but not enough is known about the taxes of the day to be sure that exemption equalled true poverty, which in its turn meant life below subsistence level for substantial periods of the year. It has been estimated that this category rarely made up less than twenty per cent of a town's adult population, and that it could reach fifty per cent. Parker states that in a medium-sized town like Kings Lynn a third of its population lived more or less permanently below subsistence level. These people leave almost no record of their way of life, and nothing remains of their houses.[155] By the time of the taking of the Hearth Taxes they probably averaged a third of the population of most towns of any size, and had been a growing problem as the increasing welter of Tudor and Stuart legislation on vagrancy and settlement demonstrated whilst failing to control the problem. There was probably a bigger proportion of them in larger than smaller towns, because of the, however wrongly perceived, opportunities for work and poor relief presented to the growing vagrant classes. Indeed, the opportunities for seasonal employment in the fields that still surrounded and dominated the economy of smaller towns were greater for their poor, whilst not presenting so much of a lure to transients. In rural areas of noted manufacture the recorded poor section of small town and village society could be quite large, ranging between about five per cent for the smallest village to over twenty per cent in the largest town of one Suffolk hundred in the early sixteenth century.[156]

It is probable that in larger towns the poor represented more of a drain than a contribution to the economy. For they had increasingly to be controlled, administered, and sometimes put into workhouses or have work found for them. Corporate attempts to put the poor to useful work were rarely more than a palliative for a few; in York, for instance, attempts to promote manufacture for the employment of the poor had been fruitless. Sometimes their bones were set at town expense, and often their burial was provided for. They certainly wanted and sometimes got, indoor and outdoor relief in cash or kind; beggars were licensed and badged. This all cost something, but it was essentially charity. There was no modern redistribution of earned and unearned income. The cost, impossible to measure, was not so great as to be allowed to distort either individual or urban economies. The terrible fact is that often the poor did not enter the economy either as givers or takers. They often simply did not matter economically, although they were of social concern, and of concern to the forces of law and order. They entered into the economy from time to time to sweep or clear or carry, and as quickly left it again. They entered the records of the day rarely, usually on the occasion of their birth or death and occasionally as they were exempted from taxation or whipped. Much is said about the role of poor in towns, but little is actually known about them quantitatively.

The same could be said of the role of rural occupations and activities by townsfolk, as distinct from the marketing of rural produce to which much attention has been devoted. It is by now a commonplace[157] observation that rural activities engaged sometimes part, and sometimes all, of townspeople's time. This is especially the case with smaller places; just as the poor were probably less absolutely important in them so rural activities were proportionately the more so. By-employment combined with farming could be as important to their inhabitants[158] as manufacturing activity could be to country-dwellers; that is not to say that they did not touch larger towns. The exigencies of harvest time seem to have affected the inhabitants of most pre-industrial English towns outside London.

London was free of most rural constraints as direct influences on its economy, though it was dependent on the rurally-born for its population; and they undoubtedly both brought with them and sustained many of the rurally born seasonal customs and traditions – like the maypole. The countryside intruded right into the town by means of its supplies being driven on the hoof down the Strand and through Temple Bar into city streets, but it did not come into the rhythm of its economic life. There were farms all around London; Fulham had its market gardens, dependent for their fertility on night-soil brought in boats from the city, while Chelsea and Tottenham had their dairies. There were farms nearby; the hamlet of Bethnal Green, away from the growing riverside parishes had many yeomen and husbandmen; Mile End had yeomen, husbandmen *and* a high proportion of the new suburban-dwelling middle class by the early seventeenth century, like knights, gentlemen, professionals, lawyers and ministers.[159] At the other end of the urban hierarchy, even tiny towns like late seventeenth-century Bury (Lancs) slowly becoming quite specialized – in this case as a textile centre – still had more people describing themselves in their wills at that time as farmers than as in textile trades.[160] The share of production generated by such rural activities in pre-industrial towns is still inadequately quantified, particularly in the case of smaller places where rural labour made up a substantial proportion of all those employed. Their presence in any numbers is a sure indicator of a low level of urban activity.

It is also extremely difficult to illuminate the economic behaviour of individuals within cities and towns. It is usually possible to learn something about the absolute wealth of a man from two major sources, inventories and tax lists, such as the 1524 lay subsidies. Unfortunately, with economic activity focused on the individual, and with the lack of business dynasties and corporate businesses leaving records, there are relatively few detailed sets of personal business papers. It is thus difficult to clothe the bare facts of occupation, wealth and standing with information on how individuals actually carried out their activities, compared with eighteenth-century figures such as the men in the Foley partnership, and important ironmasters around Birmingham like John Jennens.[161] We tend to know most, in the sixteenth and seventeenth centuries, about only the richest individuals, who stand out in tax lists or were noted by contemporaries; of the gainfully employed masses as individuals we know little.[162] In country areas it is always the 'great' people who stand out. In the Wiltshire cloth industry of the late fifteenth and early sixteenth century clothiers like Will Stumpe of Malmesbury were singled out for special mention by Leland, along with Horton of Bradford-upon-Avon, and Bayllie and Langford of Trowbridge:[163] Horton paid seventy per cent of Bradford's contribution to the 1524 lay subsidy: at the other end of the English cloth-making axis of the day were Thomas Spring at Lavenham and the Paycocks in Coggeshall.[164] Often a single individual in the smaller sixteenth-century town dominated it completely, as did 'Great' Tooley in Ipswich.[165] In Ipswich this merchant, with his trading interests in wine with the Biscayan Ports, cloth with the Low Countries and fish with Iceland, owned his great house, the garden of the old Dominican Priory, a brewhouse, and at least three other houses. In the county immediately around Ipswich he had 323 acres of farmland, and another 470 acres further to the north; he was a greater landowner than many an armigerous gentleman. Coventry in the 1520s was dominated by three rich men, Richard Master a grocer (who paid nearly one-ninth of Coventry's tax in 1524), Julian Nethermill (a draper), and Henry Pysford (a Merchant of the Staple); the three together paid over a quarter of the town's tax, while Robert Jannys (a Norwich grocer) paid nearly as much subsidy there as did the whole city of Rochester.[166] Equally in non-corporate towns like Birmingham, there were a few dominant figures in the economy in the early sixteenth century; the richest men there were William Lench (a grazier and butcher), John Shilton (a mercer), and Humphrey Symonds (a lawyer).[167] Noticeably none of the richest men then in Birmingham, at a time when Leland was already picking it out as a noted centre for iron manufacture, were ironmasters, ironmongers or metalmen.

It is not only the very richest and most dominating men that we know about, however, for we do know in surprising detail about some leading figures in smaller towns.[168] As the sixteenth century progressed, and inventory-taking became more accurate we learn more about individuals. For instance in little Darlington there is the inventory of the dominant figure in the town, John Johnson, who died in 1592; this shows the typical diversity of activity of a leading trader of the day, for he had his haberdashers' and mercers' business as well as a considerable grocers' trade and two farms.[169] Not much farther north, in Gateshead, there was the equally dominating figure of James Cole who died some ten years earlier; his son continued to diversify his father's smithing and fishing activities into lending money at interest and banking in Gateshead and Newcastle-upon-Tyne;[170] when he died in 1620 he was 'worth an immense sum in bills, bonds, and mortgages'. And in Newcastle itself a few hostmen (a term denoting involvement in the coal trade, in that town) dominated the emerging metropolis of the north in the seventeenth century; such were Sir Thomas Riddell, Sir George Selby and Thomas Liddell, men of huge wealth, as was Sir Nicholas Cole, described as 'fat and rich, vested in a sack of Sattin'.[171] It remains unclear to what extent individual figures with great riches, such as these, steered the economic course of towns; it is probable that dominant individuals, or a set of them, would have the chance actually to direct the course only of smaller towns, and that their role would be reduced as the two centuries passed and greater urban growth set in. By 1700 the age of the Olympian merchant was passing into that of the joint-stock company, the bank, and the partnership.

It must be concluded that at present we can expect to know very little about the economic behaviour of lesser men. We do know an increasing amount about the different locations within the towns of people involved in various economic activities, though in no less sketchy form than our knowledge of internal social and demographic geography, discussed in Chapter 3. As there undoubtedly were within the pre-industrial city parts which were richer or poorer, with larger or smaller households, or were more or less populous, so there was also some concentration of different economic activities within towns; this is apparent as much within generalized as specialized town economies. Concentration is a more apposite word than segregation. Since most pre-industrial towns were generalized rather than specialized in their economic activity, their internal economic geography was also generalized. In Coventry in the 1520s, by no means an economically specialized town, there was no mistaking the geographical concentration of activities in certain quarters of the city; but even in the most extreme cases of concentration, those of the butchers and the cappers, there was considerable overlapping of activities. This is exactly the same with Coventry's social structure; certain neighbourhoods near the heart of the city were biased towards the wealthier levels of society, but none was totally exclusive to higher or lower socio-economic groupings.[172] The same was the case in late-medieval Kings Lynn. Here, characteristic layout and use of building plots was the rather generalized pattern of zoning by occupation which emerged from the economically rational exploitation of the site of the town and its communications. There were not whole streets given over exclusively to one occupation, but there were certain clearly defined areas where merchants, tradesmen or craftsmen were most likely to be found – dyers and fullers near running water and fishermen on good moorings, for example.[173] In Elizabethan Winchester, the cloth trade was localized in the north-eastern part of the city, particularly in Tanner Street and Birch Street through which passed two branches of the River Itchen vital for fulling and dyeing.[174] Similarly in seventeenth-century Exeter the manufacturing quarter of the city was concentrated, in this case to the west of the line made by the City's North Street and South Street; on the slopes descending to the river, and in the low-lying 'island' district dissected by mill leats, fulling mills were to be found. This apparent dominance of manufacturing by cloth-making in Exeter impressed foreign visitors – like Count Magalotti in 1669.[175]

By far the most detailed evidence, however, for occupational segregation in the mid- and later seventeenth century is for Newcastle-upon-Tyne, from the work of Howell and of Langton.[176] Using the simple descriptive method of locational quotients, Langton is able to demonstrate that Newcastle did not have a clear pyramidal business district, and was 'four sectored'. There were concentrations of merchants and hostmen, of shipbuilders, of butchers, and others; yet, Langton argues, 'this tendency towards the spatial grouping of craft activities must not be exaggerated. Some trades were scattered through many wards, some through a few widely separated ones, and some wards contained concentration of a few trades which were in no ways affinitive. Moreover, in no case was there absolute concentration and in all trades there were 'stragglers', scattered willy-nilly across the city.'[177] Rather than strict segregation of crafts and a rigidly differentiated internal economic geography, it is clear that most towns of any size had a fairly generalized economic geography, with notable concentrations superimposed on it; the economic sectors of so many nineteenth-century towns were absent. Approaching Kendal in Westmorland in 1695, for example, the traveller would be struck by the great concentration of leather manufacturing in the High Gate area, which then stank with dressing hides and tanpits; here lived most of the cobblers, shoemakers and cordwainers of the town. Yet the activities of the rest of the town were generalized.[178] Equally, the High Street of Bristol in 1695 was lined with shops: those of a draper, a vintner, a hatter, an upholsterer, a mercer, a woollen draper, two grocers, and two milliners. Behind the High Street however, were, a variegated assortment of economic activities. This evidence comes from the 1695 tax on Births, Deaths, Marriages etc., which gives occupations only for one parish, St Nicholas, through which the High Street ran, and reveals that some of these shopkeepers were wealthy and paid at the surtax level.[179]

We would expect there to be a strong correlation between urban social and demographic geography on the one hand, and urban economic geography on the other. This is certainly the case in most towns. In Exeter, for example, at the time of the taking of the Hearth Tax, only $2\frac{1}{2}\%$ of taxpayers paid on ten hearths (the richest families); $8\frac{1}{2}\%$ paid on 6-9 hearths (almost exclusively the merchants); 19% paid on 3-5 hearths (largely master craftsmen and the more prosperous shopkeepers); 25% paid on 2 hearths (often woollen workers and journeymen-craftsmen); 45%, by far the biggest group, paid on one hearth (poor craftsmen in a myriad of trades and activities, as well as labourers).[180] There was in addition a clear spatial expression of this social diversity, with all its demographic implications. Certain levels of society and certain economic activities were concentrated in certain areas of the town, but this concentration was not the dominant feature of Exeter; it was, like its marked cloth area near the river, rather its most noticeable feature. Langton has referred to the same generalized/ specialized pattern in Newcastle. Here 'the core areas of the wealthier trades contain the wealthier members of those trades and, in addition, "creamed off" the wealthiest practioners of crafts whose membership were generally poorer. Furthermore, the core areas of poorer trades contained only the less wealthy members of those trades and the poorest practioners of crafts which were generally wealthier'.[181] At a time when London had at least 225 different occupations, in the 1690s, the picture of generalization and specialization existing side-by-side in its economic geography is naturally most advanced. There were some occupations in London which were notably concentrated, and all of them paid surtax in the 1692 Poll Tax. Glass's sample produced 26 types of occupations paying surtax, including a diamond cutter, 88 merchants and 33 haberdashers,[182] most of which were strongly localized in spatial distribution, but set in a highly generalized economic scene. It is clear that the few well-established models of socio-economic differentiation which might be applied to the pre-industrial town do not apply, at least in their pure form, to England.[183]

5

Town and Country; Town and Sea

This chapter is concerned with trade and migration. These were the strongest links which bound town and country together by land and water in pre-industrial England; two lesser ones were manufacturing, landowning and farming interests held by townsfolk in the country, or, more unusually, by countryfolk in the town. Towns could not have existed, could not have maintained themselves or grown without the two vital raw materials – people and food – which flowed increasingly into towns of any size between 1500 and 1700. London's astonishing rate of growth could certainly not have taken place without them, nor could that of many a lesser place. Towns, in addition to being consumers of food and employers of men and women, were a vital focus for the economic and social life of the country. Here goods were gathered in, sold and redistributed; here fashions were flaunted and imitated. Towns in a predominantly agrarian country with over three-quarters of the nation's people living in the countryside, were at a truly vital confluence of flows. They were diffusion centres of many of the artifacts of modernization that were changing England before the onset of industrialization.

The strong interrelationships of town and country in a predominantly rural society have been a constant theme of this book. It has been emphasized that the mores of rural society and the rhythms of the farming year pressed as urgently into towns as did foodstuffs and immigrants. The walls that surrounded even the biggest provincial cities were rarely used for defence, and were merely symbolic divides from the countryside. Gates may have been shut against travellers as the curfew bell rang, but the time had long passed since city air made men free from bondage or even slavery in England; and while the organization of society through corporate and burghal mechanisms may have differentiated town from country in a legalistic sense, for many of the smallest towns the manor court was as important as in any village. It would be difficult at first sight to tell many a little market town from a village. Braudel sums it up best when he observes:

> The essential problem at the beginning and throughout the life of towns in Europe and elsewhere, remains the same: the division of labour between the countryside and the urban centres, a division which has never been perfectly defined and which calls for continual reassessment, because the positions of the partners change incessantly. The former is always being recast in one or other direction . . . In fact town and countryside never separate like oil and water because the bond uniting them neither breaks nor pulls one way only. They separate and draw closer together at the same time, split up and then regroup . . . As for the innumerable small towns, they were barely outside the framework of country life . . . If the town did not completely surrender the monopoly of crops or stock raising to the countryside, conversely the countryside did not give up all its industrial activities in favour of nearby towns. It had its share of them, although they were generally those activities the towns were glad enough to leave to them. For a start the villages had never been without craftsmen . . . Every large village had its shoeing mill.[1]

Rural Activities, Rural Ownerships

Some townsfolk thus engaged all or part of their working year in what we would think of as 'rural' activities. Other townsfolk, rather fewer in number but greater in importance, owned, and sometimes worked, farm land. Rural influences could go even deeper than this. For example, in Norwich, England's second biggest city, in the early sixteenth century many textile workers in worsted manufacture were given the harvest month off to help get in the crops.[2] Not all of these people could have been regularly involved in rural activities, still less would have owned land. Yet the demands of harvest work ensured that help was given by city-dwellers and workers toward the continuity of their own food supply. This must not be exaggerated, as urban populations and manufacturing specialization grew over the period 1500 and 1700, agriculture too became slowly more specialized, transport systems for the inter-regional distribution of foodstuffs more integrated and the direct impact of the harvest on great cities lessened.

Many townsfolk owned a few animals or a patch of garden ground within or on the edge of a town, but this cannot be dignified with the term rural landownership. Even in the late seventeenth century in a town like Kendal, the burgage tofts (burghers lands) running down to the river were under cultivation. Scores of probate inventories for the period in Kendal show that many tradesmen kept their own animals, and engaged in a little husbandry; indeed some of them lived in what were essentially the converted farmhouses of an earlier age.[3] Earlier in the seventeenth century, and even more so in the sixteenth, husbandry was an important activity of medium-sized towns like Leicester. Husbandry in one form or another was the most general by-occupation of townsfolk of all classes, a number had their own dairies, and the town had a profoundly rural visual quality. Pigs and cows went their ways about Leicester's streets, though they were usually ringed or herded; as late as 1610 it was necessary to forbid winnowing of grain in the streets.[4] This was hardly surprising; it is clear that in 1586, for instance, among those sowing corn in the town fields were town-dwelling innholders, mercers, a tanner, and a victualler.[5] Agriculture was probably even more important earlier in the sixteenth-century; this was the case even in emerging manufacturing centres like Birmingham. Holt warns, however, that the economic significance of agriculture in slowly specializing towns like sixteenth century Birmingham should not be misunderstood:

> artisans should not be seen simply as men who combined industry with agriculture; rather, they were craftsmen to whom agriculture offered a useful element of household supply, an insurance against the future and, we may be sure, a form of recreation as a welcome alternative to the smithy. The rural aspects of the town, such as the barns, crofts and sheep-folds scattered amongst the houses, and the few rich graziers, should not be seen as other than a superficial gloss on the real business of Birmingham.[6]

A cursory inspection of the inventories of townsfolk between 1500 and 1700 in most small and medium-sized towns shows a predominance of rural activities. Rural occupations may have been less important in the larger towns but their importance in the economy of towns both large and small is difficult to calculate exactly. It may be best to regard agriculture as of supplementary rather than basic importance to the larger towns, but of fundamental importance to the economy of the many little towns which, though they might have a market, had yet to reach a population of a thousand by 1700.

Ownership of farm land was common for the pre-industrial townsman but its extent and importance to the urban economy is difficult to measure. Generally, most landownership seems naturally to have been within the immediate urban region of any town, which can be defined by a whole host of functions ranging from administrative and legal to economic. This was the natural ambit for most extra-mural urban activity. Most towns of any status exercised administrative functions (such as the courts) over the surrounding countryside, and many had a sphere of economic influence which was determined by the effective radius of their markets; this was also the sphere over which their social dominance was most marked, and their role as an information centre most noted. Most migrants to the towns were drawn from one particular area which provided the setting for an intense and fluctuating system of short-range movements, consequent on periods of urban or rural residence by individuals, or on marriages between country and town residents, or as a result of boys coming to town to learn a trade or girls to spend a period in service, before returning to their home village. Such spheres of influence were unlikely to extend more than a few miles from small towns, or further than fifteen or twenty miles from even the largest city, other than London. This was the area of local mobility. Thresholds for the spheres of influence of towns of different sizes may be expected to exist and the spheres themselves may be amenable to mapping, and even expression in a geometrical form. It is often helpful to think not of town and country in pre-industrial England, but rather of interrelated socio-economic areas that were centred on a town. This may well be the most functional way of examining, describing and analysing the space economy of pre-industrial England, but it is also as yet the most difficult way. It is almost impossible to calculate and plot these regions except in cases where sources are amenable,[7] or where detailed work on inventories, wills and parish registers has been carried out. For the moment the urban node and regional focus remains the best surrogate for that region's social and economic totality.

Within this informal region of personal contact were to be found most of the farms and estates owned by town-dwellers. Such ownership might extend only to a bit of a toft on the edge of the town or the right to graze a few beasts free of charge on town fields (as still exists for the freeman of Oxford on Port Meadow). It might on the other hand involve the extensive ownership of manors all over a large geographical region, as was the case with 'Great' Tooley of Ipswich in East Anglia.[8] Thompson has held that the spread into the suburbs that began around London in the later seventeenth century was the equivalent of the purchase of manors in the sixteenth century.[9] But this was a phenomenon which only existed only in London on any scale in the seventeenth century. In York at the time many of the principal citizens owned not only city property but also rural estates, and some resided in the country for long periods.[10] Geographic mobility through landownership was of course a predominantly outward phenomenon; urban investment in rural land was considerable and the departure of the sons of wealthy townsmen to the country either through marriage or by taking up residence on their father's estate was a well-established fact of seventeenth-century life.[11] Yet the importance of this trend must not be exaggerated; it affected only a fairly limited band of those in the upper sectors of urban society. In Winchester, for example, rural landholding was apparently confined to 'a few top members of society, and particularly to gentlemen or those with aspirations to gentility'.[12] It was probably also a feature more of the medium-sized and larger towns and cities. In smaller towns like High Wycombe in Buckinghamshire, the duality of urban occupation and rural landownership had different implications. It meant both more and less: less, because it was a much less remarkable feature, for not only the rich and ambitious owned land; more, because landownership was vitally important to the town economy of such little places. In such small towns, rural activities may have contributed as much to the town economy as to its markets and workshops, and urban residents might have been just as much landowners as merchants. In early sixteenth-century High Wycombe a townsman like Robert Ashbrooke possessed great areas of farm land around the town, and in 1524 was by far the wealthiest man in Wycombe, wealthier indeed than the landholding squires of most of the county.[13] Similarly, Gateshead was as interested in the town bull as in the town manufactures or the town trade.[14] Tiny Leighton Buzzard in Bedfordshire was no more than an embryonic town; it possessed a market and a fair, but it was a small community with an economy based in the countryside; property transfers were done in its manorial court, whose court rolls reveal as lively an interest in rural as in urban land.[15] Landownership of farmland was basic to the economic structure of such small places.

Urban Markets and Fairs

One of the most important economic functions of a town was its marketing role. This might be expressed simply in buying and selling in the urban market place and the streets in which stalls and booths were set up during fairs. Town trade was not necessarily restricted to the market and fair, however, and those looking at retail and wholesale functions in the pre-industrial town must consider inns and shops too. The inn was a place in which corn might be factored, bills exchanged and bonds entered into, forwards in commodities bought and sold and information on the state of trade passed on, and as such a focus it developed and flowered between 1500 and 1700. By the mid-eighteenth century inns had probably had their day as great centres for informal exchange, and the time of the corn-exchange and provincial bank had begun, the urban inn returning to the role of providing food, drink, accommodation and gossip. Just as the period saw an increasing division between formal market place and informal trading in inns, so it also saw the rise of the permanent shop, usually with a glass front and a display of goods. The market place, the fair and the trading inn, in pre-industrial times, were at the centre of the crossroads in economic life that the town represented;[16] they were at the centre of the cross-within-the-circle which the ancient Egyptians used as a hieroglyph with which to describe the town: '. . . every town, wherever it may be, is first and foremost a market. If there is no market, a town is inconceivable' some suggest.[17]

There were a number of constraints that generally acted as a brake on the development of urban marketing. These were related to the low population size of most towns and their functional regions. Generally poor, slow and seasonal communications – though these factors must not be over-exaggerated – hampered the volume of goods that could be carried, unless an area had access to water transport. Economies of scale in buying and selling were limited, and it was difficult in restricted trading conditions for sales and turnover to be increased by price-cutting. Clarkson feels that the market was a feeble engine of growth in the pre-industrial economy, whether in the market-place market or outside it.[18] There were urban institutional barriers to marketing, just as in corporate towns there were institutional barriers to the scale of units of production. The most important brake was undoubtedly that, given factors such as poor communications and low population, the average consumer was very poor. On the other hand town markets had advantages, for the nature of urban demand was different from that in the country; there was a concentration of demand from those in upper income brackets, more cash from those enjoying often higher wages, and relatively more elastic demand. The concentration of goods and services that such factors promoted reinforced the advantages urban markets already had for those living in the country regions round and about.

The first intention of most town markets was to provide a place for safe and fair trading. Towns, whether governed by corporation or court-leet tried to ensure this by regulating the sale of foodstuffs and manufactured goods, and often by providing shelter under which trades might sell produce. The 'Acte againste Regratours, Forestallers and Engrossers' passed in 1552 gives a taste of the sorts of activities that those in charge of markets wished to stop, in order to protect the consumer. 'Regrators' were those who brought food-stuffs for immediate resale at a higher price in nearby markets; 'engrossers' were those who bought up produce before it reached the open market, or even whilst it was still growing, in order to control the supply and make the price; 'forestallers' were those who tried to trade before the market bell had been rung, or who bought goods on the way to market trying later to resell them. The arrangement, organization and timing of a market were each aimed at making the goods that were for sale accessible to all; sales outside the market limits were frowned on, and elaborate laws for the conduct of trade were published. In provincial cities like York, attempts were made to ensure that markets were well stocked and prices were fair, es-pecially during the periodic years of scarcity of foodstuffs, like 1608, 1622, and 1630–31. Engrossers, forestallers and regrators were sought, apprehended and punished. York's corporation was evidently checking the measures that were used in markets, at the staith (quay) and in private shops too.[19] Such perfections in the control of trading was, alas, rarely achieved.

Not every town or city had a market place, or in the case of London and other great cities, enough of them. City of London authorities constantly tried, by the construction of markets, to get marketing off the streets in which it was largely conducted before the Great Fire. Newgate, Money Lane and Woolchurch markets were opened as public ones, and Leadenhall (the largest and most important of the four city retail markets) was reorganized; the city authorities at the same time abolished the old street stalls between Greenchurch Street and Lime Street.[20] In Ipswich, the Market Cross of the town was situated on the Cornhill, which was the only large space in the town that was devoted to markets. The physical layout of its marketing facilities[21] resembled Warrington in its utilization of several streets, rather than Preston which had a market place large enough to accommodate most trading, though even here

it spilled into surrounding streets.[22] In most places the space
afforded for marketing was not generous; of Leeds it was said in
1628 that 'The houses . . . are verie thicke, and close connected
together, beinge ancient meane and lowe built . . . the shambles,
with a narrow streete on both sides, much annoyinge the whole
towne; yet for theire Conveniencie, and wante of roome, not to be
avoided, or placed elsewhere'. Fiennes described Manchester as
having a 'very large Market Place' which 'takes up two streets'
length when the market is kept, for their linen cloth [and] cotton
tickings'. In Banbury the Thursday market spilled down the streets,
and it was divided into sections according to its street names: there
was Ox Market, Sheep Market, Horse Market, Flax Chipping,
Swine Market, Corn Market, etc. In Lancashire, 'the assignment of
different trades to separate sites was a feature common to all the
larger markets, among which may be included Wigan and Lancaster, but most of the weekly markets of Lancashire were so small
that segregation was unnecessary'.[23] In smaller places facilities, if
not crowded, were certainly often primitive. There could be few
more damning descriptions than that of James I about Darlington,
'Darnton i' the dirt'. The little market place of Darlington and its
surrounding streets were unpaved and after the cattle fairs they
must have been befouled by droppings;[24] squalor existed next to
richer townsfolks' houses. Most towns tried to improve their market
facilities from time to time. Many market squares were built over;
by the sixteenth century that in Bicester, Oxfordshire, had been
covered with shambles for the butchers, and the first Town House in
which courts were held and trade conducted had been built.[25]
Dudley in Worcestershire was paving some of its streets and
building a new market house in 1653;[26] and in 1691 at Walsall the
town corporation took down the old Market Crosse and built a new
Town House which was to be shelter for trading, for courts, and for
a charity school.[27]

Yet, despite such civic endeavours, the institutional and physical
facilities for marketing in towns were becoming increasingly inadequate. Partly this was due to an, albeit slow, growth in the population and economy that put a strain on existing modes of marketing
and market institutions. It was also due to the inflexibility of the
often antiquated facilities of the average market town, which proved
incapable of accommodating all the expansion in marketing; its
regulations were not sufficiently adaptable to meet growing
specialization and the slowly emerging division between retail and
wholesale trades. Open market facilities, for example, were ill-suited

to large-scale forward deals in foodstuffs; these were better carried out by private transactions outside the formal market, often in an inn. The price revolution and the growing prosperity of some people affected buildings, and altered both the marketing mechanisms and the physical aspect of towns. Thus many small English towns like the Oxfordshire markets of Thame and Banbury and new inns, as well as the new and enlarged houses built for the wealthier members of the community. This trend was particularly noted in larger towns, but also on main traffic routes.

Everitt has demonstrated the importance of thoroughfare towns: St Albans had twenty-seven inns, one of the highest figures for any town in England. The growth in the number and sizes of inns in market towns like Croydon is marked from the seventeenth century; inns on main traffic routes benefited especially from improved road surfaces and the introduction of the coach. At Banbury, eight new inns were recorded in the mid-seventeenth century, and more in the second half. Of course, these were not only used by merchants, corn badgers and malt factors coming to market. The curious traveller was growing in number, and the country gentleman was also often in town, perhaps as a magistrate or for some social event. It was their development as trading centres that represented the greatest contributions of inns to the economy.[28] The market place and the market day remained, however, the natural focus for such deals; it was the market on its appointed day which brought traders to town, sure that they would meet others of their kind. There were, according to Everitt, about 760 market towns in Tudor and Stuart England, all of which changed and adapted between 1500 and 1700.[29]

The major trend of market towns that can be seen in the pre-industrial period is one of slow rationalization of their numbers, a rationalization that paralleled the movement of some market activities out of the market place into the arena of private transactions. There were already by 1500 far fewer markets than there had been three hundred years earlier. This does not necessarily mean that there were fewer market towns as such, for the decline was due to the failure of over-speculative implantation of markets in villages in the medieval period. Yet there was also a slight decline in the numbers of market towns between 1500 and 1700, two centuries which saw relatively few new market foundations. Much more importantly, there was a slow decline in the standing of a number of markets, usually in less specialized, smaller towns. This has been brilliantly charted by Everitt.[30] Such a sequence of events was bound to occur with slowly improving transport systems, which ensured that the larger places with better locational advantages could flourish at the expense of their lesser brethren. Such changes must be set against the long-term history of the market in England, however, for markets of a traditional sort were still vitally important well into the nineteenth century. Such movement of the relative positions and standing of markets was as much a feature of thirteenth-, and nineteenth-century England as it was of the period 1500–1700. It meant no dramatic change in the urban systems of the day, simply being the result of slow alterations in the structure of national and regional marketing systems. After about 1660, there was an increased tendency for smaller market towns to decline absolutely as well as relatively, though total decline for many of them did not occur until the eighteenth century.

By 1770, Everitt tells us, while the bigger market towns were busier than ever before, many of the smaller ones, perhaps a third of the country's total, had gone.[31] Blome's great topographical work is full of references in the later seventeenth century to markets being 'very inconsiderable' or 'very mean' or 'in a manner disused'. Winchelsea presented a 'pitiful Spectacle of Poverty and Desertion'.[32] In Suffolk, the fortunes of Needham Market declined as the influence of the bigger Stowmarket, only a few miles away, increased.[33] It was places the size of Stowmarket or larger which had the scale to accommodate increased marketing, to provide a wider range of facilities, and withstand competition; lesser markets could not do so. Lancashire's county town, Preston, slowly swallowed the trade of little markets around it, like Kirkham, Chorley and Garstang.[34] It was an age of the slow concentration of marketing; many medieval trading centres were left with the appearance of mere villages.[35] On the other hand, while they often lost their tiny weekly markets, such towns might gain a retail shop or two, which in many ways carried on daily the functions previously fulfilled weekly by the market. The decline of the small market town might thus not be as serious as it seems at first sight; it was more the case that the mode of selling changed.

Some quite substantial towns like Stamford in Lincolnshire barely maintained their relative standing, and it was not only the smaller towns which suffered.[36] Some middle-sized towns were not totally protected from the exigencies of competition on their marketing facilities, as comparative locational advantages changed with alterations in regional economies. For instance, the seventeenth century saw considerable development of manufacturing in both north and south Staffordshire. This was bound to affect marketing. The county town of Stafford, and its market, did not benefit as much as might be expected from increased demand generated by these developments, and the town's economic role in the county was adversely affected by the growth of the newer manufacturing areas, for Lichfield (even though its manufactures suffered from this new industrial competition) was better fitted locationally to serve them.[37] In none of these cases, or even in that of London (whose market area was all England), did the marketing function alone lead to notable urban growth as it might have done to some extent in the medieval period. Real urban superiority was always, *inter alia,* based on adequate formal and informal marketing facilities and reasonably flourishing markets. Yet there are no cases in the pre-industrial period of any tearaway urban growth based on marketing alone; when such growth occurred, it was almost invariably because of some highly specialized activity as in shipbuilding centres or spa towns, as we saw in Chapter 4. No provincial town ever reached a position of great urban centrality simply because of market speciality; the great provincial capitals depended rather on their manufacturing or port facilities. Nonetheless, if a town had no particularly specialized manufactures, but rather a generalized array of craft, trading and service occupations, then the extent of its trade was to a large degree influenced by the size of profits made on agricultural produce sold in its markets. The food and raw material (wool, leather, etc.) markets often acted as lure for other trades, and in the extreme case represented by the capital's westward suburban expansion, the foundation of markets like Covent Garden in 1661, Hungerford in 1680 and Red Lion Court in 1688 preceded the estate planning and development phases.[38]

As the urban market system was slowly rationalized, so specialization in marketing tended to increase, reflecting regional production to some degree, but also the slow integration of a national economy with more sophisticated demands. Everitt shows how between 200 and 300 of England's markets were specializing in some product or another in the seventeenth century: over a hundred of these in corn, just under a hundred in cattle, over twenty in malt, and about a dozen in horses or in cheese and butter.[39] It was not only in food stuffs that markets found their specialization. The markets of Leeds and Exeter were famous for their cloth, with a huge turnover and great value, while people were going from all over England to the little Northamptonshire town of Kings Cliffe for turned wooden objects and tools; and wooden plates, spoons and implements were marketed on a regional and national scale from Wymondham in Norfolk.

Probably both the greatest volume and the greatest value of trade was in agricultural produce, notably corn.[40] Most towns had a market in this bulky commodity which was usually imported from the immediate vicinity. A few of them located on or near water became specialized as corn-marketing and forwarding centres. Such was the port of Chichester on the Sussex coast, or the towns like Reading and Henley that acted as collecting points for the grain travelling down river systems, such as that of the Thames. On a local or regional scale, however, most places had a variety of corn-marketing centres. In north-eastern Kent, besides the Canterbury food market itself, there were a number of other local centres such as Sittingbourne, Milton, Faversham, Whitstable, Herne, Margate and Ramsgate; together they probably consumed about twice as much corn and foodstuffs as did Canterbury, though a number of the coastal towns were also involved in serving the lucrative London market.[41] Most other goods and agricultural products had their special markets. Bark, used in the tanning process, was marketed notably in Canterbury and Maidstone in Kent, and Guildford on the River Wey in Surrey collected the bark produced from Surrey, Sussex and part of Hampshire.[42] Banbury, in the heart of midland England was equally noted for its cattle and its horse trade.[43] Many other such examples exist and they have been listed in detail elsewhere.[44] The possession of a specialized market may well have attracted extra trade to a town, particularly if associated with one or more annual fairs; however, it was unlikely by itself to engender any spectacular growth.

If a town managed to become a centre for local social activity this, too, could enhance its reputation, its size and certainly the wealth of its tradesmen. Most counties had one or more local social capitals. From both an economic and a social point of view, this function can be viewed as being concerned with marketing; marriages and society were marketed as much as goods and chattels on fair and market day. There was considerable rivalry between Ipswich and Bury St Edmunds in mid-seventeenth century Suffolk, for instance, at a time when the former's port activities were on the wane. Bury, with no particular manufacture, flourished as a social capital. Heylyn observed of it, 'Bury St Edmunds was accorded a place of much credit in Suffolk, a fine neat town, and much inhabited by the gentry who resort thither from all parts of the county'. Substantial red-brick houses were built there, and quite rich shops crowded the centre of the town by the end of the seventeenth century. A town such as Nottingham grew in social significance, as increasingly through the seventeenth century the local aristocracy and gentry gravitated to it. The social pre-eminence of the town was confirmed in 1674 when the Duke of Newcastle began the building of his great palladian mansion on the site of the old castle; it now possessed the cachet of a ducal seat and became a centre of attraction for people of quality in the neighbourhood. In Lancashire, Preston – 'Proud Preston' – subsisted, it was said, 'by many families of middling fortune . . . and it is remarkable for old maids, because their families will not ally with Tradesmen, and have not sufficient fortunes for gentlemen'. The social role of such towns was vital for their trading fortunes.[45]

It is rare that such growth led to the setting-up of new markets. Some new markets were of course founded, but only unusually as the core of new towns. In the case of the founding of Westerham in Kent, a seventeenth-century market charter merely marked the revival of an earlier trading centre. Most counties had one or two such examples. Stevenage in Hertfordshire got its market in the 1620s, as did Earith in Huntingdonshire, and Blackburn and Colne obtained their markets in Lancashire in the seventeenth century. Cumberland and Westmorland, thinly populated and not very prosperous, had their share too as the local economy slowly advanced; Hawkshead, Ambleside, Shap and Broughton-in-Furness were all seventeenth-century markets, though the most exciting foundation was on the Lowther estates at Whitehaven.[46] This far outgrew in importance by the eighteenth century the already established port town of Workington. This last town should have grown through coal marketing; it had, after all, a good haven on the Derwent, and most Cumbrian coal was going through its port in the early seventeenth century. Locationally, it was well endowed. Yet human factors affecting the small scale of urban development that might well have resulted from coal marketing, served to put a limit on much development. There were disagreements among the freeholders working the coal pits around the town, the multiple ownership of land created obstacles in the way of carting coal to the harbour, and the Lord of the Manor demanded such high payments from the working of collieries and the use of the harbour that exports declined and with them the fortunes of the town.[47]

Much of the changing fortunes of markets and the towns in which they were held, can thus be attributed to structural changes in the economy. Markets could also be rather frail economic institutions, their fortunes often greatly affected by the economic well-being of the towns in which they were situated. Long-term changes in trade could ring the death-knell for some markets, and radically affect the fortunes of the towns in which they were situated. The movement of the focus of the Mediterranean trade in the early sixteenth century from Southampton to London, with disastrous consequences for the former, is an excellent example.[48] All markets naturally were affected by changes in the domestic economy; and there were fluctuations for those concerned with foreign trade, such as the Hull and Exeter cloth trade. Plagues could wreak havoc with some markets. Hull was struck by plague in July 1637. In an attempt to minimize the spread, the town corporation ordained that all festivities at births and weddings should be banned, drinking in alehouses restrained, and church services suspended. The twice-weekly market was totally suppressed, and a special market set up on the Drypool side of the river until June the following year; similar arrangements were made in the 1643 plague outbreak. Nearby, in York, an epidemic in 1604 had completely dislocated the town's life. The markets were cancelled, the Minster was shut, the Council in the North moved to Ripon and Durham, and the assizes were held at Ripon for at least a year. 'In short, the City lost for some time all those provincial courts which brought so many visitors to buy in its shops and to lodge at its inns'.[49] Most towns of any size could withstand permanent damage to their trade from such causes. But smaller, less economically viable places could be permanently damaged by natural disasters, and their markets wiped out. The market at the tiny town of Heacham in Norfolk was destroyed by a devastating fire in the early seventeenth century; a great storm blew down the Market House at St Mary Cray in Kent in 1703,[50] it was never to be rebuilt, and the market was lost for ever. The scale of marketing at the lower end of the hierarchy of market towns was very small; their economic fortune very vulnerable to permanent damage, either from 'economic', or from 'natural' causes.

Market Areas

There are two ways of looking at the marketing facilities that a town offered: from the point of view of those in the town, and from the point of view of those in the countryside. Looked at from within, markets take on the appearance of the place where citizens obtained urban manufactured produce, and more importantly the produce of the countryside. From the outside, however, urban markets assumed a different appearance. They were places where customers from the surrounding countryside might buy things that were not available locally, such as luxury goods and a wider range of food-stuffs, and obtain services like that of a bookbinder to bind up a diary or some farm accounts, or of a watchmaker to mend a gold turnip. Both townsfolk and countrypeople looked to the market and market day as the place and the time to sell goods and services. It is clear that most towns had an area that might be regarded socially and economically speaking as tributary to them – their 'region'. The immediate three or four miles around any town would be intimately connected with it, by landownership, by outworking for urban manufacturers, by residence of those going in daily to work or sell, and by a myriad of social and economic contacts of an informal sort. Such bands of country immediately around a town could be regarded as permanently part of it in a functional sense, almost in-divisible from it. Further afield, however, there was a wider region within which people commonly looked to the town for marketing, as a social centre, for the dispensation of justice, and for the collecting of news. Each of these functions might have had a different radius, which can be measured and plotted on a map when sources survive that offer evidence; evidence for example of where stallholders came from in the surrounding countryside to sell in the town market, where subscribers to balls and newspapers dwelt, where appellants at courts lived, or where in the countryside urban tradesmen held debts. Each of these could be set on a map (some are shown on Fig. 8), and boundaries for each function drawn. Boundaries would almost certainly not be contiguous, and would overlap; and although they are a good general indication of the approximate area of a town's socio-economic tributary region they do not represent a self-contained entity. The picture was in fact far more dynamic than could be represented on a map, with people choosing to buy and sell in a variety of places.

We know a little about the periodicity with which markets were held in different places near to each other, and we know much less about the periodicity with which people moved their buying and selling activities between various towns and markets. It may well have been more frequent than has been suspected, and fluid marketing habits, while not casting doubt on the validity of the use of the functional urban region as a concept, warn against accepting such regions as rigid realities in either space or time. A farmer like

Henry Best of Elmswell in Yorkshire left a farming book which demonstrated that he showed considerable discrimination in where and when he sold his grain, and that he certainly did not belong in one urban region tributary to one town. Generally speaking, he marketed from Martinmas time (early November), and thereafter sent grain most Saturdays and Wednesdays to the markets at Beverley. But he was not tied to Beverley for an outlet. He sent his wheat sometimes to Malton; barley to Pocklington and Beverley in winter, and to Malton in summer. Market conditions varied enormously. The sale of oats at the Saturday and Wednesday markets at Beverley was always affected by the weather of the previous day, for a calm one allowed the Lincolnshire men to cross the Humber to buy oats at Beverley for re-sale in the Brigg market. Generally speaking, if barley went well at the market at Malton there was usually little for sale at Beverley, whilst if the King was at York there was a good sale to be had to brewers and bakers.[51] The choice of seller and consumer was wide; so wide that in an age where transport was slowly improving, the inflexible picture presented by the area of a town's apparent functional region as plotted on a map seems rather wooden. The band of country a few miles around any town may have been closely and permanently wedded to it, even if trips to bigger and better provided towns were far from out of the question. The country a bit further away, however, might have contained people who changed their allegiances often enough to make one hesitant before talking too firmly about the size of different urban regions. Bigger towns clearly had a greater influence than smaller ones. But it would be a mistake to attempt to draw rigid boundaries of functional regions for different towns unless there were some particular aspect to be mapped. Enough is known empirically to be certain that the picture was quite simple in broad outline, but it was likely to be more fluid in consumer loyalty than once thought.

The major trend to be seen in the development of market areas was undoubtedly that of the larger towns with better facilities increasing their influence, over the two centuries. The best example of this was of course, London, which ever widened its effective marketing range and economic influence in this period. Towards the end of the sixteenth century it was still said that the City drew its supplies 'principalie . . . from some few shires neare adioyninge',[52] although its tentacles were reaching deeper into the nation. By the seventeenth century the cloth merchants of Hull and York were complaining that 'Wee, like little fishes, are swallowed up by a great whale'.[53] By the early eighteenth century Defoe was writing that 'the magnitude of the city influences the whole nation also in articles of provisions, and something is raised in every county in England, however remote, for the supply of London; nay, all the best of every produce is brought hither; so that all the people, and all the lands in England, seem to be at work for, or employed by, or on the account of this over-grown city'.[54] At the other end of the scale were many places where market areas remained rather static. Maldon in Essex, for example, has been described as having a market area that was 'held together by kinship and by common commercial and agricultural careers'. It seemed bound together by common catastrophies, dangers, pressures, and opportunities, maintaining constant intercommunication through its wayfaring life, markets and fairs. Its market area, as most broadly defined, was very large. It reached up to north-central Essex, to the headwaters of the Stour and the Colne; westward it went ten or twelve miles out to Chelmsford and the fringes of the Roding villages which bordered on Hatfield Forest, and northwards it extended down to Epping Forest and the Thames-side villages. But this area was not exclusive to Maldon, though its influence was felt throughout it. Other towns also had their share of that countryside and its economic potential: Braintree, Brentwood, Rayleigh, and Chelmsford, besides smaller markets like Burnham-on-Crouch. Economically, Petchey observes that Maldon was 'not a centre nor dominant'.[55] This was the case with most towns, urban regions being a reality in some senses, but rather formal academic constructions in others.

Three forces seemed to affect the market area of the typical pre-industrial town. In ascending order of importance these were: transport facilities, the level of economic activity of a town and the area surrounding it, and the population of a town and the area surrounding it. The second and third forces are obviously closely inter-connected, while transport is perhaps the least important. Most transport to market on a regular basis was on men's backs, on packhorses and in wagons; or on small, slow boats plying on what were usually unimproved rivers. Values and volumes of both are likely to remain elusive. Generally, heavy and low value goods could either simply not be carried because of their bulk, or only at such costs as to make road transport impossible. Of roads and road transport in the sixteenth century very little is known, and very little may ever be known. Though we have knowledge about the condition of Elizabethan highways (to use the contemporary term), we can detect an increased interest in them and their use.[56] If road surfaces only improved slowly, and road-building technology lagged behind even the slow advances in agricultural or industrial techniques, the sorts of vehicles travelling on them did slowly improve. Heavy duty stage wagons and then sprung coaches for passengers and higher value parcels were introduced. More than anything else there was an improvement in the regularity of the carrying systems travelling on the roads. Stage wagons lumbered over the clays from Ipswich to London on a regular basis from the 1590s. Regularity meant that tradespeople could depend on goods reaching their towns at certain times, and was probably as important a leap forward as most improvements in actual transport technologies between 1500 and 1700. By the 1630s carriers' networks were so well established that the first directory detailing them, Taylor's *Carriers Cosmographie*, was published; he covered wagoners and carriers, as well as the men involved on the developing foot post.[57] The trend in improving roads and building-up carrying networks in the seventeenth century was fostered by the demands of the towns. Road conditions were by then quite good enough to permit the running of complex systems of regular carrying services;[58] Oxford, Ipswich, Cambridge, Kendal[59] and most other provincial towns by the seventeenth century could rely on regular transport of goods, even if this became costlier and slower in winter months when poor drainage slowed down men, beasts and carts on the roads of the day. Much of the carrying centred on London.

Seasonality also affected the carriage of heavier, often lower cost goods by water to and from towns. In the summer months water levels might be too low to afford easy passage of even tiny boats across shoals and shallows; in winter floods and ice could impede progress. All the year round mills, fish traps and weirs presented their own peculiar problems in hindering river navigation. Despite these problems, Willan concludes that 'The difference in cost between road and river transport suggests that goods would be carried by water when that was possible and convenient . . . river transport leaves very little evidence of its nature and extent. Just as it is difficult to determine the state of the roads, so it is difficult to determine the state of the rivers'.[60]

The five major rivers of England were the Thames, Severn, Great Ouse, Trent and Yorkshire Ouse. Many of England's greatest towns were on or near these rivers which were tidal, and free from hazards for navigation within their tidal limits. Off them radiated many lesser rivers, presenting natural and human impediments to navigation which were often also considerable barriers to trade. There were as yet no canals to improve this situation; navigation and improvement schemes were generally slight in their effect on towns. This was certainly the case on the Wey in Surrey[61] and the upper Medway in Kent.[62] Occasionally towns on much-improved stretches of water could benefit greatly, however. Guildford in the seventeenth century, for example, already had a considerable trade in agricultural products and timber destined for London. There was also an important trade in ordnance and gunpowder made locally on the Tillingbourne stream at Chilworth. The opening of the Wey navigation greatly eased the problems of transporting the powder, which hitherto had to be carried by cart overland to Weymouth, and thence by boat to London; barges on the navigation were also carrying rags and papers to and from the paper mills at Stoke and Byfleet. The possession of a really improved head of navigation must have widened Guildford's effective economic region, and Defoe, with his eye for commerce and trade, shows how timber was brought there from Surrey, Sussex and Hampshire.[63] The effects of such improvements to navigation on towns was limited by the small number and size of such schemes; there were certainly no urban creations consequent on them in the sixteenth and seventeenth centuries, as there were in the eighteenth century, with canal ports, like Goole.[64]

Those towns which benefited from river transport, and had large regions linked to them because they had this facility, were essentially those on tidal rivers. York is a case in point,[65] as is Hull. Ignoring for the moment the rapidly declining seaport role of the former city, and the rapidly increasing role of the latter, both benefited greatly because of the navigable river on which they were situated. York collected lead from Derbyshire, which was joined by grain, butter and cloth, and sent downstream. Hull imported coal, wine, haberdashery and grocery goods which it trans-shipped for distribution up the Ouse system to York and other towns. At the other end of England, Severn-side towns benefited in the same way. Much of the development in the West Midlands iron trades between the mid-sixteenth and the mid-seventeenth century was reflected in the changing nature of the trade carried on the Severn and channelled through its ports. In the sixteenth century, the boats going downstream carried raw materials to the Bristol craftsmen, and boats coming upstream brought luxury goods, like wine, to Worcester. From the early seventeenth century the trade changed, for the ships going downstream carried manufactured metal goods, like nails, and some trade seemed to begin to bypass older corporate towns, where the ironmongers' trade was diminishing.[66] Much was

sold direct to London dealers. The greatest part of the trade
between Bristol and its Severn riverine hinterland was essentially
carried out below Worcester, especially at the cereal markets of
Tewksbury (also important for leather) and at Gloucester. Dyer
sees the sixteenth-century trade between Bristol and Worcester as
one of the 'colonial' sort already demonstrated for the metal trades,
although this relationship changed in the seventeenth century. This
change was a reflection of the great economic developments taking
place in the upper valley, some of which were independent of larger
downstream towns like Worcester.[67] However, river ports continued
to gain from the overall growth of the economy. As late as the 1750s
Dr Pococke observed on his travels of Shrewsbury, that 'This towne
being one of the highest to which the Severn is navigated, tho' it is
navigable thirty miles higher, is the reason why it is in so flourishing
a condition, as it supplies the country about with many goods
brought from Bristol; and many people come here to go by water to
Worcester, Glocester [sic], Bristol and Bath, and so take coach or
other carriage from Worcester to London'.[68] The effective
hinterlands of towns like Bristol and Shrewsbury were vastly
enhanced because of the possibilities of the two-way speedy carriage
of goods, some like coal too heavy for economic land carriage. Location on a river was as important to urban fortunes and urban market
areas as could be location on the 'great river around England' to
ports.

The size, economic strength and spacing of markets were much
more likely to be affected by levels of local and regional economy,
and population size, than transport. The maps in Figure 9 based on
Everitt's calculations, show something of the numbers of market
towns in south and eastern England; and also the average market
areas of market towns in different counties. Naturally there were
more market towns in southern and eastern England, particularly
along the west–east axis stretching from Devon and Cornwall to
East Anglia, the traditional area of richest farming and manufacturing activity and densest population since medieval times. Even
within these areas there were parts of counties which had few
market towns, as was the case in the Weald, or the sandy areas of
the Norfolk–Suffolk borders. Population and economy are far more
important factors than simple area, and market towns sizes and
market areas were closely related to them. Everitt feels that:

> . . . the ideal distribution of market towns in England would have been at
> a distance of eight or ten miles apart, varying with the density of popula-
> tion and the kind of husbandry of the area. Such a distance would afford

time for the unmounted countryman to walk to market, transact his business, and reach home again by daylight. But even in a county like Kent, where towns were numerous, many folk lived twelve or fifteen miles from their nearest market; there was not a single market town in the Isle of Thanet, the Stour Levels, or the Forest of Blean.[69]

The market areas of towns would vary not only with their own economic importance and 'pull', and with the competition of other a 'jacent local or regional centres, but also with local levels of population and economy. They could also vary for different products. Corn, for example, with its relatively great weight, was likely to be marketed for local consumption at a number of small markets in any one region. That region, however, might contain one great social, administrative and luxury goods centre whose market area for these was the whole of the region, together with one or two specialized markets for horses or cloth which might have a national as well as regional pull. Though corn was carried over great distances by

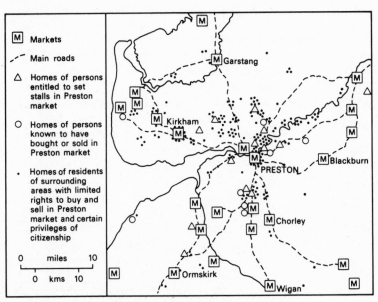

8   Market connections of Preston, Lancashire
    (Based on H. B. Rodgers, 'The market areas of Preston in the sixteenth and seventeenth centuries', *Geographical Studies*, III (1956), 46–93

water for export, most corn sellers and buyers went no more than five to ten miles by land to local markets. Livestock could travel much further more cheaply, and thus the 'livestock radius' of a town might be three or four times as great as its corn radius; high value goods like cloth could have huge, almost nationwide market areas. There is, for example, evidence of linen cloth made in Lancashire being sold in Coventry, Banbury, Witney, Cambridge, Bedford, Newbury, Wellingborough, Northampton, Bury St Edmunds and Daventry, and as far as Southampton.[70]

The trading area of a market town was much influenced by the competition and attractiveness to the consumer of nearby centres, which would present 'intervening opportunities' to the seller or buyer travelling to market. In the case of Worcester, its market area (from the evidence of debts owed to Worcester tradesmen) was an elliptical one, stretching twenty-five miles east–west, and fifteen miles north–south. The maximum distance any regular trader came was between twelve and fifteen miles. The market towns of Droitwich, Bromsgrove, Kidderminster, Stourbridge, Halesowen and Bewdley cut off a large section of north Worcestershire from the city's direct influence, while beyond them were other thriving commercial centres like Birmingham and Wolverhampton. Equally, the city's influence was restricted to the south by Ledbury, Tewksbury, Pershore and Evesham, with Gloucester and Bristol on the Severn behind them. On the other hand, good market centres were fewer to the east and west; in the east there was little before Alcester and to the west to Hereford, Leominster and Ludlow. Worcester's sphere of influence for cattle, however, was much larger than for its traders and shopkeepers, and reached deep into Wales.[71]

In the less populated and prosperous area of the north-west, the market area of Preston can be seen from the evidence in Figure 8, based on work by Rodgers.[72] Like Worcester, it had thrice-weekly markets. No market was held closer than seven miles to the west or south of Preston, and only one (Blackburn) was less than twelve miles away to the east or north. Villages at a considerable distance from Preston preferred to bypass lesser centres like the smaller weekly market at Kirkhaven to get to the bigger centre. Villagers pleaded in 1655 for better drained roads through Markham, so that they could not be ' . . . debarred from the benefitt of the Marquette at Preston'.[73] Its growth as a legal centre (having Quarter Sessions and the Chancery Court of the Duchy of Lancaster) and a growing social role led to it being called 'Proud Preston'; it showed the common tendency of larger, well-located towns to acquire new regional functions by the seventeenth century, to dominate lesser towns and to widen their effective 'market' areas for different functions.[74] Midland centres like Loughborough in Leicestershire served a bigger radius in the seventeenth century and got the grant of more

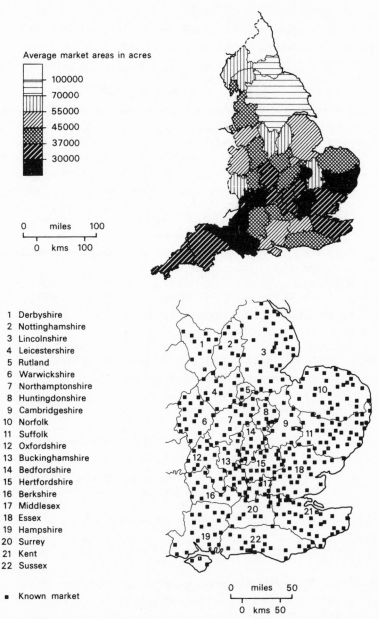

Average market areas in acres

100000
70000
55000
45000
37000
30000

0   miles   100
0   kms   100

1 Derbyshire
2 Nottinghamshire
3 Lincolnshire
4 Leicestershire
5 Rutland
6 Warwickshire
7 Northamptonshire
8 Huntingdonshire
9 Cambridgeshire
10 Norfolk
11 Suffolk
12 Oxfordshire
13 Buckinghamshire
14 Bedfordshire
15 Hertfordshire
16 Berkshire
17 Middlesex
18 Essex
19 Hampshire
20 Surrey
21 Kent
22 Sussex

■ Known market

0   miles   50
0   kms   50

9   Market areas in England and market towns in south-eastern England, 1580–
1640
(Based on A. Everitt, 'The marketing of agricultural produce', in J. Thirsk (ed.),
The Agrarian History of England and Wales, IV, *1500–1640*, 1967)

fairs.[75] In Cheshire, smaller markets were squeezed out by Chester's greater economic and social centrality; it dominated the Wirral, though with some competition from the growing port of Liverpool, and took over the marketing facilities for the inhabitants of the Aldford and Coddington areas. The market area for most towns in Cheshire was above the average of seven miles which lay between them. There is a 1672 list of stall holders in Macclesfield Market, similar to that used for Preston (see Fig. 8), which showed that it attracted traders from a wide area of East Cheshire. Traders were clearly attracted from other market towns in the area, especially from Stockport in the north. Two people came from Derbyshire, and one from Lancashire, some fifteen miles away. It is clear that Macclesfield's market area overlapped considerably with the market areas of Stockport, Knutsford and Congleton; the town drew traders to a lesser extent from the directions of Leek and Chapel-en-le-Frith.[76] The twenty-two markets of late medieval Cheshire had been reduced to a dozen by the eighteenth century.[77]

In Sussex by the end of the seventeenth century East Grinstead had gained considerably by the decay of Crawley's market, as did Horsham. Both extended their hinterlands north into Kent and Surrey. The market area of Lewes by the early eighteenth century appears to have trebled in size since the early sixteenth century, taking over the marketing functions of decayed centres like Ditchling. Cowley observes of Sussex that, generally speaking, 'the mid-seventeenth century may be taken as the period by which most of the smaller centres had either decayed completely or were at least in advanced stages of decay';[78] such were Hailsham, Broadwater, Pevensey or Seaford. Travel in the Weald can not have been quite as bad as contemporaries made it out to be; access to larger centres that were further away was obviously quite possible. Those Sussex markets that survived and flourished into the eighteenth century were the older, traditional centres, which had the advantages of good communications. These were generally situated on, or in close proximity to the main routes to London, and it seems that it was the capital's influence which helped to confirm and underpin their positions. On the other hand, the typical pattern for many smaller places which lost their markets, like Burwash or Rotherfield, was to keep their fairs into the eighteenth century, and to gain shops.[79] The urban fair and urban shop must now be considered.

Fairs and Shops in Town and Country

The role of the fair in towns is extremely difficult to measure. Most towns had at least one, and sometimes several fairs a year. Lists of them, like contemporary lists of markets, abound.[80] Everitt feels that 'The importance of these wholesale trade fairs to English towns from the late sixteenth to the early nineteenth century would be difficult to exaggerate, but we know remarkably little about them'.[81] They certainly helped, as did markets, to bind town and country together, and brought country people into town. Like markets, many fairs began to fail by the sixteenth century. In his *Description of England*, Harrison had noted as early as 1577 that many fairs had become 'paltry' events; little was brought or sold at them apart from 'foode, drinke, pies and some pedleric trash'.[82]

Undoubtedly many fairs were as important for social as for wholesale activities. There were some fairs of huge national and international importance, such as the Stourbridge cloth fair just outside Cambridge, or St Bartholomew's Fair at Smithfield in London. These were picked out for special mention in a proclamation of Charles I made at Woodstock, Oxfordshire in 1625, aimed at limiting that year's plague outbreak: 'remembering that there are at hand two fairs of special note and unto which there is usually extraordinary resort out of all parts of the Kingdom, the one kept in Smithfield, near to the City of London, called Bartholomews Fair, and the other near Cambridge called Stourbridge Fair, the holding whereof at the usual times would in all likelihood by the occasion of further danger and infection in other parts of the land'.[83] There was a significant regional difference in the numbers of fairs and of fair towns – for many fairs were held outside towns, sometimes on hilltops or at cross roads. Hodgen writes:

> One of these regions, composed of the counties of the eastern plain and fenland, and lying northeast of the road running from London to Manchester through Leicester was served by only a few fairs held in widely separated communities. In the other, composed of the counties of the English heartland, the fairs were far greater in number and the fair sites in close proximity. South of this commercial borderland, which was itself marked with many fairs, there were 364 fair towns and 675 fairs; north of the economic frontier, however, there were only 95 fair towns and only 147 fairs. Indeed, three of the counties south of the boundary, namely Kent, Essex and Wiltshire, with 20% of the fairs, were better supplied with trading facilities than the eleven counties north of the boundary, with 17% of the fairs.[84]

Most authorities feel that fairs were of great economic importance in towns when they had a substantial wholesale function, although they are understandably unable to quantify this assumption. Dyer said of Worcester that 'the four annual fairs held at Worcester were of very considerable economic importance . . . like all towns Worcester depended on its flourishing markets to buy its food and sell much of its own produce, and on its fairs to widen that contact with the rural hinterland, that exchange of goods between town and country which was the basis of the urban economy'.[85] In Cheshire, the fair was not defunct as a commercial institution even in the eighteenth-century; markets and fairs were the time-pieces of the local community, major trading institutions, and great social occasions, and their centrality was only slowly challenged.[86] In some towns, however, fairs were not very important. In High Wycombe in Buckinghamshire in 1527 the burgesses attempted to revive the Fair held at St Thomas's day in Easton Street; they forbade anyone else in the town to open up shop on that day, so that all trade would be confined to the fair. This regulation was not a success and neither was the fair.[87] Such little urban fairs were often much less economically vital than those held on rural sites, like the St White Down Fair in Somerset. This was a great cattle and horse market held on an open down at a meeting point of important routes; almost every parish within eight miles, and most within eight and sixteen miles was involved, although few people attended from further afield.[88]

If town fairs often suffered at the hands of their country cousins, so town markets could lose some of their functions to village shops, whose steady growth was one of the great trading phenomena of the sixteenth and seventeenth centuries.[89] The growth of shopkeeping as an occupation was noted in Chapter 4. Their spread into the countryside from the sixteenth century was a further example of the close interrelationships between town and country, in this case showing the spread of an urban innovation into the villages of pre-industrial England. By the late seventeenth century rural shopkeepers became a common feature of many larger villages in Wiltshire[90] and Lincolnshire.[91] With the spread of a monetary economy and the price revolution, many rural as well as urban shopkeepers became issuers of tokens. In seventeenth-century Buckinghamshire 191 different tradesmen issued tokens, many of them living in little villages.[92] Far from all the token-issuers in seventeenth-century Sussex lived even in decayed market towns; many tokens were issued from village shops. Not all token-issuers were necessarily shop owners, however. The occupations of thirteen of the issuers of tokens in High Wycombe are known: 7 of them were innkeepers, 1 a lace buyer, 1 a carpenter, 1 a draper, 1 a clothmaker, 1 a grocer and 1 a tanner.[93] Willan notes for mid-seventeenth century provincial England and Wales 7,787 different trading tokens issued by 6,575 issuers; they came from 1,534 places, about twice as many places as there were market towns in 1640. The distribution of the places issuing tokens reflected to some extent population, and also the general level of regional economic development. At least 300 locations in England which were not market towns had token-issuers who were definitely shopkeepers; these were widely distributed but were especially numerous in Kent, Suffolk, Sussex, Surrey and Norfolk, much less so in Cambridgeshire, Derbyshire, Essex, Hampshire, Lincolnshire, Middlesex and Wiltshire. Willan concludes that an 'obvious and trite' conclusion can be drawn, 'that, in general shops outside market towns were more numerous in those counties where market towns were fewer in number and more scattered. At least it shows that, even if market day were a shopping day, in many places it was not necessary to go to market to shop'.[94] It may be overstating the case to say that 'tokens may provide the nearest thing that we can get to a directory of shopkeepers before the appearance of the national directories in the 1780s', for wills and inventories can be as useful too as rather more detailed evidence. It might also be overstating the case to say that the penetration of shops into the country, and thus of an urban mode of sale into a rural setting, represented the beginnings of the urbanizing of countryside.[95] Whatever the case, it is a quite wellcharted process, even if not yet fully understood or evaluated. In East Anglia the spread of distributive trades was a noted feature of the two centuries.[96] In the sixteenth century, apart from in towns, they were generally to be found only in the larger villages such as South Creake in Norfolk, or Botesdale and Stratford St Mary in Suffolk. During the seventeenth century they spread quite markedly, even to little places like Briston in Norfolk and Hepton in Suffolk. Some of the people who died in these places and were recorded as 'grocers' may have been retired or landowning townsfolk, but such an explanation is insufficient entirely to account for the spread. These village trades were understandably supplemented by the activities of travelling chapmen and pedlars of small wares. By the end of the seventeenth century few villages in Norfolk or Suffolk could have been far from some shop, be it in a town or another village. The trend was noted with scant approbation by some contemporaries.[97] The village shop could be an extraordinary mixture. John Woods of

Gedney in the neighbouring county of Lincolnshire was known as a 'tobacconist', but his activities were much wider, from the evidence of the inventory taken after his death in 1683. They apparently included barbering, and the sale of grocery and general goods, ranging from sugar to hats and wigs. 'The extraordinary mixture', the Barleys write of him, 'given in the inventory as it is quoted here, gives a true picture of the village shop catering for every need'.[98] Some of the supplies for such shops came by water; some by river and quite a lot by sea from other parts of the country. Thus another component of this examination of rural–urban relationships is the part played by ports.

Ports

In many ways more is known about the trade of ports than of any other type of English pre-industrial town.[99] Thanks to the existence of the Port Books, which recorded for customs purposes the shipments of goods in and out, it is possible to examine in some detail both the inland and the foreign trade of ports in a way impossible for most inland towns, which did not usually keep a record of the passage of goods. The predominant movement was of small lots of goods for redistribution inland, ports thus binding themselves to the countryside of quite large areas, as well as to inland towns for whom they served an entrepôt role. This seaborne trade was an integral part of the total inland trade of the country that generally focused on towns. Navigable rivers almost invariably had ports at or near their mouths from which goods brought downriver could be shipped along the coast or abroad in return for goods coming upstream. Not every port had navigable water communication inland, however, and those that did not communicated directly overland. Naturally the hinterland for ports of this type was very much smaller than for towns like Bristol or Kings Lynn, at the mouth of considerable river systems. For instance, in the sixteenth century the merchant Tooley sent goods from Ipswich over a wide area by land; but nothing like as far as merchants in Hull, from where the Ouse allowed trading deep inland into Yorkshire.[100]

Most south and east coast ports, from Dorset around the coast to Norfolk, had poor inland water communication and relied on land carriage inland. They were thus tied to their countryside and at one level simply represented a special case of ordinary market towns. Market towns collected and redistributed goods over an area related to their size, regional population density and economy. Similarly, a port distributed goods that happened to be brought by sea, but often finished their journey by land rather than water. At the lowest level they differed from market towns only by their location on the coast, and by the fact that the mode of carriage for much of their trade was seaborne. Indeed, if it had a market, the port might perform functions for its immediate region which were the same as any other town. Ports had their freemen, their apprentices and their immigrants, like any other town. They were also engaged in forwarding goods inland, just as small inland market towns might play their role in forwarding goods up and down the functional economic chain between village and city. What marks them out, however, is the fact that in the coasting trade around England ports acted as collecting and distributing centres for heavy goods such as coal and timber which were impossible to transport cheaply by land. In addition, they were the point of entry into the local marketing system for goods that issued directly from abroad. These could be exotic without being 'luxury', and were as likely to be Flemish onions or tiles as fortified wines.

Yet not all of this vital coasting trade was transported inland *via* port towns. The sea was treated like a great river around the country; and like rivers it was seasonal in its uses, for the winter months could be hazardous even for vessels hugging the coast. Goods in parcels that seem amazingly small to modern eyes were landed on the coast for despatch inland, in exactly the way that they could be offloaded here and there on the banks of rivers and not necessarily at a town. Around Exeter, for example, coasting goods were offloaded not only at little ports, with no great urban life, like Starcross, Lympstone and Countess Wear, but also at little creeks like Kenton, Powderham and Cockwood, settlements possessed of no vestiges of urban life.[101] The small scale of such places, which did not necessarily even have vessels of their own, is aptly illustrated in a description of Workington on the Cumbrian coast in the 1560s: 'An other Creke, hath a Towne, nere scituate the same, called Workington of XXX householders . . . There is there several vessels called pickerdes of the burden of VII or VIII Tonnes . . . their trade commonlye is used to goe to Chester and Liverpole with herrings to make sale there, and to bye salte'.[102] The trade of such places, if it came under the aegis of the customs of an appointed port, might be only indirectly recorded, being subsumed into the figures of the 'headport'.[103] Although it was usually small in volume such trade was of considerable local importance.

Going around the coast of England from east to west, towns like

Grimsby, Blakeney, Brighton and the Cornish ports provide instructive examples of the activities of little port towns. At Grimsby, for example, in the course of the first half of the sixteenth century, the town's fortunes continued to deteriorate, but the trade in coal, corn and grocery goods played a significant part in the economy not only of the town itself, but of villages fifteen or twenty miles inland, as at the village of Walesby, where there was a road called 'Grimsby Gate'. Without this trade it is clear that the town would have been of little significance, for fishing and shipbuilding were of minimal importance.[104]

At Blakeney, one of a chain of little ports on the north Norfolk coast, local trade was small scale but important for an area inland.[105] In one half year in 1587, Blakeney got coal from Newcastle, and in this it was typical of a chain of places located on the Newcastle-upon-Tyne to London trade route, receiving loads of this desirable, but expensive to transport, domestic fuel. Having little wood, Blakeney imported timber for building from Arundel in Sussex at the same time. Fish came from Blyth on the north-east coast, and oats from Lynn. Grocery goods came from London, while a whole range of vegetables and building materials came from the Low Countries. Out of the port went malt, rye, peas, butter and saffron. Not all of this trade was consumed by or generated in the town of Blakeney itself; it was largely concerned with the north Norfolk rural hinterland.

On the Sussex coast, Brighton by 1680 had been appointed a legal quay of the port of New Shoreham, in spite of its location on a harbourless stretch of coast much exposed to the sea, where boats often had to be drawn up on the beach. The volume of maritime trade was modest. For example, between 1661 and 1689 an average of thirty-six coastwise cargoes and eight foreign cargoes passed through Brighton each year; eighty-five per cent of the coasters visiting the port brought coal from the north-west, while some brought luxury goods from London. Salt and wine were also offloaded direct from Portugal and the Bay of Biscay.[106] However, Brighton did not flourish overmuch as a town by this trade, and seems to have had a fairly limited hinterland, like other little ports such as Hastings and Rye. Like all market towns, such ports suffered increasingly in the seventeenth century from the competition of other towns, and the rationalization of their roles. But in an area where few canals were to be constructed in the eighteenth century, and where the advent of turnpiking did not greatly ease the problems of the carriage of heavy goods, these south coast ports nevertheless retained their importance. They did not feel the loss of the foreign and volume coasting trade that established ports like Ipswich or Southampton increasingly suffered at the hands of London in the seventeenth century. Their trade was of a different sort; it was too small to be worth organizing from London, yet of great importance to the surrounding areas.

A county like Cornwall was far away enough to be relatively untouched by London, as was the provincial metropolis of Bristol in the late seventeenth century. Ports which returned Port Books in Cornwall were Looe, Fowey, Truro, Penryn, Falmouth, Helford, Penzance, St Ives and Padstow; there were a great number of supporting creeks, quays and landing places. All of them were deeply engaged in importing coal, in this case mainly from South Wales, and it was used increasingly not only for heating in the home, but also for smithy work, the metalliferous smelting industry, malt-making and brewing. Like the little ports of Sussex, the Cornish ports imported their coal and wine direct; like them too they were small and intimately connected with their local hinterland in their dual role of local market centres and specialized ports for coastal and foreign imports of high bulk or high value.[107]

Such ports, little more than marketing centres for a section of countryside in most cases, were unlikely to grow to any great size, or to achieve much functional specialization from such local, if seaborne, trade. However, for a number of towns growth in size and specialization did stem directly from large-scale coasting and foreign trade. Most ports of any size were involved in, and benefited from, both coasting and foreign activities; though some of these which had been important as late as the fifteenth century had relapsed into a local torpor for a number of reasons. The Cinque Ports are obvious examples, and Boston another. At one time the port of Boston was second in importance only to London, but by the seventeenth century its trade was much smaller than Hull's. The great inland area once served by Boston had come to depend on the rivers of the Humber and Thames. Boston now exported mainly the produce of a limited hinterland, and imported goods apparently purely for local consumption.[108]

Between 1500 and 1600 a number of ports, however, grew to considerable importance partly on the coasting trade. These were predominantly places some way around the coast from London, whose influence was slowly destroying much of the trade of ports nearby like Ipswich, as more and more trade was won by London merchants and carried in London shops. Newcastle, Hull and

Chichester are good examples, though others would be Kings Lynn, Liverpool and Bristol. Newcastle developed in the pre-industrial period to one of the major coasting ports in England, especially in the coal trade; indeed, the basis of its size, prosperity and variety of manufactures lay in coal. Coal was vital to much of the rest of England, and Newcastle supplied most of the eastern and southern coasts of the country with it. It was able to weather trade depressions which might otherwise have seriously affected its economic vitality and urban standing, because of its highly specialized role, which was unlikely to be disrupted by foreign or home competition, or by secular changes in the national economy, for demand for coal was fairly inelastic and inclined only to grow. For example, the years 1509–33 saw a series of crises which led to the decline of the Newcastle wool trade; but in absolute terms its general trade probably expanded rather than declined during these crisis years,[109] for production of and demand for coal, and to a lesser extent lead, exported through it remained high. The spectacular growth of the east-coast coal trade attracted much attention from contemporaries, and so did the rise of Newcastle as a town consequent upon it. Celia Fiennes by 1697 saw it as a 'notable town' that 'most resembles London of any place in England'.[110] Its trade in textiles and skins, so important in the early sixteenth century, was being taken over by Hull, while coastal coal exports shot up. It is a striking commentary on the economic life of the port that in 1616 only two of the principal hostmen, Alexander Davison and Robert Bewick, engaged in a large foreign trade in commodities other than coal. As Willan observes: 'Newcastle was a very odd town by Elizabethan standards. It was larger, with a population of perhaps 10,000 and its economy rested on the mining and shipping of coal. It is curious that the "backward" north should have contained in Newcastle perhaps the largest purely industrial town in the country and in the Mines Royal the biggest integrated mining and manufacturing concern in the country'.[111]

Other nearby northern ports were being increasingly drawn into the net of London's demand at the same time as Newcastle's coal trade grew.[112] For example, from the early years of the seventeenth century, and with dramatically increasing pace after 1660, the port of Stockton[113] emerged as the most important commercial centre between the Humber and the Tyne, and Whitby was engaged in the building of ships for the Newcastle coal trade, using much imported timber. The Newcastle trade meant that some of the east-coast ports operated in two directions, both north to Newcastle and south to

London. Hull, for instance, got its coal from Newcastle, sending in return grain and malt; but grain, butter, cheese and lead also went south to London, from whence came a great mass of miscellaneous grocery and haberdashery goods.[114] Kings Lynn, too, looked both ways; it got large amounts of coal from Newcastle, and like Hull sent grain back north, as well as south to London, and in years of scarcity in the mid-sixteenth century even as far west around the coast as Bristol. Grocery goods, iron, soap and wine came from London, some of which was re-shipped inland up the Ouse, or sent on to other ports like Boston and Newcastle.[115]

Hull, like many other English ports, reached a nadir of activity in the fifteenth century.[116] Unlike Boston, its trade and its urban fortunes revived in the pre-industrial period, though this was based as much on foreign as on coasting trades. In the latter, Hull men took part in the London–Newcastle trade, and also the export of lead out of Derbyshire round the coast; butter and cheese from both Derbyshire and Cheshire travelled the same way. The cheese was largely Cheshire cheese, brought across England for shipment from Hull, rather than through west-coast ports; it was an easy journey from the producing areas to the Trent, and thence to the sea. Coal, lead and provisions were the only important elements in Hull's coastal traffic before the middle of the seventeenth century, but after the Civil War this traffic underwent an enormous expansion. Out of Hull in increasing numbers went saws, nails and edge tools from the Sheffield area, as well as cloth from the towns of the West Riding. In came raw materials for their textile manufactures, as well as grocery and luxury goods, and tobacco.[117] Yet it is unlikely that Hull would have risen to the pre-eminence it achieved as a specialist port, and thus its size and standing as a town, on coastal trade alone. Newcastle may well be the only port to have won its status in this way, because of its peculiar advantages as the unique centre of a coastally borne coal trade that was always in demand. Hull got its particular uban impetus from foreign trade. It had links with the Low Countries and especially the Baltic, with timber and flax, pitch, tar and potash. By the seventeenth century, Hull was probably second to only London in the Baltic and Northern trade; in Davis's view, 'essentially Hull was the port connecting the north of England with northern Europe'.[118] It is unlikely that the coasting and local trade could have produced the Hull of the eighteenth century,[119] with its important manufacturing and processing industries, often based on imported goods, and its growing commercial expertise. Alongside shipbuilding, provisioning and related trades were oilseed crushing,

paint manufacture, sugar refining and a range of other miscellaneous activities. There was no clear-cut distinction between
trade and industry, most of those involved in the latter being
merchants. As in other commercial centres of any size, the need for
credit and a simple system of payments led to the foundation of
banks, all but one of which were linked with a major merchant
house.[120]

Shorn of much of their foreign trade by London, coastal ports involved in more than local trade were unlikely to grow much above
the average as towns. Chichester on the Sussex coast is a fine case in
point. It was dependent almost entirely on the coastal, and by the
end of the seventeenth century foreign, export of corn. The external
structure of the coastal malt trade was far from simple. Chichester
lay near the edge of the area supplying London with corn by sea; the
period 1656–1731 witnessed the gradual capture of the Chichester
malt trade by the London market from the ports of Exeter,
Plymouth and Dartmouth. In the second half of the seventeenth
century its coastwise corn exports were more than equal to those of
all the other Sussex ports combined, and in Kent only Sandwich and
Margate exported more malt than Chichester.[121] But Chichester
had very little foreign trade to provide the basis of a more
sophisticated coasting trade, or to generate much special urban
growth. With exceptions such as Newcastle-upon-Tyne, foreign
trade was the major force behind such expansion.

At the most a dozen of the towns of pre-industrial England gained
all or a large part of their size, economic vitality and special function
from foreign trade, generally through both export and import.
Whilst their merchants and traders redistributed and supplied the
inland market towns with imported goods, many of which were
destined to be sold to countryfolk, others were involved in processing
imported goods, and manufacturing articles based on them. The
spin-off of these activities was as likely to generate marked urban
centrality and size as was the manufacturing of textiles or metal
goods in inland centres. Such was the case with traditional centres
like Bristol, the port–metropolis of the west, and with the newer
centres with an interest in the colonial trade in the later seventeenth
century like Liverpool or, to a lesser extent, Whitehaven. In about
1600 the chief ports of England, as measured by the customs
revenue generated from them, were in descending order: London,
Hull, Exeter, Bristol, Newcastle, Plymouth, Lyme Regis,
Southampton and Dartmouth.[122] The customs revenue in 1614 at
London was £105,131, fifteen times as much as that in the next

highest yielding port, Hull, where it was £7,664. Towards the end of
the century, there had been great increases in trade, as is shown by
London's yield of £569,531 in 1676. The second most important port
by this measure was by then Bristol, with £65,908; it had overtaken
Hull and Exeter which were following it some long way behind with
£20,213 and £17,038 respectively, though these two ports were being
closely pressed by Plymouth in fourth place with £16,564.
Plymouth, like Bristol, was growing from the colonial trade, and it
was the western ports which expanded fastest, benefiting from the
'Americanization' of English overseas trade.

By far the greatest growth up to 1700 – though it was to be out-
paced thereafter by Liverpool – was to be found at Bristol. After
1660 Bristol acquired a seemingly ever expanding role as a major
participant in the Atlantic trade by engaging in the tobacco and
sugar trades, in the Newfoundland fisheries, and in the African slave
trade.[123] This growth was built on the firm base of a western port,
important since medieval times.[124] The subsidy returns of the 1520s
found the economy of Bristol relatively on an ebb, like most towns of
the day. It was then clearly a great English provincial city, ranking
with its eastern and northern counterparts Norwich and York. Yet it
did not have any special manufacture, and whilst its trade with
Ireland and the Continent (especially France and Spain) was important, it was not of a scale to raise it in overall wealth to the level
of Norwich. In the 1520 lay subsidies, it had only half the wealth of
that city, though just 300 less taxpayers.[125] Camden saw Bristol not
long after as being 'so populous and well inhabited withall, that next
after London and Yorke, it may of all cities in England justly
challenge the chiefe place'.[126] Its seaborne trade was not solely
foreign, of course. The ports of South Wales and the western peninsula supplied it with wool, cloth, skins and foodstuffs. In return they
received miscellaneous goods like groceries, wine, spices, iron, and
soap. Bristol did not receive those varied cargoes from London,
which was a feature of the trade of most other English ports; instead
it distributed its own to the Welsh ports, and for the towns up its
extensive Severn river hinterland.

Up to the mid-seventeenth century, Bristol's trading base and
trading patterns remained substantially the same; like most international ports it went through difficult periods, such as the trade
depressions of the 1620s.[127] From the 1650s, however, whilst her
longer-established trade with Ireland, France and the Iberian
peninsula continued to flourish, the first signs of burgeoning
American and West Indian trades could also be seen; in 1659–60

this shipping represented about one-seventh of the total, one-sixth in 1667–68 and by 1686–87 between a quarter and a third of all that going into Bristol. Tobacco was vital, much of it for re-export, and sugar was of growing importance too, though not yet at its eighteenth-century level, whilst slaving was not important until after 1698. Between the beginning and end of the century covering this development, Bristol's population grew from 12,000 to 20,000. Many of the business community of Bristol were involved in trading overseas; not merely merchants but linen drapers, soap boilers, mercers, clothiers, grocers, writers and innkeepers.[128] The tonnage of shipping entering the port from the West Indies rose from 1,900 in 1670 to 5,200 in 1700. The rum, slaves, tobacco and sugar which were to be the main ingredients of Bristol's great prosperity of the eighteenth century were thus firmly established as the main parts of its trade by the late seventeenth century, although a constant part of the overseas trade remained with Ireland, going to Dublin and the ports around the southern coast like Cork, Limerick, Waterford and Youghall.[129]

The colonial trade had an electric effect on the size and status of those ports like Bristol which already were of substantial size and importance. It also was to imitate the startling growth of one western port which had been a tiny and insignificant place in the early sixteenth century, Liverpool, whose trade had been entirely dominated hitherto by the port of Chester inland on the river Dee. Chester acted in the sixteenth century as a distributive centre for goods to northern Wales, rather in the same way as Bristol did for southern Wales, though it was clearly of less importance than Bristol. Unlike Bristol, Chester was dependent on London for its luxury goods and special products, such as wine, iron, fuller's earth, soap, hops and dyestuffs. Willan suggests that 'the arrival of the London ship must have been like the arrival of the great ship from Amacon'.[130] Though Chester did a certain amount of coastal trade with Liverpool, from which it received imported Irish goods, it had a considerable trade itself with Ireland. In the early seventeenth century, it was clear that the north-west had no ports of the first rank or indeed any towns of a size to compare with Bristol or Newcastle. There were only the two ports of second-class importance; Chester, specializing in the cloth and London trade, and Liverpool with the import trade from Ireland. But their foreign trade combined was tiny compared with that of such provincial ports as Hull, Exeter or even small places like Weymouth and Lyme Regis.[131] If there was to be marked growth based on ports, it could only have been in one of the two on the north-west coast. The region was not big, populous or economically strong enough to support two major ports, and it would have needed some international trade of nation-wide importance to hoist even one of them to urban prominence. Chester began to suffer as a port because of the effects of silting on its navigation, and this was not the only difficulty it experienced, for there seemed to be insufficient driving force from inside the town itself. In Armour's view, the problems were especially related to the deadening influence of the guilds, together with the relatively small size of Chester's hinterland.[132] By the end of the century it was clearly in decline as a port and scarcely larger than it had been in 1600. Navigational problems alone – Camden said 'the sea is not so favourable as it had been, and the town has lost the advantage of a harbour which it enjoyed heretofore' – did not slow Chester's growth. By the end of the seventeenth century, and from 1660 in particular, it was suffering competition from Liverpool.

Liverpool had always been important in the Irish trade in the sixteenth century. Leland tells us that 'Irisch marchants cum much thither as to a good haven . . . At Lyrpole is smale custume payid that causith marchantes to resorte. Good marchandis at Lyrpole and most Yrish yarn that Manchester men do by ther.'[133] Throughout the sixteenth century, the Irish trade remained Liverpool's principal 'foreign trade'; it was involved with importing barley, rye, wheat, flax, linen, yarn, skins and tallow. Exports were of cloth, pewter cups and metal implements, and re-exported goods from London and Chester. By the seventeenth century some salt and wine were being imported from France, together with iron and salt from Spain. On this trade Liverpool survived rather than prospered, and remained very small. But from the mid-seventeenth century both trade and the town shot up in size. Nowhere is there a more graphic example of what trade could do to a town. In 1650 Liverpool had only 6 streets there; in 1667, 11; in 1677, 18; in 1697, 28; in 1708, 34; and a further 16 streets were built between 1708 and 1725. As its trade was transformed, so Liverpool town changed in size, prosperity, and regional importance. The new-found prosperity was based on entry into the North American and West Indies trade at exactly the same time as Bristol's sugar-baking developed from the late 1660s; in 1667, Allyn Smith, a London sugar baker settled in Liverpool and started work.[134] It was quite clear to contemporaries what caused the increase of Liverpool's size and prosperity. Of the reasons Edward Moore wrote:

amongst which are divers merchants and tradesmen, whose trade and traffic, especially into the West Indies, makes it famous; its scituation affording in greater plenty, and at reasonabler rates than most parts of England such exported commodities proper for the West Indies, as likewise a quicker return from such imported commodities, by reason of the sugar bakers and the great manufacture of cottons in the adjacent parts, and the reason for that it is found to be the convenientest passage to Ireland, and divers considerable counties in England with which they have intercourse of traffick.[135]

This colonial trade had a spin-off right through the town's economic structure. Shipbuilding and ancillary trades grew, as well as manufactures connected with the increase in the rock-salt trade from nearby. Rock salt had been discovered at the same time as the West Indies trade was growing, but did not develop in commercial importance until after 1690.[136] Liverpool's urban growth was based on tobacco and sugar, not on salt. Its rapid development was a marvel to Defoe, to Fiennes and to Pocock, whose pages are decidedly empty of many tales of rapid and noticeable urban growth.[137] The systematic expansion of Liverpool, and other ports further from London like Bristol and Whitehaven, 'represented a rationalization of marketing procedure in which a new emphasis on consumer imports was matched by an efficient reorganization of distribution patterns'.[138] Yet that reorganization of distribution patterns, and the parallel growth of ports to a marked regional independence was not fully to develop until the eighteenth century. For most of the sixteenth and seventeenth centuries London dominated the trades and the ports of the country, as it dominated its politics, society and economy.

London throughout the sixteenth and seventeenth centuries had tended to exert a considerable pull on nearby ports, swallowing up much of the important foreign trade of ports in eastern and southern England. Those such as Dunwich, Aldeburgh, Orford, Woodbridge, Colchester and Maldon were reduced to a largely tributary role of supplying London with foodstuffs. In the early sixteenth century London was clearly dominant in the foreign trade of the country, one more factor adding to her national centrality.[139] Most port activity was limited to quite a small area of the north bank of the Thames, between Queenhithe and Tower Dock or Wharf. The total frontage of the legal quays was only about 2,000 feet, and the activity crammed into this small space made up the Elizabethan port of London. Coastal shipments of coal and corn could be legally landed elsewhere in London, however. The export of cloth in particular was a notable feature of trade, whilst imports consisted of all the international goods which made up London's entrepôt and redistributive trade. As London grew in the seventeenth century,[140] so did its trading activities, its port and its influence on the trade of the other coastal ports of England, particularly those between Kings Lynn and Southampton. Its export trade blossomed further,[141] with less reliance on intermediary continental ports like Antwerp and more direct trade with France, Spain and the Mediterranean. Certainly the impression gained from looking at the Port Books which record London's trade is that the city merchants supplemented their overpowering trade in textiles less by dealing in other English products than by trading in foreign commodities. By the mid-seventeenth century London was re-shipping East Indies goods to Russia, Germany and the Netherlands, Virginia tobacco to the Baltic and European manufactures to Africa and the Americas. It was increasingly the great emporium, not only for world trade, but for much of England too. Only Bristol and late-seventeenth century Liverpool stood out as receiving relatively few cargoes of imported foreign goods *via* London which most other English ports depended on. Willan thinks it could be argued that the national coasting trade made a contribution to London in supplying its people with food, and its manufacturers with an outlet for their products to provincial markets.[142] Soap and ironmongery, both London made, certainly did go out from London on the coastal trade, but most goods issuing out of London were imported, not London manufactures. The resemblance between the cargoes of miscellaneous goods imported from the Continent and recorded in the Port Books, and those shipped along the coasts is too close to be coincidence. This confirms that London was essentially a distributive centre for imported goods. Given the concentration of foreign trade in London, such a role would make sense. A national market was emerging for imported goods from London, just as there was one to meet London's insatiable demand for food which drew most ports in England into direct contact with her, and led her to dominate much of their trade at least until the development of Bristol and Liverpool from the mid-seventeenth century. This overwhelming superiority of London's port was both a function of, and a contributing factor to, her great growth and urban dominance in pre-industrial England, and it helped bind the countryside of England to her.

Immigration

London also dominated the migratory system of pre-industrial England that bound town and country together. Just as there was a national market for foodstuffs and goods, so there was a national market for men and women, carried by land and water. The great importance of migration for towns, as we saw in Chapter 3, was that it made urban growth possible. This also had a spatial expression which we must now consider.

London was at the centre of the national migratory system, as it was of every other facet of national life. Much movement, however, was very local, being within the radius of a few miles around a town. This was the area of most urban landownership, and where marriage partners were often to be found too, as well as goods sold and debts for rural and urban products contracted. It is important to separate long-distance migratory movements from the local and often temporary ones which might be thought of as purely local mobility, intimately connected with local rural conditions, centred on the market and town. Most places had their little migration fields from within which much of their labour would be recruited, an area which reflected long-established rural–urban relationships. Movements such as this did not lift the locally mobile out of their immediate social, economic or geographical context. Many smaller towns of a thousand people or so, with intimate connections with the immediate countryside in occupation and landownership, were quite like country areas in their fertility and mortality patterns, and more like them in administration and society too. Such places needed – and attracted – the long-range migrant much less than did larger towns and cities. They were much more affected by deeply embedded local mobility at a time when many of their inhabitants laboured daily in the town fields, when their activities were concerned with the provision of a few services, perhaps a shop or two, and a little market. In the movement of people from country to town in pre-industrial England, it seems that there was a distinct trend down a gradient of movement that stretched from real migration to purely local mobility.[143] Every place, from London to a tiny market centre, would have its own pattern of local mobility, impinging directly on the immediate area. But it would only be to the larger places – county capitals, ports, provincial cities, and London itself – that migratory movement on any scale took place, lifting the rural migrant permanently out of his own rural context into a new, urban one.

It would be pedantic to attempt to draw any firm line of demarcation between 'migration' and 'mobility', as those terms are used here; the boundary is obviously a shifting and ill-defined one. But by treating all recorded movement into towns in exactly the same way,

there is the risk of confusing local mobility with much more important longer-range and semi-permanent or permanent flows. Local
mobility was transient, and much less is known about it than longer-
range migration. The arena of local mobility for most towns like
Ipswich or Maldon, was very small, being only five or six miles in
radius.[144] In Elizabethan Buckinghamshire, short-distance migration was always more common than long-distance migration, and
also more complex, since factors such as marriage, kinship obliga-
tions, and inheritance customs were much more operative than was
likely to be the case over longer distances, except perhaps where the
wealthier gentry were concerned.[145] At the other end of England, at
Bury, Lancashire, in the later seventeenth century this pattern was
still the same; most migration, even of the poor members of society
subject to the rigours of the settlement acts, was within a five or six
mile radius.[146] Similar patterns are to be found around the little
town of Maldon in seventeenth-century Essex.[147] It can hardly be
dignified with the title of migration, and should rather be accepted
as a permanent feature of pre-industrial rural–urban relationships,
as much for towns like Shrewsbury or Wem in Shropshire as for the
parishes connected to them.[148]

People moving further were also typical of pre-industrial society,
but they did not necessarily go to towns. Some might be vagrants
flitting from village to village.[149] Others would be migrant agricultural workers whose movements, long- and short-range might
not impinge on towns at all. In England, as in France or Spain,
there could sometimes be considerable temporary long-range
treks; in Spain in 1640, one contemporary observed, 'there passes
every year a great quantity of haymakers, reapers, cattle gelders,
and other workers who relieve their households of the burden of
feeding them and bring back some profit to their families'.[150] These
also could pass by towns in England. But undoubtedly the most important actual migrant streams did involve towns, and whilst the
numbers of migrants may have fluctuated from year to year, the
paths along which they travelled and the spheres of influence of the
towns to which they were attracted, did not alter greatly. One constant was the sphere of local mobility; the other was the spheres
around towns, and predominant streams of long-distant migration
to them. Hägerstrand suggests that, 'When analysing migration and
area we must not look for transient factors but try to lay bare the
secular constants;'[151] to which might be added the fact that the
spatial constants, like so much in pre-industrial life, were changing
but slowly.

Patterns of Migration

A variety of sources exist which give the places of origin of migrants.
All of them are selective, and were discussed in Chapter 3.[152] The
most dominant spatial pattern was that of migration to London, the
migratory node or pivot of the country. There was a tremendous
flow of people into London who were lifted out of their home environment from the stage of local mobility into that of the capital,
power-house of the process of modernization. This of course had
tremendous demographic implications in a period when London
could not replace itself, and yet grew from a population of around
60,000 in 1500 to 200,000 in 1600, 400,000 in 1650 and approaching
700,000 by 1750. But the flood of immigrants also integrated
country and capital to an increasing degree. Probably upwards of
one million came to London between 1550 and 1750.[153] At certain
times half the natural increase of provincial England was absorbed
by London, many of the immigrants being very young. The data for
London at the end of the seventeenth century and in 1851 show a
strong similarity in the large proportion of single males and females
entering it. This would be expected with a relatively high age at first
marriage, and particularly in the largest urban centre, with substantial employment opportunities for young unmarried men and
women and with a heavy emphasis on apprentice opportunities for
young men. No less important is the fact that the London apprenticeship system brought together young men from all over the
country to the largest urban centre in Western Europe, and certainly one of the major intellectual centres of the period.[154] People even
in remote upland villages such as Myddle in Shropshire were surprisingly familiar with the capital. The Rector of that village,
Gough, spoke familiarly of London and his visits to it, and gives in
his memoirs of the parish charming little potted biographies of
young migrants; there is not always a happy ending to these movements, and often immigrants aspirations were not met: 'Michaell
(Jukes) was sett apprentice in London but for some misdemeanor,
came to an untimely end . . .' Another locally born London apprentice was Humphrey Hall who 'was a silversmith in London and is
there marryed; he is a strong man, and a skillful workman, butt he
loves drink too well to be rich'. Philip Foden went to London, too,
and met equal ill fortune: 'Philip Foden was a Drawer (*sic*) in
London, and afterwards married there and became a Vintner, but
he broake and soon after dyed.'[155] London was a great magnet[156] for
the young and thus the evidence of apprentice indentures may be

quite a good surrogate for much of the movement which took place.

It is clear that there was a considerable influx of people from the nearby Home Counties. There were other well-established patterns of movement, too, especially from the poorer uplands of northern and western England. One sample of the apprentices enrolled in eight different city companies between 1630 and 1660 shows that only about four in every ten were from the London area.[157] A quite high proportion of long-range migrants entered the lowly Stationers' Company between 1562 and 1640.[158] A more comprehensive picture for the later seventeenth century can be obtained by examination of the 1,600 persons admitted to Freedom of the City by apprenticeship in the year 1690. Of those entering in that year, as was the case with the Stationers' Company earlier, only about twenty per cent of those admitted were London born, while about ten per cent came from the northern and western English Counties. Immigrants from the Home Counties (Middlesex, Essex, Surrey, Kent, Buckinghamshire and Berkshire) supplied only about another quarter of the whole; thus longer distance immigrants made up the greater part of those enrolled that year.[159] Many of those coming from the north and west were born in areas of considerable demographic pressure and economic difficulty. Whatever source is used, this pattern is replicated. Some 89 per cent of the deponents in Cressey's study of the riverside extra-mural parishes between 1580 and 1640 came from outside London. Eleven per cent had travelled further than 50 miles, and 38 counties are recorded as places of origin for immigrants. This study, using the deposition books from the Archdeaconal Courts, was for part of the growing eastern suburbs that stretched from Spitalfields to Limehouse. Being outside the closely controlled city, this area was an obvious home for the immigrant.[160]

Whilst there were significant numbers of migrants from places beyond 30 or 40 miles away from London, and a lot of these from the Highland Zone (Table 11) the picture did not remain static. There seems to have been a notable contraction taking place in the seventeenth century in the area from which London drew its recruits. The records of apprentices going into the Carpenters and Fishmongers companies show that while the Highland Zone had supplied some forty per cent in the earlier part of the seventeenth century, this had dropped to twenty per cent or less by 1700.[161] Whilst specialized occupations probably continued to draw from all over the country,[162] the middle of the seventeenth century saw a contraction in the numbers coming from the northern counties, although those from most other regions remained fairly stable. This overall geographical shift during the seventeenth century was due in part to shifts in the population and to changes in birth rates for different parts of the country.[163] Recruitment from the Home Counties seems to have risen. By the 1690s London and the Home Counties were providing about half of the total of those admitted to freedom by apprenticeship. Shorter-distance migration was becoming increasingly common elsewhere in the country because of the attraction exerted by the other growing towns upon the increased population of their own catchment areas, especially in parts of the north and west, which by 1700 were experiencing quite rapid population growth.[164] These 'areas of difficulty' were becoming 'areas of opportunity' for their local young; there were now attractive intervening economic opportunities, mitigating London's lure.

Table 11: GEOGRAPHICAL ORIGINS OF APPRENTICES IN SOME LONDON COMPANIES, 1630–60

Company	Number	London	London and Home Counties	Midlands	North	East	South and West
Armourers	399	21·30	42·10	28·82	12·03	2·25	11·52
Bakers	1049	6·51	35·02	32·63	12·37	2·96	14·06
B/Surgeons	374	24·33	47·86	22·19	12·03	5·39	8·82
Butchers	390	12·56	34·87	36·66	10·00	4·10	13·84
Carpenters	528	12·31	34·84	34·84	9·84	1·32	15·34
Founders	255	17·32	31·76	22·74	18·03	5·88	13·72
Joiners	1709	16·21	40·84	32·70	10·06	2·04	10·59

This table is based on that on p.204 of Smith, S. R. 'The social and geographical origins of the London Apprentices, 1630–1660', *Guildhall Miscellany,* IV (1973), 195–206

Migration to most provincial centres was undoubtedly smaller in volume, and more restricted spatially, than that taking place to the capital. There is no reason to suspect that the mortality of Bristol or Norwich, with populations of not more than 30,000 by 1700, was running at a lower level than that of London for much of the period. So they too must have depended on migrants for their economic and demographic health. Very few English counties failed to send at least some migrants to early sixteenth-century Bristol, with large numbers coming from northern and western counties. London was far from unique in attracting long-range migrants; Bristol drew many of its immigrants from counties on the trade route up the Severn, and northern and western counties supplied nine or ten per cent of the total immigrants to Bristol, and about five per cent of those to Norwich.[165] Norwich drew considerable numbers of immigrants from the West Riding of Yorkshire, Westmorland and Cumberland, many of them entering her clothing trades, and some returning with their new-found skills to help build up local manufactures. By contrast to Bristol and Norwich, Newcastle drew its apprentice immigrants from a much more restricted area in the north-east, though some immigrants came up the coast from ports with which Newcastle had regular coasting links.[166]

The migration fields of towns of different sizes clearly interacted with one another. In East Anglia, for example,[167] Norwich drew immigrant apprentices from over a wide area, covering the whole of the region, especially within about thirty miles. The ports of Great Yarmouth and Ipswich had much more restricted migration fields, drawing most of their permanent immigrants from within fifteen miles, although some came by sea from further ports. This difference is a reflection of their lesser size and standing compared to Norwich, which obviously had a much greater attraction to immigrants. There was a fairly regular fall-off in numbers of migrants in most directions away from Norwich, though in the direction of Great Yarmouth, twenty-two miles away to the east, its migration field was much more restricted. Fewer people came from this area, which was Yarmouth's own migration field. Naturally, fewer people also came from the thinly populated 'poor sands' of north Norfolk, the Breckland, and the sandy heaths of inland coastal Suffolk. On the other hand far more migrants came from the area to the north-east of Norwich, where a good deal of worsted manufacture was carried on, and with which the city had considerable trade links which would encourage migration.

Turning to the north of the country, to the other great provincial city of York, only a quarter of those recorded as entering the city freedom in the course of the sixteenth century came from the city. Of the rest, half came from Yorkshire itself, especially from within ten miles of York. Beyond this, there was a markedly localized pattern; an important stream of migrants came from the north-west, especially Swaledale and Wensleydale and from as far away as Westmorland (just those 'areas of difficulty', in fact, which sent apprentices in noticeable numbers to Norwich). Far fewer came from the East Riding, where Hull was a big counter-attraction – in exactly the same way as Yarmouth was a counter-attraction to Norwich. Few came from the West Riding also, where there was the local attraction of the growing cloth industry. Many migrants may

have been attracted by the considerable trade in stockings and textiles up and down the Ouse,[168] in exactly the same way as Bristol's
trade up the Severn seemed to encourage long-distance migration
from counties fluvially connected to it. One in ten immigrant
freemen came from Cumbria to York, where the soil was poor and
the population large. Kendal cloth found its way to York, and
Kendal men came the same way. It would therefore seem that the
migration patterns to the greater English provincial cities were
similar to, though much more restricted than, London's. They had
their strong local links in the immediate twenty or thirty miles
around, but equally had important longer-range connections.

Lower down the urban hierarchy, just as migration was less important to smaller towns demographically, it was more restricted in
spatial extent. There were exceptions to this. A university city such
as Oxford would have nationwide contacts,[169] in its case notably
again from the poorer counties of Highland England, whence came
about a third of all apprentices, with very few on the other hand
issuing from the southern and eastern counties. But most county
capitals had rather restricted local migration fields. Tudor and
Stuart Worcester, for example, was an important county capital and
textile-manufacturing centre, yet it drew most of its immigrant
freemen from within ten or fifteen miles.[170] The same was true of late
seventeenth-century Leicester, where nearly sixty per cent of all
immigrant apprentices came from less than ten miles away. Most
longer-distance immigrants came from counties quite nearby.[171]
Neither Worcester nor Leicester had any marked long-range
streams of immigrants coming to them, whether from upland
England or elsewhere, to compare with those going to London or the
three great provincial cities of York, Norwich or Bristol. In Kent,
most immigrants came from within twenty miles to the county
capital of Canterbury, while smaller places like Maidstone or
Faversham got most of theirs from within ten miles.[172] Long-
distance migrants were not, however, completely precluded from
travelling to a small cathedral city like Canterbury of no great
national standing; it was neither a port like Bristol nor a textile
centre like Norwich, yet between 1580 and 1640 people came to it
from Yorkshire, Lancashire and Cheshire. Their numbers were
so small, however, that it would be wrong to suggest that any
permanent long-range migration field existed. Local migration was
important to the life of smaller towns, as it also was to growing
manufacturing centres like Birmingham. Here, in the sixteenth and
seventeenth centuries, most immigrants were local. Nine-tenths of

all those settling in Birmingham with a Settlement Certificate between 1686 and 1726 came from no further than twenty miles away.[173] Even such a burgeoning manufacturing centre had a largely restricted and local 'pull'. Other Black Country towns like Walsall and Wolverhampton also attracted many local immigrants. Birmingham was a strong pole of attraction, but the Staffordshire coalfield parishes replaced any net outflows by short-distance immigration from the agricultural parishes of nearby counties.[174] Most apprentices going to the nearby small textile centre of Kidderminster were equally local, though quite a number left the area to go to the Black Country.[175]

Overall, there appears to have been a system of rural–urban migration that was characterized by a declining size of migration fields related to the decline in size of towns down the urban hierarchy. On this basic spatial pattern were superimposed important long-range networks of movement, both inland and coastal, particularly from the north and west of the county to the south, to London, and to the greater provincial cities. As the two centuries passed, there is evidence that this longer-range movement declined in importance, with greater economic opportunities occurring in parts of the north and west. Further, the free movement of poorer people was being increasingly controlled by Settlement Acts, which tended to inhibit migration.

6

Towns in the National Urban System – East Anglia

The Region and its Towns

Discussion of English pre-industrial towns has so far concentrated on national generalizations about their population, their economy, and their external relations. This has naturally been shaped to a considerable degree by the work that has chanced to be done by geographers and historians. It is impossible, however, to paint a clear picture of urban characteristics – as far as sources permit – without descriptive and explanatory generalizations about a large number of towns of different sizes on a comparative basis, something not attempted hitherto in urban studies of pre-industrial England. It would be impossible, because of the size of the task, to attempt this for the whole of the kingdom. Equally, it would be difficult to sample a number of different towns all over England of different sizes and sorts, for this would demand a foreknowledge of urban structures that we do not yet have, in order to permit proper sampling design; the interrelationships between towns of various sizes might in addition be obscured because of regional differences. A distinct area for study is therefore necessary, in order to try to exemplify the generalizations that have been suggested in the preceding chapters.

East Anglia – comprising the counties of Norfolk and Suffolk – is used as such an area. All the towns of East Anglia can be examined within a fairly coherent regional framework. This region itself has the advantage, for these purposes, of containing towns drawn from the whole diverse range of types in the English pre-industrial urban system, excepting only the great capital which was undergoing its own extraordinary growth, transformation, and centralization. East

Anglia contained the largest city of provincial England, Norwich, and thus had an urban system ranging right down to the level of the smallest towns, merging imperceptibly as they did into villages and the rural life of the region.

Although the character and landscapes of Norfolk and Suffolk have been left relatively untouched by the effects of subsequent industrialization, from medieval times they made up a notably populous economically important and wealthy area. East Anglia was one of the power-houses of the pre-industrial English economy, and was probably England's most modernized region. Cloth and other manufactures flourished in the towns and in the countryside, which also had its diversified agricultural activity. Some of the products of manufacturing and agriculture travelled overland to other quarters of the realm, but probably the greater part left *via* important ports like Great Yarmouth, Ipswich and Kings Lynn for London, the north-east and abroad, as well as from a myriad of minor ports, creeks and landing places. East Anglia comprised a coherent area, undisturbed by the direct influence of London, in contrast with counties nearer to the capital, like Essex or Middlesex. The capital's tentacles did however penetrate the coast of these counties; for example, by swallowing the indigenous trade of Ipswich as it had done that of the Essex ports, and by drawing much of the East Anglian cloth into its centralized marketing system that dominated the nation's trade in textiles.

Sources

Within this region, the occupational structures of all East Anglian towns can be examined and related to their population size, in order to construct a basic comparative urban framework; within this framework, their less systematic attributes such as markets, administrative and other functions can be examined. This comparative approach is a vital task for urban historical geography, as Smith has suggested.[1] Throughout, discussion is based on the only large-scale analysis of urban occupations within a region, that has yet been carried out for pre-industrial England.[2] Earlier discussion has demonstrated how important the records of corporate towns are in elucidating their occupational and economic structure, and such is certainly the case for East Anglia. But for smaller, non-corporate towns without freemen's rolls or the indenture papers of apprentices, wills and probate records are the only remotely systematic source. This is even the case for many of the smaller East Anglian boroughs which had some corporate life, and left some corporate records. Their paucity bears witness to everything from lack of corporate vigour to the ravages of damp and fire on ill-stored records. The low level of activity in many such towns needed little control, and thus left little record. The amount of information that they yield is low, particularly in decaying centres like Dunwich.[3] It would surely, even if such records were to be found for all boroughs, beg the question of urbanism to accept them as prime sources. Neither walls (as in the case of decaying Castle Acre in Norfolk) nor pieces of parchment embodying the privileges of a borough (as in the case of Dunwich in Suffolk) necessarily made a town in pre-industrial society.

Wills, and to a lesser extent, probate inventories, prove to be the only source yielding occupational information in any way consistent in time and space for towns in East Anglia. Other surviving sources giving occupational information are more biased, and can only be regarded as supplementary to that provided by these ecclesiastically administered records. In East Anglia they survive for the Archdeaconries of Norwich, Norfolk, Sudbury and Suffolk, for the Doicese of Norwich, in the records of the Prerogative Court of Canterbury, and in the papers of a number of ecclesiastical peculiars.[4]

Over 150,000 wills appear to survive for the region. However, a considerable variety of problems exist with regard to both the cover,[5] and the interpretation,[6] of wills and the occupational information that they contain. Will-making may have increased over the course of these two centuries, reflecting changes in well-being, status or literacy, while the level and accuracy of recording similarly improved; but the occupational designations in wills contain many pitfalls. In order to gain some idea of how valid it is to use wills as a source on such a large scale, the occupational information given by wills for Norwich can be tested against that given in the Freemen's records for that city, since the two sources are independently derived. Freedom to trade was a jealously guarded privilege, and records of those admitted to it represent the best possible source of the range of occupations in existence. The same people who were freemen were likely also to leave wills. Since many of the statistical characteristics of both bodies of material are unknown, only non-parametric tests can be used to see how closely the information derived from these two different sources does correlate. For each of the three periods in which East Anglian towns are discussed in this chapter (1500–99, 1600–49 and 1650–99) some fifty of the top occupations in the Freemen's lists were ranked against a similar number of those given in wills. Despite a few wide divergences in ranks for some occupations – for example Glovers ranked fifteenth amongst the numbers of Freemen enrolled in the sixteenth century yet thirty-fourth amongst will-leavers – highly significant correlations at the 0·01 level of probability were obtained. (The results were between 1500–99 $r_s = \cdot 8894$; 1600–49 $r_s = \cdot 9722$; 1650–99 $r_s = \cdot 9937$). Neither of the lists from which these coefficients are derived are censuses, nor do they include the poorer sector of society, but nonetheless they can be accepted as the best possible occupational sources. From these results wills can be regarded as providing at least as good a general indication of the occupations present in Norwich as are contained in the Freemen's lists. (Between 1500 and 1599 wills give 109 different occupations and the Freemen's register 143; between 1600 and 1649 the former 98 and the latter 120; but between 1650 and 1699 the number given in wills rises to 121 while that from Freemen lists drops to 114). The further implications that can be drawn must be very cautious, however.

Wills remain the most comprehensive available source for the whole region between 1500 and 1700, and are the best archive that can be created from the range of available sources, in order to try to resolve the simple problem of describing the East Anglia urban system. Other records are only supplementary. For instance, corporate records on any scale survive for only five towns, Norwich, Great Yarmouth and Kings Lynn in Norfolk, and Bury St Edmunds and Ipswich in Suffolk; they may record the admission of freemen often with their occupation,[7] or that of apprentices to employment.[8] Local[9] and national government[10] lists and census-style documents compiled in response to religious or political enquiries, or recording the administration of the poor laws and poor relief,[11] can often yield much for individual years, but these unfortunately are usually for different towns at widely separated dates. A host of other miscellaneous records can be of use, ranging from the books of town court depositions[12] before the corporations, to records of entertainments[13] paid for by the borough which chance, *inter alia*, to tell us the occupations of those involved.

Change in the East Anglian Urban System

The information yielded by these sources enable a comparative examination of the urban system of East Anglia over 200 years to be made. Certainly betwen 1500 and 1700 this area seems to have been relatively stable, and to have been one for which 'change' rather than 'decline' or 'growth' is a more appropriate term in any discussion of the structure and interrelationships of its towns. It thus seems to fit into the general framework developed earlier for the towns of England as a whole.[14]

The two centuries are broken down into periods, in order to describe and analyze the changing system. These are 1500–99; 1600–49; and 1650–99. There were sometimes quite fundamental short-term fluctuations affecting the towns of East Anglia; these ranged from slumps in manufactures[15] to disastrous fires[16] and plagues. Thus some short-term changes of the urban system consequent on secular trends like changes in the terms of trade for textile manufactures, or unexpected and chance events like the devastation of a fire, are rather obscured by this approach. Indeed, considerable lengths of time are, as it were, held steady in order to make a preliminary survey of the urban structure of the region possible. This approach depends on considerable periods of time being used in order to get a picture of the whole system from the few available sources, particularly for the smaller centres. Thus a period of fifty years or so is necesssary if the integration of evidence for the smallest with the largest towns is to be made possible. A hundred years may seem a rather long period, but its use for the sixteenth century in this study was entirely constrained by sources. Occupational information on any scale is very scarce for the period before 1500,[17] and it increases only slowly in volume as the years pass. 1550 thus might have been more practical starting point, but in order to preserve as much information as possible a longer period is used. In particular this makes possible the retention of information on occupations that are important indicators of relative urban status and activity, as more sophisticated occupations spread slowly and erratically down through the system into the smaller towns, and even the villages of pre-industrial East Anglia.[18] Many of these had an already old-established basic local craft structure reinforcing employment in both agriculture and the manufacture of worsteds and woollens.[19] It is certainly the case that in structural studies of this kind, 'An exceptional craft is just as important as a predominating trade',[20] in indicating urban status. Exceptionally indicative occupations in association in any place are very important when seen against the background of the ubiquitous pre-industrial agricultural occupations. Lastly, the division employed has the advantage of supplying similar numbers of occupations for each of the three periods employed, and therefore of giving 'samples' in quasi-quantitative terms related to growing population, (see Table 1). For between 1650 and 1699 the number of wills, and the proportion giving occupational information did increase, but only roughly in proportion to the growing size of the population. The division of the two centuries adopted depended most of all on the availability of sources and reasoned compromises made with them. The stability of the system itself makes such a study as this possible. Movements within the urban system seldom represented anything more than perturbations and slow readjustments, rather than dramatic alterations of course.

The sixteenth and seventeenth centuries in East Anglia, when looked at in the context of long-term urban, as well as economic development, could be thought of as simply representing the maximum adjustment of a pre-industrial urban system. The precursors of future movements in its towns consequent on 'the industrial revolution' can be seen, but to a much lesser extent than in other parts of the country which were to bear the full brunt of industrialization. Indeed, the structure of East Anglian towns, as represented here, may have been broadly typical of many other parts of pre-industrial England, although there were many differences between regions, and indeed between towns of different sizes, complexity and shape. The sixteenth century opened with a nationwide urban malaise, as we saw in Chapter 2, which wealthy and economically advanced East Anglia undoubtedly shared. This was followed by the initiation of some change and growth after the stagnation of the fifteenth century, although the chronology and causes of these secular movements are still open to debate regionally as well as nationally. Towns of all sizes in East Anglia, even Norwich, seem to have been in a far from flourishing state at the time. In Norwich buildings were in decay and the destruction wrought by fires, in a setting where the thatched roof was still prevalent, was often long unrighted. The Mayor and Corporation were reduced to ordering that if vacant land was not rebuilt, or at least surrounded by a stone wall, it should revert to the corporation:[21] such regulations would not have been necessary in a buoyant urban economy. That city's great cloth manufacture was in a poor way, too.[22] Not much store should be set on the tales of urban woe told by urban petitioners against taxes or for state relief, but we must pay at least some attention to the statutes of the realm. In early sixteenth-century East Anglia, some were deeply preoccupied with problems of the decay of the urban environment. For instance,

Forasmuche as there have ben in tymes past divers and many beautiful Houses of Habitaecion within the walls and libertyes of the Cities Burroughes and Townes of . . . Ipswich . . . Great Yarmouth . . . and nowe are fallen downe decayed and at this day remaine unreedified and doo lye as desolate and vacante grounds, many of them nygh adioyning to the high stretis replennyshed withe much unclennes and filthe with pittes, sellers and vaultis lying open and uncovered, . . . and some houses be feoble and very like to fall down dangerous to passe by, which decayes are to the great impoverishing and hinderance of the same boroughs and towns.[23]

Such patent ills – which must have been indicative of economic and demographic stagnation – could be put right by the civic authorities (as in the case of Norwich) if the owners did not do so. Even the smallest towns received this sort of attention; the 'Towne of Dunwich in the Countie of Suffolk' was another place to be examined,[24] although many of its particular problems can be attributed solely to the ravages of the eroding sea.

The beginning of the sixteenth century was thus no more a period of great buoyancy in the urban system of East Anglia than in the nation as a whole. As the sixteenth century passed, however, greater activity and prosperity was possible for some, if not all of the towns of the two counties, and indeed the whole country.[25] Larger towns all over the region had probably been fairly complex in a structural sense for a considerable time; in the latter half of the thirteenth century about 130 trades were practised in Norwich, for example.[26] Even lesser places were quite occupationally sophisticated by the seventeenth century. Change was certainly in the air in the urban system as the century developed, and paralleled the upsurge of population to the end of the sixteenth century, erratic though that was. During this time the population of Norfolk and Suffolk increased from around 200,000 in the 1520s to over 250,000 in 1600 and 305,000 in 1700. This was a movement in which the region's towns, having high death rates but being 'fed' by immigration, at the very least kept pace.

Table 12 shows that around a quarter of the region's population lived in places thought of here as towns, a proportion slowly increasing to reach about a third by 1700. Parallel with this growth there had been a continued movement down through the urban system of crafts and occupations that had once seemingly been the preserve of larger towns.[27] This process extended into the villages[28] of East Anglia to some extent also. Certainly a much more complex urban structure had emerged by the end of the seventeenth century in what

Table 12: THE TOWNS OF EAST ANGLIA 1520–1670s (ROUNDED FIGURES)

	Population 1524–25	Per cent change	Population 1603	Per cent change	Population 1670	Overall per cent change
Norwich N	8,000	37	15,000(?)	81	20,000(X)	150
Kings Lynn N	4,500(?)	33	8,000(?)	50	9,000(?)	100
Gt Yarmouth N	4,000(?)	37	8,000(?)	81	10,000(X)	150
Bury St Edmunds	3,550	26	4,500	37	6,200	74
Ipswich S	3,100	61	5,000(?)	58	7,900	154
Wymondham N	1,450	10	1,600	93	3,100	113
Hadleigh S	1,500	16	1,750(?)	20	2,100	40
Beccles S	1,200	−8	1,100	59	1,750	45
Sudbury S	1,200	12	1,350	48	2,000	66
Dunwich S	1,150	−26	850	−64	300	−73
Little Walsingham N	1,100(X)	−27	800(?)	6	850	−22
Aylsham N	1,100	−36	700(X)	92	1,350	22
Lavenham S	1,050	14	1,200	25	1,500	42
Long Melford S	1,000	15	1,150	56	1,750	75
Woodbridge S	950	15	1,100	31	1,450	52
North Walsham N	800	12	900	77	1,600(X)	100
Diss N	800	−12	700	114	1,500	87
Lowestoft S	750	33	1,000	0	1,000	33
Thetford N	700	28	900(?)	33	1,200	71
Attleborough N	700	7	750	40	1,050	50
Mildenhall S	700	42	1,000	90	1,900	171
Aldeburgh S	700	85	1,300(X)	−50	650(X)	−7
Bungay S	650	61	1,050	14	1,200	84
Southwold S	650	38	900(?)	50	1,350	107
East Dereham N	600	83	1,100	36	1,500	150
Swaffham N	600	41	850	23	1,050	75
Stoke-by-Nayland S	600	—	—	—	—	—
Framlingham S	550	36	750	33	1,000	81
Nayland S	525	57	825	—	—	—
Debenham S	500	0	500	0	500	0
Stowmarket S	500	60	800	75	1,400	180
Eye S	500	0	500	70	850	70
Harleston N	400	75	700(?)	21	850	112
Fakenham N	400	25	500	45	725	81
Needham Market S	400	37	550(?)	27	700	75
Downham Market N	350(X)	0	350(X)	185	1,000	185
Wickham Market S	350	50	525	4	550	57
Loddon N	325	23	400	75	700	115
Holt N	325	23	400	50	600	84
Woolpit S	325	23	400	6	425	30
Ixworth S	300	66	500	10	550	83
Burnham Market N	275	−9	250	40	350	27
Halesworth S	250	140	600	66	1,000	300
Gorleston S	250	—	—	—	550	120
Cromer N	225	133	525	−71	150(X)	−33
Saxmundham S	200	0	200(X)	212	625	212
Watton N	175	71	300(?)	50	450	157
Wells N	—	—	1,300	15	1,500	—
Foulsham N	—	—	500	30	650	—
Total	50,225		65,425		98,375	

Note: (?) = Estimated figure from partial source. (X) = Figure from doubtful source.
N = Norfolk. S = Suffolk.

was still one of the wealthiest and most populous parts of the country; a considerable transformation had taken place.

Towns in the Sixteenth Century

Even the largest provincial towns were more important as centres of distribution and manufacture than they were of consumption. In this way they were almost a different breed of urban animal from London, whose major role as a centre of consumption made it unique in pre-industrial England. The nineteenth-century Norfolk antiquarian and paper-chase runner, Walter Rye, wrote of 'the curious information' that could be gained from the Norwich Freemen's Books as to the numbers of trades that were carried on by their citizens. He felt that this number was ' ... only to be accounted for by the fact that in olden days, if a countryman wanted an out-of-the-way article, he could not get it easily sent him from London, or any other centre, as he can now'.[29] It is probable that the provisioning of pre-industrial towns, except in famine years, was much less of a problem than was the town's problem of meeting the needs of their hinterlands, where was situated the biggest market for goods.[30] In sixteenth-century Norfolk and Suffolk about three-quarters of the population lived outside, though usually within close reach, of some town (Fig. 10); by 1700 this proportion had only declined a little. Towns presented a market place for such country folk, and redistributed goods into the country *via* travelling chapmen, and later through urban-provisioned rural shops.

The range of economic activities that towns embraced is indicated by the presence or absence of different occupations as shown on Figure 11. All available information on the presence of occupations has been gathered and ranked against the towns for which it survives, by the technique of scalogram analysis. These scalograms can be related to the size of towns (see Table 12 and Figure 12) in order to get some idea of the regional standing and importance of all East Anglia's towns. Scalogram analysis is a very simple non-parametric ranking tecnnique by which towns and occupations can be set the one against the other, providing both a good description of the urban hierarchy and a starting point for wider discussion of their role. Total numbers involved in any occupation are not taken into account; presence or absence of occupation in any town is all that is considered in the analysis. Such a technique is of wide applicability in the historical and social sciences, whether in the eighteenth-

10 Locational map of the towns of East Anglia in the sixteenth and seventeenth centuries
(Based on J. Patten, 'Population distribution in Norfolk and Suffolk during the sixteenth and seventeenth centuries', *Trans. Institute British Geographers*, 65 (1975), 45-65)

century Netherlands,[31] nineteenth-century U.S.A.,[32] or the urban geography of twentieth-century Australia.[33] In essence, scalograms rank order subjects (e.g. towns in rows on graphs like Fig. 11) and items (e.g. occupations in columns on graphs like Fig. 11) simultaneously, so that if the universe of attributes considered (in this case all the occupations of all the town-dwellers in East Anglia)

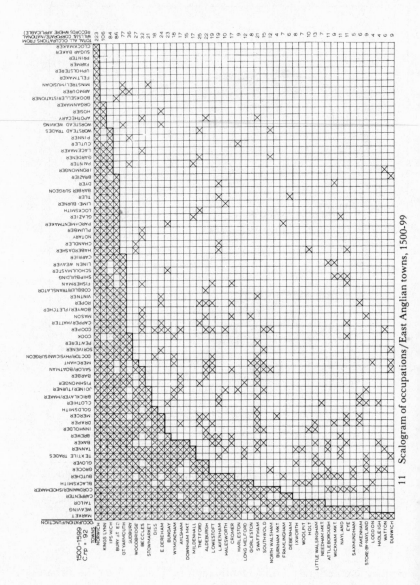

11　Scalogram of occupations/East Anglian towns, 1500–99

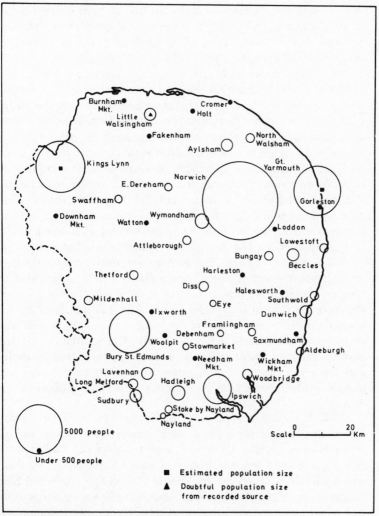

12 Population size of towns in East Anglia, 1524-25
(Based on Patten, 'Population distribution in Norfolk and Suffolk')

contains a single acceptable variable than this last will always be obtained, whatever sample is taken. The most important statistical point is that from any sample inferences may be drawn about the whole universe of attributes. Besides this invaluable property the method is visually excellent, presenting an easily assimilated picture of the configuration of the data. All occupations and towns above the cutting point, or heavy black line, on the graph are said to 'scale'; 'missing' occupations above the line, or those present below it, are thought of as 'errors' in the relationship which has to meet but one real statistical demand, a 'coefficient of reproducibility' (c_{rp}) always of more than 0·90.

The pattern shown on Figure 11 is of a steadily progressing complexity of places entering the scale (above the black line, or cutting point) according to their relationship with the increasing number of occupations entered. Ubiquitous occupations such as husbandman or labourer are not included; on the other hand the possession of a market is included as just one more economic attribute and given no special weighting. This ranking of towns by their occupational structure on a simple presence or absence basis facilitates visual and statistical comparison of occupational information drawn from different sources of different dates, and for towns of different sizes. It obscures much, not least the numbers of people involved in the various occupations and their relative standing in urban economies, as well as secular changes. But such an approach presents the best starting point – and nothing more is claimed for it – for regional economic analysis of towns; it gives an *entré* into the comparative structure of towns of a far wider nature than that permitted by, for example, direct comparisons of the numbers involved in different occupations enumerated in freemen's lists. The occupations plotted here stand as mere proxies for the dynamic urban economic whole, and conclusions drawn from them must not only be cautious, but also cannot be far-reaching. Nonetheless, important outlines can be drawn.

Norwich, as might be expected, heads the scale of the forty-seven towns that are shown. These vary greatly in the numbers of recorded occupations in them up to a maximum of 223; and in population size from a few hundred to at least 8,000 people. Norwich, which contained nearly five per cent of the total population of East Anglia in the 1520s (when London must have had a similar proportion of the population of the country as a whole) was dominant. At the other end of the scale, towns like Loddon, having markets though they did, seemed to be merging into the characteristic size and structure of places that might more properly be thought of as villages. There was clearly a close relationship, as might be expected, between total numbers of occupations and town size; this can be clearly seen on Figures 13 and 14; at the lower end of these figures the regular relationship begins to break down, where there was an 'equipossible' area in which the log-linear relationship ceases, and where the transition from town to village probably occurred. The chances of entry into the scalogram, and thus into consideration as towns on these graphs at the lower end, was probably governed by chance survival of sources from a small possible sample. The criteria for urbanity assumed here is thus an ordered association of occupations (usually, but not always, in-

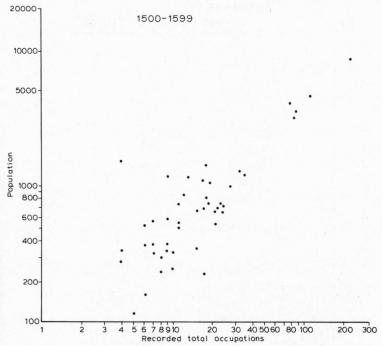

13   Relationship of recorded total population/recorded total occupations, 1500-99

cluding a formal market function), which is highly significant in a statistical as well as a empirical sense. There was a correlation ($r_s =$ 0·635) that is highly significant. Figure 14 which shows this, graphically relates the information on population size given on Table 12 to the scalogram ranking of towns and occupations on Figure 11. It is clear from this evidence that types of occupations such as weaver or tailor had a good chance of being found in almost every East Anglian town. Other occupations were restricted to larger and more important places, but these were not necessarily just the most sophisticated of trades and services. Tudor contemporaries thought that every town should 'be replenished with all kinds of artificers; not only clothiars, which as yet weare oure naturall occupation, but with cappers, glovers, paper makers, glasiers, painters, goldsmithes, blacke smithes of all sortes, coverlet makers, nedle makers, pinners . . .'; naturally towns at the head of the urban hierarchy were likely to have all or most of these occupations, as Figure 11 shows. There were also likely to be rather less economically important, but equally specialized occupations at the

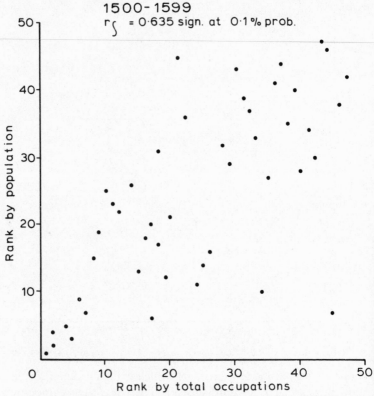

14   Relationship of town's rank by population/rank by occupation, 1500-99

very bottom of the occupational hierarchy which would only be found in the largest and most economically complex towns. Needs that were served in the home or not served at all in small towns or villages, were in enough demand in the largest towns to lead to the setting up of specialized, if low order, occupations representing divisions of labour. The shoemaker in some little town probably sold some ready-made shoes, made up others to order and mended and repaired worn articles. But it was only in the five largest towns of East Anglia, Norwich, Kings Lynn, Great Yarmouth, Ipswich and

Bury St Edmunds, that specialized and apparently whole-time cobblers, shoe repairers and translators (who literally took shoes made for one size and 'translated' them to fit another foot) can be found. In a way, such specialized trades are just as important as those of a rich grocer or vintner as indications of urban standing and specialization; the townsfolk of large towns lived by taking in each others' washing, to use Lewis Mumford's immortal phrase, just as much as they thrived on distributing and redistributing goods to surrounding social and economic hinterlands.

There seems to have been quite a clear fourfold urban hierarchy in East Anglia in the sixteenth century. At its top and standing by itself was Norwich in Norfolk, a great provincial city; the next level was of the four county and/or port towns of Kings Lynn and Great Yarmouth in Norfolk, Ipswich and Bury St Edmunds in Suffolk; below these places were some forty lesser towns. A number of them were quite large, and had economical importance over a reasonably wide area, like Wymondham in Norfolk or Hadleigh in Suffolk, with their noted marketing or manufacturing specialities. Many more were tiny with sometimes declining markets and few economic functions, being hardly distinguishable from villages; such were Woolpit in Suffolk and Loddon in Norfolk. Certainly there was a qualitative difference between the biggest and smallest of these market towns, though it is difficult to draw a clear line between them.[34]

Norwich was much more than a county town, and ranked with Bristol, York and Newcastle-upon-Tyne as one of the biggest and most important provincial cities of the realm.[35] Over the sixteenth century 223 different occupations were recorded in a city which was a great market and fair centre. The richness and variety of the city's life could probably only be matched by that of Bristol, apart from London. Not only was there the full range of village and small-town activities like tailoring and carpentering, together with notable textile manufactures, but also a whole host of high-level distributive and service activities, and representatives of the developing professions. There were merchants, grocers, mercers and vintners, notaries, apothecaries and doctors, as well as lesser services, only to be found then in larger towns, like barbers and cobblers. A number of parchment-makers are evidence of the continued importance of one way of conveying information, and printers and stationers herald the advent of another. The first books were being printed in Norwich in the 1570s by one Antony de Solemne, who came from the Low Countries,[36] and later became a freeman.[37] Other immigrants helped to transform the Norwich textile industry[38] with the introduction of the 'New Draperies', an innovation which gave the kiss of life to its flagging textile trades in mid-century. Textiles were of great importance to the city's economy, though it was no more dependent on one industry than any other pre-industrial town. Manufacturing of the old and the new draperies was merely an overlay on the city's economy, albeit an important one. Had Norwich not had its noted cloth manufacture it would undoubtedly still have been a great provincial city comparable with York in status.

Other innovations of importance from across the North Sea were brick and tiling techniques which helped increasingly to replace the timber-framed and thatched buildings that still crammed the city, new vegetables and fruits that were used first of all in suburban market gardening,[39] and many trading links.[40] Nowhere else in East Anglia, and perhaps nowhere nearer than London itself, could be found such luxury specialized trades as upholsterers, clockmakers, or refineries of exotic goods such as sugar-bakers, as early as the sixteenth century. In the latter part of the century, in the 1570s and 1580s, a rare opportunity occurs to illustrate what was probably approaching the total array of occupations of most Norwich townsfolk, the poor as well as the better-off. (See Tables 13 and 14.) This is based on a householders list of 1589, possibly for muster purposes; a list of strangers living in the town, largely from the Low Countries, taken in 1568; and a so-called 'census' of the poor taken in 1570. About 150 of the 223 occupations listed for the whole of the sixteenth century are recorded in these; 223 may be a rather artificially high number, some of the occupational names simply being different ones that were used for the same activity. This total of 150 shown in Table 13 is still greater than for other provincial cities like York, where apparently only between 90 and 100 trades were practised at any one time, though about another 50 occupations were mentioned occasionally throughout the sixteenth century.[41] These lists support the evidence of great occupational complexity derived from other sources such as wills and shown on the scalogram (Fig. 11). In particular Figure 14 reveals fascinating details of the everyday activities of the poor of the city, numerically large though economically less important than those who took up their freedom. The poor never became free, usually had not served apprenticeships nor left wills, and thus were left out of the records which were used to construct, for example, Figure 11. Of course, some people who had become free appeared in the lists of the poor, being luckless weavers or cappers, for example. In addition, there are many poor in trades like

Table 13: THE OCCUPATIONAL STRUCTURE OF NORWICH IN THE LATER
SIXTEENTH CENTURY

	From the Lists of Strangers, 1568	From the 'Census' of the Poor, 1570*	From the 'Census' of the City, 1589
Aquavita Seller	—	1	—
(Alderman	—	—	11)
Apothecary	—	—	7
Armourer	1	—	1
Attorney	—	—	7
Bagmaker	—	1	—
Baker	1	6	23
Barber	—	2	13
Basket maker	—	3	3
Bell founder	—	—	2
Boatwright	—	1	4
Bodger	—	5	—
Bonesetter	—	—	1
Bookbinder	—	1	—
Bookseller	4	—	—
Bowyer	—	1	3
Brewer	—	4	33
Builder	1	—	—
Butcher	—	5	36
Cabinet maker	1	—	—
Capper	1	1	—
Calenderer	—	2	4
Carpenter	11	9	35
Carter	—	2	3
Carrier	—	1	9
Carver	—	—	2
Chandler	—	1	—
Chimney-sweep	—	1	—
Clasp-maker	—	1	—
Clerk	—	2	—
Clothier	—	—	1
Clothworker	—	—	1
Clothsherman	1	—	—
Cobbler	—	31	28
Comber	—	—	4
Cook	—	—	4
Cooper	—	1	9
Cordwainer	—	17	48
Cornmerchant	1	—	—
Corvisor	—	—	1
Currier	1	1	7
Cutler	1	—	8
Dealer in cloth and Bays	1	—	—
Doctor	—	—	1
Dornix-weaver	9	—	13
Draper	6	—	16
Dyer	5	1	7

	From the Lists of Strangers, 1568	From the 'Census' of the Poor, 1570*	From the 'Census' of the City, 1589
Embroiderer	—	1	1
(Esquire	—	—	2)
Factor for Merchant Aliens	1	—	—
Feltmaker	—	—	2
Fisherman	—	—	14
Freshwater Fisherman	—	1	—
Fishmonger	—	—	5
Fletcher	—	1	2
Freemason	—	—	1
Fringemaker	8	—	—
Fuller	12	—	—
Furbisher	—	1	—
Gardener	2	3	4
Gatherer of Coney skins	—	1	—
(Gent.	—	—	28)
Glazier	1	5	13
Glover	—	7	22
Goldsmith	—	2	4
Grocer	—	—	60
Haberdasher	—	1	10
Hairweaver	—	1	1
Hatter	—	8	26
Haymaker	—	1	—
Hempspinner	3	—	—
Hosier	—	—	6
Husbandman	1	1	21
Innholder	—	—	5
Innkeeper	—	—	3
Ironmonger	—	1	2
Joiner	—	1	11
Keelman/Boatman	—	3	3
Knacker	—	1	1
Keepers of . . .	—	2	—
Labourer	—	119	161
Laceweaver	—	6	1
Lathervyver	—	1	1
Lime-burner	8	1	1
Linen-weaver	—	1	—
Locksmith	1	—	6
Maker of Horns and spoons	—	1	—
Maltster	—	—	11
Mariner/Seaman	1	1	1
Mason	—	10	19
(Mayer	—	—	1)
Mercer	—	—	2
Merchant	27	—	15
Midwife	1	—	—
Miller	—	2	7
Minister	5	—	—
Mouldmaker	1	1	—

	From the Lists of Strangers, 1568	From the 'Census' of the Poor, 1570*	From the 'Census' of the City, 1589
(Nobilis	1	—	—)
Notary	—	—	1
Painter	—	2	6
Parchmentmaker	—	1	2
Patten-maker	—	—	2
Ped-maker	—	5	5
Pewterer	—	1	4
Physician	1	—	—
Pinner	—	—	4
Pipe filler	—	1	—
Ploughman	—	1	—
Plumber	—	—	3
Pointmaker	—	1	1
Potter	1	—	—
Printer	2	—	—
Quarry Picker	—	1	—
Reeder	—	5	8
Roper	—	—	1
Russell weaver	—	3	—
Sadler	—	—	4
Sawyer	—	8	3
Sayweaver	1	—	8
Schoolmaster	5	—	6
Scrivener	2	—	9
Shepherd/Herdsman	1	2	—
Sherman	—	6	14
Shoemaker	5	—	3
Silkweaver/silkfringe weaver	2	—	—
Silversmith	—	1	—
Skinner	—	1	3
Slaughterman	—	1	—
Slaymaker/wright	—	2	4
Smith	13	1	23
Spicebreadmaker	—	1	—
Spindlemaker	—	1	1
Stainer	—	1	—
Stationer	—	—	3
Surgeon	2	—	2
Sutor (sic)	1	—	—
Tailor	18	18	111
Tanner	—	1	—
Tawyer	—	1	—
Thatcher	—	1	—
Tiler	—	2	3
Tinker	—	1	1
Tipler	—	—	2
Traveller in small wares	—	1	—
Turner	—	—	1
Twisterer	—	—	3

	From the Lists of Strangers, 1568	From the 'Census' of the Poor, 1570*	From the 'Census' of the City, 1589
Upholsterer	—	—	1
Waterman	—	1	—
Weaver	60	9	193
Wheelwright	—	—	1
Woolchapman	—	—	1
Woolcomber	166	2	—
Woolenweaver	—	1	—
Workman	1	—	—
Worsted sherman	—	1	—
Worsted weaver	—	62	12
Wright	—	1	—
Valuer	1	—	—
Yeoman	—	—	13
TOTALS	401 in 47 occupations	453 in 93 occupations	1,286 in 106 occupations

Total of 2,140 people in 159 different types of occupation, or status designation, overall.

*Census' of Poor taken from tables in J. F. Pound 'An Elizabethan census of the Poor,' *Univ. of Birmingham Hist. Jnl.*, VIII, (1961–2) 135–161.

Table 14: NORWICH OCCUPATIONS OF THE POOR IN 1570,* NOT REPRESENTED IN THE FREEMEN'S REGISTERS 1500–99

Acqua-vita seller	1	Boatwright (1 will, 1500–99)	1
Bodger	5	Chandler (2 wills, 1500–99)	1
Chapman (2 wills, 1500–99)	1	Chimney Sweep	1
Gatherer of Coney Skins	1	Haymaker	1
Keepers of Institutions	2	Laceweavers	6
Mariner (1 will, 1500–99)	1	Mouldmaker	1
Maker of Horns and Spoons	1	Pipe Filler	1
Ploughman	1	Quarry Picker	1
Shepherd	2	Silversmith	1
Slaughterman	1	Slaywright (1 will, 1500–99)	1
Spicebreadmaker	1	Spindlemaker	1
Tawyer	1	Traveller in Small Wares	1
Thatcher	1	'Wright'	1
Woolcomber (1 will, 1500–99)	1		

*Taken from J. F. Pound 'An Elizabethan census of the Poor', *Univ. of Birmingham Historical Journal*, VIII, (1961–2), 135–61.

Acquavita Sellers, Chimney Sweeps and Quarry Pickers,[42] such people produced little, and earned less. They rarely had enough to contribute to taxes like the lay subsidies, or to the city's wealth; indeed they were more of a drain on the city's resources, as well as a social nuisance and a prospective civic danger, always to the forefront of the corporate mind of the city fathers.

Such people represented one half of the urban dual economy, and sometimes must have outnumbered the more productive half. The fact that the poor were rarely entered in documentary records, save when they were whipped or put into a house of correction or buried at civic expense, certainly affects the completeness of the records of occupational structures; on the other hand, this fact is in itself an indication of just how ineffective they must have been in town economics. In the biggest cities, such as Norwich, they collected in great number, regulated and sometimes supported by better off citizens. Pickpockets, thieves, and prostitutes must have flourished in its daily markets, and in its fairs, as well as in the great annual cattle fair held just outside Norwich at Norsham St Faith. In its size, its sophisticated economic complexity, its manufactures and trade, and its poor, Norwich was clearly aping the role in its East Anglian region which London had begun to play for the nation as a whole.

The four towns in the second level of the hierarchy, Bury St Edmunds, Kinds Lynn, Ipswich, and Great Yarmouth, were of major importance in their counties, and the last three of them were also seaports with important links around the coastal trading network and overseas. They were smaller than Norwich, and less occupationally sophisticated, but they stand out clearly above the rest of East Anglia's towns. They played a role in their regions that is characterized in Camden's description of Ipswich in the early sixteenth century; he wrote that it was 'a faire town resembling a city, situate in a graunde somewhat low; which is the eie (as it were) of this shire . . .'[43] Town houses for the gentry were being built in Bury St Edmunds by the end of Elizabeth's reign.[44] Their economic and social influence was much more restricted than that of Norwich, and some of them had the sort of regional influence that it did. Norwich, for example, drew apprentices from all over sixteenth-century East Anglia, while these four towns had much more restricted migration fields, drawing young apprentices mostly from within about fifteen miles in their own counties.[45] Yet whilst their regional 'pull' was more limited than that of Norwich, they had a large number of different occupations and were notable centres of trade, manufacture, and (in the case of ports) seaborne trade and fisheries. Kings

Lynn was the node of a great riverine corn and malt marketing system; Great Yarmouth was an important centre for shipbuilding and the North Sea herring fisheries, and played its part in the coaling trade from Newcastle and the north-east, as did Kings Lynn; Ipswich had a major role in the sixteenth century in exporting cloth, though this was to decline in the next century as the cloth manufactures of its Suffolk–Essex manufacturing hinterland declined. It also played a vital role in supplying London with food, notably butter and cheese. All three also played the typical inland county town role that Bury St Edmunds had for West Suffolk. It had no noted manufactures, but like many other English county towns rather was the economic, administrative, legal and social capital of its shire.

Great Yarmouth and Ipswich, like Norwich, were amongst those towns which were in a state of some economic stagnation at the beginning of the sixteenth century. Yarmouth was having trouble clearing its silting haven, and a stream of petitions went up to the monarch for relief because of it;[46] Ipswich suffered from fluctuations in foreign trade. Bury seems to have suffered for a while from its decline as a pilgrimage centre, and it certainly declined for a while from effects of the Reformation, which closed the great abbey which the town had long supplied; the abbey itself had employed people engaged in about forty different occupations, ranging from tailors to plumbers.[47] It must have been quite difficult for these redundant workpeople to be quickly absorbed into the town's economy after 1539. Nonetheless, it had its substantial markets, fairs and tradespeople; an annual guild procession through the town in 1492 contained about forty occupations proceeding under different flags.[48] Bury, like Ipswich, had its Grocers and Vintners, Cappers and Hatters, Physicians and Surgeons. Like Ipswich, Great Yarmouth and Kings Lynn, economic recovery came quite quickly for Bury St Edmunds after the mid-century; all four were the buoyant regional centres they had been in medieval times throughout the seventeenth century. Their role shows great continuity.

Filling in the broad urban network supplied by these four towns focusing on Norwich were another forty lesser towns, ranging from Sudbury in Suffolk, centre of an internationally important textile manufacturing industry, right down to tiny places like neo-rural Watton in a largely agricultural part of Norfolk. Such places as these more immediately touched the economic and social lives of most of the countryfolk of East Anglia than did Norwich or the county towns. Almost all were market towns with at least one weekly market; some had fairs in or hard by them. Places like Wymondham in Norfolk were noted as the centre for trade in manufactured goods, in this case for wooden goods like spoons, plates, taps and spigots,[49] and a number of wills of Wymondham 'turners' and 'spooners' survive; others like Hadleigh in Suffolk were deeply involved in actual manufacture, and were to remain so – with the stability typical of the pre-industrial urban system – for very long periods of time. In early Tudor times and in Stuart England,[50] Hadleigh was 'a prosperous town consisting in the trade of clothing'. Others like Woodbridge were important ports on the coasting trade. Particular involvement in some trade or manufacture must have contributed considerably to the population and economy of such places. Indeed most of the larger places outside of Norwich and the county towns had some such speciality. Yet they were also engaged in much more local activities that were the sole rationale for lesser places, like Ixworth or Woolpit in Suffolk with populations of 300 or 400 each, a market and half a dozen non-agricultural occupations which were at the bottom end of the rank relation expressed by the continuum of points shown on Figure 13. There may well be no clear break between larger and smaller market towns that can be imposed on this simple descriptive rank-size continuum, yet clearly another Suffolk town like Beccles with a parish population of at least a thousand, flourishing markets and at least thirty non-agricultural occupations, was a markedly different sort of place in character from Ixworth or Woolpit. Beccles was a major local service centre as much as Ixworth or Woolpit were clearly minor local service centres. Such major centres in the sixteenth century tended to have a population of approaching or more than 1,000, and tended to have more than twenty or so non-agricultural occupations concerned with manufacture or service. They stand quite high in the scalogram shown in Figure 11. Many of their occupations are above the cutting line on the scalogram, and are thus, as scaling occupations, indicators of the economic standing of such places. Besides carrying the agricultural and village-level functions that towns of whatever size did, they generally possessed an association of trades which suggest fair internal and local regional demand, as well as some manufacturing speciality, such as linen in and around Bungay in Suffolk. They commonly had only the occasional representative of such occupations, offering only basic services like tailoring, carpentering, cordwaining, and shoemaking.

Sometimes, however, the expected relationship between population size and numbers of occupations is not apparent; this may be attributable on the one hand to deficiencies in sources, or on the other to more tangible reasons. Dunwich on the Suffolk coast was quite a large town in the sixteenth century, yet it had relatively few recorded occupations; most of its wills were rather poor, and it stands right at the bottom of the towns considered here. (See Fig. 11.) It was suffering terribly from coastal erosion, and its decline can be reasonably attributed to this. Camden said that Dunwich 'lieth (as it were) desolate', and Leland stressed the effects of the rages of the sea on the fading port.[51] Most places, however, conformed to a generally stable rank-size relationship within the four broad categories of town outlined. Within this stable relationship the fortunes of individual towns could fluctuate, though rarely as dramatically as was the case with Dunwich. Sudbury's fortunes as a cloth-collecting centre, for example, went up and down over the sixteenth century as terms of foreign trade fluctuated; and some of the ports suffered setbacks from privateers. Much more seriously, particularly for the smaller and less resilient towns, were the effects of episodic disasters such as fires and plagues. Larger towns such as Norwich, Kings Lynn and Yarmouth[52] also suffered from fires and plagues, the effects of which were heightened by crowded intermural conditions, but being more robust, they could quite quickly recover. Lesser places, even some major marketing centres, could suffer longer setbacks. Beccles had a disastrous fire in 1586;[53] Southwold was burnt 'pitifully' in 1596;[54] and the great fire of East Dereham in 1581 apparently burnt nearly every house in the town, causing a total loss claimed to be £14,000.[55] It took some time for these places to reassert themselves. Plagues severely hampered the little port of Lowestoft in the same way in 1547, 1579 and 1585;[56] and disrupted the trade of much larger places. Great Yarmouth was hit by plague in 1578, and immediately not only was all traffic prohibited between that port and Norwich inland up the River Yare, but the Mayor of Newcastle wrote asking that no more boats be sent from Yarmouth for coal.[57]

In between such catastrophic events, the everyday life of small towns was quiet and regular, focusing on the weekly markets and having close links with their surrounding countryside. Little ports like Blakeney, which does not enter into consideration amongst the towns on the scalogram, must have been as quiet as many tiny places which had small weekly markets, but similarly *cannot* be thought of as truly urban by the criteria adopted here. Blakeney must have woken up when the coasting boats came in, and gone to sleep when they left. Besides a little fishing and seafaring, the occupations of its people were limited in extent, and the considerable trade that came through Blakeney[58] seemed to leave relatively little impact on it; this was the case with many other small ports around the Norfolk and Suffolk coast, they were really landing places for the import of coastal goods from London together with coal from Newcastle, and for the export of largely agricultural produce. Such passing trade did not touch them as much as might be expected. The same was true of little inland places with dying markets such as Thorpe[59] and Fransham[60] in Norfolk, both called 'Market' in the wills of people dying in them in the early sixteenth century, but neither seeming to have a significant hint of urban life in them. There were a number of declining markets in both Norfolk and Suffolk. (See Table 15.) The attractions of such places for trade would have been very small, and those with goods to sell or money to spend would have by-passed them in order to go to larger and more lively urban centres. They suffered from the competition of larger places and the fact that more and more goods and services could actually be obtained in rural areas.[61] Most small areas in East Anglia such as Babergh Hundred in Suffolk could show the whole range of settlements; it had villages composed entirely of farmers; some having manufacturing workers as well; other villages which were working as service centres and markets; as well as clearly urban places like Sudbury.[62]

Slowly improving communications increased the centrality and attractiveness of larger centres. Carrying services in East Anglia seem well-established at least as early as the fifteenth century, though this is not to say that travel and trade was without its hazard. There were few 'main' roads as such, and those that were in existence were poorly maintained and difficult in winter. Equally, few navigable waterways penetrated into the heart of the region. Even on the short River Yare which symbiotically linked Norwich and Great Yarmouth, trade seasonality was a problem, and silting considerable in mid-century.[63] This in the end benefited Great Yarmouth's status as a port for, as was the case with Hull and York, the inland provincial capital of Norwich could no longer directly receive larger sea-going vessels, but had to rely on transhipment from Yarmouth. Roads were slow and seasonal; Will Kemp, a noted late sixteenth century long-distance dancer, danced from town to town for wagers in 1599, and tells that the road to Long Melford was a 'long myle' and found the highway beyond Clare 'both farther and fouler'.[64] Yet this did not prevent regular carrying services by stage wagon as early as 1564 from Ipswich *via* Stowmarket to London,[65] and people came from all over England to the great annual cattle fair at Horsham St Faiths, north of Norwich; a London draper is recorded as dying there in the 1510s.[66] Equally, much of the trade inland from the thirty ports, creeks and landing places on the Suffolk coast and the thirteen on the Norfolk coast,[67] went overland quite easily, if not on surfaces that we would immediately recognize as roads. It would be wrong to make too much of the newness of improved communications in the sixteenth century, just as it is clear that many villages and towns had quite complex occupational structures in the fourteenth century. The Poll Tax lists of the 1380s show this clearly for the thirteenth century, as much for well-developed Suffolk[68] as for less-developed Yorkshire.[69]

It would be a great mistake to assume that the urban system in sixteenth-century East Anglia was any different in its major lineaments from that of the fourteenth century; the stability of the urban pattern into the sixteenth century is the remarkable thing to note, and not the forging ahead of Norwich, the decline of some small market towns, or Dunwich being washed into the sea.

The Early Seventeenth Century

The beginning of the seventeenth century was one of civil and foreign peace for East Anglia as it was for the rest of the country. However, the first half of the century saw economic disasters in the shape of a slump in the cloth trade and it saw 'natural' disasters in the constant return of plagues and fires. Both hit towns hard, but nonetheless, the region and its towns – largely untouched by the Civil War – were certainly more populous and probably more prosperous than had been the case in the 1520s. It is possible to get rough estimates of population from the imperfect data of the 1603 communicant returns; it is extremely difficult, however, to get any figures for regional or urban prosperity, such as those which can be derived from the lay subsidies of the 1520s. The sources do not exist. Nonetheless it clearly was prosperous; Sir Thomas Wilson, writing of the country around 1600, for example, noted that south Norfolk was very rich. He exclaimed over the numerous gentry that abounded there with a lot of money to spend; such were the conditions reported around the prosperous major market centre of 'Windhame' (Wymondham) in Norfolk.[70]

Certainly there were more people in the two counties, and after a century of considerable if erratic population rise the population was about 250,000. About 65,000 of these lived in the towns that are discussed here, which were becoming steadily larger and more crowded; about a quarter of the population of East Anglia can be defined as urban in the early seventeenth century, a larger proportion than in the early sixteenth century. The increase in population in the rural areas since then had been about 23 per cent, while the towns increased their population by 40 per cent (see Table 12 and Figure 15). Urban population growth was proceeding at a greater rate than overall regional and rural population growth.

There was none of the urban decay apparent to greet the new century, compared with the scene of town's turpitude at the beginning of the sixteenth century. Disruptions in foreign trade because of war had their effect, though the Civil War was to leave the towns of the region largely untouched; the most marked trends were the continuing above-average growth of the regional capital, Norwich, set against a background of considerable stability in the urban systems, a picture in which the occasional example of long-term decay such as the final consignment of Dunwich to urban oblivion is very much the exception. This is clear from an examination of the urban structure of the early seventeenth century in comparison with the sixteenth century. There was very little change in the spatial relationship of towns, although the inexorable process of the decline of the smaller towns continued, as economies of scale provided by larger ones ensured that their locational and economic advantages were capitalized upon.

This relative urban stability is reflected by the occupational structure of towns betwen 1600 and 1649 (see Figs. 11 and 16). The kinds of occupations recorded are not very dissimilar to those recorded in the sixteenth century; the relative numbers of occupations that the different classes of town had were alike too. Two towns drop out of the scalogram altogether; these were Stoke-by-Nayland and Gorleston. Stoke-by-Nayland like other Suffolk broadcloth towns, was suffering from a decline in home and foreign demand for its produce in the face of the lighter New Draperies, while Gorleston, hard by Yarmouth, was increasingly being overshadowed by that port. The deficiencies of sources probably account for the fact that the Norfolk seaport of Wells-next-the-sea, which had not entered the scalogram in the sixteenth century, appears with a reasonably well-defined occupational structure in the early seventeenth century (see Fig. 16); the little Norfolk market town of Foulsham now also merits consideration. Foulsham was typical of numerous little places at the bottom end of the scalogram, lurking in

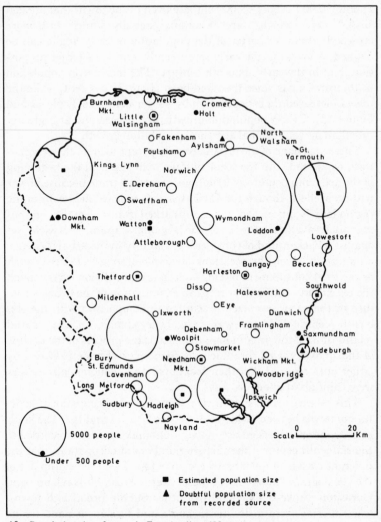

15   Population size of towns in East Anglia, 1603
     (Based on Patten, 'Population distribution in Norfolk and Suffolk')

the half-light of settlement life between true 'village' and true
'town'; chance in the method of selection dictated Foulsham's inclu-
sion and the exclusion of other little places like it. Not too much
significance should be put on this chance quality; it merely illustrates the difficulty of imposing a clear rural–urban break, and
thus gives a clear indication that no such break existed in pre-
industrial England. A few occupations had declined in importance

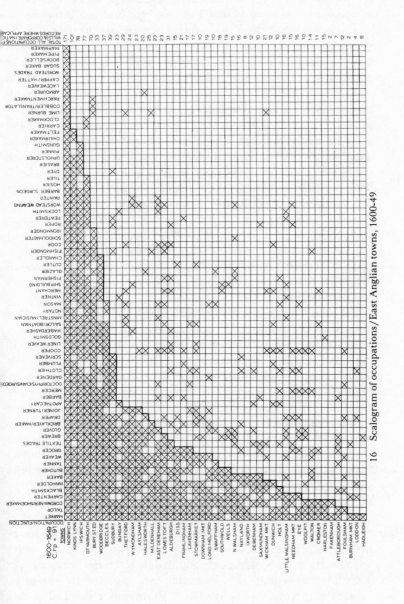

16 Scalogram of occupations/East Anglian towns, 1600-49

too, notably that of the furriers, and the manufacturer of traditional weapons by the Bowyers and Fletchers. By contrast, a number of new, more sophisticated occupations appear for the first time in the early seventeenth century. Chairmakers, for example, appear in East Anglian towns for the first time, while such occupations as pipemaker and even mapmaker appear in Norwich. Norwich in 1600 had a population of about 15,000, over 7 per cent of the population of Norfolk, and over 4 per cent of that of the whole region. The provincial capital had far more different occupations than had any other East Anglian town. The total number of different occupations noted for the early seventeenth century was 171;[71] this was less than the 223 for the sixteenth century, a fact which undoubtedly reflects both the differing length of the periods themselves, and a greater standardization of occupational nomenclature,[72] though there continued to be a myriad of different names for the occupations of those engaged in the manufacture of the 'new draperies', for example. It was probably often the case that two or more names were used for what in fact was basically the same occupation. Textiles remained a vital part of Norwich's life, though it in its turn remained more than just a textile town.

The four county towns and ports remain clearly differentiated from Norwich, and from the major and minor local towns that lay below them in the urban system. There was neither any change in the basic fourfold structure that characterized the urban system, nor any shifting of towns from one level to another, nor any interregional change. Certain of the county towns had quite sophisticated occupations such as gunsmith or upholsterer for the first time. The social capital of Bury St Edmunds had a confectioner in the early seventeenth century when that specialized trade was apparently to be found nowhere else in East Anglia, including Norwich. Some slight changes in rank by these occupational criteria took place. For instance, Great Yarmouth now ranked above Bury St Edmunds, having seven more recorded occupations. This is attributable to its livelier economy as a port, with a number of specialized and diversified shipbuilding and shiprepairing trades, as well as numerous merchants. It also appears to have grown larger by now than Bury, although population estimates for both are doubtful throughout the sixteenth and seventeenth centuries. Ipswich and Kings Lynn, like Great Yarmouth, continued to lack any concentration of manufacturing crafts to compare with Norwich's textiles, though merchants and shipowners were of great importance in all three ports.

Major local service centres such as Woodbridge or Bungay by the first half of the seventeenth century generally had their grocers, brewers, and a number of apothecaries; there was a continuous process of filtering-down of occupations from larger to smaller towns. Most of the minor local service centres had a basic occupational array of bakers, butchers, innholders (many of whom did their own brewing in smaller towns) and other simple trades, as well as the occasional apparently more sophisticated trade such as the vintner at Little Walsingham in Norfolk, or the goldsmith apparently working (though possibly it was his retirement home) in the little Suffolk town of Harleston. At the beginning of the seventeenth century there were mercers at Holt and Woolpit, both probably involved, in the fashion typical of those ostensibly called 'grocer/mercer/draper', in selling more than the restricted range of goods (in this case higher quality textiles) that their name would suggest.

The ranking of individual occupations (see Fig. 16) is as stable as that of towns; the ranking of the different occupations in the early seventeenth century correlates highly significantly with their ranking in the sixteenth century (r_s = 0.75). However, this correlation does obscure some considerable and significant changes in rank. For example, the high-level trade of apothecary had risen by some forty places in the ranking, and those practising newer divisions of the distributive trades like haberdasher or hosier also rose in standing significantly, the former by twenty and the latter by eleven places. The occupations which had an element of profession or service in them were becoming far more important and widespread than before; only five towns had apothecaries in the sixteenth century, whilst during the seventeenth century they were to be found in eleven towns. Doctors, physicians, surgeons and scriveners also rose slightly in rank, and were to be found in more places. These sorts of occupations were fast becoming diagnostic of the urban centrality and dominance of larger places. They are usually only found in association with other key indicator occupations such as market gardening, then largely restricted to in and around larger East Anglian towns.

In the case of craft activities, the importance of shoemakers, tailors, carpenters, and so on had been long established in smaller towns and many villages. Two occupations, those of baking and innholding or alehouse keeping, were to be found in twice as many towns in the early seventeenth century as had been recorded during the sixteenth century, when only sixteen towns had them. The decline in home-baking and brewing that this represents is token both of increased town size, and increased demand. Building trades also rose in importance as the demands for water supply and drainage (plumbers) and the use of new building materials (brickmakers, tilers) were felt in larger towns. The most advanced trades such as soap-boiling were still to be found only in the largest towns, even though the chandlers who distributed their goods were widely found. Sugar-baking was still apparently unique to Norwich.

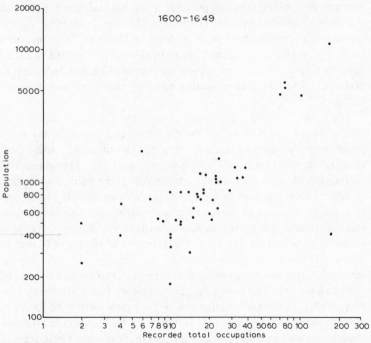

17 Relationship recorded total population/recorded total occupations, 1600-49

Manufacturing activities remained much the same as they had been in the sixteenth century. Tanners, cordwainers and the rest were basic to the urban economy. The cloth trade, however, suffered considerably in the early seventeenth century from disruption and difficulties consequent on political upheavals abroad, the spread of new manufactures, protective practices by the Dutch and the collapse of Cockayne's project. As East Anglia's major manufactured export, its fortunes were bound to affect the region's towns. Export statistics reveal years of acute difficulty for the East Anglian trade, much of which was urban, in the 1620s and 1630s and the number of apprentices entering the depressed textile manufactures of Norwich plumetted in the early seventeenth century.[73] A number of these and other movements are naturally obscured in the static and comparative approaches adopted here. However, with probably no more than 10 or 20 per cent of Norwich's workforce involved in textiles, it is unlikely that such short-term setbacks would have caused any long-term structural changes in the occupational patterns, and the places of occupations involved in the textile trades on the scalogram for the early seventeenth century remained largely unchanged.

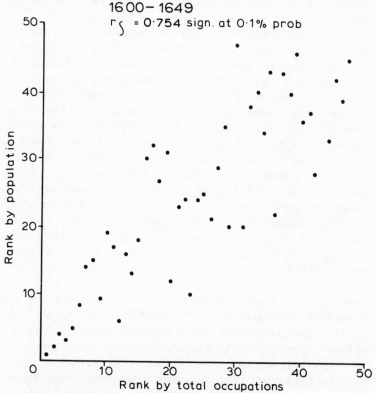

18 Relationship of town's rank by population/rank by occupation, 1600-49

The relation between occupations and population size expressed graphically in Figures 17 and 18 is, as was the case during the sixteenth century (see Figs. 13 and 14), a close one. The gap in size between Norwich and the county towns had however widened to over 5,000; and the gap between them and the largest local service centres had grown from only 1,500 to at least 2,500 (see Table 12). This sort of change is reflected as a slight steepening of the scatter of points representing towns shown on Figure 17, compared to those on Figure 13 for the sixteenth century; a number of towns such as Aylsham and Halesworth shown on Figure 17 and Figure 18 had rather more occupations (see Fig. 16) than their size might lead to expect, whilst Hadleigh had considerably fewer; it is difficult to adduce any particular reasons for this; it may have been due to the exigencies of sources. The association between the rank of towns when measured by total population and when measured by total occupations, is highly significant statistically, $r_s = 0.754$ (see Fig. 18).

The strong impression of stability which has been given must not be allowed to obscure certain important trends in local urban economies. Changes in the distributive system were undoubtedly important, with the rapid spread of the shop being one of the most distinctive features of the seventeenth century, not only in the towns, but also in the villages of East Anglia.[74] This was not always viewed favourably by contemporaries, who regarded shopkeepers as 'great burthens', parasitic middlemen, little better than the forestallers and regrators who so infuriated those in control of agricultural marketing in town markets. Shops and shopkeepers became established when the daily level of demand rose above that which could conveniently be satisfied by the weekly market and by the travelling chapmen whose stock, loaded on a horse or two, could not have been as varied as that offered in provincial shops. There was a time-lag in the diffusion of the shop from one level of the urban hierarchy down to the next, but villages quite quickly got a 'grocer', a 'mercer' or a 'draper' who, as their inventories show, in fact acted much more as general traders in textiles, dry goods and spices. The dominance over large areas which urban merchants had was gradually lost to these lesser shops, and the merchants and mercers of East Anglian towns (like Worcester[75]) suffered to a degree from a growing economic independence in the countryside. It would be wrong to think of the shop as a purely urban phenomenon, even in the sixteenth century. On the other hand, towns certainly did have a much greater assortment of shops, some of which were becoming purely retail, rather than being involved in both making and selling.

There were changes in urban agricultural marketing, too. These changes were twofold: the continued decline of the smallest market towns which did not have the scale of operation to ensure their survival, and the movement of transactions out of the formal market place and into the inn and the shop. It is as difficult to find the exact number of markets in operation at any time as it is to find true differences between the smallest 'town' and the largest 'village'. In the 1610 edition of Camden[76] twenty-seven 'Mercat' towns are listed and Peter Heylyn in 1641 and 1652[77] gives the same number, possibly simply drawing from Camden's list; however, one early seventeenth-century list gives thirty-one,[78] as does Everitt.[79] The market at tiny Heacham[80] in Norfolk died a sudden death, as we noted in the last chapter, extinguished by a great fire which destroyed the market house; and place names like Pulham 'Market' linger on, when clearly no active market was by then in existence. On the other hand, new markets were being founded, as in the case of 'Falsham'[81] (the Foulsham which entered the scalogram for the early seventeenth century), whilst long-established yet non-chartered ones as at Attleborough in Norfolk were struggling for formal recognition.[82]

The shop was gradually taking over some of the functions of the market place. Shops began to handle dry and grocery goods, whilst the handling of raw produce and provisions remained the role of the open market, although some of the dealing in corn left the open market for unrestricted dealing in inns. Perishable foodstuffs began to be sold in shops, for example in Yarmouth in the plague year of 1631, when it was thought by the town authorities that the disease was being brought from Norwich, it was ordered that fruit should be sold only in the open market 'as much fruit ... was kept by pettifoggers and others, and sold in small shops'.[83] It is probable that the role of the travelling chapman and pedlar decreased in importance in Norfolk and Suffolk, just as it had done in Lincolnshire in the early seventeenth century,[84] and the mobile grocers or mercers market stalls also declined in the face of an increasingly articulated distributive system from the fixed point of the shop. It is wrong to think simply in terms of shops gaining at the expense of markets, but a change in the relationship between the two had definitely taken place. It is probable that the phrase 'market town' meant something rather different in the early seventeenth century than it had done in the early sixteenth century. The difference was found as much in the way that goods were sold, as in the increased volume and variety. Those places with small agricultural markets and little else were facing severe problems by the seventeenth century.

Ports, the nodes for the distribution of 'sea cole' and imported goods, as much as for shipbuilding and fishing, were equally open to

changes in economic fortune and structural alterations. Particularly for the Suffolk ports, the influence of London was vital in
digesting much of their foreign trade. Other factors could intervene
too; the collapse of the Baltic trade, and the widespread switch to
the New Draperies meaning the decline of the broadcloth manufacture of its hinterland, radically altered the fortunes of Ipswich.
Ipswich continued, however, with lesser ports like Woodbridge, to
be vital in supplying London with agricultural produce like butter
and cheese.[85] Ipswich also suffered from the unwelcome attentions
of the Dunkirkers, just as the fisheries of Yarmouth and its trade
were much disturbed by the Dutch.[86] Ports that were further away
around the coast, such as Kings Lynn, were able to resist the incur-
sions of London, and large amounts of Wealden iron were shipped
direct to Kings Lynn in the early seventeenth century, whereas ports
nearer to London such as Ipswich had theirs re-shipped from the
capital.[87]

Overall, there was urban growth between the sixteenth and
seventeenth century, but a growth which was remarkably stable in
its advance. Figure 19 shows this change, relating percentage population change between 1524 and 1603 to the rise or fall in rank by
total numbers of occupations for each town between 1500 and 1599,
and 1600 and 1649; it can be seen that most changes in population
size were accompanied by fairly small rank changes. Some of these
rises and falls are easy to explain. Framlingham in Suffolk rose
modestly in rank by total occupations and rose modestly in population size too. Attleborough in Norfolk dropped in ranking by
occupations dramatically, and its population – after a century which
had seen considerable growth overall in East Anglia – had risen but
little; much of this must be attributed to the temporary loss of its
market, and a great fire which destroyed much of the town. Other
changes are apparent, but less easy to explain. Swaffham in Norfolk
for example, had one of the greatest losses in rank (by twenty-two
places) measured by total occupations, yet experienced average
population growth. Such occupations as it earlier had, e.g. doctor or
fishmonger, were no longer to be found, yet it could not have been
suffering from the competition of nearby markets, as the nearest,
such as East Dereham or Downham Market were in fact some way
away, and Watton was of no significance. It is equally difficult to
explain the noted population increases of Cromer and Halesworth,
for one had a few less occupations, the other a few more.

There were only slight changes in transport and communications
that would radically alter urban functional and space-relations.

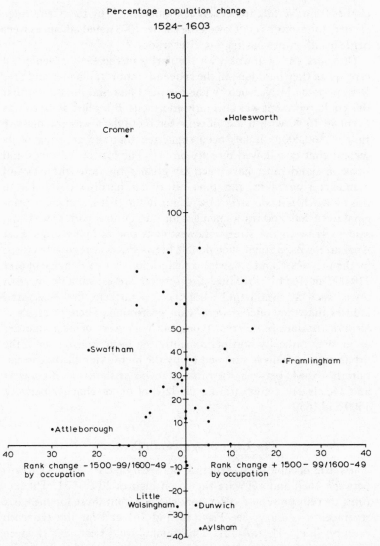

Percentage population change
1524– 1603

19 Urban change by population and occupation, 1524-1603

Slow improvements in transport, as in the case of changes in the distributive system, were evolutionary, not revolutionary. Little happened to East Anglia's transport net[88] to compare with what happened in the eighteenth century.[89] Road distances and stages in East Anglia, and elsewhere, were well known by the beginning of the seventeenth century;[90] a mother could with certainty send clothes from Norfolk to her son at Cambridge,[91] by the 'Cambridge carrier, Johnsons', and 'Cowell the carrier'. No noted advances were made in either the coasting[92] or river trades.[93]

Disasters struck towns with regularity in the early seventeenth century as they had done in the sixteenth century; plagues and fires were periodic in Norwich.[94] The financial loss and disruption that this could represent was obviously enormous. Bury St Edmunds was burnt in 1608, with a loss of what for those days was the massive sum of £60,000;[95] it has been suggested that the granting of its second charter followed directly on it.[96] The loss of buildings and stock in hand must have been far greater by value than loss of manufacturing 'plant' and 'tools'. Bury had hardly recovered from this blow when it was struck by plague in the 1630s, and many principal townsfolk and tradesmen left for the country, with grass being said to grow in the streets. Lowestoft is one of many other East Anglian towns to suffer such double blows.[97] It was regularly visited by the plagues,[98] and an awful conflagration caused damage of over £10,000 in 1644.[99] Primitive fire services were available in most towns such as Swaffham,[100] but the few buckets, fire hooks and ladders that they offered were scant protection. There were many local disruptions of different types, but none were of such an order as to alter radically and permanently the basic lineaments of the urban system. This is summed up by the highly significant correlation ($r_s = 0.84$) between the ranks of towns as shown on Figures 11 and 16, clearly demonstrating the lack of major changes between 1500 and 1650.

The Later Seventeenth Century

The basic occupational structure and size of East Anglia's towns between 1650 and 1699 are shown on Figures 20 and 21. The pictures therein presented differ only slightly from those for the early seventeenth century (see Figs. 15 and 16) and for the sixteenth century (Figs. 11 and 12). This qualitative assessment is given strong quantitative backing by the statistically significant correlation between the ranks of towns in the early seventeenth century (Fig. 16) and the later seventeenth century (Fig. 20); the rank correlation is $r_s = 0.89$. Some changes did, of course, occur. Nayland, a small cloth-making town in the by now totally declined broadcloth manufacturing area of the Suffolk–Essex borders drops out of consideration altogether, whilst Gorleston returns to it. Apart from these, only five towns changed rank by ten places or more, and only

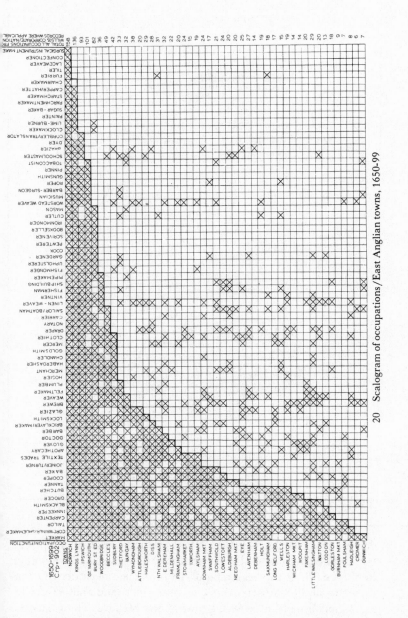

20 Scalogram of occupations/East Anglian towns, 1650-99

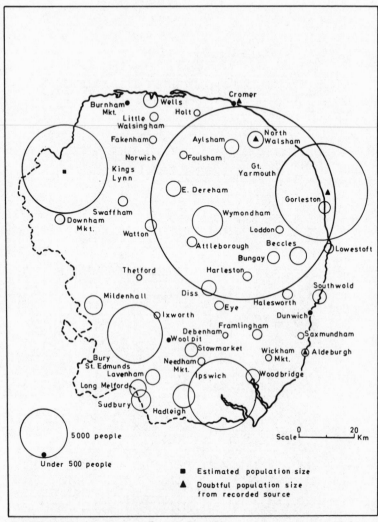

21 Population size of towns in East Anglia, 1670s
    (Based on Patten, 'Population distribution in Norfolk and Suffolk')

one of these changes (see Fig. 20) was by more than fifteen places,
the jump back to its earlier sixteenth century level of Attleborough
from its nadir at the beginning of the seventeenth century. By contrast two declining ports, Dunwich and Wells, and another declining Suffolk broadcloth weaving town, Long Melford, fell by between
ten and fourteen places. The rank position of the first eight towns
remained completely unaltered; their regional urban primacy and

functional interrelationships were remarkably stable over two centuries.

There is also a highly significant correlation ($r_s = 0.81$) between the ranks of the different occupations in the early and late seventeenth centuries (cf. Figs. 16 and 20), although a certain amount of re-sorting did occur. The then old-fashioned occupation of Armourer no longer appears, but more modern occupations like tobacconist and surgical-instrument maker appear for the first time. One or two very considerable rises in standing of occupation do occur; bookseller rose by twenty-three places in the scale and was a highly significant indicator of urban sophistication and standing, for booksellers were to be found only in Norwich and in the four county capitals and ports (Kings Lynn, Great Yarmouth, Ipswich and Bury St Edmunds). No smaller town had one, though books were undoubtedly sold from stalls on market day, and inventories reveal that country shopkeepers – grocers, drapers, or whatever – sometimes had bibles and primers amongst their stock. In an age of pamphlet literature, more ephemeral publications telling of strange happenings or obscure theological disputes circulated too. Also restricted were ironmongers, scriveners, pewterers, and cooks, found, like booksellers, only in these five places. Whilst brickmakers and bricklayers now ranked eighteenth amongst the occupations, masons had fallen by seventeen places since the early seventeenth century; this was due to a considerable change in building materials and techniques. Apothecary now ranked fourteenth amongst the scaling occupations; they were to be found in the top five towns, and in sixteen others, including such little places like Woolpit in Suffolk. The number of occupations recorded as present above the cutting point had increased markedly; the implication of this is that more towns had a larger number of different occupations in significant association than ever before. There was also a much greater number of scaling occupations below the cutting point on Figure 20: there were now about 250 of these compared to 200 in the early seventeenth century. This suggests that a variety of occupations like Doctor or Haberdasher were percolating down through the urban system in a rather random way, not related particularly either to the size of a town, or the association of trades in it. Contemporaries in seventeenth-century pamphlets wrote of trade being more 'diffused'[101] and this clearly seems to have been the case from the evidence presented in Figure 20.

At the same time as this process can be discerned, East Anglia's towns were getting bigger. Between 1603 and the 1670s the region's population rose by over 20 per cent from about a quarter of a million to more than 300,000, a growth which probably continued slowly until the end of the seventeenth century and one in which towns had more than their share. About a third of the population of East Anglia lived in towns by the 1670s, as opposed to about a quarter in 1600. Their rate of growth, over 40 per cent was much faster than the 10–15 per cent experienced by country areas, and this quickening pace of urbanization must have been fed to a great extent by rural–urban migration. The relationship between town size and town occupations remained close (see Figs. 22 and 23); the line of points on these graphs had steepened a little, and its base had moved (on Fig. 23) to the right of the graph, illustrating in this way the fact that the smallest towns had increased their basic numbers of

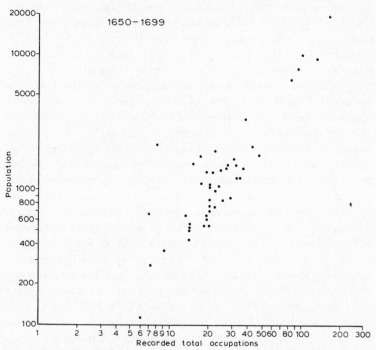

22   Relationship recorded total population/recorded total occupations, 1650-99

occupations. The correlation between the rank of towns by population and their rank by total occupation remained highly significant statistically ($r_s = 0.685$), as might be expected.

Amongst the towns, Norwich maintained its dominance; it had over 11 per cent of Norfolk's population in the 1670s and some 6 per cent of that of the whole region. The gap between it and the next largest town (Kings Lynn) had widened to over 10,000 people (see Table 12); the gap between the four county and port towns and the largest major service centre remained fairly constant in comparison with the early seventeenth century, at about 3,000. Certainly the five largest towns were dominant in their occupational structure, and Norwich towered above them all. Its centrality within the region

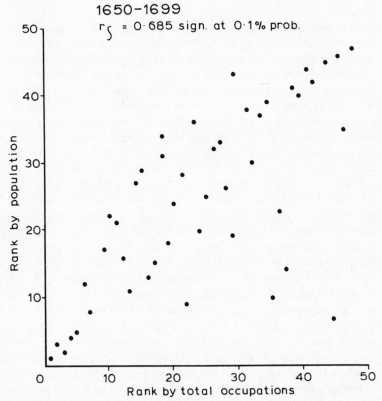

23   Relationship of town's rank by population/rank by occupation, 1650-99

was complete, despite the mixed fortunes of its cloth manufactures[102] and the muted heralds of their future long-term decay that were appearing. Norwich naturally had every scaling occupation as shown on Figure 20, and there were people at work in activities (like the making of surgical instruments) to be found in no other East Anglian towns. It had numerous fishmongers, gunsmiths, tobacconists, booksellers, clockmakers and confectioners, selling from retail shops as well as making and selling from workshops. It was the administrative and religious capital of East Anglia, with numbers of scriveners, notaries and lawyers busy with conveyancing urban property and rural estates, preparing lawsuits and drafting wills. The city itself, struggling to retain corporate control over its economic activity, could expand without restriction as buildings began to fill up open ground within the walls and spread into suburbs.[103] It was the social capital of Norfolk, if not of all of East Anglia.

The four county towns and great ports aped Norwich, and enjoyed considerable growth in population and occupations at or above the mean. Kings Lynn was developing a basic urban equipment quite like that of Norwich, and the gap between them in occupation complexity seems to have narrowed, even though the gap in size between them had widened, and the actual numbers of people involved in the different occupations in Norwich was undoubtedly larger than in Kings Lynn. Kings Lynn, Great Yarmouth, Ipswich and Bury St Edmunds had a wide selection of high-level urban activities such as upholsterers, scriveners, and tobacconists. The latter trade represents a high level of urban demand at a time when most country shopkeepers stocked tobacco; this demand came both from those rural shopkeepers looking to the urban tobacconists for their wholesale stock, and from the townsfolk themselves who demanded the selection that they could offer. Equally, the big towns all had their booksellers, one bookseller had a regular stall on Great Yarmouth market.[104] There were schoolmasters, too, and those recorded must have represented the tip of the iceberg of popular education run by vicars, curates and in Dame Schools. None of the four had any noted manufacturing interests, but they had the tailors and carpenters that most small towns and many villages had as a matter of course; as well as blacksmiths who were also involved in a range of general metal working. There was increasing division in the metal trades, and the later seventeenth century saw locksmiths, for example, rising to prominence in larger towns.

Bury St Edmunds fed on its role as a county and social capital, with substantial houses being built in it during the later seventeenth century. Fiennes enthused over the new house of a rich apothecary in Angel Square, and both Heylyn in the 1650s and Defoe after the turn of the century noted how it manufactured little and depended most on the gentry for its livelihood.[105] The other three in its class were ports, and benefited from that role. Kings Lynn was a con-

siderable centre for the refining of imported raw materials by sugar-
bakers or starchmakers, and for the distribution of their finished
products inland, not only into East Anglia, but also into its vast
midland hinterland. Sea coal brought down the coast from
Newcastle-upon-Tyne followed the same route inland up the Ouse
river system. Lynn seems to have become far more important than
Yarmouth or Ipswich as a port; by its own assessment, stridently set
down in a petition against foreigners (i.e. Dutch and Dunkirkers)
who were disrupting trade, it claimed to supply all the 'northern
ports' with grain and ten inland counties with salt and coal.[106] Defoe
graphically describes its trade.[107] Kings Lynn and Great Yarmouth
between them accounted for over fifty per cent of Newcastle-upon-
Tyne's coasting trade in coal[108] down the east coast, and were vital
links in the chain between Newcastle and Hull to London. In comparison with Kings Lynn and Great Yarmouth, Ipswich was quite
rapidly losing its stature as a port and centre for shipbuilding, a
decline which had begun in the early seventeenth century. This
process was apparently very noticeable by Defoe's day; he contrasted the state of prosperity when he first visited Ipswich in 1688
with that of apparent decay in 1724; he thought it by then thinly
populated in relation to its extent.[109] Ipswich colliers no longer
played much of a role, and London totally dominated its trade.
Fiennes in 1698 said that there was little trade, and that the coal
ships went away empty with no cargo.[110] Long-term decline as a
port had set in, although Ipswich was large and complex enough as
a county capital and market centre to resist total urban decline. The
possession of important ports undoubtedly made the urban system
of East Anglia very different from inland regions, and made a
number of its towns larger and more prosperous than they otherwise
would have been.

The economic complexity of the larger local towns increased
notably. There is every indication that the pace of commercial activity in them was quickening, particularly in the larger areas. The
volume of inland commerce, largely unsung in domestic records
compared to the wealth of information for foreign trades which survives in the Port Books, was much greater,[111] if only because of the
fact that there were more people in village and town alike. For instance, 35 of East Anglia's 47 towns had grocers recorded, compared with only 25 in the early seventeenth century; in addition,
grocers were now to be found in 77 villages.[112] Money circulated
faster, though there was a lack of adequate small change. Great Yarmouth corporation minted brass farthings for its poorer people, and

its traders offered their own tokens[113] as did those of much smaller places like Swaffham;[114] grocers were notorious token-issuers. No one in East Anglia by the late seventeenth century was very far from a grocer's shop, for they are recorded at 112 places in all during the later seventeenth century, in nearly one in ten of all of East Anglia's settlements.

The larger local centres consolidated their position, and places like Beccles, Bungay and Woodbridge commanded the attention of travellers such as Fiennes, Defoe and Kirby.[115] Some new manufacturing trades of local importance, such as feltmaking and hosiery had spread into a number of them, as well as trades such as locksmithing. Many towns like East Dereham or Beccles now had full-time carriers operating out of them; earlier in the seventeenth and in the sixteenth century much carrying seems to have been done on a part-time basis by farmers and others. They generally benefited from improved and more regular transport systems, though there is no evidence that road surfaces or river carriage became easier; the cost of transporting goods to Bungay was greatly increased by the need to carry them overland when the little River Waveney became so clogged that passage was restricted at Beccles, ten miles away downstream [116] (see Fig. 24). Whilst epidemic diseases abated somewhat in their effects on the larger towns, fires continued to wreak havoc. Swaffham in Norfolk was burnt so badly in 1669 that there is barely a house in the town standing today that was built earlier than that date; East Dereham was burned in 1679 to the cost of £19,443;[117] and Bungay was burned in 1652, and again in 1688, when only one street was left untouched and £30,000 worth of damage was caused.[118] Appeals for relief for Bungay were intoned from pulpits not only in the churches of east Anglia, but even in St Margaret's Westminster.[119] The Great Fire of Southwold in 1659 destroyed 238 houses, the Town Hall and most of the town records with it.[120] We owe Southwold's present-day urban landscape to that fire, for it was rebuilt – an early example of quasi-town planning – with a series of great greens separating the houses to act as fire breaks.[121] Thetford was burned in 1667, and was again decimated in 1697.[122] Nonetheless, all the larger local centres survived such knocks, for they had the long-established centrality and functions that enabled them to maintain their positions, rather as the much larger Ipswich had the urban resources to withstand the decay of its seaborne trade. Though some did not do very well, there is no case of a town in the 'major local service centre' category entering total decline. For example, local inhabitants lamented Thetford's decay

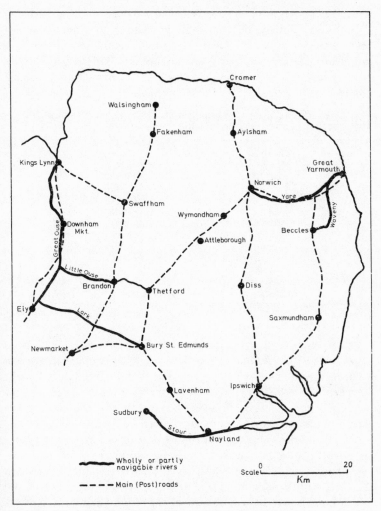

24 Major communications in Norfolk and Suffolk, sixteenth and seventeenth centuries

from its former glories, laying the blame on poor communications because of the difficulties of river navigation and the lack of manufactures,[123] but nonetheless it remained an important centre for the less populated western parts of Norfolk.[124] Sudbury in Suffolk, once such an important collecting and finishing centre for the broadcloth industry, survived the slump and maintained its occupational structure and population in the later seventeenth cen-

tury; it was, however, to be called populous and poor by Defoe.[125]
Perhaps only Attleborough's rise in the scale by thirty-one places is
really noteworthy, as the town was re-establishing its position as a
major local centre between Wymondham and Thetford in Norfolk
after it had lost its market and been hit by fires. Lesser secular
changes are obscured in this static approach.

Table 15: PLACES WITH MARKETS RECORDED AT SOME TIME IN NORFOLK
AND SUFFOLK, NOT IN SCALOGRAMS (FIGS 11, 16, 20)

In Norfolk	In Suffolk
Castle Acre	Bildeston
Cawston	Blythburgh
Cley	Botesdale
East Harling	Brandon
Heacham	Clare
Hickling	Haverill
Hingham	Mendlesham
New Buckenham	Orford
Reepham	
Snettisham	
Worstead	

Taken from Everitt's lists, pp. 474–75 in Thirsk, J. (ed.) *An Agrarian History of England and Wales*, Vol. IV, *1500–1640* (1967)

In the case of the lesser local towns, there do seem to have been
cases of lasting decline; they did not have the advantages of
centrality and scale which larger places did. They were caught
between the twin pincers of the attractiveness of larger, better
equipped and increasingly accessible towns, and the competition
from the shops springing up in rural villages offering much that they
and their markets supplied, but much nearer to hand. Such places
as Ixworth in Suffolk, with a population of between 500 and 600,
were simply too small to stand up to such competition. Wickham
Market, with a population of 550, certainly felt the pinch of the
better equipped nearby market town of Framlingham, with a population of over 1,000 and only a few miles away. Many of the
smaller towns were on their way to the obscurity which had earlier
overtaken other little places like Blythburgh in Suffolk. Once, this
town had had merchants' houses, had maintained a gaol for the
division of Beccles, and had been the site of both Quarter Sessions
and Annual meetings of the clergy. It kept its right to hold a market
for a while, but seems by the seventeenth century to have had no
vestiges of urban life; the same was true of a number of other places
in both counties, which are not considered towns by the criteria
adopted here[126] (see Table 15).

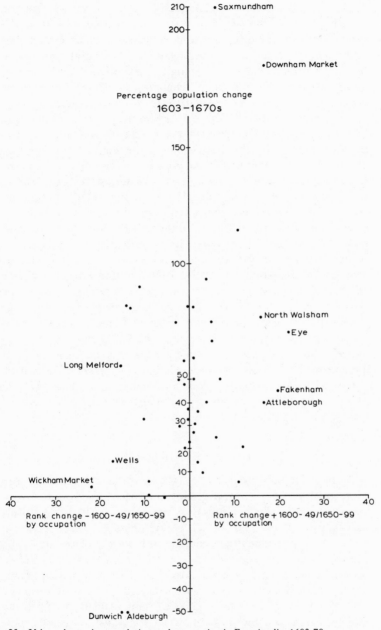

25 Urban change by population and occupation in East Anglia, 1603-70s

Figure 25 illustrates the changes in the urban system that had occurred between the early and later seventeenth century. It is, with the exception of the urban renewal of Attleborough and the decline of the ports of Dunwich (washed away) and Aldeburgh (increasingly cut-off from the sea by a shingle spit), difficult at present to ascribe reasons for all these changes; as usual in historical geography the deficiencies of sources must be responsible for some of the movements shown. For example, Saxmundham and Downham Market experienced percentage population increases between 1603 and 1670s (see Table 12 and Fig. 24) that were far greater than any other places and greater than their increase in rank by occupations would suggest; this was almost certainly due to underestimates of population size based on the 1603 Communicant returns for these towns. North Walsham, Eye and Fakenham all seem to have improved their position considerably. On the other hand, Long Melford, once a great broadcloth manufacturing centre, seems to have remained populous, but become poorer as its rank by numbers of occupation fell. Wells, a little Norfolk port, was clearly not doing very well in common with other tiny ports around the coast in facing competition from larger ones. Its Norfolk neighbour Cromer had done even worse with a massive 71 per cent fall in population (which takes it off the foot of Figure 25 altogether); it only had a market and a handful of recorded occupations, Defoe noted it just for lobsters.[127] Just as the static comparative statistical approach adopted here tends to obscure secular changes, so those that are plotted are not always easy to explain without much further detailed local work.

Two Centuries of Stability

It is not at all paradoxical to hold the view that the years between 1500 and 1700 were a time of great stability for East Anglian towns, yet were years which also saw great advances in some towns, generally the larger ones, which became notably more modern in terms of the pre-industrial economy and society of the day. The successful, larger towns were different in character from the often decayed centres which saw the turn of the sixteenth century. Their urban economies were much more advanced, perhaps as advanced as they could be in a pre-technical manufacturing world using largely organic sources of raw material and power. Certainly communications between towns, other regions and the capital were as well developed as they could be before the onset of the turnpike and the canal which accompanied industrialization. Information diffused quite quickly in an increasingly literate age. Towns looked very different by 1700, too; their monasteries and religious houses had largely vanished; bold brick fronts with stone copings and dressings replaced many half-timbered façades, and sat under tiled rather than thatched roofs. Old houses which did remain were endlessly subdivided, for towns had larger populations crammed inside the old urban area where open ground vanished, although some suburban growth had also taken place.

Yet stability there was. The outlines and interrelationships of the urban system remained substantially the same in 1700 as they had been in 1500. There had been no major disruptions, no urban disasters, no noted new urban growth. Certain movements in the system had taken place, but they were movements remarkable either for their rareness or for their regional insignificance. There were occasional dramatic falls from urban grace such as the decline of Dunwich, or Attleborough's sufferings from fires and troubles with market rights, but such movements as these were of little regional significance, for there were plenty of other towns in East Anglia to take up the slack. At the bottom end of the urban hierarchy it is true that there was the decline of a number of little market towns, as larger towns began to offer better services and nearby large villages themselves became better equipped. Such a movement is interesting in the historical geography of marketing and service provision, and is one further illustration of the impossibility and undesirability of attempting to differentiate by size or in a functional sense between small town and large village in pre-industrial England; but it was of little importance to the basic outlines of the urban system. There were still lots of other mildly prosperous little towns; the whole business was just a stage in the constant process of 'shaking-out' of less successful, less well located small towns, a process that had been going on since medieval times, and was to go on well into the railway age. Such movements as these left the urban system unaltered; Norwich dominated all in 1700 as in 1500, being supported by Kings Lynn, Great Yarmouth, Ipswich and Bury St Edmunds, which county and port towns together with Norwich provided the basic frame for the urban system at both dates. The network was filled in by lesser towns, some clearly more important than others in 1700 as in 1500. There was remarkably little change in this basic pattern, and towns very rarely changed their status significantly.

Although the relative status of towns did not change, they had become more modern. It was naturally the larger ones which became most modern, for they increased in size the fastest, and it was scale, not specialization that by and large conferred economic and social advance on towns then, as now. Urban rates of growth were quicker than rural rates by 1700, when a third of East Anglia's population lived in towns compared to less than a quarter in 1500. Its people were thus technically more 'urbanized' although many of the towns in which they lived were still both small and semi-rural. The quality of true urbanity was to be found only in the larger towns, and Norwich in particular was growing at a great pace, even in the seventeenth century which saw slower and less certain growth of population overall. The biggest twenty towns increased by about 25 per cent in population between the 1520s and 1603, and by 55 per cent between 1603 and the 1670s. The lesser towns experienced a relatively greater increase of 35 per cent between the 1520s and 1603, but a much smaller one of only 20 per cent between 1603 and the 1670s compared to that of the bigger towns. Norwich alone grew faster than either group of towns during both periods (Table 12). There were parallel increases in the number and complexity of urban occupations. The faster growth rate of smaller towns in the sixteenth century over the larger ones probably reflected their greater activity in a period of noted population increase before the larger towns had capitalized on their complexity and levels of provision and manufacture, and before shops and services had begun their spread into villages. By the seventeenth century modernization meant increasing change for the larger towns. The economic and social behaviour of their inhabitants, their spatial behaviour and locational decisions were clearly very different from what they had been in the sixteenth century, providing the mix for later urban advances that were to be felt much more in other, industrializing areas of the country. Such behaviour, which really helps explain the structural pattern and changes outlined in the East Anglian example, should be the focus for the next large scale study; the pre-industrial town is of great importance in the evolution of England's urban system, and deserves increasingly detailed examination.

Notes and References

Chapter 1   *The English pre-industrial town*

1   W. G. Hoskins, 'English provincial towns in the sixteenth century',
     Trans. Roy. Hist. Soc., 5th Ser., 6 (1956), 1-19

2   W. J. McCaffrey, *Exeter 1540-1640* (Cambridge, Mass., 1956)

3   J. W. F. Hill, *Tudor and Stuart Lincoln* (Cambridge, 1956)

4   T. Atkinson, *Elizabethan Winchester* (1963)

5   A. D. Dyer, *The city of Worcester in the sixteenth century* (Leicester, 1973)

6   J. F. Pound, 'Government and society in Tudor and Stuart Norwich,
     1525-1675', Unpubl. Ph.D. thesis, Leicester University (1974)

7   C. J. M. Moxon, 'Ashby-de-la-Zouch: a social and economic survey of
     a market town 1570–1720', Unpubl. D. Phil. thesis, Oxford Univer-
     sity (1971)

8   A. B. Rosen, 'Economic and social aspects of the history of
     Winchester, 1520-1670', Unpubl. D. Phil. thesis, Oxford University
     (1975)

9   P. Ramsey, *Tudor economic problems* (1963), see esp. Chapter III, 82-113

10   A. Thompson, *The dynamics of the Industrial Revolution* (1973); L. A.
     Clarkson, *The pre-industrial economy in England 1500-1750* (1971); B. A.
     Holderness, *Pre-industrial England: economy and society 1500-1750* (1976);
     D. C. Coleman, *The economy of England, 1450-1750* (Oxford, 1977)

11   H. Miskimin, 'Agenda for early modern economic history', *Journal of
     Economic History,* 31 (1971), 176-77; W. Frances Carter (ed.) *An
     historical geography of the Balkans* (London, 1977), 176-87

12   See for example J. De Vries, *The Dutch Rural Economy in the Golden Age,
     1500-1700* (Yale, 1974)

13   R. A. Butlin, 'Land and people, c. 1600', being pp. 142-67 of T. W.
     Moody, F. X. Martin and F. J. Byrne (eds.), *A new history of Ireland.
     III, Early modern Ireland, 1534-1691* (Oxford, 1976); see also his 'Irish
     towns in the sixteenth and seventeenth centuries', being pp. 61-100 of
     R. A. Butlin (ed.) *The development of the Irish Town* (London, 1977)

14   H. Carter, 'Urban systems and town morphology' in E. G. Bowen,
     H. Carter and J. A. Taylor, *Geography at Aberystwyth* (Cardiff, 1969),
     220

15   H. Carter, *The towns of Wales* (Cardiff, 1965), 220

16 *Ibid.* 32-50

17 P. Wheatley, 'What the greatness of a city is said to be; reflections on Sjoberg's pre-industrial city', *Pacific Viewpoint*, 4 (1963), 163-88

18 Hoskins, 'Provincial towns'; see also J. Cornwall, 'The people of Rutland in 1522', *Trans. Leics. Hist. and Arch. Soc.*, 37 (1961-62), 7-28

19 P. Clark and P. A. Slack (eds.) *Crisis and order in English towns, 1500-1700* (1972); see also *idem, English towns in transition 1500-1700* (Oxford, 1976); P. Clark, *The early modern town* (Open University, 1976); P. Corfield, 'Urban development in England and Wales', being pp. 214-47 of D. C. Coleman and A. H. John (eds.), *Trade, government and economy in pre-industrial England* (London, 1976); A. D. Dyer, 'Warwickshire towns under the Tudors and Stuarts', *Warwickshire History*, III (1977), 122-35

20 C. W. Chalklin *The provincial towns of Georgian England* (1974); *idem*, 'The making of some new towns', being pp. 229-52 of C. W. Chalklin and M. A. Havinden (eds.), *Rural change and urban growth 1500-1800* (1974)

21 C. Phythian-Adams, review of A. D. Dyer, *The city of Worcester in the sixteenth century*, being pp. 63-64 of *Urban History Yearbook* (Leicester, 1974)

22 C. Phythian-Adams, review of, M. M. Rowe and A. M. Jackson (eds.) *Exeter freemen 1266-1967*, Devon and Cornwall Record Society, Extra Series, 1 (Exeter, 1973) being p. 103 of *Urban History Yearbook* (Leicester, 1974)

23 S. G. Checkland, 'English provincial cities', *Economic History Review*, 2nd Series, 4 (1953-54), 200

24 E. E. Lampard, 'The history of cities in the economically advanced areas', *Economic Development and Cultural Change*, 3 (1954-55), 81-136

25 Hoskins, 'Provincial towns'; Checkland, 'English provincial cities'; Lampard, 'History of cities'

26 J. C. Russell, *Medieval regions and their cities* (Newton Abbott, 1972)

27 E. J. Hobsbawm, 'From social history to the history of society', *Daedalus*, 101 (1969), 34

28 John Patten, 'Urban life before the Industrial Revolution', *Geographical Magazine* (December 1970), 205-13

29 Clark and Slack, *Crisis and order*, 1-6

30 John Adams, *Index Villaris, or an Alphabetical List . . .* (1690); Anon. 'A step to the Bath with a character of the Place' (1700)

31 William Harrison, *Description of England* (ed. F. J. Furnivall, 1877-1908), 259

32 MacCaffrey, *Exeter*, 275

33 G. Botero, *Treatise concerning the causes of the magnificance and greatness of cities . . .* (1606), 275

34 J. Styrpe, *Survey of London*, II (1720), 87

35 J. Tate, *The medieval English borough* (Manchester, 1936), 349

36 S. Thernstrom, 'Reflections on the new urban history', *Daedalus*, 102 (1971), 359; B. Robson, *Urban growth* (1975), 3, 12

37 J. Gottmann, *Virginia at mid-century* (New York, 1955), 83

38 *Ibid.*

39 Dyer, *Worcester*, 14

40 W. E. A. Axon, *The annals of Manchester* (Manchester, 1886), 59

41 C. Gill, *History of Birmingham,* I (1952), 26

42 R. A. Holt, 'The economic development of Birmingham before 1553', Unpbl. M.A. thesis, Birmingham University (1975), 26

43 G. O. Cowley, 'Some market towns 1550-1750', Unpubl. M.A. thesis, London University (1965), 7

44 J. S. Cogswell (ed.) 'Reasons against a general sending of Corne . . .' *Norfolk Archaeology,* 20 (1921), 19

45 A. Everitt, 'The Banburys of England', *Urban History Yearbook,* (1974), 29

46 D. M. Palliser and A. C. Pinnock, 'The markets of medieval Staffordshire', *North Staffs Jnl. of Field Studies,* II (1971) 49-64

47 R. H. Hilton, *The English peasantry in the later Middle Ages,* (Oxford, 1975), 85

48 A. R. Bridbury, *Economic growth: England in the later Middle Ages* (1962), 40; see also H. Pirenne, *Medieval cities: their origins and revival of trade* (Princetown, 1952)

49 Bridbury, *Economic growth*

50 D. J. B. Shaw, 'Urbanism and economic development in a pre-industrial context – the case of southern Russia (seventeenth and eighteenth centuries)', Unpbl. paper at the I.B.G. Historical Geography Research Group, Spring Symposium (1974), 2

51 G. Sjoberg, *The pre-industrial city; past and present,* (Glencoe, Ill., 1960)

52 See, for example, Wheatley, 'The greatness of a city'; *idem,* 'The concept of urbanism', being pp. 601-37 of *Man, settlement and urbanism* (1972); *idem, The pivot of the Four Quarters* (Edinburgh, 1971); T. H. McGee 'The rural–urban continuum debate, the pre-industrial city and urban migration', *Pacific Viewpoint,* 5 (1964), 159-81; W. D. Mc-Taggart, 'The reality of urbanism' *Pacific Viewpoint,* 6 (1965), 220-24

53 Wheatley, 'Concept of urbanism', in *Man, settlement and urbanism,* 601

54 Clark and Slack, *Crisis and order.*

55 K. H. Burley, 'Economic development of Essex in the later seventeenth and early eighteenth centuries', Unpbl. Ph.D. thesis, London University (1957), 7-8

56 Burley, 'Economic development of Essex'

57 On attitudes to the identity of towns see Yi-Fu Tuan, *Topophilia* (Englewood Cliffs, N.J., 1974), 150-91

58 E. Moir, *The discovery of Britain: the English tourists 1540-1840* (1964), 24, 19

59 C. Fiennes, *The journeys of Celia Fiennes* (ed. C. Morris) (1947), *passim;* D. Defoe, *A tour through the whole island of Great Britain,* ed. G. D. H. Cole (1927), *passim*

60 W. Camden, *Brittania,* transl. P. Holland (1610)

61 C. Gill, *A history of Birmingham,* I (1951), 44; W. Smith, *The Particular Description of England* (1879), 38

62 J. Leland, *The itinerary . . ., ed.* L. Toulmin-Smith V (1909), 94

63 W. Farror and J. Brownbill, 'Manchester', in *V. C. H. Lancaster,* IV (1911)

64 Quoted in R. Howell, *Newcastle-upon-Tyne and the Puritan revolution* (Oxford, 1967) 1; 'The travels of Peter Mundy', Vol. V; *The Hakluyt*

Society, 2nd Series, LXXVIII (1936) II. I am most indebted to Dr. H. S. A. Fox for this reference.

65 Hist. Man. Comm., 13th Report, Appendix II, Portland ii, 307-9

66 Cal. S.P. Dom. Eliz., 1547-80, **XXXVII**, 259

67 Cal. S.P. Dom. Eliz., 1581-90, 402

68 L. Sutherland, 'When was the Great Plague? Mortality in London, 1563 to 1665', being pp. 287-320 in D. V. Glass and R. Revelle (eds.), *Population and social change* (1972), 290

69 Quoted in C. Platt, *The English medieval town* (1976), 222-23

70 E. Lamond (ed.), *A Discourse of the Common Weal of This Realm of England* (Cambridge, 1893)

71 W. C. Hazlitt, *Inedited Tracts. Illustrating the Habits, Opinions and Occupations . . .* (1868), 13, 78

72 A. G. Dickens, 'Tudor York', being pp. 117-59 of *V. C. H. York* (1961), 159

73 F. V. Emery, 'England *circa* 1600', in H. C. Darby (ed.) *A new historical geography of England* (Cambridge, 1973), 295

74 Camden Miscellany, 'A relation of a short survey of the western counties', *Camden Society,* III (1888), 49

75 C. Phythian-Adams, 'Ceremony and the citizen', in Clark and Slack, *Crisis and order*

76 J. Taylor, 'A Discovery . . .', *Spenser Society Publications,* II (1868)

77 Camden Miscellany, 'A short survey', 43

78 *Ibid.* 39

79 A. Everitt, 'The marketing of agricultural produce', in J. Thirsk (ed.) *The agrarian history of England and Wales,* IV 1500-1640 (Cambridge, 1967)

80 *Ibid.* 559

81 J. A. Chartres, 'The place of inns in the commercial life of London and Western England, 1660-1760', Unpubl. D.Phil. thesis, Oxford University (1973)

82 See, for example D. Cressey, 'Occupations, migration and literacy in East London, 1580-1640', *Local Population Studies,* 5 (1970), 53-60

83 Anon. *Lamtable News . . .* (1585)

84 See, for just one discussion, P. Laslett, *The World we have lost* (1966), *passim*

85 Patten, 'Urban life'

86 W. B. Stephens (ed.), *History of Congleton* (1970), 138

87 D. Ward, *Cities and immigrants* (New York and London, 1971), 9, 14

88 Sjoberg, *Pre-industrial city*

89 D. J. Johnson, *Southwark and the City* (1969), plate facing 130

90 A. Dulley, 'People and housing in the Medway towns, 1687-1783', *Archaeologia Cantiana,* 77 (1962), 161; P. Ripley 'The trade and social structure of Gloucester 1600-1640', *Trans. Brist. and Glos. Arch. Soc.,* XCIV (1976), 119-20

91 Sjoberg, *Pre-industrial city*

92 J. E. Vance, 'Land assignment in pre-capitalist, capitalist and post-capitalist cities', *Economic Geography,* 47, 101-20

93 *Ibid.* 103, 105

94 J. Langton, 'Residential patterns in pre-industrial cities; some case

studies from seventeenth-century Britain', *Trans. Inst. Brit. Geog.*, 65 (1975), 1-27; see also his 'Late medieval Gloucester: some data from a rental of 1455', *Trans. Inst. Brit. Geog.* N.S., vol 2 (1977), 259-77

95 Langton, 'Residential patterns', 8-9
96 D. V. Glass, 'Notes on the demography of London at the end of the seventeenth century', *Daedalus,* 97 (1968), 583
97 Langton, 'Residential patterns', 11
98 *Ibid.* 16-18, 21
99 Langton 'Late medieval Gloucester', *passim*
100 W. J. Petchey, 'The Borough of Maldon, Essex, 1500-1688', Unpubl. Ph.D. thesis, Leicester University (1972)
101 Taylor, 'A Discovery'; M. B. Rowlands, 'Masters and men in the small metallurgical trades of the West Midlands, 1660-17.00', Unpubl. Ph.D. thesis, Aston University (1972), 49
102 Laslett, *World we have lost,* 57
103 F. Braudel, *Capitalism and material life, 1400-1800* (1973), 373, 374
104 F. Braudel, *The Mediterranean and the Mediterranean world in the age of Philip II* (1975), Vol. II, 325
105 C. M. Cipolla, *Before the Industrial Revolution. European society and economy, 1000-1700* (1976), 143

Chapter 2   *Antecedents, patterns and forces for change*

1 C. Platt, *The English medieval town* (1976), 15
2 R. H. Hilton, *The English peasantry in the later Middle Ages* (Oxford, 1975), esp. Ch. V. 'The small town as part of peasant society', 76-94
3 A. R. Bridbury, *Economic growth: England in the later Middle Ages* (1962
4 A. Everitt, 'The Banburys of England', *Urban History Yearbook* (1974), 30-35
5 See for example M. W. Beresford, *New towns of the Middle Ages* (1967); and H. S. A. Fox, 'Going to town in thirteenth century England', being pp. 69-78 of A. R. H. Baker and D. B. Harley (eds.), *Man made the land* (Newton Abbot, 1973), 69
6 A. Crossley, *V. C. H. Oxfordshire,* X (1972), 62; J. I. Leggett, 'The 1377 Poll Tax Return for the City of York', *Yorkshire Archaeological Journal,* XLIII (1971), 128-46
7 F. V. Emery, *The Oxfordshire landscape* (1974), 201
8 M. W. Beresford, 'Founded towns and deserted villages in the Middle Ages', being pp. 79-92 of Baker and Harley, *Man made the land*
9 R. E. Glasscock, 'England circa 1334', being pp. 136-85 of H. C. Darby (ed.) *A new historical geography of England* (Cambridge, 1973), 185
10 R. A. Donkin, 'Changes in the early Middle Ages', being pp. 75-135 of Darby, *A new historical geography,* 133
11 S. C. Thrupp, *The merchant class of medieval London* (Chicago, 1948); see also R. S. Scholfield, 'The geographical distribution of wealth in England, 1334-1649', *Economic History Review,* 2nd Series, XVIII (1965), 508
12 E. Veale, 'Craftsmen and the economy of London in the fourteenth century', being pp. 133-51 of A. E. J. Hollaender and W. Kellaway (eds.), *Studies in London History* (1969), 133

13   T. Atkinson, *Elizabethan Winchester* (1963), 16

14   V. Hansen, 'The pre-industrial city of Denmark', *Geografisk Tidsshrift*, 75 (1976), 52-53

15   Fox, 'Going to town', in Baker and Harley, *Man made the land*, 70-75

16   Bridbury, *Economic growth*

17   This passage is based on information kindly supplied to me by Mr P. Rutledge; see his 'A 15th century Yarmouth Petition', *Great Yarmouth and District Archaeological Society Bulletin*, 46 (1976), two mimeographed sheets, *passim*

18   32 H VIII c.19

19   W. Hudson and J. C. Tingay, *The records of the City of Norwich*, 11 (1910), lxx-lxii

20   M. Sellers, 'York in the sixteenth and seventeenth centuries' *Eng. Hist. Rev.*, XII (1897), 437-47

21   N. Bartlett, 'The expansion and decline of York in the later Middle Ages', *Econ. Hist. Rev.*, 2nd Series, XII (1959), 17-33

22   In *V. C. H. Yorkshire, The City of York* (1961)

23   D. M. Palliser, 'Some aspects of the social and economic history of York in the sixteenth century', Unpubl. D.Phil., Oxford University (1968)

24   Quoted in A. Raine, 'York Civic Records', VI, *Yorkshire Archaeological Society, Record Series*, XII (1946), 17

25   J. W. F. Hill, *Tudor and Stuart Lincoln* (Cambridge, 1956), 19-20

26   A. A. Ruddock, 'London capitalists and the decline of Southampton in the early Tudor period', *Econ. Hist. Rev.*, 2nd Series, II (1949-50), 137-51

27   M. K. Dale, 'Social and economic history 1066-1509', being pp. 31-54 of *V. C. H. Leicestershire*, IV (1958), 52-4

28   E. Gillet, *A history of Grimsby* (1970), 115-16

29   *Ibid.* 116

30   Hudson and Tingay, *City of Norwich,* lxxii

31   W. J. Petchey, 'The Borough of Maldon, Essex', Unpubl. Ph.D. thesis, Leicester University (1972), 52

32   R. B. Outhwaite, *Inflation in Tudor and early Stuart England* (1969), *passim*

33   Platt, *The English medieval town,* 181

34   V. Parker, 'The making of Kings Lynn from the eleventh to the seventeenth century', Unpubl. Ph.D. thesis, Sheffield University (1969), 79

35   A. D. Dyer, *The City of Worcester in the sixteenth century* (Leicester, 1973), 163

36   Petchey, 'Maldon, Essex'

37   P. Clark and P. A. Slack (eds.), *Crisis and order in English towns 1500-1700* (1972), 40

38   *Ibid.* 6-7

39   A. R. Bridbury, 'Sixteenth-century farming', *Econ. Hist. Rev.*, 2nd Series, XXVII (1974), 543

40   C. Phythian-Adams, 'Ceremony and the citizen', being pp. 57-85 of Clark and Slack, *Crisis and order,* esp. 57

41   J. A. Chartres, 'The place of inns in the commercial life of London

and Western England', Unpubl. D.Phil. thesis, Oxford University (1973), 686
42 Dyer, *Worcester*
43 Bridbury, *Economic Growth*
44 Dyer, *Worcester*
45 A. R. H. Baker, 'Changes in the later Middle Ages', being pp. 186-247 of Darby, *A new historical geography*, 241
46 P. Burke, 'Some reflections on the pre-industrial city', *Urban History Yearbook* (1975), 19-20
47 E. E. Lampard, 'Historical contours of contemporary urban society; a comparative view', *Journal of Contemporary History*, 4 (1969), 3
48 See, for example, Scholfield, 'Geographical distribution of wealth'
49 P. Wheatley, *The pivot of the Four Quarters: a preliminary enquiry into the origins and character of the ancient Chinese city* (Edinburgh, 1971), XV
50 R. Millward, 'The Cumbrian town between 1600 and 1800', being pp. 202-28 in C. W. Chalklin and M. A. Havinden (eds.), *Rural change and urban growth* (1974), 204
51 P. H. Ramsey, Review, *History*, 58 (1973), 273
52 For example L. A. Clarkson, *The pre-industrial economy in England 1500-1750* (1971)
53 See, for example H. H. Lamb, 'Our changing climate past and present', *Weather*, 14 (1959), 299-318, and M. L. Parry, 'Secular climatic change and marginal agriculture', *Transactions Institute British Geographers*, 6 (1975), 1-13; *idem, Climatic change, agriculture and settlement* (Folkestone, 1978)
54 B. A. Holderness, *Pre-industrial England: economy and society from 1500 to 1750* (1976), 3
55 *Ibid.*
56 E. E. Lampard, 'Historical aspects of urbanization', being pp. 519-54 of P. M. Hauser and L. F. Schnore, *The study of urbanization* (New York, 1966), 548
57 D. C. Coleman, 'Textile growth', being pp. 1-21 of N. B. Harte and K. G. Ponting (eds.), *Textile history and economic history* (1973), 9
58 I. S. W. Blanchard, 'Commercial crisis and change: trade and the industrial economy of the North East, 1509-32', *Northern History*, VIII (1973), 64-85; C. Wilson, *England's Apprenticeship* (1967), 40, 53
59 B. E. Supple, *Commercial crisis and change in England 1600-1642* (1959), 2-3
60 J. E. Pilgrim, 'The cloth industry in Essex and Suffolk, 1558-1640', Unpubl. M.A. thesis, London University (1939), 193
61 S. Porter, 'Fires and pre-industrial towns', *The Local Historian*, 10 (1973), 395; *idem*, 'Fires in Stratford-upon-Avon in the sixteenth and seventeenth centuries', *Warwickshire History*, III (1976) 97-105
62 Quoted in D. Defoe, *A tour through the whole island of Great Britain* (ed. G. D. H. Cole, 1927), 485
63 W. G. Hoskins, *Industry, trade and people in Exeter, 1688-1800* (Manchester, 1935), 13
64 E. L. Jones, 'The reduction of fire damage in southern England 1650-1850', *Post-Medieval Archaeology*, 2 (1968), 144
65 *Ibid.*

66   *Ibid.* 146
67   Gillet, *Grimsby,* 115
68   Anon. (1585)
69   Anon. (1675)
70   A. Everitt (ed.), *Perspectives in English urban history* (1973), 6
71   J. Baskerville, in *Historical Manuscripts Commission, Portland. MS.* II, 308-9
72   D. J. Johnson, *Southwark and the City* (1969), 128
73   A. Crossley, *V. C. H. Oxfordshire,* X, 8
74   J. Sprigge, *Anglia Rediviva* (1647), 251
75   M. B. Weinstock, 'Blandford in Elizabethan and Stuart Times', *Notes and Queries for Somerset and Dorset,* XXX (1975), 118
76   C. A. F. Meekings, *Dorset Hearth Taxes, 1662-64* (Dorchester, 1951), XXXI
77   C.S.P.D. 1665-6, 523; D. Palliser, 'Death and disease in Staffordshire, 1540-1670', in Chalklin and Havinden, *Rural change and urban growth;* L. A. Clarkson, *Death, disease and famine in pre-industrial England* (1975), 71; see also W. H. McNeill, *Plagues and people* (Oxford, 1977), 226-27
78   D. M. Palliser, 'Epidemics in Tudor York', *Northern History,* VIII (1973), 54
79   R. Howell, *Newcastle upon Tyne and the Puritan revolution* (Oxford, 1967), 7
80   J. E. O. Wilshere, 'Plague in Leicester, 1558-1665', *Trans. Leicester Archaeological and Historical Society,* XLIV (1968-9), 45-71
81   E. W. J. Kerridge, 'Social and economic history, 1509-1660', *V. C. H. Leicester,* IV (1958), 107-8
82   W. Hutton, *The history of Derby* (1891) 233; idem. *The history of Birmingham* 6th edn. (1835), 51
83   P.R.O. Calendar of Treasury Books, ii, 296
84   P. Slack, 'Some aspects of epidemics in England 1485-1640', Unpubl. D.Phil. thesis, Oxford University (1972), 162
85   A. L. Merson, 'Southampton in the sixteenth and seventeenth centuries', being pp. 218-227 in F. J. Monkhouse (ed.), *A survey of Southampton and its region* (1964), 224; M. J. Groombridge, 'Calendar of Chester Council Minutes 1603-42', *Record Society of Lancashire and Cheshire,* 106 (1956), XXXIV
86   T. Sowler, *A history of the town and borough of Stockton-on-Tees* (Teesside, 1972), 78-79
87   N. Griffin, 'Epidemics in Loughborough, 1539-1646', *Trans. Leicestershire Archaeological and Historical Society,* XLIII (1967-8), 30
88   L. J. Ashford, *The history of the borough of High Wycombe* (1960), 132
89   Worcester Quarter Sessions Rolls, part 1, *Worcester Historical Society* (1899), 229
90   Hill, *Lincoln,* 92
91   P. McGrath, 'Merchants and merchandise in seventeenth century Bristol', *Bristol Record Society,* XIX (1955), XIX-XX
92   F. W. P. Manders, *A history of Gateshead* (1973), 16-17
93   Quoted in Howell, *Newcastle*
94   *Ibid.* 274, 282
95   Quoted in *ibid.* 274

96   Groombridge, 'Chester Council Minutes'
97   A. Jorevin de Rocheford, 'Description of England and Ireland, 1672',
     reprinted in *Antiquarian Repertory*, 4 (1809), 586
98   J. S. Roper, *Dudley, the town in the sixteenth century*, Dudley Public
     Library Transcripts, 5 (1974), 8-11
99   Dyer, *Worcester*, 255
100 C. Gill, *A history of Birmingham*, Vol. 1: *Manor and Borough to 1865*
     (1951), 52-54
101 K. R. Adey, 'Seventeenth-century Stafford: A county town in decline',
     Midland History, II (1974), 156-57
102 J. Simmons, *Leicester past and present*, Vol. 1: *Ancient Borough to 1860*
     (1974)
103 Crossley, *V. C. H. Oxfordshire*
104 E. A. L. Moir, *The discovery of Britain: the English tourists 1540-1840*
     (1964), 26-27; see also H. Belasyse, 'An English Traveler's First
     Curiosity . . . 1657', *Hist. Manuscripts Commission, Various Coll.*, II
     (1903)
105 Ashford, *High Wycombe*, 134-5
106 W. B. Stephens (ed.), *History of Congleton* (1970), 138
107 W. G. Hoskins, 'Harvest fluctuations and English economic history,
     1480-1619', *Agricultural History Review*, XII (1964), 28-46; see also
     Parry, *Climatic Change, Agriculture and Settlement*
108 Hoskins, 'Harvest fluctuations', 29
109 *Ibid.* 36
110 East Sussex Record Office, QO/EW 7p, 100
111 T. S. Willan, *River navigation in England, 1600-1750* (1936), 18-21; *idem*
     'Chester and the navigation of the Dee, 1600-1750', *Jnl. North Wales
     Architectural, Archaeological and Historical Society*, NS XXXII (1938);
     G. M. Hayes-Thomas, 'The port of Chester', *Transactions Lancashire
     and Cheshire Antiquarian Society*, LIX (1947)
112 C. N. Parkinson, *The rise of the Port of Liverpool* (1952)
113 F. N. G. Thomas, 'Portsmouth and Gosport: A study in the historical
     geography of a naval port', Unpubl. M.Sc. (Econ.) thesis, Liverpool
     University (1961), 9
114 R. H. Morris, *Chester in the Plantagenet and Tudor Reigns* (Chester, 1893), 74
115 E. A. Wrigley, 'Mortality in pre-industrial England: the example of
     Colyton, Devon, over the centuries', pp. 244-73 of D. V. Glass and
     R. Revelle (eds.), *Population and Social change* (1972)
116 W. G. Hoskins, 'The population of an English village 1086-1801: A
     study of Wigston Magna', *Transactions Leicester Archaeological and
     Historical Society*, XXXIII (1957), 15-35
117 Clarkson, *Death, disease and famine*, 28
118 *Ibid.*
119 J. J. Spengler, 'Demographic factors and early modern economic
     development', *Daedalus*, 97 (1968), 437
120 E. A. Wrigley, 'Modernization and the Industrial Revolution in
     England', *Journal of Interdisciplinary History*, III (1972), *passim*
121 D. C. North and R. P. Thomas, *The rise of the western world: a new
     economic history* (Cambridge, 1973); but see also a searching review by
     R. M. Smith in *Journal of Historical Geography*, 1 (1975), 111-12

122 F. J. Fisher, 'London's export trade in the early seventeenth century'
     Econ. Hist. Rev., 3 (1950)
123 Clarkson, *Death, disease and famine*, 16
124 A. Thompson, *The dynamics of the Industrial Revolution* (1973), 41
125 See R. A. Holt, 'The economic development of Birmingham before
     1553', Unpubl. M.A. thesis, Birmingham University (1975). *passim;*
     Hutton, *Birmingham*
126 Hutton, *Birmingham*, 55-57
127 Thompson, *Industrial Revolution*, 34
128 P. M. Tillot (ed.) *V. C. H. The City of York* (1961), 215
129 S. McIntyre, 'Towns as health and pleasure resorts; the development
     of Bath, Scarborough and Weymouth, 1700-1815', Unpubl. D.Phil.
     thesis, Oxford University (1973), 2
130 Thomas, 'Portsmouth and Gosport', 9
131 *Ibid. passim*
132 Clark and Slack, *Crisis and order*, 31
133 E. Ekwall (ed.), *Two early London subsidy Rolls* (Lund, 1951), *passim*
134 *Ibid.* 81-89
135 J. Stow, *A Survey of London, written in the year 1598* (rev. ed. by W. J.
     Thomas, 1842), *passim*
136 R. R. Steel, *Bibliotheca Lindesiana V or Tudor and Stuart Royal Proclama-*
     tions (Oxford, 1910), 158
137 M. Wilson (ed.), *Strange island: Britain through foreign eyes 1395-1940*
     (1935), 25
138 *Ibid.* 42
139 *Ibid.* 49
140 F. Braudel, *Capitalism and material life* (1972), 411
141 *Ibid.* 411-12
142 *Ibid.* 391
143 K. H. Burley, 'Economic development of Essex in the seventeenth and
     eighteenth centuries', Unpubl. Ph.D. thesis London University,
     (1957), 385
144 J. Gottmann, 'The dynamics of large cities', *Geographical Journal*, 140
     (1974), 254-61
145 *Ibid.*
146 E. E. Lampard, 'The history of cities in the economically advanced
     areas', *Economic Development and Cultural Change*, III (1955), 131
147 Thompson, *Industrial Revolution*, 39
148 C. E. Schorske, 'The idea of the city in European thought', being pp.
     95-114 of O. Handlin and J. Burchard, *The historian and the city*
     (Cambridge, Mass., 1966), 96
149 E. A. Wrigley, 'A simple model of London's importance in changing
     English society and economy 1650-1750', *Past and Present*, 37 (1967),
     44-70
150 G. D. Ramsay, *The city of London in international politics at the accession of*
     Elizabeth Tudor (1975), 33
151 Wrigley, 'A simple model'
152 J. H. Andrews, 'Some statistical maps of Defoe's England',
     Geographical Studies, III (1956), 33-45
153 John Patten, 'Urban life before the Industrial Revolution',

Geographical Magazine (December 1970), 208

154 E. E. Lampard, 'Urbanization and social change; on broadening the scope and relevance of urban history', being pp. 225-47 of Handlin and Burchard, *The historian and the city,* 240-41

155 H. Otsuka, 'The market structure of rural industry in the early stages of the development of modern capitalism', being pp. 457-72 of *Second International Conference of Economic History, Aix-en-Provence,* Vol. II (Paris, 1965), 471

156 A. B. Rosen, 'Economic and social aspects of the history of Winchester, 1520-1670', Unpubl. D.Phil. thesis, Oxford University, (1975), 279

157 Adey, 'Seventeenth-century Stafford', 152

158 M. Gray, 'The history of Bury, Lancashire, from 1660-1876', Unpubl. B.Litt. thesis, Oxford University (1963), *passim*

159 H. C. Whitford, 'Expos'd to sale: the marketing of goods and services in 17th century England, as revealed by Advertisements . . .' *Bull. New York Public Library,* LXXI (1967), esp. 495-505, 517; see also P. Borsay, 'The English urban renaissance: the development of provincial urban culture, c. 1680-1760', *Social History,* 5 (1977), 581-603; M. Falkus, 'Lighting in the Dark Ages of English economic history: town streets before the industrial revolution', being pp. 248-73 in D. C. Coleman and A. H. John (eds.), *Trade, government and economy in pre-industrial England,* (London, 1976)

160 H. C. Darby, 'England in the age of the improver' being p. 381 of Darby, *A new historical geography*

161 *Ibid.* 382

162 C. Chalklin, *The provincial towns of Georgian England* (1974), *passim*

163 *Ibid.* 25

164 *Ibid.* 2

Chapter 3 *Town populations*

1 The estimates of annual population increments for Europe and England are from J. J. Spengler, 'Demographic factors in early modern development', *Daedalus,* 97 (1968), 434, 436; F. Braudel, *The Mediterranean and the Mediterranean world in the age of Phillip II* (1975)

2 F. Braudel, *Capitalism and material life 1400-1800* (1967)

3 *Ibid.* 411-12

4 F. W. Carter, 'Urban development in the Western Balkans, 1200-1800', being pp. 147-95 of F. W. Carter (ed.) *An historical geography of the Balkans* (1977), 176-77, 181

5 R. Lee, 'Population in pre-industrial England: An econometric analysis', *Quarterly Journal of Economics,* LXXXVII (1973), 581

6 John Patten, 'Village and town: an occupational study', *Agric. Hist. Rev.,* 20 (1972)

7 J. Sheail, 'The regional distribution of wealth in England as indicated in the 1524-25 lay subsidy returns', Unpubl. Ph.D. thesis, London University, (1968); see also, John Patten, 'Population distribution in Norfolk and Suffolk during the sixteenth and seventeenth centuries', *Trans. Inst. Brit. Geog.* 65 (1975), 45-65

8 Sheail, 'Regional distribution of wealth', 119

9 P. N. Dawe, 'A Dorset lay-subsidy roll 1522-3 (*recte 1525*)', *Somerset and Dorset Notes and Queries*, 26 (1955)

10 A. C. Chibnall and A. V. Woodham, 'Subsidy roll for the county of Buckingham around 1524', *Buckinghamshire Record Society*, 8 (1950); J. Cornwall, 'The people of Rutland in 1522', *Trans. Leics. Hist. and Arch. Soc.*, 37 (1961-62)

11 L. F. Salzmann, 'Early taxation in Sussex', *Sussex Arch. Collections*, 98 (1960), 29-43; 99 (1961), 1-19

12 Anon. 'Suffolk in 1524', *Suffolk Green Books*, X (1910), 19 (in fact edited by S. H. A. Hervey)

13 J. Cornwall, 'The lay subsidy rolls for the county of Sussex, 1524-25', *Sussex Record Society*, 56 (1956)

14 *Ibid.* XXVII

15 R. Fieldhouse, 'Social structure from Tudor lay subsidies and probate inventories', *Local Population Studies*, 12 (1974), 12-13

16 A. R. Bax, 'The lay subsidy assessments for the county of Surrey in 1593 or 1594', *Surrey Archaeological Collections*, XVIII (1903), 161-214; XIX (1906), 39-101

17 J. Amphlett, J. W. W. Bund and F. J. Eld (eds.) 'Lay subsidy rolls, 1280-1603', *Worcestershire Historical Society*, 8-13 (1893-1902), 2

18 W. A. Carrington, 'Subsidy for the Hundred of Scarsdale, 1599', *Journal of the Derbyshire Archaeological and Natural History Society*, 24 (1902), 5-25

19 J. B. Harley, 'Population trends and agricultural development from the Warwickshire Hundred Rolls of 1279', *Econ. Hist. Rev.*, 2nd Series, XI (1958-9), 8-18

20 L. M. Munby, 'Hertfordshire population statistics, 1563-1807', *Herts. Local History Council* (Hitchen, 1964); *idem* 'The population of Hertfordshire before 1801', *Transactions East Hertfordshire Archaeological Society*, 14 (1955-61) *passim*

21 J. E. Cornwall, 'An Elizabethan Census', *Records of Buckinghamshire*, 16 (1959), 258-73

22 R. Pickard, *The population and epidemics of Exeter in pre-census times* (Exeter, privately printed, 1947)

23 P. Ripley, 'The parish register evidence for the population of Gloucester, 1562-1641', *Transactions Bristol and Gloucestershire Archaeological Society*, XCI (1972), 199-206

24 For example A. Jessop, 'The condition of the Archdeaconry of Suffolk and Sudbury in the year 1603', *Proceedings Suffolk Institute of Archaeology*, 6 (1888), 361-400

25 Patten, 'Population distribution in Norfolk and Suffolk', 54

26 *Ibid.* 56

27 R. Stewart-Brown, *The inhabitants of Liverpool, from the fourteenth to the eighteenth century* (Liverpool, 1930). For another study utilizing the Protestation returns, see D. A. Kirby. 'Population density and land values in County Durham during the mid-seventeenth century', *Trans. Inst. Brit. Geog.*, 57 (1972) 83-98

28 K. R. Adey, 'Seventeenth-century Stafford: A county town in decline', *Midland History*, II (1974), 154

29   S. A. H. Burne (ed.), 'A subsidy roll of 1640', *Collections for a History of Staffordshire* (1942), 155-68

30   J. T. Driver (ed.), 'A subsidy roll for the hundred of Macclesfield, 1610', *Transactions of Lancashire and Cheshire Antiquarian Society*, 62 (1953), 54-67

31   P. Slack, 'Poverty and politics in Salisbury 1597-1666', being pp. 164-203 of P. Clark and P. Slack (eds.), *Crisis and order in English towns 1500-1700* (1972)

32   J. Patten, 'The Hearth Taxes, 1662-89', *Local Population Studies*, 7 (1971), 14-27

33   E. Ralph and M. E. Williams (eds.), 'The inhabitants of Bristol in 1696', *Bristol Record Society Publ.*, XXV (1968)

34   D. V. Glass, 'Two papers on Gregory King', being pp. 159-202 in Glass and D. E. C. Eversley, *Population and History* (1965); see also P. E. Jones and A. V. Judges, 'London population in the late seventeenth century', *Econ. Hist. Rev.*, VI (1935-36), 45-58

35   H. A. Whitney, 'Estimating pre-census populations: a method suggested and applied to the towns of Rhode Island and Plymouth Colonies in 1689', *Annals Association American Geographers*, 55 (1965), 179-89

36   Patten, 'Hearth Taxes'; R. Howell, 'Hearth Tax returns: short guides to records, 7', *History*, 49 (1964)

37   S. Coleman (ed.), 'The Hearth Tax returns for the Hundred of Blackbourne, 1662', *Proceedings Suffolk Institute of Archaeology*, XXXII (1972)

38   E. J. D. Morriss, 'The Hearth Tax in Chester', *Journal of the Chester and North Wales Archaeological and Historical Society*, XXXVI (1946), 31-43

39   M. M. B. Weinstock, 'Hearth Tax returns, Oxfordshire, 1665', *Oxfordshire Record Society*, XXI (1940)

40   R. Welford, 'Newcastle householders in 1665', *Archaeologia Aeliana*, VII (1917), 49-76

41   E. Dwelly and R. Holworthy, 'Hearth Tax for Somerset 1664-65' (Dwelly's National Records, I, Fleet, 1916)

42   E. Grogan, W. N. Lander *et al.* (eds.), 'The Staffordshire Hearth Tax', *Collections for a History of Staffordshire* (1921), 41-173; (1923), 47-256; (1925), 155-242; (1927), 1-79

43   C. A. F. Meekings, 'Surrey Hearth Tax 1664', *Surrey Record Society*, XVII (1950)

44   M. Walker (ed.) with introd. by P. Styles, 'Hearth Tax Returns', *Warwickshire Records Publications* (1958); see also, P. Styles, 'The social structure of Kineton Hundred in the reign of Charles II' *Trans. and Proc. Birmingham Arch. Soc.*, 78 (1962), 96-117

45   Glass, 'Two papers on Gregory King', in Glass and Eversley, *Population and history*

46   G. O. Cowley, 'Sussex market towns 1550-1750', Unpubl. M.A. thesis, London University (1965) 56

47   A. Everitt, 'Urban growth, 1570-1770', *The Local Historian*, VIII (1968-69), 118

48   Cowley, 'Sussex market towns'

49   E. Gillett, *A history of Grimsby* (1970), 67

50   C. W. Chalklin, *The provincial towns of Georgian England* (1974), 3
51   Glass, 'Two papers on Gregory King', in Glass and Eversley, *Population and history*, 177
52   C. W. Chalklin, 'A seventeenth-century market town, Tonbridge', *Archaeologia Cantiana*, 76 (1961), 152
53   Cowley, 'Sussex market towns'
54   C. A. F. Meekings, *Dorset Hearth Tax, 1662-64* (Dorchester, 1951), XXX-XXXII
55   *Ibid*. XXX
56   H. C. Darby, 'The age of the improver, 1600-1800', being pp. 302-88 in Darby, H. C. (ed.) *A new historical geography of England*, (Cambridge, 1973), 361
57   R. A. Butlin (ed.), *The development of the Irish town* (1977), 93
58   D. E. C. Eversley, Appendix B in E. A. Wrigley (ed.) *An introduction to English historical demography* (1966), 266
59   John Patten, 'Population distribution in Norfolk and Suffolk', 62
60   G. S. L. Tucker, 'English pre-industrial population trends', *Econ. Hist. Rev.*, 2nd Series, XVI (1963), 205-18
61   P. Deane and W. A. Cole, *British economic growth, 1688-1959* (1964), 3; see also, B. R. Mitchell and P. Deane, *Abstract of British Historical Statistics* (Cambridge, 1962), *passim*
62   Deane and Cole, *British economic growth*, 7
63   S. Kuznets, 'Capital formation in modern economic growth, and some implications for the past', *Third International Conference of Economic History* (Paris, 1968), 30-31
64   Deane and Cole, *British economic growth*, 7-8
65   R. A. Holt, 'The economic development of Birmingham before 1553', Unpubl. M.A. thesis, Birmingham University (1975), 108
66   C. Gill, *History of Birmingham*, I (1951), 49, 56
67   H. Hamilton, *The English brass and copper industries to 1800* . . . (1926), 125
68   *Ibid*. 129
69   L. A. Clarkson, *The pre-industrial economy in England, 1500-1750* (1971), 47
70   *Ibid*.; see also, W. G. Hoskins, 'The population of Exeter', *Devonshire Notes and Queries*, XX (1938-39), 292-27
71   J. D. Chambers, 'Population change in a provincial town: Nottingham 1700-1800', in L. S. Pressnall (ed.), *Studies in the Industrial Revolution* (1968): J. A. Johnston, 'Developments in Worcester and Worcestershire 1563-1851', *Trans. Worc. Arch. Soc.*, 3rd Series, 5 (1976), 53
72   G. C. F. Forster, 'From the foundation of the borough to the eve of the Industrial Revolution', being pp. 131-45 of *Leeds and its region* (1967)
73   Sir W. Petty, 'Political arithmetic (1690)' in C. H. Hull (ed.), *The economic writings of Sir William Petty*, I (1899), 272
74   P. M. Frost, 'The growth and localization of rural industry in south Staffordshire, 1560-1720', Unpubl. Ph.D. thesis, Univ. of Birmingham University (1973) 283-84
75   E. A. Wrigley, 'A simple model of London's importance in changing English society and economy, 1650-1750, *Past and Present*, 37 (1967), 44-70

76 A. H. French, *et al.* 'The population of Stepney in the early seventeenth century', *Local Population Studies,* 3 (1969), 39-52

77 *Ibid.* 47

78 J. M. Beattie, 'The pattern of crime in England 1600-1800', *Past and Present,* 62 (1974), 47-95; C. A. Edie, 'New buildings, new taxes and old interests: an urban problem of the 1670s', *Jnl. British Studies,* 6 (1967), 35-63

79 R. L. Morrill, 'The development of spatial distribution of towns in Sweden: an historical predictive approach', *Annals Assoc. American Geographers,* 53 (1962), 103

80 J. D. Chambers, *Population, economy and society in pre-industrial England* (1972), 103

81 For example P. Slack, 'Vagrants and vagrancy in England 1598-1664', *Econ. Hist. Rev.,* 2nd Series, XXVII (1974), 360-79

82 J. Hicks, *A theory of economic history* (1969), 134-35

83 John Patten, *Rural–urban migration in pre-industrial England,* School of Geography, Oxford Research Paper, 6 (1973), *passim*; see also *idem,* 'Patterns of migration and movement of labour to three pre-industrial East Anglian towns', *Journal of Historical Geography,* 2 (1976), 111-29

84 Example for Gloucester, see Ripley, 'The population of Gloucester'

85 R. F. Peel, 'Local intermarriage and the stability of rural population in the English Midlands', *Geography,* XXVII (1942), 28

86 Slack, 'Vagrants and vagrancy', esp. 361

87 J. F. Pound, 'The Norwich Census of the poor, 1570', *Norfolk Record Series,* 40 (1971), 42

88 Patten, *Rural-urban migration*

89 J. Cornwall, 'Evidence of population mobility in the seventeenth century', *Bulletin Institute Historical Research,* XL (1967), 143-52

90 P. Clark, 'The migrant in Kentish towns, 1580-1640', being pp. 117-63 of Clark and Slack, *Crisis and order*

91 Much of the discussion of individual sources is based on Patten, *Rural–urban migration,* 11-22

92 I. G. Doolittle, 'The effects of the plague on a provincial town in the sixteenth and seventeenth centuries', *Medical History,* 19 (1975), 333-41

93 Slack, 'Vagrants and vagrancy', 374

94 See for example C. Creighton, *A History of epidemics in Britain* (2 vols., 1965); J. F. Shrewsbury, *Plague in the British Isles* (1971); see also M. W. Flinn, 'The stabilization of mortality in pre-industrial western Europe', *The Journal of European History,* 3 (1974), 286

95 Doolittle, 'Effects of plague', 334

96 D. M. Palliser, 'Death and diseases in Staffordshire 1540-1670' in C. W. Chalkin and M. A. Havinden (eds.), *Rural change and urban growth 1500-1800* (1974), esp. 71-72

97 Wrigley, 'A simple model', 47

98 M. F. Hollingsworth and T. H. Hollingsworth, 'Plague mortality rates by age and sex in the parish of St Botolphs Without, Bishopsgate, London, 1603', *Populations Studies,* 25 (1971), 131-46

99 D. F. McKenzie, 'Apprenticeship in the Stationers' Company 1550-1640', *The Library,* 5th Series, 13 (1958), 292-98

100 D. V. Glass, 'Socio-economic status and occupations in the City of London at the end of the seventeenth century', pp. 373-89 in A. E. Hollaender and W. Kellaway (eds.), *Studies in London History* (1969)

101 Pattern, *Rural–urban migration,* 31

102 M. Power, 'The urban development of East London (1550-1700)', Unpubl. Ph.D. thesis, London University (1971), 75-85

103 Glass, 'Status and occupations' in Hollaender and Kellaway, *London History,* 389

104 Anon. 'A bibliography of lists of apprenticeship', *Genealogists Magazine,* 7 (1935-7)

105 Glass, *op cit.*; S. R. Smith, 'The social and geographical origins of the London apprentices', *Guildhall Miscellany,* 4 (1973), 195-206

106 S. R. Smith, 'The London apprentices as seventeenth century adolescents', *Past and Present,* 61 (1973), 160; *idem* 'The social and geographical origins of the London apprentices 1630-1660', *Guildhall Miscellany,* IV (1973), 195-206

107 Glass, 'Status and occupations', in Hollaender and Kellaway, *London History,* 377

108 *Ibid.* 386

109 A. D. Dyer, *The city of Worcester in the sixteenth century* (Leicester, 1973) esp. 27, 48 and 183

110 D. Hollis (ed.), 'Calender of the Bristol Apprentice Book, 1532-1569; pt 1, 1532-42', *Bristol Record Society,* 14 (1948)

111 Clarkson, *Pre-industrial economy',* 32

112 Flinn, 'Stabilization of mortality', 285

113 G. C. F. Forster, 'York in the seventeenth century', being pp. 160-206 in *V.C.H. City of York* (1961), 162

114 Dyer, *Worcester*; Forster, 'York'; E. A. Wrigley, 'Mortality in pre-industrial England', reprinted in D. V. Glass and R. Revelle, *Population and social change* (1972), 259-60, 269

115 D. R. Palliser, 'Epidemics in Tudor York', *Northern History,* VIII (1973), 46

116 P. Slack, 'Some aspects of epidemics in England, 1485-1690', Unpubl. D. Phil. thesis, Oxford University (1972), IV

117 *Ibid.* 12-22

118 *Ibid.* 112

119 N. Griffin, 'Epidemics in Loughborough 1539-1640', *Trans. Leics. Arch. and Hist. Soc.,* XLIII (1967-68), 24-34

120 J. E. O. Wilshere, 'Plague in Leicester, 1558-1665', *Trans. Leics. Arch. and Hist. Soc.,* XLIV (1968-69), 45-61

121 H. Dane, 'The story of a thousand years; a chronology of Faversham's history . . .', *Faversham Papers,* 5 (1968), 13

122 T. Atkinson, *Elizabethan Winchester* (1963), 213-16

123 Adey, 'Seventeenth-century Stafford', 159

124 The 'sweat' may have been influenza, see R. S. Roberts, 'A consideration of the nature of the English sweating sickness', *Medical History,* IX (1965)

125 See for example F. J. Fisher, 'Influenza and inflation in Tudor England', *Econ. Hist. Rev.,* 2nd Series, XVIII (1965)

126 A. B. Appleby, 'Disease or Famine? Mortality in Cumberland and

Westmorland 1580-1640', *Econ. Hist. Rev.*, 2nd Series, XXVI (1973), 403-32

127 *Idem* 'Nutrition and disease: The case of London, 1550-1750', *Journal of Interdisciplinary History*, VI (1975), 1-22
128 *Ibid.* 19
129 J. D. Chambers, *Population, society and economy in pre-industrial England* (1972), 94; see esp. chs. 1 and 4
130 *Ibid.* 65
131 Gill, *Birmingham*, 49, 60-61
132 W. G. Rimmer, 'The evolution of Leeds to 1700', *The Thoresby Miscellany*, 14 (1967), 118
133 For example in Dyer, *Worcester*
134 Chambers, *Pre-industrial England*, 65
135 E. A. Wrigley, 'Family limitation in pre-industrial England', *Econ. Hist. Rev.*, 2nd Series, XIX (1966), 82-104
136 *Ibid.* 66
137 Clark and Slack, *Crisis and order*, 17
138 J. Langton, 'Residential patterns in pre-industrial cities', *Trans. Inst. Brit. Geog.*, 65 (1975); Clark and Slack, *Crisis and order*
139 Langton, 'Residential patterns'
140 Chambers, *Pre-industrial England*, 67
141 John Webb (ed.), *Poor relief in Elizabethan Ipswich*, (Suffolk Record Society, 1966)
142 M. J. Power, 'East London housing in the seventeenth century', being pp. 237-62 in Clark and Slack, *Crisis and order*, 237
143 I. Sutherland, 'When was the Great Plague?, Mortality in London, 1563 to 1665', being pp. 287-30 in Glass and Revelle, *Population and social change*, 302
144 D. V. Glass, 'Notes on the demography of London at the end of the seventeenth century', being pp. 275-85 in Glass and Revelle, *Population and social change*, 277-80
145 Glass and Nevelle, 'London inhabitants within the walls, 1695', *London Record Society Publications*, 2 (1966)
146 Glass, 'Status and occupations', in Hollaender and Kellaway, *London History*, 374
147 D. W. Jones, 'London merchants and the crisis of the 1690s', being pp. 311-55 in Clark and Slack, *Crisis and order*, 311
148 Palliser, 'Epidemics in Tudor York', 46
149 Forster, 'York', 165
150 Ralph and Wilhams, 'Inhabitants of Bristol'
151 W. G. Hoskins, *Industry Trade and people in Exeter, 1688-1800* (1935), 116
152 Slack, 'Epidemics in England', 114-41
153 *Ibid.* 189-90
154 Hoskins, *Provincial England*, 92
     V. C. H. Leicester, 158-59
155 Clark, 'The migrant in Kentish towns 1580-1640', being pp. 117-63 in Clark and Slack, *Crisis and order*, 142
156 Fieldhouse, 'Social structure', 10-13
157 J. D. Purdy, 'The Hearth Tax returns for Yorkshire', Unpubl. Ph.M. thesis, Leeds University (1975), 328, 360; M. Thorpe, 'Lichfield: a

study of its growth and functions; *Staffordshire Hist. Coll.* (1950-51), 171-97

158   Patten, 'Village and town', 6
159   Langton, 'Residential patterns'

Chapter 4   *Town occupations and town economies*

1   P. Heylyn, *Cosmographie* (1652), 22-271
2   D. Defoe, *A plan of the English commerce* (1728), 20-27
3   G. D. H. Cole, *People and places* (1948)
4   W. Hutton, *The history of Birmingham* (Birmingham, 6th edn 1835), 109
5   W. G. Hoskins, *Provincial England: essays in social and economic history* (1963), 88; D. Charman, 'Wealth and trade in Leicester in the early sixteenth century' *Trans. Leicester Arch. Soc.*, XXV (1949), 69-97; E. W. J. Kerridge, 'Leicester, social and economic history, 1509-1660', *V.C.H. Leicester* IV, 76-109; J. A. Jenkin and C. T. Smith, 'Social and administrative history, 1660-1835', being pp. 153-200 in *ibid.*
6   John Patten, 'Urban occupations in pre-industrial England', *Trans. Inst. Brit. Geog.* N.S. 2 (1977), 296-313
7   G. C. F. Forster, 'York in the Seventeenth Century', *V.C.H. City of York* (1961), 167
8   John Patten, 'Occupations in the East Anglian countryside, 1500-1700', in R. A. Butlin, and H. S. A. Fox, (eds.) *Change in the countryside*, Institute of British Geographers, Special Publication (*forthcoming, 1978*)
9   Anon. *The trade of England revived and the abuses thereof rectified* (London, 1681)
10   J. Webb, *Poor relief in Elizabethan Ipswich*, Suffolk Records Society Publication (1966)
11   P. Clark, 'The migrant in Kentish towns 1580-1640', being pp. 117-63 in P. Clark and P. Slack, *Crisis and order in the English town 1500-1700* (1972); P. Slack, 'Vagrants and vagrancy in England, 1598-1664', *Econ. Hist. Rev.*, XXVIII (1974), 360-78
12   These are extensively examined in John Patten, 'Urban occupations'
13   See for example C. Phythian-Adams, 'Sources for urban history: 3. Records of the craft guilds', *Local Historian*, IX (1971), 267-74 or M. M. Rowe and A. M. Jackson (eds.), *Exeter Freemen, 1266-1967*, Devon and Cornwall Record Society, Extra Series 1 (Exeter, 1973)
14   W. M. Rising and P. Millican (eds.), 'Apprentices indentured at Norwich, 1510-1752', *Norfolk Record Society*, XXIX (1959)
15   John Patten, 'The urban structure of East Anglia in the sixteenth and seventeenth centuries', Unpubl. Ph.D. thesis, Cambridge University (1972), 89-90
16   Such as the wills printed in an extensive series by The British Record Society
17   East London History Group, 'The population of Stepney in the early seventeenth century', *East London Papers*, II (1968), 75-93
18   Such as the 1522 'Muster of Harness'; see John Patten, 'Village and town: an occupational study', *Agricultural History Review*, 20 (1972), 1-16, and, for an early seventeenth-century muster, see A. J. Tawney

and R. H. Tawney, 'An occupational census of the seventeenth century', *Econ. Hist. Rev.*, V (1934), 25-64

19 Such as the 1695 Tax on Births, Deaths, Marriages etc.; see D. V. Glass, 'Socio-economic status and occupations in the City of London at the end of the seventeenth century', being pp. 373-392 of A. J. Hollaender and W. Kellaway (eds.), *Studies in London History* (1969); or E. Ralph and M. E. Williams, 'The inhabitants of Bristol in 1696', *Bristol Record Society Publication*, XXV (1968)

20 John Patten, 'Freemen and apprentices', *Local Historian*, 9 (1971), 232; C. J. Palmer, *The history of Great Yarmouth by H. Manship* (Great Yarmouth and London, 1854), 230

21 J. Webb, *Great Tooley of Ipswich* (1962)

22 M. M. Rowe and G. E. Trease, 'The 1572 Bill of an Exeter apothecary', *Devon and Cornwall Notes and Queries*, XXXII (1971)

23 Phythian-Adams, 'Records of the craft guilds', 269

24 Kerridge, 'Leicester', 76-89

25 C. R. Elsington, 'Records of the Cordwainers' Scoiety of Tewkesbury, 1562-1941', *Trans. Bristol and Glouces. Arch. Soc.*, LXXXV (1966), 164-74

26 W. L. Goodman, 'Woodworking apprentices and their tools in Bristol, Warwick, Great Yarmouth and Southampton, 1535-1650', *Industrial Archaeology*, IX (1974), 376-411

27 D. G. Vaisey, 'A Charlbury Mercer's Shop, 1623', *Oxoniensia*, 31 (1966), 107-16

28 D. C. Coleman, 'London Scriveners and the estate market in the later seventeenth century', *Econ. Hist. Rev.*, 2nd Series, 4 (1951)

29 E. Lamond, *A discourse of the Commonwealth of this Realm of England* (Cambridge, reprinted 1893), *passim*

30 Alan MacFarlane, *The family life of Ralph Josselin, a seventeenth century clergyman* (Cambridge, 1970); idem., *The diary of Ralph Josselin, 1616-83* (1976)

31 For example T. S. Willan, *An eighteenth century shopkeeper: Abraham Dent of Kirkby Stephen* (Manchester, 1970) *passim*

32 P. Clark, *The early modern town* (Open University, 1976)

33 D. J. Johnson, *Southwark and the city* (1969), *passim*

34 E. Kerridge, 'Leicester', 89-90

35 S. Unwin, *Industrial organization in the sixteenth and seventeenth centuries* (1904), 10

36 C. Hill, *The century of revolution 1605-1714* (1947), 205

37 S. Kramer, *The English craft guilds and the government*, Columbia University Studies, 23 (New York, 1905), 146

38 For example J. H. E. Bennett, 'The Rolls of the Freemen of the City of Chester, Part 1, 1392 to 1700', *Lancashire and Cheshire Record Society*, 51 (1906); or on Exeter, Rowe and Jackson, *Exeter freemen*

39 For example F. W. Dendy, 'The struggle between the merchant and craft guilds of Newcastle in 1515', *Archaeologia Aeliana, VII* (1911), 77-101

40 Begin:.ing with the work of M. Sellers, 'The city of York in the sixteenth century', *E.H.R.*, IX (1894), 275-304; idem 'York in the sixteenth and seventeenth centuries', *Eng. Hist. Rev.*, XII (1897), 437-47

41 R. B. Dobson, 'Admission to the Freedom of the City of York in the later Middle Ages', *Econ. Hist. Rev.* (1973), 1-27
42 D. M. Palliser, 'The trade guilds of medieval York', pp. 86-116 of Clark and Slack, *Crisis and order*, 86
43 *Ibid.* 87
44 *Ibid.* 90, 92
45 E. Gillet, *A history of Grimsby* (1970), 104-5
46 *Ibid.*
47 J. R. Kellet, 'The breakdown of guild and corporate control over the handicraft and retail trade in London', *Econ. Hist. Rev.*, 2nd Series, X (1958), 382
48 D. W. Jones, 'London merchants and the crisis of the 1690s', being pp. 311-55 of Clark and Slack, *Crisis and order*, 311, 318-19
49 For comparison with Paris, see R. Larmour, 'A merchant guild of sixteenth century France: the grocers of Paris', *Econ. Hist. Rev.*, 2nd series, XX (1967), 467-81
50 A. B. Rosen, 'Economic and social aspects of the history of Winchester, 1520-1670', Unpubl. D.Phil. thesis, Oxford University (1975), VI, 115-18; D. M. Palliser, 'Some aspects of the social and economic history of York', Unpubl. Ph.D. thesis, Oxford University (1968), 168
51 D. C. Coleman, *Industry in Tudor and Stuart England* (1975), 16
52 *Idem.* 19
53 L. A. Clarkson, *The pre-industrial economy in England 1500-1750* (1971), 78
54 *Ibid.* 88-89
55 A. J. and R. H. Tawney, 'An occupational census'
56 R. J. A. Shelley, 'Wigan and Liverpool pewterers', *Trans. Hist. Soc. Lancashire & Cheshire*, 97 (1946), 1
57 W. G. Hoskins, 'English provincial towns in the sixteenth century', *Trans. Roy. Hist. Soc.*, 5th ser., 6 (1956), 15
58 Patten, 'Urban Occupations', *passim*
59 Rosen, 'Winchester', 198-201, 298
60 D. M. Palliser, 'York under the Tudors', being pp. 39-59 in A. M. Everitt, (ed.) *Perspectives in English urban history* (1973), 53; D. G. Vaizey, 'Probate inventories of Lichfield and district, 1568-1680', *Coll. for a History of Staffordshire*, Series 5 (1969)
61 Jenkin and Smith in *V.C.H. Leicester*, 158
62 A. Crossley, 'A history of the county of Oxford', *V.C.H. Oxford*, X, 5-127; on the leather trades see L. A. Clarkson, 'The leather crafts in Tudor and Stuart England', *Agricultural History Review*, XIV (1966), 25-39
63 C. J. M. Moxon, 'Ashby-de-la Zouch, a social and economic survey of a market town, 1570-1720', Unpubl. D.Phil. thesis, Oxford University (1971), p. 1 of Abstract
64 Patten, 'Occupations in the East Anglian countryside'
65 R. Blome, *Brittania* (1673), 57
66 W. B. Stephens, (ed.) *History of Congleton* (1970), 51-55
67 F. W. D. Manders, *A history of Gateshead* (1973), 31-32
68 L. J. Ashford, *The history of the borough of High Wycombe from its origin* (1960), 146-50, 122-3

69 J. Cornwall, 'The people of Rutland in 1522', *Trans. Leicester Hist. &*
    Arch. Soc., 37 (1961-62), 7-28
70 *Ibid.* 8
71 G. O. Cowley, 'Sussex market towns, 1550-1750', Unpubl. M.A.
    thesis, London University (1965), 219, 244
72 *Ibid.* 210, 217-18
73 G. H. Kenyon, 'Petworth towns and trades, 1610-1760', pt. 1, *Sussex*
    Arch. Coll., XCVI (1958), 35-107
74 *Ibid.* 45
75 *Ibid.* 62
76 Cowley, 'Sussex market towns', 217
77 C. E. Brent, 'Employment, land tenure and population in eastern
    Sussex, 1540-1640', Unpubl. Ph.D. thesis, Sussex University (1973),
    353
78 *Ibid.* 309-10, 343
79 C. W. Chalklin, 'The making of some new towns, c. 1600-1720', being
    pp. 229-52 in C. W. Chalklin and M. A. Havinden, *Rural change and*
    urban growth (1974), 230-31
80 *Ibid.*
81 A. A. Ruddock, 'London capitalists and the decline of Southampton
    in the early Tudor period', *Econ. Hist. Rev.*, 2nd Series II (1949-50),
    137-51
82 A. L. Merson, 'Southampton in the sixteenth and seventeenth cen-
    turies', being pp. 218-277 of F. J. Monkhouse (ed.), *A survey of*
    Southampton and its region (1964), 224; see also *idem* 'A calendar of
    Southampton Apprenticeship registers, 1609-1740', *Southampton Record*
    Series, XII (1968)
83 A. T. Patterson, 'A history of Southampton, 1700-1914', *Southampton*
    Record Series, II (1966), 5
84 F. N. G. Thomas, 'Portsmouth and Gosport: A study in the historical
    geography of a naval port', Unpubl. M.Sc. thesis, London University
    (1961)
85 Clarkson, *Pre-industrial economy*, 85
86 D. C. Coleman, 'Naval dockyards under the later Stuarts', *Econ. Hist.*
    Rev., VI (1953)
87 Chalklin in Chalklin and Havinden, *Rural change and urban growth*, 231
88 C. Armour, 'The trade of Chester and the state of the Dee navigation
    1600-1800', Unpubl. Ph.D. thesis, London University (1956)
89 A. Dulley, 'People and houses in Medway towns, 1687-1783',
    Archaeologia Cantiana, 77 (1962), 161-67
90 *Ibid.* 165
91 Kenyon, 'Petworth towns and trades'
92 Dulley, 'Medway towns', 166-7
93 John Patten, 'Population distribution in Norfolk and Suffolk during
    the sixteenth and seventeenth centuries', *Trans. Inst. Brit. Geog.*, 65
    (1975), 45-65
94 33 H. VIII c. 15
95 F. Walker, 'The historical geography of south-west Lancashire',
    Chetham Society, 2nd Series, C111 (1939), 33-69; see also N. Lowe, 'The
    Lancashire textile industry in the sixteenth century', *Chetham Society*,
    3rd Series (1972)

96   D. C. Coleman, 'Textile growth', being pp. 1-21, of N. B. Harte and K. G. Ponting, *Textile history and economic history* (1973)

97   See M. E. François, 'The social and economic development of Halifax 1558-1640', *Proc. Leeds Philosophical and Literary Society, Literary and Historical Section*, XI (1966), 217-80

98   W. T. Wild, 'An historical geography of the west Yorkshire textile industry to c. 1850', Unpubl. Ph.D. thesis, Birmingham University (1972), 75-6

99   W. G. Rimmer, 'The evolution of Leeds to 1700', *Thoresby Miscellany*, 14 (1967), esp. 108-9

100 G. C. F. Forster, 'From the foundation of the borough to the eve of the Industrial Revolution', being pp. 131-14 in *Leeds and its region* (1967), 134-36

101 Rimmer, 'Leeds', 109

102 J. F. Pound, 'The social and trade structure of Norwich 1525-75', *Past and Present*, 34 (1966); see also K. J. Allison, 'The Norwich Hatters', *East Anglian Magazine*, 16 (1957), 134-38

103 A. D. Dyer, *The city of Worcester in the sixteenth century* (Leicester, 1973), 133, 111

104 Jenkins and Smith, in *V.C.H. Leicester*, 168

105 J. Simmons, *Leicester past and present, I: Ancient borough to 1860* (1974), 97

106 A. W. A. White, 'Economic growth in eighteenth century Warwickshire', Unpubl. Ph.D. thesis, Birmingham University (1972), 257

107 W. Smith, *A particular description of England* (1588)

108 C. Gill, *History of Birmingham* (1952), 44-45

109 *Ibid.* 45

110 R. Pelham, 'Migration of the Birmingham iron industry', *Birmingham Arch. Soc. Trans.*, LXVI (1945-6), 146

111 J. S. Roper, *Dudley, the town in the sixteenth century*, Dudley Public Libraries Transcript, 4 (1974)

112 M. B. Rowlands, 'Masters and men in, the small metallurgical trades of the West Midlands, 1660-1760', Unpubl. Ph.D. thesis, Birmingham University (1972)

113 R. Plot, *Staffordshire* (1686), 375-76

114 Rowlands, 'Masters and men', 96, 49

115 S. McIntyre, 'Towns as health and pleasure resorts; the development of Bath, Scarborough and Weymouth, 1700-1815', Unpubl. Oxford D. Phil. (1973), 30, 7; J. A. Patmore, 'The spa towns of Britain', being pp. 47-69 in R. P. Beckinsale and J. M. Houston (eds.), *Urbanization and its problems* (Oxford, 1968); E. Deane, *Spadacrene Anglica, or the English Spaw Fountaine* (1626); M. Stanhope, *Cures without care* (1632)

116 P. R. James, *The baths of Bath in the sixteenth and early seventeenth centuries* (1938), 89

117 H. Chapman, *Thermae rediviae* (1673), 15

118 C. Morris (ed.), *The journeys of Celia Fiennes* (1949), 21

119 McIntyre, 'Health and pleasure resorts', 180-82, 293-97

120 C. I. Hammer, 'The mobility of skilled labour in late Medieval England: some Oxford Evidences', *Vierteljahrshrift für Sozial und Wirtschaftsgeschichte*, 63 Band, Heft. 2 (1976), 196

121 C. W. Chalklin, *The provincial towns of Georgian England* (1974), 11
122 S. I. Mitchell, 'Urban markets and retail distribution 1730-1815, with particular reference to Macclesfield, Stockport and Cheshire'. Unpubl. D.Phil. thesis, Oxford (1974), 24
123 P. J. Bemrose, 'Newcastle under Lyme: its contribution to the growth of the North Staffordshire pottery industry, 1650-1800', Unpubl. M.A. thesis, Keele University (1972), *passim*.
124 E. M. Veale, 'Craftsmen and the economy of London in the fourteenth century', being pp. 133-51 of Hollaender and Kellaway, *London History,* esp. 143
125 *Ibid.* 149
126 H. C. Darby, 'The age of the improver 1600-1808', being pp. 302-88 in H. C. Darby (ed.) *A new historical geography of England* (Cambridge, 1973), 387
127 For example F. J. Fisher, 'The development of the London food market, 1540-1640', *Econ. Hist. Rev.,* V (1935), 46-64
128 E. A. Wrigley, 'A simple model of London's importance in changing English society and economy, 1650-1750', *Past and Present,* 37 (1967), 44-70; *idem* 'Modernization and the industrial revolution in England', *Journal of Interdisciplinary History,* III (1972)
129 L. Stone, 'English and United States Local History', *Daedalus,* CI (1971), 131; W. G. Hoskins, *The age of plunder* (1976), 95
130 Wrigley, 'A simple model'
131 G. D. Ramsay, *The city of London in international politics at the accession of Elizabeth Tudor* (1975), 33
132 *Ibid.* 12
133 E. Howes, *Stowes Annales* (1631), 948, col. 1
134 Cal. S. P. (Venice and Northern Italy), XV, 257
135 J. L. Archer, 'The industrial history of London 1603-40', Unpubl. M.A. thesis, London University (1934), 41-42
136 J. Cornwall, 'English country towns in the fifteen-twenties', *Econ. Hist. Rev.,* 2nd Series, XV (1962-3), 68
137 Howes, *Stowes Annales,* 948, col. 1
138 D. Davis, *A history of shopping* (1966)
139 D. Alexander, *Retailing in England during the Industrial Revolution* (1970), *passim*
140 *Ibid.*; R. Scola, 'Food markets and shops in Manchester 1770-1870', *Journal of Historical Geography,* I (1975), 153-67; T. S. Willan, *The inland trade* (1976); Patten, 'Occupations in the East Anglian countryside'
141 N. J. Williams, 'Tradesmen in early-Stuart Wiltshire', *Wilts. Arch. & Nat. Hist. Soc., Record Branch,* XV (1959)
142 D. G. Vaisey, 'A Charlbury mercer's shop, 1623', *Oxoniensia,* XXI (1966), 107-16
143 F. C. Morgan, 'Inventory of a Hereford Mercer's Shop, 1689' and 'Inventories of a Hereford Saddler's Shop, 1692 and 1696', *Trans. Woolhope Naturalists Field Club,* XXXI (1947), 181-200, 253-68
144 T. S. Willan, *An eighteenth century shopkeeper, Abraham Dent of Kirkby Stephen* (Manchester, 1970)
145 Ipswich & East Suffolk Record Office C7/2/5; see also J. Brome, *Travels over England, Scotland and Wales* (1700), 119

146 K. Charlton, 'The professions in sixteenth century England', *Univ. of Birm. Hist. Journal,* XII (1969-70), 41; D. C. Coleman, 'London scriveners and the estate market in the late seventeenth century', *Econ. Hist. Rev.,* IV (1951), 221-30

147 T. D. Whittet, 'The apothecary in provincial guilds', *Medical History,* 8 (1964), 245-73

148 There are three admirable thesis on East London: K. G. T. McDonnell, 'The economic social structure of the parishes of Bromley, Hackney, Stepney and Whitechapel from the thirteenth to the sixteenth century', Unpubl. Ph.D. thesis, London University (1958); J. L. Archer, 'The industrial history of London 1603-1640', Unpubl. M.A. thesis, London University (1934); M. Power, 'The urban development of East London, 1500-1700', Unpubl. Ph.D. thesis, London University (1971)

149 East London History Group (1968), *op. cit. passim*

150 D. J. Johnson, *Southwark and the City* (1969), *passim*

151 A. R. Bridbury, *Economic growth: England in the later Middle Ages* (1962); J. Sheail, 'The regional distribution of wealth in England as indicated in the 1524-5 Lay Subsidy', Unpubl. Ph.D. thesis, London University (1968)

152 W. B. Stephens, 'Merchant companies and commercial policy in Exeter 1625-1688', *Trans. Devonshire Assoc.,* XXXVI (1954), 139

153 P. Corfield, 'A provincial capital in the late seventeenth century: the case of Norwich', being pp. 263-310 of Clark and Slack, *Crisis and order,* esp. 282

154 See W. G. Hoskins, *The age of plunder* (1976), esp. 99, 105-20, 226-29

155 V. Parker, 'The making of Kings Lynn from the eleventh to the seventeenth century', Unpubl. Ph.D. thesis, Sheffield University (1969), 27

156 John Patten, 'Village and town', 1-16

157 P. Styles, 'The social structure of Kineton Hundred in the reign of Charles II', *Trans. and Proc. Birmingham Arch. Soc.,* 78 (1962), 96-117

158 For example Vaisey, 'A Charlbury mercer's shop'

159 A. H. French, *et al.* 'The population of Stepney in the early seventeenth century', *Local Population Studies,* 3 (1969), 39-52, esp. p. 51

160 M. Gray, 'The history of Bury, Lancashire from 1660 to 1876', Unpubl. B.Litt. thesis, Oxford University (1963), 33, 64

161 B. L. C. Johnson, 'The Foley Partnerships', *Econ. Hist. Rev.,* 2nd Series, IV (1951-52), 322-40, *passim*

162 See K. Thomas, 'Work and leisure in pre-industrial society', *Past and Present,* 29 (1964), 50-66

163 V. C. H. Wiltshire, *4,* 146-47

164 B. McClenaghan, *The springs of Lavenham and the Suffolk cloth trade in the fifteenth and sixteenth centuries* (Ipswich, 1924)

165 Webb, *Great Tooley, passim*

166 Hoskins, 'Provincial towns', 6-7

167 R. A. Holt, 'The economic development of Birmingham before 1553', Unpubl. M.A. thesis, Birmingham University (1975), 80

168 D. M. Palliser and A. Selwyn, 'The stock of a York Stationer in 1538', *The Library,* XXVII (1972), 207-19

169 N. Sutherland, *Tudor Darlington* (1974), 66
170 F. W. D. Manders, *A history of Gateshead* (1973), 55
171 R. Howell, *Newcastle-upon-Tyne and the Puritan Revolution* (Oxford, 1967), 14-18
172 C. Phythian-Adams, 'Ceremony and the citizen', being pp. 57-85 of Clark and Slack, *Crisis and order*, esp. 65
173 Parker, 'The making of Kings Lynn', 51-52
174 Atkinson, *Elizabethan Winchester*, 199
175 E. A. G. Clarke, 'The ports of the Exe Estuary 1660-1860', Unpubl. Ph.D. thesis, Exeter University (1960), 24-25
176 Howell, *Newcastle;* J. Langton, 'Residential patterns in pre-industrial cities', *Trans. Inst. Brit. Geog.*, 65 (1975)
177 Langton, 'Residential patterns', 18
178 J. D. Marshall, 'Kendal in the late seventeenth and eighteenth centuries', *Trans. Cumb. & Westm. Antiq. & Arch. Soc.*, LXXXV (1976), 189
179 Ralph and Williams, 'Inhabitants of Bristol', 135-53
180 W. G. Hoskins, *Industry, trade and people in Exeter, 1688-1800* (Manchester, 1935), 115-19
181 Langton, 'Residential patterns', 21
182 D. V. Glass, in Hollaender and Kellaway, *London History*, 382-83
183 G. Sjoberg, *The pre-industrial city, past and present* (Glencoe, Ill., 1960); J. E. Vance Jnr., 'Land assignment in pre-capitalist, capitalist and post-capitalist cities', *Economic Geography*, 47 (1971), 101-20

Chapter 5 *Town and country, town and sea*

 1 F. Braudel, *Capitalism and material life 1400-1800* (1967), 376-79
 2 K. J. Allison, 'The Norfolk worsted industry in the sixteenth and seventeenth centuries, pt I', *Yorkshire Bull. Econ. & Soc. Res.*, 12 (1960), 74
 3 J. D. Marshall, 'Kendal in the late seventeenth and eighteenth centuries', *Trans. Cumb. & West. Antiq. & Arch. Soc.*, LXXXV (1976), 189
 4 *V. C. H. Leicester*, IV, 99-100
 5 *Ibid.* 102
 6 R. A. Holt, 'The economic development of Birmingham before 1553', Unpubl. M.A. thesis, Birmingham University (1975), 120-21
 7 H. B. Rodgers, 'The market area of Preston in the sixteenth and seventeenth centuries', *Geographical Studies*, III (1956), 46-53
 8 J. Webb, *Great Tooley of Ipswich*, (1962)
 9 F. M. L. Thompson, *Hampstead: building a borough, 1650-1964* (1974)
10 *V. C. H. City of York*, 180
11 J. T. Evans, 'The decline of oligarchy in seventeenth-century Norwich', *Jnl. British Studies*, XIV (1974), 58
12 A. B. Rosen, 'Economic and social aspects of the history of Winchester, 1520-1670', Unpubl. D.Phil. thesis, Oxford University (1975), 126-27
13 L. J. Ashford, *The history of the borough of High Wycombe from its origins to 1880* (1960), 91
14 F. W. D. Manders, *A history of Gateshead* (1973), 33

15 A. Jones, 'Land and people at Leighton Buzzard in the later fifteenth century', *Econ. Hist. Rev.*, 2nd Series, XXV (1972), 19-25

16 J. Gottmann, 'The city is a crossroads', *Ekistics*, 204 (1972), 308-9

17 Braudel, *Capitalism and material life*, 389

18 L. A. Clarkson, *The pre-industrial economy in England, 1500-1750*, (1971), 22

19 For example Anon. *The lawes of the market*, (publ. by the City Printer, 1653); *V.C.H. York*, 168

20 A. B. Robertson, 'The open market in the city of London in the eighteenth century', *East London Papers*, 1 (1958), 19-20

21 M. Reed, 'Ipswich in the seventeenth century', Unpubl. Ph.D. thesis, Leicester University (1973), 14

22 Rodgers, 'The market area of Preston'

23 M. W. Beresford, 'Leeds in 1628: A "Ridinge Observation" from the City of London', *Northern History*, X (1975), 135; *V.C.H. Oxfordshire*, X (1972), 58; S. H. Tupling, 'Lancashire markets in the sixteenth and seventeenth centuries, pt 1', *Trans. Lancs. & Ches. Antiq. Soc.*, 58 (1945), 20

24 N. Sunderland, *Tudor Darlington* (1974), 16

25 F. Emery, *The Oxfordshire landscape* (1974), 194

26 J. S. Roper, *Dudley, the town in the sixteenth century* (1974), 5

27 F. W. Willmore, *The history of Walsall* (Walsall and London, 1887), 192

28 M. Lobel, 'Some reflections on the topographical development of the pre-industrial town in England', being pp. 141-63 in F. G. Emmison and W. B. Stephens, *Tribute to an antiquarian* (1976), 157-8; A. Everitt, 'The English urban inn' in A. Everitt (ed.) *Perspectives in English urban history* (1973), 94, 104; T. M. James, 'The inns of Croydon 1640-1840', *Surrey Arch. Coll.*, 68 (1971), 109-29

29 A. Everitt, 'The marketing of agricultural produce', being pp. 466-92 of J. Thirsk (ed.), *The agrarian history of England and Wales*, IV, *1500-1640* (1967), 467

30 *Ibid. passim*

31 A. Everitt, 'Urban growth, 1570-1770', *Local Historian*, 8 (1968), 118-25

32 R. Blome, *Brittania* (1673), esp. 227

33 John Patten, 'Urban life before the Industrial Revolution', *Geographical Magazine*, XLII (1970), 213

34 Rodgers, 'The market area of Preston'

35 As listed for different counties in, for example, J. O'Donnell, 'Market centres in Herefordshire 1200-1400', *Trans. Woolhope Nat. Hist. Field Club*, XL (1971), or D. M. Palliser and A. C. Pinnock, 'The markets of medieval Staffordshire', *North Staff. Jnl. of Field Studies*, 11 (1971)

36 J. Thirsk, 'Stamford in the sixteenth and seventeenth centuries', being pp. 58-76 of A. Rogers, *The making of Stamford* (Leicester, 1965)

37 K. R. Adey, 'Seventeenth century Stafford: A county town in decline', *Midland History*, 11 (1974), 166

38 A. B. Robertson, 'The suburban food markets of eighteenth century London', *East London Papers*, 2 (1959), 24

39 Everitt, 'Urban growth', 120

NOTES AND REFERENCES

323

40 N. S. B. Gras, *The evolution of the English corn market from the twelfth to the eighteenth century* (Cambridge, Mass. and London, 1915)

41 D. Baker, 'The marketing of corn in the first half of the eighteenth century: north-east Kent', *Agric. Hist. Rev.*, 18 (1970), 127

42 L. A. Clarkson, 'The English bark trade, 1660-1830', *Agric. Hist. Rev.*, 22 (1974), 136-52

43 Emery, *Oxfordshire Landscape*, 199

44 Everitt, 'Agricultural produce', in Thirsk, *Agrarian history*, IV

45 P. Heylyn, *A help to English history* . . . (1652), 356; J. D. Chambers, 'Three essays on population and economy of the Midlands', being pp. 308-51 of D. V. Glass and D. E. C. Eversley (eds.), *Population and history* (1965), 341-2; J. D. Chambers, *Population, society and economy in pre-industrial England* (1972), 47

46 R. Millward, 'The Cumbrian town between 1600 and 1800', being pp. 202-28 of C. W. Chalklin and M. A. Havinden (eds.), *Rural change and urban growth 1500-1800* (1974), 210-11

47 *Ibid.*

48 A. A. Ruddock, 'London capitalists and the decline of Southampton in the early Tudor period', *Econ. Hist. Rev.*, 2nd Series, 11 (1949-50), 137-51

49 *V.C.H. Yorkshire, East Riding*, Vol. 1 (1969), 155-6; D. M. Palliser, 'Epidemics in Tudor York', *Northern History*, VIII (1973), 56

50 Everitt, 'Urban growth', 121

51 K. L. McCutcheon, 'Yorkshire fairs and markets to the end of the eighteenth century', *Publications of the Thoresby Society*, XXXIX (1940), 137-38

52 S.P.D. Eliz., ccliv, 1595

53 H. Heaton, *The Yorkshire woollen and worsted industries* (Oxford, 1920), 16

54 D. Defoe, *Complete English tradesmen* (1727), 328-9. See also F. J. Fisher 'The development of the London food market 1540-1690', *Econ. Hist. Rev.*, V (1935), 46-64

55 W. J. Petchey, 'The Borough of Maldon, Essex, 1500-1688', Unpubl. Ph.D. thesis, Leicester University (1972), 284, 289. I am most grateful to Dr Petchey for allowing me to quote from his important thesis

56 T. S. Willan, *The inland trade* (Manchester, 1976), 2, 3

57 J. Taylor, *The Carriers Cosmographie* (1637)

58 J. A. Chartres, 'Road carrying in England in the seventeenth century: myth and reality', *Econ. Hist. Rev.*, 2nd Series, XXX (1977), 87-88

59 E. J. Pawson, *Transport and economy* (London, 1977), 35-48

60 Willan, *Inland trade*, 14; see also his map of navigable rivers, facing p. 1 in *ibid.*

61 M. Nash, 'Early seventeenth-century schemes to make the Wey navigable, 1618-1651', *Surrey Arch. Coll.*, LXVI (1969), 33-40

62 C. W. Chalklin, 'Navigation schemes on the upper Medway, 1660-1665', *Jnl. Transport Hist.*, V (1961), 105-15

63 M. Nash, 'Barge traffic on the Wey navigation in the second half of the century', *Jnl. Transport Hist.*, VII (1966), 218-24

64 J. D. Porteous, *Canal ports. The urban achievement of the canal age* (1977), *passim*

65   Willan, *Inland trade*, 15
66   M. B. Rowlands, 'Masters and men in the small metallurgical trades of the West Midlands, 1660-1760', Unpubl. Ph.D. thesis, Aston University, Birmingham (1972), 24-26
67   A. D. Dyer, *The city of Worcester in the sixteenth century* (1973), 60-62
68   J. J. Cartwright (ed.), 'The travels through England of Dr Richard Pococke', *Camden Society*, NS., xlii (1887-8), VI
69   Everitt, 'Agricultural produce', in Thirsk, *Agrarian history*, IV, 498
70   *Ibid.* 499; N. Lowe, 'The Lancashire textile industry in the sixteenth century', *Chetham Society*, 3rd Series, XX (1972), 58-9, 61
71   Dyer, *Worcester*, 68-71
72   Rodgers, 'The market area of Preston'
73   R. Sharpe-France, 'The highway from Preston into the Fylde', *Trans. Hist. Soc. Lanc. & Ches.*, XCVII (1945), 33
74   *Ibid.* 112
75   G. H. Green and M. Green, *Loughborough markets and fairs through seven and a half centuries* (Loughborough, 1964), 25
76   S. I. Mitchell, 'Urban markets and retail distribution, 1730-1815, with particular reference to Macclesfield, Stockport and Chester', Unpubl. D.Phil., Oxford University (1974)
77   D. Sylvester and G. Nutty (eds.), *The historical atlas of Cheshire* (Chester, 1958), 27
78   G. O. Cowley, 'Sussex market towns, 1550-1750', Unpubl. M.A. thesis, London University (1965), 164
79   *Ibid.* 174, 144
80   J. Adams, *Index villaris* (1690); R. Grafton, *A little treatise containing many proper tables and rules* (1571); N. Scarfe, 'Markets and fairs in seventeenth century Suffolk', *The Suffolk Review*, 3 (1965), 11-15
81   Everitt, *Urban history*, 6
82   W. Harrison, *A description of England, 1577* (ed. F. J. Furnivall) (1877), 34; N. F. Hulbert, 'A survey of Somerset fairs', *Proc. Somerset Arch. and Nat. Hist. Soc.*, 82 (1937), 154-55
83   C. Walford, *Fairs past and present: a chapter in the history of commerce* (1883), VI, 44
84   M. T. Hodgen, 'Fairs of Elizabethan England', *Economic Geography*, 18 (1942), 393
85   Dyer, *Worcester*, 74, 80
86   Mitchell, 'Urban Markets'; see also Richardson, 'The Medieval fairs and markets of Yorkshire', *Borthwick Inst. Hist. Res.*, 20 (1961), 1-35
87   Ashford, *High Wycombe*, 92
88   J. H. Harmer, 'Trading at Saint White Down Fair, 1637-1649', *Somerset Arch. & Nat. Hist. Soc.*, 112 (1968), 61-70 *passim;* Hulbert, 'Somerset fairs'; I. F. H. Jones, 'Somerset fairs', *Proc. Som. Arch. & Nat. Hist. Soc.*, XCI (1945), 71-81; W. Robertshaw, 'Notes on Adwalton fair', *Bradford Antiquary*, NS.5 (1927), 51-70
89   R. B. Westerfield, *Middlemen in English business particularly between 1660 and 1700* (New Haven 1915); D. Davis, *A history of shopping* (1966)
90   N. J. Williams, 'Tradesmen in early-Stuart Wiltshire', *Wilts. Arch. & Nat. Hist. Soc.*, Records Branch, XV (1959)

91   B. A. Holderness, 'Rural Tradesmen, 1660-1850: A regional study in Lindsey', *Lincs. Hist. & Arch. Soc.*, VII (1972)

92   G. Berry, 'New Light on the seventeenth century token issues of Chepping Wycombe', *Records of Buckinghamshire*, XVIII (1967), 150-63

93   *Ibid.* 152; see also *Idem* 'Notes on the seventeenth century token issues of Chesham', *Records of Bucks.*, XVIII (1970), 422-36

94   Willan, *Inland trade*, 85-89, esp. 88-89

95   *Ibid.* 89

96   John Patten, 'Changing occupational structures in the East Anglian countryside 1500-1700', in R. A. Butlin and H. S. A. Fox (eds.), *Change in the Countryside*, Institute of British Geographers, Special Publication, (*forthcoming*, 1978)

97   Anon. *The trade of England revived* (1681), 34

98   L. B. and M. W. Barley, 'Lincolnshire shopkeepers in the sixteenth and seventeenth centuries', *The Lincolnshire Historian*, 2 (1962), 20-21

99   R. C. Jarvis, 'Sources for the history of ports', *Jnl. Transport Hist.*, III (1957), 76-93

100 Webb, *Great Toolev*, 93-115

101 E. A. G. Clark, 'The ports of the Exe estuary, 1660-1860', Unpubl. Ph.D. thesis, Exeter University (1960), 48-72

102 P. H. Fox, 'Cumberland ports and shipping in the reign of Elizabeth', *Trans. Cumb. & West. Antiq. Soc.*, NS. 21 (1921), 74

103 On the appointment of ports, creeks and landing places see, e.g., R. C. Jarvis, 'The appointment of ports', *Econ. Hist. Rev.*, 2nd Series, XI (1959), 455-66, or *idem*. 'The appointment of ports in Cumberland, Westmorland and Lancashire – north of the sands', *Trans. Cumb. & West. Antiq. & Arch. Soc.*, XLVII (1947), 128-69

104 E. Gillet, *A history of Grimsby* (1970), 98-99

105 B. Cozens-Hardy, 'The maritime trade of the port of Blakeney, Norfolk, 1587-1590', *Norfolk Record Society*, VIII (1936), 17-37

106 J. H. Andrews, 'The trade of Brighton in the second half of the seventeenth century', *Surrey Notes and Queries*, XIV (1954) 46-51; C. E. Brent, 'Employment, land tenure and population in eastern Sussex, 1546-1750', Unpubl. Ph.D. thesis, Sussex University (1973), 296

107 J. A. Whetter, 'Cornish trade in the seventeenth century: an analysis of the Port Books', *Jnl. Royal Institution of Cornwall*, 14 (1964), 388-413

108 R. W. K. Hinton, 'The port books of Boston, 1601-1640', *Lincs. Record Society*, 50 (1956), V

109 I. S. W. Blanchard, 'Commercial crisis and change: trade and the industrial economy of the north-east, 1509-1532', *Northern History*, VIII (1973), 84-85

110 C. Morris (ed.), *The journeys of Celia Fiennes* (1947), 209; See also D. C. Coleman, *Industry in Tudor and Stuart England*, (1975), 46-48

111 Willan, *Inland Trade*, 32

112 R. Howell, *Newcastle-upon-Tyne and the Puritan revolution* (Oxford, 1967), 20-23

113 T. Sowler, *A history of the town and borough of Stockton-on-Tees* (1972), XXIII

114 Willan, *Inland trade*, 32-33
115 *Ibid.* 33
116 R. Davis, 'Trade and shipping of Hull, 1500-1700', *East Yorks. Local History Series*, XVII (1964)
117 *Ibid.* 15
118 *Ibid.* 27
119 G. Jackson, *Hull in the eighteenth century; a study in economic and social history* (1972)
120 See a review of *ibid.* by W. E. Minchinton, in *Am. Hist. Rev.*, 78 (1973), 436
121 J. H. Andrews, 'The port of Chichester and the grain trade, 1650-1750', *Sussex Arch. Coll.*, XCII (1954), 100, 103
122 J. J. Bourhis, 'Le trafic du port de Dartmouth 1599-1641', Unpubl. thesis, Diplome d'etudes supérieures d'histoire moderne, Universite de Bretagne Occidentale, Brest (1972) (There is a copy of this in the library of the Institute of Historical Research, University of London)
123 W. E. Minchinton, *The growth of English overseas trade in the seventeenth and eighteenth centuries* (1969), 1-69
124 J. W. Sherborne, 'The port of Bristol in the middle ages', *Historical Association, Bristol*, XIII (1965), *passim*
125 J. Sheail, 'The regional distribution of wealth as indicated in the lay subsidy returns of 1524-5', Unpubl. Ph.D. thesis, London University (1968), 198
126 W. Camden, *Brittannia* (1610), 237
127 J. D. Gould, 'The trade depression of the early 1620s', *Econ. Hist. Rev.*, 2nd Series, VII (1954-55), 81-90
128 P. McGrath, 'Merchants and merchandise in seventeenth century Bristol' *Bristol Record Series*, XIX (1955), IX-XXI
129 W. Minchinton, 'The port of Bristol in the eighteenth century', being pp. 127-59 of P. McGrath (ed.), *Bristol in the eighteenth century* (1972), 128-29
130 Willan, *Inland trade*, 39
131 W. B. Stephens, 'The overseas trade of Chester in the early seventeenth century', *Trans. Hist. Soc. Lancs. & Ches.*, CXX (1968), 23, 34
132 C. Armour, 'The trade of Chester and the state of the Dee Navigation', Unpubl. Ph.D. thesis, Leeds University (1956), 11, 111
133 L. Smith Toulmin *The itinerary of John Leland in or about the years 1535-1543, parts IX, X and XI* (1910), 40-41
134 D. J. Pope, 'Shipping and trade in the port of Liverpool, 1783-1793', Unpubl. Ph.D. thesis, Liverpool University (1970), 1-11
135 R. Gladstone, *Notes on the history and antiquity of Liverpool* (Liverpool, 1932), 20
136 J. C. Barker, 'Lancashire coal, Cheshire salt and the rise of Liverpool', *Trans. Hist. Soc. Lancs. & Ches.*, CIII (1951), 83-101
137 Defoe, *English tradesmen;* Morris (ed.), *Fiennes;* Cartwright (ed.), 'Pococke'
138 P. G. E. Clemens, 'The rise of Liverpool 1665-1750', *Econ. Hist. Rev.*, 2nd Series, XXIX (1976), 213

139 B. Dietz, 'The port and trade of early Elizabethan London. Documents', *London Record Society*, VIII (1972), IX-XX

140 E. A. Wrigley, 'A simple model of London's importance in changing English society and economy 1650-1750', *Past and Present*, 37 (1967), 44-70

141 F. J. Fisher, 'London's export trade in the early seventeenth century', *Econ. Hist. Rev.*, 2nd Series, III (1950), 151-61

142 Willan, *Inland trade*, 41

143 John Patten, *Rural–urban migration in pre-industrial England*, School of Geography, Oxford Research Paper, 6 (1973), 24

144 M. Reed, 'Ipswich in the seventeenth century', Unpubl. Ph.D. thesis, Leicester University (1973), *passim;* W. J. Petchey, 'The Borough of Maldon, Essex, 1500-1688', Unpubl. Ph.D. thesis, Leicester University (1972), *passim*

145 H. Hanley, 'Population mobility in Buckinghamshire, 1578-1583', *Local Population Studies*, 15 (1975), 36

146 M. Gray, 'The history of Bury, Lancashire from 1660 to 1876', Unpubl. B.Litt. thesis, Oxford University (1964), 38, 41

147 E. G. Thomas, 'The treatment of poverty in Berkshire, Essex and Oxfordshire 1723-1839', Unpubl. Ph.D. thesis, London University (1970), 220-21

148 R. Gough, *Antiquities and memoirs of the parish of Myddle, County of Salop* (Shrewsbury, 1875); see also D. G. Hey, *An English rural community, Myddle under the Tudors and Stuarts* (Leicester, 1974)

149 P. Clark, 'The migration to Kentish towns, 1580-1640', being pp. 117-63 in P. Clark and P. Slack (eds.), *Crisis and order in English towns 1500-1700* (1972); or P. Slack, 'Vagrants and vagrancy in England, 1598-1664', *Econ. Hist. Rev.*, 2nd Series, XXVIII (1974), 360-78

150 F. Braudel, *The Mediterranean and the Mediterranean world in the age of Phillip II*, Vol. I (1975), 418

151 T. Hägerstrand, 'Migration and area', *Lund Studies in Geography*, Series B 13 (1957), 79-80

152 Patten, *Rural–urban migration*

153 Wrigley, 'A simple model'

154 D. V. Glass, 'Socio-economic status and occupations in the City of London at the end of the seventeenth century', being pp. 373-89 of A. E. Hollaender and W. Kellaway (eds.), *Studies in London History* (1969), esp. 377, 386

155 Gough, *Parish of Myddle*, 54, 143, 162

156 P. Spufford, 'Population mobility in pre-industrial England II: The magnet of the metropolis; III: Conclusion', *Genealogists' Magazine*, XVII (1974), 9, 10

157 S. R. Smith, 'The social and geographical origins of the London apprentices, 1630-60', *Guildhall Miscellany*, IV (1973), 195-206, esp. 199

158 C. Blagden, 'The Stationers' Company in the Civil war period', *The Library*, 5th Series, 13 (1958), 1-17

159 Patten, *Rural–urban migration*

160 D. Cressey, 'Occupation, migration and literacy in East London', *Local Population Studies*, 5 (1970), 53-60

161   L. Stone, 'Social mobility in England, 1500-1700', *Past and Present*, 33 (1966), 31-32

162   L. G. Matthews, 'London's immigrant Apothecaries, 1600-1800', *Medical History*, 18 (1974) 262-74

163   Smith, 'London apprentices', 202-3

164   D. C. Coleman, *The economy of England, 1450-1750* (1977), 98

165   D. Hollis (ed.), 'Calendar of the Bristol Apprentice Book, 1532-1569 (pt. 1 1532-1542)', *Bristol Record Society*, 14 (1948); 'Apprentice indentures at Norwich, 1510-1672', *Norfolk Record Society*, **XXIX** (1959)

166   Howell, *Newcastle*, 19

167   John Patten, 'Patterns of migration and movement of labour to three pre-industrial East Anglian towns', *Journal of Historical Geography*, 2 (1976), 111-29

168   D. M. Palliser, 'Some aspects of the social and economic history of York in the sixteenth century', Unpubl. D.Phil. thesis, Oxford University (1968), 66-76 and map in end pocket

169   C. I. Hammer, 'The mobility of skilled labour in late medieval England: some Oxford evidence', *Vierteljahrschrift für sozial und Wirtschaftsgeshcichte*, 63 Band, Heft 2 (1976), 201

170   A. D. Dyer, 'The city of Worcester in the sixteenth century', Unpubl. Ph.D. thesis, Birmingham University (1966), 304-10, 484 and 490

171   *V. C. H. Leicester*, IV (1958), 193

172   Clark, 'Migration to the Kentish towns', in Clark and Slack, *Crisis and order*

173   C. Gill, *A history of Birmingham*, I (1951), 60-61

174   P. M. Frost, 'The growth and localization of rural industry in South Staffordshire 1560-1720', Unpubl. Ph.D. thesis, Birmingham University (1975), 337-42, 539

175   K. McP. Buchanan, 'A note on Kidderminster apprentices', *Trans. Worcester Arch. Soc.*, NS. XX (1943), 43-45

Chapter 6   *Towns in the national urban system – East Anglia*

(Note: The 'Bury St. Edmunds and West Suffolk Record Office' and the 'Ipswich and East Suffolk Record Office' are now branches respectively of the Suffolk Record Office).

1   C. T. Smith, *An historical geography of Western Europe before 1800* (1967), VIII

2   John Patten, 'The urban structure of East Anglia in the sixteenth and seventeenth centuries', Unpubl. Ph.D. thesis, Cambridge University (1972), esp. 72-131, for a fuller discussion of sources and their interpretation and analysis

3   See for example, *Historical Manuscripts Commission Report*, VII (1914)

4   PREROGATIVE COURT OF CANTERBURY
     Wills enrolled in the Prerogative Court of Canterbury

Vol. I	1383-1558	(A-J)	(1893)
II	1383-1558	(K-Z)	(1895)
III	1558-83		(1897)
IV	1584-1604		(1901)
V	1605-19		(1912)

VI	1620-29	(1912)

P.C.C. *Probates and Sentences, ed. John Mathews and George Mathews*

Vol. I	1630-34	(1902)
II	1635-39	(1903-4)
III	1640-44	(1905-6)
IV	1645-49	(1906-8)
V	1650-51	(1909-10)
VI	1652-53	(1911-13)

Wills enrolled in the Prerogative Court of Canterbury (cont.)

Vol. VII	1653-56	(1925)
VIII	1657-60	(1936)

Wills, Sentences and Probate Acts, 1661-70 (incl.)
by J. H. Morrison (1935)

1 vol.	1661-1670

Wills enrolled in the Prerogative Court of Canterbury (cont.)

Vol. IX	1671-75	(1942)
	1676-85	(1948)
	1686-93	(1955-56)
	1694-1700	(1959-60)

(See also: *A list of Wills, Administration, etc. in the Public Record Office, London, England, twelfth to nineteenth century* (Magna Carta Book Company, Baltimore, 1968)

(Other printed volumes covering some of the above years are John Mathews and George Mathews, *P.C.C. Probates and Sentences, 1620-1624*, vol. 1 (1914); also for 1654-1655, vol. VII (1914-25) and 1655, vol. VIII (1926-8); J. H. Morrison, *P.C.C. Register Scroope Abstracts and Index* (1934)

CONSISTORY COURT OF NORWICH

Wills at Norwich, 1370-1550 Norfolk Record Society, XVI, Pt. I (1943)

Wills at Norwich, 1370-1550 Norfolk Record Society, XVI, Pt. II (1944)

Wills at Norwich, 1370-1550, Norfolk Record Society, XVI, Pt. III (1945)

Wills at Norwich, 1550-1603, Norfolk Record Society, XXI (1950)

Wills at Norwich, 1604-1686, Norfolk Record Society, XXVIII (1958)

Wills at Norwich, 1687-1750, Norfolk Record Society, XXXIV (1965)

ARCHDEACONRY COURTS

Norwich: Norfolk and Norwich Record Office, Registers of Wills from *Liber Fuller alias Roper,* 1469-1503, to *Liber Fenn, 1699-1700. (Liber Blomefield, 1653-1660* contains the Local copies of those enrolled by the P.C.C., printed in Wills enrolled in the Prerogative Court of Canterbury, vol. VII, 1653-1656, and vol. VIII, 1657-1660, Index Library, 1925, British Record Society, 1936).

Norfolk: Norfolk and Norwich Record Office, Registers of Wills from *Liber 1460-1509* to *Liber 1697-1699.* There are no Registered copies of wills for the years 1615-24, 1627-9, 1637-59. The Original Wills were consulted. These are in bundles for single years, but in two years together for 1628-6, 1647-8, 1649-50 and 1651-52.

Suffolk: The Registered Copies of Wills for this Archdeaconry are indexed on cards, Ipswich and East Suffolk Record Office:

IC/AA3/1	(1440-1620)
IC/AA3/2	(1621-1660)
IC/AA3/3	(1661-1735)

A number of wills enrolled before the Borough Court of Ipswich, a practice which died out by the seventeenth century, are calendared in *Proceedings Suffolk Institute of Archaeology,* vol. 15 (1915), pp. 291-304.

Sudbury: Bury St Edmunds and West Suffolk Record Office, Register Books of Wills, Court of the Sacrist of St Edmund's Abbey for the Peculiar of Bury St Edmunds, becoming the Episcopal Commissary Court for Bury St Edmunds, 1539, from *Liber Pye 1491-1509* to *Liber Sunday, 1540-66;* and Archdeaconry Court of Sudbury, including after 1566 the Episcopal Court of Bury St Edmunds (the latter court was not formally joined to the former until 1844, but for practical purposes the probate business of recording wills was merged from 1566), from *Liber Fuller, 1462-1530* to *Liber Coe 1696-1699.* (There is a Ms. calendar of these wills by *V. B. Redstone* (undated); Bury St Edmunds Wills and Archdeaconry of Sudbury Wills, Ipswich Reference Library, Suffolk Collection, Redstone Papers, Box 1, *viz.*:

1.1	1529-55
1.2	1556-69
1.3	1570-90
1.4	1591-1611
1.5	1611-1626
1.6	1627-1642
1.7	1643-1652
1.8	1660-1674

and Box 2, *viz.*:

1.9	1674-1707)

PROBATE INVENTORIES: CONSISTORY COURT OF
NORWICH

*Norfolk and Norwich Record Office, Norwich
Diocesan Records (Typescript Lists)*

c. 929	3 bar
c. 929	3 bar
c. 929	3 bar
c. 929	3 bar

ARCHDEACONRY COURTS

*Norfolk and Norwich Record Office, Typescript Lists
Ipswich and East Suffolk Record Office (Typescript Lists)*

F.E. 1/1
F.E. 1/2
F.E. 1/3

(These are consolidated with Wills and Admonitions for the Suffolk Archdeaconry in the index IX/AA 3/1-3).

Bury St Edmunds and West Suffolk Record Office: Calendars of Probate Inventories, 592/1-4.

5   Patten, 'Urban structure of East Anglia', 97-103
6   *Ibid.* 104-26

7   P. Millican (ed.), *The Freemen of Norwich, 1548-1713* (Norwich, 1934);
    J. F. Pound, 'The social and trade structure of Norwich, 1525-75',
    Past and Present, 34 (1966); 'A calendar of the Freemen of Kings Lynn
    1292-1836', *Norfolk & Norwich Arch. Soc.*, Add. Papers (1913); 'A
    calendar of the Freemen of Great Yarmouth, 1429-1800', *Norfolk &
    Norwich Arch. Soc.*, Add. Papers (1910)

8   W. M. Rising and P. Millican, 'Apprentices indentured at Norwich,
    1510-1752', *Norfolk Record Society*, XXIX (1959); appendix of appren-
    tice indentures in Millican, *Freemen of Norwich; Norfolk and Norwich
    Record Office* C.4/258–C.4/357, and Great Yarmouth Corporation
    Assembly Books 1614-37; Ipswich and East Suffolk Record Office
    A.IX-4 for 1571-1651

9   For example a list of householders for Norwich taken in 1589, Norfolk
    and Norwich Record Office, Aylsham Collection, 156

10 For example lists taken of foreign strangers at Kings Lynn in 1571,
    Public Record Office, S.P.D. 12.78, fos. 47-8, and at Great Yarmouth in
    the same year S.P.D. 12.78, fos. 25-34

11 For example J. F. Pound, 'An Elizabethan census of the poor', *Univ.
    Birmingham Hist. Jnl.*, VIII (1962) 135-61; J. Webb, 'Poor relief in
    Elizabethan Ipswich', *Suffolk Records Society*, IX (1966), 122-40

12 For example *Ipswich and West Suffolk Record Office*, Petty Court Books,
    A.V. 12/5 (1505-7), A.V. 12/7 (1508-13) and A.V. 12/8 (1520-24,
    1527-31)

13 For example bills for entertainment at Bury, *Bury St Edmunds and East
    Suffolk Record Office*, D.6/3/2

14 R. M. Hartwell, *The industrial revolution and economic growth* (1971), 21,
    31-33

15 For example, J. B. Mitchell, *Historical geography* (1954), 247-50

16 For example A. Suckling *The history and antiquities of the county of Suffolk*,
    I (1846), 12-13

17 For example, there are a handful of wills in existence proved before
    the 1470s in the archdeaconries of Norwich and Norfolk, covering the
    county of Norfolk. Before 1500 only three or four registers of wills
    survive for either archdeaconry, and the number of wills in them
    which give occupational designations for the deceased are few. *Norfolk
    and Norwich Record Office*, Archdeaconry Registers, *op. cit.*

18 See, for one Suffolk Hundred, John Patten, 'Village and town: an
    occupational study', *Agric. Hist. Rev.*, 20 (1972), 1-16, and *idem*,
    'Changing occupational structures in the East Anglian countryside,
    1500-1700', in R. A. Butlin and H. S. A. Fox (eds.), *Change in the
    countryside* Institute of British Geographers, special publication
    (*forthcoming*, 1978)

19 Patten, 'Village and town'

20 P. E. Jones, 'Local assessments for parliamentary taxes', *Jnl. Soc.
    Archivists*, 4 (1970), 58

21 W. Hudson and J. C. Tingay, *The records of the city of Norwich*, II (1910),
    LXX-LXII

22 K. J. Allison, 'The Norfolk worsted industry in the sixteenth and
    seventeenth centuries, pt 1', *Yorks. Bull. Econ. & Soc. Research*, 12
    (1960), 79, and Pound, 'Social and trade structure of Norwich', 58

23   32 H.VIII c.18

24   33 H.VIII c.36: The useful preambles of such statutes give indications
      of decay in the earlier sixteenth century in towns in other regions; this
      information can be found in the appropriate parts of O. Ruffhead,
      Statutes at large, new ed. rev. by C. Runnington, 14 vols. (1786-1800)

25   A fact which is borne out in the standard texts for the time on a
      countywide scale; see, for example, P. Ramsey, *Tudor economic problems*
      (1963), esp. ch. III, 'Industry and the towns'

26   Hudson and Tingay, *City of Norwich,* **XXV-XXVII**

27   Patten, 'Village and town', *passim*

28   Patten, 'Changing occupational structures'

29   W. Rye, *A history of Norfolk* (1885), 157; see also his *An autobiography of
      an ancient athlete and antiquary* (Privately printed with plates, Norwich,
      1916)

30   A. Everitt, 'The food market of the English town, 1660-1760', being
      pp. 56-71 of *Third International Conference of Economic History* (Paris,
      1968), 59-61

31   H. K. Roessingh, 'Village and hamlet in a sandy region of the
      Netherlands in the middle of the 18th century: an application of the
      Guttmann Scalogram technique to socio-historical research', *Acta
      Historiae Neerlandica,* 4 (1970), 105-29

32   G. Shapiro, 'Myrdal's definitions of the "South". A methodological
      note', *American Sociological Review,* 13 (1948), 619-21; L. Adrian,
      'Urban change in East Anglia in the nineteenth century', Unpubl.
      Ph.D. thesis, Cambridge University (1966)

33   D. N. Parkes, 'The Guttmann Scalogram: an empirical appraisal in
      urban geography', *Australian Geographical Studies,* **VII** (1969), 109-36

34   Patten 'Village and town', 11

35   J. F. Pound, 'The social and trade structure of Norwich, 1525-75', *Past
      and Present,* 34 (1966), 49-64; K. J. Allison, 'The Norfolk worsted in-
      dustry in the sixteenth and seventeenth centuries, pt. 1', *York. Bull.
      Econ. & Soc. Research,* 12 (1960)

36   'W. R.' (presumably Walter Rye), 'A note on early Norwich
      typography', *Norfolk Antiquarian Miscellany,* 111 (1885-87), 249

37   Millican, *Freemen of Norwich,* 111

38   Allison, 'The Norfolk worsted industry'

39   For example W. Rye, 'The Dutch refugees in Norwich', *Norfolk Anti-
      quarian Miscellany,* 111 (1885-7), 185-248; W. J. C. Moens, 'The
      Walloon Church of Norwich: its registers and history', *Publication of
      the Huguenot Society of London,* I (1887-88)

40   D. L. Rickwood, 'The Norwich Accounts for the Customs and
      Strangers, goods and merchandise, 1582-1610', *Norfolk Record Society,*
      XXXIX (1970), 81

41   D. M. Palliser, 'Some aspects of the social and economic history of
      York in the sixteenth century', Unpubl. D.Phil. thesis, Oxford
      University (1968), 272-73

42   Pound, 'Census of the poor', 135-61; B. Cornford, 'Inventories of the
      poor', *Norfolk Archaeology,* **XXXV** (1970) 118-25

43   W. Camden, *Brittania* (1610, 1637), 464

44   A. Everitt, 'Change in the provinces: the seventeenth century', *Dept.*

English Local History, University of Leicester, Occasional Papers, 2nd series,
1 (1969), 25

45 John Patten, 'Patterns of migration and movement of labour to three
    pre-industrial East Anglian towns', *Journal of Historical Geography,* 2
    (1976), 111-29

46 H. Manship (ed. C. J. Palmer), *A booke of the foundation of Great Yar-
    mouthe* (Great Yarmouth, 1847); C. J. Palmer, *The history of Great Yar-
    mouth . . .* (London and Great Yarmouth, 1856)

47 Yates, R. 'An illustration of . . . St Edmund's Bury . . .' (1805) 202-6

48 V. B. Redstone, 'Chapels, chantries and guilds in Suffolk', *Proc. Suffolk
    Inst. Arch.,* XII (1904), 9

49 A. Everitt, 'The marketing of agricultural produce', in J. Thirsk (ed.),
    The agrarian history of England and Wales, IV, 1500-1640 (1967), 496

50 S.P.D. Car. 1, vol. 330, no. 90

51 Camden, *Brittania,* IV, 466; Leland, *The itinerary,* II, 28

52 Leland, *The itinerary,* IV, 122; Hudson and Tingay, II, *City of Norwich,*
    lxxxvi, cxxiv-viii

53 E. G. R. Taylor, *Late Tudor and early Stuart geography 1583-1650* (1934),
    96

54 R. Wake, *Southwold and its vicinity* (Great Yarmouth, 1839), 10

55 N. Boston and E. Puddy, *Dereham* (Dereham, 1952)

56 E. Gillingwater, *An historical account of the ancient town of Lowestoft*
    (1791), 58-59

57 Palmer (ed.), Manship, *Great Yarmouthe,* 221

58 B. Cozens-Hardy, 'The maritime trade of the port of Blakeney, Nor-
    folk, 1587-90', *Norfolk Record Society,* VIII (1936)

59 Norfolk and Norwich Record Office, Norfolk Archdeaconry, Liber 6,
    1515-23

60 *Ibid.* Liber Gloys, 1509-19

61 Patten, 'Village and town'

62 Patten, 'Urban structure of East Anglia, 1-16

63 N. J. Williams, 'The maritime trade of the East Anglian ports, 1550-
    90', Unpubl. D. Phil. thesis, Oxford University (1952), 72

64 C. G. Grimwood and S. A. Kay, *History of Sudbury* (Sudbury, 1952),
    100

65 A. G. H. Hollingsworth, *History of Stowmarket* (Ipswich, 1844), 121

66 N.N.R.O. Liber Gloys 1509-19, fo. 350; he *might* conceivably have
    been a returned resident, or have owned lands there, however.

67 B. M. Stow, Ms. 570, fo. 207-8

68 Edgar Powell, *The rising in East Anglia in 1381 with an appendix containing
    the Suffolk Poll Tax lists for that year* (1896); I owe this reference to Mr
    James Campbell of Worcester College, Oxford

69 A. Raistrick, 'A fourteenth century regional survey', *Sociological
    Review,* XXI (1929), 241-49

70 Sir T. Wilson, *The state of England Anno Dom. 1600* (ed. F. J. Fisher),
    Camden Society Publication, LII (1936), 12

71 Patten, 'Urban structure of East Anglia'

72 John Patten, 'Urban occupations in pre-industrial England', *Trans.
    Inst. Brit. Geog.,* NS. 2 (1977), *passim*

73 Patten, 'Urban structure of East Anglia', 207

74 See, in particular, the evidence presented in Patten, 'Changing occupational structures'
75 A. D. Dyer, *The city of Worcester in the sixteenth century* (Leicester, 1973), 131-32
76 Camden, *Brittania* (1610), 471
77 P. Heylyn, *A help to English history* (first pub. 1641; edn. of 1652), 319
78 C. M. Hood (ed.), *The chorography of Norfolk* (Norwich, 1938), 73-7
79 Everitt, 'Agricultural produce', in Thirsk, *Agrarian history*, IV, 474
80 *Ibid.* 472
81 Hood, *Chorography of Norfolk*, 73-74
82 C.S.P.D. 1639/40, 252
83 Palmer (ed.), Manship, *Great Yarmouthe*, 222
84 L. B. Barley and M. W. Barley, 'Lincolnshire shopkeepers in the sixteenth and seventeenth centuries', *The Lincolnshire Historian*, 2 (1962), 7-21
85 R. Reyce (ed. F. Harvey), *Suffolk in the XVII century: the Breviary of Suffolk 1618 . . .* (1902), 42
86 Patten, 'Urban structure of East Anglia', 209
87 T. S. Willan, *The English coasting trade, 1600-1750* (1958), 71
88 J. Parkes, *Travel in England in the seventeenth century* (Oxford, 1925)
89 E. J. Pawson, *Transport and economic growth* (London, 1977) *passim*
90 G. T. Scott, 'Roads in England and Wales in 1603', *Eng. Hist. Rev.,* XXXIII (1918), 234-43
91 R. Hughey (ed.), 'The correspondence of Lady Katherine Paston, 1603-27', *Norfolk Record Society,* XIV (1941)
92 Willan, *Coasting trade*
93 T. S. Willan, *River navigation in England, 1600-1750* (1936); *idem,* 'River navigation and trade from the Witham to the Yare 1600-1750', *Norfolk Archaeology* (1938), 53
94 Hudson and Tingay, *City of Norwich,* cxxiv-viii
95 H. R. Barker, *History of Bury St Edmunds* (Bury, 1885), 37; Gillingwater, *Lowestoft,* 281-2
96 M. D. Lobel, *The Borough of Bury St Edmunds* (Oxford, 1935)
97 Gillingwater, *Lowestoft,* 280-81
98 A. Suckling, *The history and antiquities of the County of Suffolk,* II (1848), 68
99 Gillingwater, *Lowestoft,* 61-62
100 W. B. Rix, *Swaffham* (Norwich and Swaffham, 1931), 53
101 C. Hill, *Reformation to Industrial Revolution* (1969), 171
102 P. Corfield in P. Clark and P. A. Slack (eds.), *Crisis and order in the English town, 1500-1700* (1972)
103 See also C. A. Edie, 'New buildings, new taxes and old interests, an urban problem of the 1670s', *Jnl. British Studies,* 6 (1967), 35-63
104 C. J. Palmer, *The Perlustration of Great Yarmouth . . .* 1 (1872), 81
105 Morris (ed.), *Fiennes,* 151-2; Defoe, *English tradesmen,* vol. 1, 51-3; Heylyn, *A help to English history,* 356
106 C.S.P.D. 1655-6, fo. 210-11
107 Defoe, *English tradesmen,* vol. 1, 73-74
108 Willan, *Coasting trade,* 62-63
109 Defoe, *English tradesmen,* vol. I, 40-45

110 Morris (ed.), *Fiennes*, 143-44

111 A. Everitt, 'The food market of the English town 1660-1760', *Third International Conference of Economic Historians* (1968), 58; see also T. S. Willan, *The inland trade* (Manchester, 1977), *passim*

112 Patten, 'Changing occupational structures'

113 Palmer, *The history of Great Yarmouth,* (1856), 95-96

114 Rix, *Swaffham,* 72; Willan, *Inland trade*

115 Morris (ed.), *Fiennes;* Defoe, *English tradesmen;* J. Kirby, *The Suffolk traveller* (Ipswich, 1735), *passim.*

116 E. Mann, *Old Bungay* (Bungay, 1934), 147

117 N. Boston and E. Puddy, *Dereham* (Dereham, 1952), 48-49

118 S. Porter, 'Fires and pre-industrial towns', *The Local Historian,* 10 (1973), 396

119 Mann, *Old Bungay,* 198-207

120 Historical Manuscripts Commission Report, VII (1914), 114

121 Porter, 'Fires and pre-industrial towns', 396

122 A. L. Hunt, *The capital of the ancient kingdom of East Anglia . . . Thetford* (1870), 288-90

123 T. Markin, *The history of the town of Thetford* (1779), *passim;* Hunt, *Thetford, passim*

124 Morris (ed.), *Fiennes,* 150

125 Defoe, *English tradesmen,* vol. 1, 48

126 Patten, 'Urban structure of East Anglia', 239-43

127 Defoe, *English tradesmen,* vol. 1, 72

Index

Included in this index are all textual references to specific place-names, persons and systematic discussions; excluded are references to counties. Figures in *italics* refer to a figure or table on the specified page.

LONDINVM FER
GLIAE REGN

Clarkenwell

Smythe Fydd

The Temple

Paris Garde

Lambeth

LONDINVM ad flu